THE COMMON SCIENTIST
IN THE SEVENTEENTH CENTURY

THE COMMON SCIENTIST IN THE SEVENTEENTH CENTURY

A Study of the Dublin Philosophical Society

1683–1708

by

K. THEODORE HOPPEN

Lecturer in History in The University of Hull

THE UNIVERSITY PRESS OF VIRGINIA
CHARLOTTESVILLE

The University Press of Virginia
© 1970 K. Theodore Hoppen

First published 1970

Standard Book Number: 8139-0292-4

Library of Congress Catalog Card Number: 72-98307

Printed in Great Britain

To
MY MOTHER
and
THE MEMORY OF MY FATHER

Contents

To the several advantages which Europe has within these latter centuries experienced from the cultivation of science and polite literature, this kingdom unfortunately has remained in a great measure a stranger. As no Irishman's partiality will deny this, so no man's prejudice should be suffered to make it an occasion of illiberal imputation on the capacity of Irishmen, while in the state of the country so many local peculiarities may be found fully sufficient to account for it. The important changes which took place in the government upon the invasion of Henry the Second were not carried on with so little disturbance, as to permit the nation to apply itself immediately to the peaceful employments of literary inquiry, nor could it reasonably be presumed, that two classes of inhabitants entirely dissimilar in their inclinations and habits, and afterwards more widely separated by a difference in religion, should be readily prevailed on to lay aside their mutual enmity, and unite in the pursuit of speculative science.

Reverend Robert Burrowes, F.T.C.D.,
Transactions of the Royal Irish Academy, 1787.

Foreword

This is a study in the institutional development of science during the late seventeenth and early eighteenth centuries. The foundation and growth of the Royal Society in England has occasioned much recent discussion, and while the Philosophical Society which flourished at Dublin in the years between 1683 and 1708 was smaller and less distinguished than its London contemporary, it shared many of the attitudes of English and European science, and is remarkable as the first credible organization of its kind in Ireland. The Dublin Society certainly included men of great ability, such as George Berkeley, William Molyneux, and William Petty. However, its real importance lies in its reflection of the attitudes and standards of the ordinary scientist of the time. The history of science, as Professor Butterfield has pointed out, 'could never be adequately reconstructed by a student who confined his attention to the few men of supreme genius',[1] and this work is therefore an attempt to chart the beliefs and outlooks of the common scientist of the period, of the mass of contemporary natural philosophers who played an important part in spreading the ethos of the scientific revolution, and who found their most characteristic expression in the philosophical societies of the late seventeenth century. Many of the experiments and observations undertaken by the Dublin Society were crude and even grotesque, but a sympathetic approach will, it is hoped, show that deep and fundamental issues often lay behind the superficially commonplace. As no group of this kind can operate in isolation, it is important to examine the general intellectual background against which the society and its members prosecuted their studies. In the case of Ireland this background, which is hereafter discussed in some detail, was comparatively unhelpful, and as a result the members were forced to rely heavily on the advice and assistance of the Royal Society, of which many of them were to become fellows.

[1] H. Butterfield, *Man on His Past* (Cambridge, 1955), p. 32.

Any writer who discusses aspects of the history of ideas in the seventeenth century is faced with an established terminology, which although sometimes misleading, has become so widely used that it would be confusing to introduce alternatives. In the course of this work therefore expressions such as 'Ancient' and 'Modern', 'New Learning' and 'New Philosophy', will be found, terms which imply a degree of precision and intellectual stratification which in reality did not exist. The men who claimed to be supporters of the New Learning varied widely in outlook, and were often prepared to abandon rational scientific beliefs when faced with disturbing religious or mystical phenomena. Indeed, even within the scientific sphere itself, credulity and scepticism were inextricably mingled together.

The so-called battle between the Ancients and the Moderns was never a clash between absolute darkness and perfect light. But the historian cannot ignore the existence of tension simply because to him the issues upon which it was based seem marginal and unclear. There is no lack of evidence to suggest that contemporaries believed a conflict was taking place, and it is above all what men themselves believe is happening that influences their outlook and even their conduct.

At present I am preparing an annotated edition of the minutes, letters, and other papers of the Dublin Philosophical Society, which will include most of the archival material upon which the present study is based. Work on this is fairly well advanced and it is hoped that the edition, to be published by the Irish Manuscripts Commission of Dublin, will not be long delayed.

I am grateful to the staffs of the libraries in which I have worked, and particularly to those at the National Library of Ireland, Trinity College Dublin, the Royal Irish Academy, the British Museum, the Royal Society of London, the archives of the Town of Southampton, the Bodleian Library, and Cambridge University Library, all of whom treated me with a courtesy which my importunate questioning hardly deserved.

My greatest debt in the writing of this work is to my friend Dr Hugh F. Kearney of the University of Sussex, whose constant help and encouragement it only very dimly reflects. Mr Michael Millerick and my colleague Dr J. L. Price very kindly read the manuscript and saved me from many errors. My colleague Dr H. A. Lloyd was good enough to read the proofs and to make a number of useful observations. Other scholars also have been generous in their assistance, and I should like to thank Professor R. Dudley Edwards, Professor Irvin Ehrenpreis, Mr F. V. Emery, Professor A. R. Hall, Mr W. R. Le Fanu, Mr William O'Sullivan, Dr J. G. Simms, and Professor T. Desmond Williams. Even if I have, perhaps obstinately, not always accepted their advice, this work owes much to their friendly interest.

University of Hull   K. T. H.

Abbreviations

B.M.	British Museum, London.
Bodl.	Bodleian Library, Oxford.
D.N.B.	*Dictionary of National Biography.*
H.M.C.	Historical Manuscripts Commission.
Ir. MSS Comm.	Irish Manuscripts Commission.
Minutes	Followed by date and folio number indicates the minutes of the Dublin Philosophical Society in B.M. Add. MS 4811.
Oxford Minutes	Followed by date and page number indicates the minutes of the Oxford Philosophical Society printed in R. T. Gunther, *Early Science in Oxford*, vol. IV.
P.T.	*Philosophical Transactions of the Royal Society of London.*
R.I.A.	Royal Irish Academy, Dublin.
R.S.	Royal Society of London.
Southampton	Southampton Civic Centre Archives.
T.C.D.	Trinity College Dublin.

Note on Dates

Unless otherwise indicated, all dates
are in the old style, save that the year
has been taken as beginning on
1 January.

Chapter 1
Background and Beginnings

I. THE ENGLISH BACKGROUND

The optimistic hope that the new philosophy would make man a happier being, in body as well as in intellect, underlay and promoted that mental attitude congenial to scientific change which was one of the features of organized thought in seventeenth-century Europe. It gave added impetus to the progression towards the experimental method, which, although already present in the sixteenth century, only came into full flower during the hundred years that followed. When Thomas Sprat suggested in 1667 that while the old philosophy 'could only bestow on us some barren terms and notions, the new shall impart to us the uses of all the creatures and shall inrich us with all the benefits of fruitfulness and plenty',[1] the supporters of the latter were certainly on the offensive, although their opponents were still capable of making loud, often rude, and occasionally effective assertions of conservative disagreement. This growing confidence was reflected in the flood of pamphlet and other literature published in England between the years 1640 and 1690.

There were, however, also important political and economic forces involved in the shaping of the scientific movement. But Puritanism and the rule of the Commonwealth in England were factors conditioning men towards change, rather than direct propellents of the scientific method. Puritanism was of course in essence a spiritual phenomenon, and its concomitant political and social characteristics were incidental rather than central to its basically religious message. Puritanism could never more than till the ground for a new scheme of thought, the seed for which had to come from other, sometimes alien, philosophies of progress. T. K. Rabb is near the truth when he asserts that the stimulus given by Puritans to 'the New Learning was due not to any inherent Puritan tendency, but rather to the revolutionary's natural adoption of the convenient, ready-made, and Baconian philosophy'.[2] It seems certain however that the Puritan stress on education, especially when practical and useful, helped to disseminate more widely the new ideas of the natural philosophers. But any precise statement about the exact relationship between cause and effect is difficult to formulate with accuracy. For instance, the Puritan's utilitarian outlook may itself have come about as a result of, or at least been given added impetus by, contemporary Baconian writings. The scientific movement was therefore rather in the nature of a perpetual chain-reaction, than one in which it is easy to isolate definite first causes.

William Petty, a founder fellow of the Royal Society of London and first president of the Dublin Philosophical Society, who, 'besides Wilkins and Boyle, was as much responsible for the promotion of the new science as any of his contemporaries',[3] was not alone in his eagerness to emphasize the usefulness of the new philosophy, especially when prosecuted by means of intensive use of physical experiment. In a pamphlet of 1648 he suggested the establishment of a 'Gymnasium Mechanicum' for the advancement of all 'mechanical arts and manufactures', which would make 'trades miraculously prosper, and new inventions . . . more frequent than new fashions in clothes', and the members of which would 'pursue the means of acquiring the publick good and comfort of mankind a little further'.[4] Some twenty years later Petty's views on this point had become more precise. In a booklet refuting those who accused the Royal Society of engaging in useless undertakings, he wrote, 'I have therefore, to streighten this crooked stick, bent it and my present discourse the quite contrary way, *viz.* to the sails and shapes of ships; to the carpentry and carriages; to mills, mill-dams, bulwarks; to the labour of horses, . . . which are handled in this exercise to prevent further imputation of needless nicety', and went on to assert that he had 'declined all speculations not tending to practice'.[5] The fact that Petty thought it important to demonstrate in detail the errors of those attacking the Royal Society, indicates the contemporary vigour of opposing arguments, which were not always in themselves irrational or without foundation.

The serious scientific experiments dragged behind them a

heterogeneous crowd whose only passion was for the obviously marvellous or bizarre. For these men the less understandable any phenomenon was, the more interesting it became. Mary Astell, writing in the last decade of the century, echoed earlier authors. 'What discoveries do we owe to their labours? It is only the discovery of some few unheeded varieties of plants, shells, or insects, unheeded only because useless.'[6] While Astell criticized only the lunatic fringe of scientific activity, Henry Stubbe was less discriminating, and condemned all modern learning. He conceived a particular hatred for Francis Bacon, because, like so many others, he considered him to have been the prime mover and direct source of the English exemplar of the New Learning. So pervasive and pernicious did Stubbe consider Bacon's posthumous influence that he felt it necessary to point out that 'no law ever made him our dictator, nor is there any reason that concludes him infallible'.[7]

But if the so-called virtuosi indulged in useless, if interesting, activities, the leaders of scientific advance claimed to be firmly practical. Robert Boyle, besides Newton the outstanding figure of the time, declared in 1663, 'I should not have neer so high a value as I now cherish for physiology, if I thought it could onely teach a man to discourse of nature, but not at all to master her; . . . I shall not dare to think my self a true naturalist, till my skill can make my garden yield better herbs and flowers, or my orchard better fruit.'[8] Robert Hooke, for a time Boyle's laboratory assistant, was also convinced that if the new philosophy were properly pursued, all the 'universal metaphysical natures, which the luxury of subtil brains has devis'd, would quickly vanish, and give place to solid histories, experiments, and works'.[9] Thomas Sprat, although himself no scientist, wrote one of the best defences of the contemporary scientific method in *The History of the Royal Society*, in which he never tired of describing his subject as an institution 'that prefers works before words'.[10] But some enthusiasts for the New Learning went further, and by overstating their case, presented an easy target for the arrows of antagonists. Samuel Parker, an opponent of Cambridge Platonism, had nothing but contempt for the whole corpus of ancient knowledge, the new methods being 'unquestionable, and therefore must needs render all lesser evidence vain and unnecessary'.[11]

B

In any case the argument from utility is most commonly found among the propagandists of science. Those who themselves brought about major intellectual advances were at least as concerned with abstract speculation as with matters of use. Furthermore the nature of scientific change in the seventeenth century cannot be properly understood without reference to the fundamental ambivalence which typified it. Boyle for example was deeply concerned with problems which had formed the core of Hermetic teaching, while Newton's chronological studies owed as much to medieval number mysticism as they did to modern mathematics.

This is not to deny the existence of real struggle and meaningful dispute. One hardy perennial in this field concerned religion. The Royal Society in particular came under severe censure from those who regarded it, not only as having no real interest in sound belief, but far worse, as tolerating fanaticism and papism. Sprat merely emphasized the point when he mentioned how at the society 'the divine, the Presbyterian, the Papist, the Independent, and those of orthodox judgement, have laid aside their names of distinction, and calmly conspir'd in a mutual agreement of labors and desires'.[12] Stubbe was quick to react to this passage. 'I believe it is not displeasing to them,' he wrote, referring to the Roman Catholics, 'to see how friendly the Protestants and Papists converse . . . in this assembly, and it must needs raise their hopes of bringing things to a closer union, when they perceive the strangeness, that ought to be, and hath been, betwixt them, taken off. . . . I say, how great benefit popery may draw hence, I cannot well comprehend.'[13] He himself, as was righteously pointed out, stood firmly on the rockbed of the establishment, namely, 'the present monarchy, the Church of England, the universities, and my own faculty'.[14] Stubbe's writings, although strident in tone, were not as influential as he imagined them to be, and while it is true that he became a sort of leader for those of like view, it was in the main an uninspiring captaincy. As early as 1671 John Beale could claim that 'the wings of the Stubbians are already broken and their reputation withers'.[15]

Throughout this period of controversy, many of those interested in the new philosophy formulated schemes for combining themselves into colleges or societies, so that, by means of mutual help they might advance the cause of scientific learning. One such institution had already been in existence since late Elizabethan times, namely London's Gresham College, founded in 1596. This provided a focus for science outside the universities, but its organization and its staff of seven celibate professors lecturing to the public, were far too modest to satisfy the demands of the 'Bacon-faced generation'.[16] The many schemes and plans produced are evidence that Gresham College was not enough, although its very existence gave it an advantage over the always elaborate and often impracticable dreams of the projectors. But despite the obvious eagerness to establish new scientific institutions, an eagerness not at all dimmed by the Restoration, John Flamsteed, one of Gresham's professors, was in 1681 lecturing to almost non-existent audiences. His friend William Molyneux of Dublin, on hearing his complaints, agreed that:

'Tis pitty so noble a designe should fall to the ground, and 'tis a shame for the gentry of London to suffer the great professors of that colledge to read sometimes to almost bare walls, were a seditious balling fanatick in the pulpit he would have a thick audience to hear his infernall doctrine, whilst the celestiall discourses of a learned astronomer or other mathematician are heard but by a few and perhaps by them neglected.[17]

The archetype for most of these schemes was Bacon's *New Atlantis*. Although already in the late sixteenth century John Dee had gathered a group of like-minded men about him at his house in Mortlake, the idea of scientific strength through finely organized cooperation was in England essentially a Baconian concept. But Bacon was often misunderstood by his admirers. He 'professed no such narrow utilitarianism as later went under his name. . . . "Works themselves are of greater value as pledges of truth than as contributing to the comforts of life." . . . Knowledge should not be sought as . . . "a shop for profit and sale".'[18] But as so often in the past, the misunderstandings were to become more important in their effects than the realities which they distorted. It would however be wrong to stress too strongly these interpretative mistakes on the part of Bacon's would-be disciples, for the whole matter was one of emphasis rather than fundamentals.

Samuel Hartlib, a German living in England, was foremost among the projectors. He was not a scientist, but one of those

Puritan thinkers who became enthusiasts for the New Learning. Among others, John Evelyn, Robert Hooke, and the poet Abraham Cowley, can also be mentioned as having made important contributions in this field.[19] The Royal Society was the rather pale outcome of these schemes, and perhaps the most significant point about its foundation was the timing of that event. It was established not under the Puritan Commonwealth, but in the company of restored monarchy.

The precise origins of the Royal Society have been, and still are, a matter of some dispute. Until recently most historians had relied on an account given in 1678 by the mathematician John Wallis, who, in the course of an angry argument with another fellow over a quite different matter, mentioned that the first meetings had taken place at London 'about the year 1645'.[20] Thomas Sprat, John Evelyn, and Henry Oldenburg (the first and tireless secretary of the society) all however maintained that the first meetings were held at Oxford.[21] Sprat was writing about the mid-1660s and Evelyn in 1661. They were thus much nearer in time to the events described than was Wallis. Sprat's *History of the Royal Society* was corrected before publication by a committee of fellows which included Viscount Brouncker, Sir Robert Moray, John Wilkins, and John Evelyn. And while these may have been interested in publicizing Royalist Oxford rather than Puritan London as the society's place of origin, Sprat's account merits lengthy quotation.

It was therefore, some space after the end of the Civil Wars at Oxford, in Dr Wilkins his lodgings, in Wadham College, . . . then the place of resort for vertuous, and learned men, that the first meetings were made, which laid the foundation of all this that follow'd. The university had, at that time, many members of its own, who had begun a free way of reasoning; and was also frequented by some gentlemen, of philosophical minds, whom the misfortunes of the kingdom, and the security and ease of a retirement amongst gownmen, had drawn tither. Their first purpose was no more, then onely the satisfaction of breathing a freer air, and of conversing in quiet one with another, without being ingag'd in the passions, and madness of that dismal age. . . . For the truth of this, I dare appeal to all uninterested men, who knew the temper of that place. . . . The most constant of them, were Doctor Seth Ward, the present Lord Bishop of Exeter, Mr Boyl, . . . Dr Bathurst, [and] Dr Christopher Wren, ... Their meetings were as frequent, as their affairs permitted: their proceedings rather by action, then discourse; cheifly attending some particular trials, in chymistry, or mechanicks: they had no rules nor method fix'd. . . . Thus they continued . . . till about the year 1658. But then being call'd away to several parts of the nation, and the greatest number of them coming to London, they usually met at Gresham College, . . . where there joyn'd with them several eminent persons of their common acquaintance.[22]

While these meetings were the direct forerunners of the Royal Society, other institutions, particularly Gresham College itself and the College of Physicians, had some influence on its foundation. The exact nature of the rôle played by Gresham College is a matter of dispute. Professor McKie states categorically that 'such historical facts as may be gathered about Gresham College in late Elizabethan and early Stuart times suggest that it was the matrix in which the Royal Society originated and in which it was formed and moulded'.[23] Miss Syfret, on the other hand, tends to the view that 'the evidence does not seem to warrant either the conjecture that Gresham College was the direct cause or immediate stimulus of the meetings in 1645'.[24] Gresham College certainly helped to create a receptive atmosphere. To claim that it did more than this, would be wishful thinking. The connection with the College of Physicians was one both of personnel and ideology. It has been established that of the eighty-two members of the college in the period 1603–25, at least twenty-seven had serious scientific interests. As these eighty-two constituted almost the entire authorized medical profession in London, the fact that nearly a third of them were practising scientists shows clearly that the Royal Society was the culmination, not the initiator, of the scientific movement in England. Of the 115 original fellows mentioned in the society's second charter of 22 April 1663, twenty-four were physicians. In the years immediately following another fifteen were to join. At the Restoration the College of Physicians only had sixty-two members, so that about 60% of its membership had been elected to the Royal Society in the early years of the latter's existence.[25]

There had of course been scientific societies in Europe long before the foundation of the Royal Society in 1660.[26] One of the earliest was the Accademia dei Lincei established at Rome in 1601. But perhaps the most important and influential was the

Accademia del Cimento, which flourished at Florence between 1657 and 1667. This group enjoyed powerful ducal support and had among its members men as distinguished as Vincenzo Viviani and Alfonso Borelli. It produced an account of its experiments in 1666, which was translated into English by Richard Waller, F.R.S., under the title *Essayes of Natural Experiments made in the Academie del Cimento* (London, 1684). A severely scientific group, its conclusions were strictly limited by the necessities of observed evidence rather than dependent on little more than the whims of speculative imagination. In this the Royal Society could not emulate the Florentine academy, if only because its membership included persons whose interests were oriented more in the direction of the obviously bizarre and strange than towards genuine scientific research. 'The universal curiosity manifested by the early members . . . towards unfamiliar natural phenomena of every description proved a source of weakness. They cast their net too widely and forfeited the advantages of united and prolonged concentration upon a limited set of problems.'[27] In France too there had been several scientific groups of varying formality, notably those formed under Mersenne, Montmor, Justel, and the Abbé Bourdelot.

That the founders of the Royal Society were conscious of their debt to these continental academies is evident from the first entry in the Journal Book of the society, dated 28 November 1660. 'It was proposed that some course might be thought of to improve this meeting to a more regular way of debating things, and according to the manner in other countryes, where there were voluntary associations of men into academies for the advancement of various parts of learning.'[28] The society obtained its second charter from Charles II in April 1663, when it first adopted the title of 'The Royal Society of London for Improving Natural Knowledge'. King Charles, to whom many books were dedicated by fellows of the society in terms of fulsome praise, graciously declared himself *Fundator et Patronus* of the new academy. He presented its mace, granted it a distinguished coat of arms, and equally graciously regretted his inability to provide more substantial support. The king had no deep interest in science and his small measure of involvement was due mainly to his friendship with some of the royalist founder members. The English society was therefore, unlike some of those on the continent, which were often subsidized by wealthy patrons, forced to provide its own finance.

The aims of the infant society were succinctly expressed by Robert Hooke, one of its most brilliant members. They were:

To improve the knowledge of naturall things, and all useful arts, manufactures, mechanick practises, engines, and inventions by experiments (not meddling with divinity . . .). To examine all systems, theories, principles, hypotheses, elements, histories, and experiments, . . . practised by any considerable authors ancient or modern. In order to the compiling of a complete system of solid philosophy for explicating all phenomena produced by nature or art.[29]

The society, according to Hooke, was to eschew hypotheses until this work was finished. It was to question all doctrines, 'adopting nor adhering to none till by mature debate and clear arguments, . . . the truth of such experiments be demonstrated invincibly'. But in fact the Royal Society was quite unable to live up to Hooke's narrow and magisterial ruling.

The number of fellows in the society, which had stood at 131 during the latter part of 1663, rose to 215 by 1673.[30] During the decade 1663–73 an effective administration had been evolved, and membership had increased by 64%, while the most important of the communications received were being published in the *Philosophical Transactions*, founded in 1665 by Henry Oldenburg, and one of the first journals of its kind.[31] After 1675, however, the number of members began to decline. By 1680 it had fallen to 199, and in the June of that year John Evelyn wrote to Samuel Pepys begging him for:

One half-hour of your presence and assistance toward the most material concern of a society which ought not to be dissolved for want of a redress. . . . You know we do not usually fall on business till pretty late in expectation of a fuller company, and therefore if you decently could fall in amongst us by 6 or 7 it would, I am sure, infinitely oblige . . . the whole society.[32]

Also by 1680 the arrears of the fellows' contributions had reached £3259 5s. 6d., while two years later they were higher still. The average ordinary annual income, which during the period 1667–70 had been £246 2s. 3d. (with an average fellowship of 203), fell to £166 11s. 7d. in 1676–80 (with an average fellowship of 199). Each member was supposed to pay the sum of 52s. each year in satisfaction of the weekly impost of 1s. But in the period 1676–80 the average yearly payment per fellow was as low as 12s. 8d.[33] So serious did the committee of the society consider the situation, that during these years several fellows, having fallen into excessive arrears, were expelled. A memorandum headed 'Proposals for the Advancement of the R. Soc.', which probably dates from about this time, put the matter plainly.

If the members of the R.S. do nothing, seldome come to meetings, and when they come 'tis only as to a play to amuse themselves for an hour or so, yet if they pay their contribution which by their subscription they are unavoidably obliged to do, they take themselves to be (and indeed in respect of those who scandalously refuse payment are) good members.[34]

Although the society was still producing excellent work in the 1680s, this, when compared with the achievements of the previous decade, was a period of decline. By 1690 the fellowship had sunk to 136, the lowest it was ever to reach, and only two or three new members were being admitted each year.[35] But two important events took place in this decade which show that scientific interest in Britain had not declined as disastrously as a study of the Royal Society alone might lead one to believe. The two occurrences were the foundation, in the same month of the year 1683, of the Philosophical Societies at Oxford and Dublin.

II. THE IRISH BACKGROUND

The Philosophical Society at Oxford was successor to that which had flourished in the 1650s, and there had always been intermittent scientific activity in that city throughout the period 1660–83. During the great plague of 1665 so many of the London scientists withdrew to Oxford that Robert Boyle wrote to Oldenburg that he 'did not know why we might not, though not as a society, . . . renew our meetings. . . . I offered them my lodging, where over a dish of fruit we had a great deal of pleasing discourse, and some experiments that I shew'd them.'[36] And later during the early months of 1683 'an ingenious assembly' was meeting at Oxford to discuss philosophical matters.[37] The first meeting of the formally constituted Philosophical Society did not however take place until 26 October, and from then until 3 June 1690 regular minutes were kept of its transactions.[38]

The Dublin Philosophical Society, although founded in the same year of 1683, was not, unlike the Oxford group, based on any important or lengthy scientific tradition. Ireland had in the main been relatively unaffected by the revolution in thought that had been sweeping through Europe during the first three-quarters of the seventeenth century. There had of course been some writers and philosophers of merit living and working in Ireland before 1683, but they had on the whole had little organic relation to Irish life. Archbishop Ussher of Armagh, intellectually the most imposing figure of this early period, combined moderate religious Calvinism and academic modernity in a manner more typical of the contemporary Dissenter than of bishops of the established church.[39] He gave financial assistance to Samuel Hartlib, who as well as being publisher of Petty's *Advice*, acted as a one-man clearing-house for advanced ideas in education, religion, and the sciences. In 1641 he paid the publishing costs of Arnold and Gerard Boate's *Philosophia Naturalis* (Dublin, 1641), being in agreement with the book's strongly anti-Aristotelian tone.[40] When in 1640 Dr Prideaux expressed fears over some of John Dury's pansophist writings, 'having certain information dass der Ertzbischof [Laud] doth not altogether' approve, his friend Constantine Adams, 'to shade off this needlesse fear, . . . did instance unto him in the ArchB. of Armach'.[41] Ussher also tempted Nathanael Carpenter to Dublin as schoolmaster of the king's wards. Carpenter, who was deeply influenced by William Gilbert and sympathetic to the new astronomy, is best known as author of *Philosophia Libera* (Frankfurt, 1621), which contains a long and detailed attack on the peripatetic school of natural philosophy. Himself a scientist of some ability, he pleaded for an openness of vision and a receptiveness to new ideas, though he later regretted having neglected divinity for the study of mathematics.[42]

But Ussher himself was no scientist, and knew relatively little of the New Learning's techniques and justification. His correspondence with the English mathematician Henry Briggs and with the astronomer John Bainbridge was concerned largely with the help the new science could provide for his own historical and chronological studies.[43] Thus while he was obviously interested in Briggs's remark of 1610 on Kepler's 'making scarce any use of any former hypotheses',[44] his historical frame of mind made him extremely susceptible to arguments of precedence and development. As he told William Camden in 1614, 'And in every truth, when the matter is meerly historical, . . . I have no right to use mine own invention, but simply to produce what I find delivered by them that went before me.'[45] None the less Ussher's interest in science did lead him to acquire some of the manuscripts belonging to John Dee, Edward Wright, and John Bainbridge.[46]

In the antiquarian field Sir James Ware, who died in 1666, was pioneering the systematic study of Ireland's past. In his association with Duald MacFirbis, the Gaelic scholar, he anticipated the Dublin Society's interest in Celtic studies, which it too fostered through contact with native scholars such as Roderic O'Flaherty and Teague O'Roddy. But despite the work of Ussher, Carpenter, Ware, and others, the only scientific book in the modern manner relating to Ireland written before the Restoration was Gerard Boate's *Irelands Naturall History*, published at London by Samuel Hartlib in 1652. Although the book had the severely practical aim of attracting Cromwellian planters to Ireland, it none the less 'represents a parting of ways not only for Irish geography but for a wider field in Britain and the rest of Europe'.[47] Breaking away from the old chorography, Boate based his views on observation and verifiable fact. He himself had not been to Ireland before completing the book, but had relied on the excellent descriptions sent by his brother Arnold, a friend of Hartlib's and a firm believer in 'the true experimental natural philosophy', who had, through Ussher's influence, obtained appointment as Surgeon-General for Ireland. The Boates were not Irish, however, coming originally from Holland, a country then well known for the excellence of its geographers.

But these were only isolated incidents, and when Robert Boyle was in Ireland during the 1650s, he held it to be 'a barbarous country, where chemical spirits were so misunderstood and chemical instruments so unprocurable, that it was hard to have any Hermetic thoughts in it.'[48] In February 1654 Samuel Hartlib wrote to Boyle, who was then in Ireland.'Sir, you complain of that barbarous . . . country, wherein you live. . . . [Surely] Dr Child, Mr Worsley, Dr Petty, Major Morgan, (not to mention others),

. . . would abundantly cherish in you many philosophical thoughts, and encourage you, perhaps more vigorously, than I can do at this distance, . . . to venture even upon divers . . . experiments for the advancement both of health and wealth.'[49] Boyle followed Hartlib's advice, at least to the extent of conducting anatomical experiments with Petty, who was as yet not involved in the organization of the Down Survey.[50]

This survey, the most remarkable scientific work undertaken in Ireland before the Restoration, was begun early in 1655 and completed in March 1656. It tabulated and described the whole country, and although modern research has shown that it underestimated the area of lands confiscated by the Commonwealth, it was the first truly modern survey of Ireland and a milestone in the science of cartography.[51] The Down Survey had however been preceded by others, and it was in the field of practical mathematics that Ireland first experienced the workings of modern science. Already in the late sixteenth century at least three surveyors of distinction, Robert Lythe, Paul Ivye, and John Browne, were active in Ireland, which was then being assiduously mapped under the direction of Sir Henry Sidney, Lord Deputy from 1566 to 1571. Indeed between 1580 and 1603 'more maps were drawn of that country and its provinces and districts than of English regions',[52] while in the seventeenth century men like William Forster and Henry Osborne worked in Ireland, both as surveyors and mathematicians. Osborne, to whom William Molyneux dedicated the second part of his *Dioptrica Nova* (London, 1692), was himself an Irishman and lived in County Meath.[53] He corresponded with a number of English scientists including Robert Hooke, who supplied him with a telescope.[54] In 1654 he produced a seven page pamphlet in which he described a 'more exact way to delineate the plot of any spacious parcel of land', in an attempt to correct the inefficient surveying methods then in use.[55] Complementing the activities of the surveyors was the work of the military engineers, at least some of whom seem to have been of higher than average competence.[56]

Thus in the first half of the seventeenth century Ussher, Carpenter, and some others were trying to introduce a more 'modern' intellectual atmosphere into Ireland. But despite their undoubted abilities, they stand out so prominently largely as a result of the flatness of the surrounding countryside. The proof of their lack of success is that the research of the Boates, the experiments of Boyle and Petty, and of course the latter's survey work, are the only real signs of concerted scientific effort in Ireland during the period 1640–60. Exaggeration is dangerous, but with the evidence at hand no other conclusion can be reached than that the scientific scene in pre-Restoration Ireland was one in which inertia, rather than movement, was clearly the dominant feature. Ireland, as a result of its political, economic, and social condition, could not in the first half of the seventeenth century provide a congenial context within which the natural philosopher might readily work.

The output of Irish printers and publishers before the Restoration does not reflect any pronounced interest in the New Learning. The overwhelming majority of books printed in Ireland during the period 1601–1700 appeared at Dublin, and Dublin printing therefore demands the most serious attention. As far as can be discovered the number of books and pamphlets produced at Dublin can be tabulated as follows:[57]

1601–1625	38
1626–1650	93
1651–1675	193
1676–1700	525

Most of these publications were of a religious nature and the number devoted to science, using that term in the widest possible sense, was very small. The earliest work of a scientific nature printed at Dublin was Dermot O'Meara's *Pathologia Haereditaria Generalis* (1619). O'Meara was a graduate of Oxford and an honorary fellow of the London College of Physicians.[58] His book is old-fashioned in presentation and argument, and relies heavily on the doctrines of Hippocrates and Galen. Other notable Dublin publications in some way connected with the development of natural philosophy were Gerard and Arnold Boate's *Philosophia Naturalis* (1641), Nathaniel Henshaw's *Aero Chalinos: Or a Register for the Air* (1664), William Molyneux's *Six Metaphysical Meditations of Descartes* (1680), Edward Wetenhall's *Judgement of the Comet* (1682), Patrick Bellon's *The Irish Spaw* (1684), William Molyneux's *Sciothericum Telescopicum* (1686), Charles Allen's *The Operator for the Teeth* (1686), Jacobus Sylvius's

Novissima Idea de Febribus (1686), and Henry Davis's *Practical Gauging* (1687).

But these publications were few in number. They appeared as follows:

1601–1625	1
1626–1650	1
1651–1675	4
1676–1700	14

The other towns which maintained presses during the seventeenth century, Kilkenny, Cork, Waterford, and Belfast, failed to produce a single book of scientific interest before 1701. Of course not all books written by Irishmen appeared in their native land. A number of important works were published at London. They include the Boates' *Naturall History* (1652), the *Speculum Matricis: Or the Irish Midwives' Handmaid* (1670) by the Cork physician James Wolveridge, which was probably the first work in English on its subject, Allen Mullen's *Account of the Elephant* (1682), Timothy Byfield's *The Artificial Spaw* (1684), and William Molyneux's *Dioptrica Nova* (1692). Petty's valuable statistical writings relating to Ireland were also published at London. Medical works were however the most numerous in this category, and mention should be made of books by the two most prominent Irish physicians to practise for a time in late seventeenth-century England. They were Edmund O'Meara, who published his attack on the neurological theories of Thomas Willis at London in 1665 under the title *Examen Diatribae T. Willisii de Febribus* (reprinted Amsterdam, 1667), and Bernard Connor, whose principal medical works are the *Dissertationes Medico-Physica* (Oxford, 1695) and *Evangelium Medici* (London, 1697). O'Meara was, like his father, a fellow of the London College of Physicians, and Connor was admitted to the Royal Society in 1695.[59]

One of the few significant points of contact in Ireland between science and a popular audience is to be found in the activities of almanac writers. Irish almanacs of this period, contain, as do their English counterparts, a *mélange* of historical, prophetical, geographical, political, and astronomical information. They vary greatly in quality. But their combination of comparatively accurate – if basic – astronomical matter and purely egregious nonsense, reflects, to a greater extent than is sometimes supposed, the peculiarly confused state of contemporary science in general. Because they are not the sort of book usually preserved in libraries, many have certainly been lost. Notwithstanding this, the fact that only three Irish almanacs have survived for the period 1601–60, as compared with twenty-one for the last forty years of the century, indicates a considerable growth of interest in this field after the Restoration. The actual years of publication strengthen this view.

1612	1	1683	1	1694	1
1636	1	1684	2	1695	2
1646	1	1685	2	1696	1
1665	1	1686	1	1697	2
1666	1	1691	1	1699	2
1679	1	1692	1	1700	1[60]
1681	1				

It can be noted therefore that the publication of Irish almanacs seems to have been virtually suspended during the period of parliamentary and Cromwellian rule. In England, however, almanac makers flourished under the Long Parliament. One of them, John Booker, wrote from a defiantly Puritan standpoint, attacking 'episcopal chaplains', and praising the 'liberty given by the noble parliament now [1646] resident at Westminster for the advance of any man's learning'.[61] Booker had no parallel in Ireland and, with the exception of a pro-Catholic almanac printed at Waterford in 1646,[62] nothing of note seems to have appeared between 1636 and 1665.

The work of almanac makers does provide some evidence of mathematical and astronomical activity in seventeenth-century Ireland. William Farmer, author of the earliest surviving Irish piece, the *Prognosticall Almanacke* of 1612, described himself as a 'chirurgian' and 'practitioner in the mathematicall artes',[63] while the most famous of the Irish astrologers of the time, John Whalley (1653–1724), claimed the title of 'student in physick and mathematicks'.[64] Whalley became active at Dublin in 1682, and soon reached so considerable an eminence that he was consulted by the government for his astrological information as to the whereabouts of the Duke of Monmouth in 1685.[65]

Almanac makers did not confine themselves to the written

word. Most of them engaged in teaching, specializing particularly in mathematics and astronomy. In 1685 Whalley was available for consultation at the *Golden Last* on the Upper Coomb.[66] One year later he was selling nostrums and teaching 'arithmetic, geometry, trigonometry, navigation, gauging, [and] measuring' at the same address.[67] John McCombe and Andrew Cumpsty were similarly engaged at the *Sign of the Royal Exchange* on the Wood Quay in 1692.[68] Again, in Whalley's most substantial production, his English edition of Ptolemy's astrological treatise the *Quadripartitum*, dedicated to the English astrologer John Partridge and to 'Michael Cudmore, doctor of physick at Drogheda' in Ireland, he recommended Solomon Grisdale and Jonathan Hill, 'masters of the mathematical school next door to the post office in Fishamble Street, Dublin'. It is interesting to note that as well as teaching the usual wide range of mathematical 'arts', these two also claimed competence in the extremely practical fields of 'merchant's accompts and bookkeeping, either after the Italian, Dutch, or English manner'.[69]

Even the authorities in Dublin had, by the time of James II, been convinced of the necessity of providing some practical training in mathematics for those wishing to become navigators or surveyors. In January 1688 the corporation, conscious of 'there being noe free schoole kept in this cittie for teaching poor youth the mathematicall sciences, as there is in most other countries, the erecting of which would be a great benefit to seamen, surveyors, and others', granted an annual salary of twenty pounds to one Patrick Bourke, and put a room at his disposal for the foundation of such a school.[70]

After the Restoration, Petty, that 'most rare and exact anatomist . . . excelling in all mathematical and mechanical learning',[71] began his series of experiments with double-bottom ships. In all he made four attempts to build such a catamaran-type vessel over a period of twenty-five years. The first, a complete failure, was launched early in 1662. Later in the same year he built the *Invention II*, the most successful ship he was ever to construct. It twice sailed from Dublin to Holyhead in Wales and back, and won him a wager of £50. Viscount Brouncker, the first president of the Royal Society, wrote to Petty in November 1662, asking him to report to those fellows of the society then in Dublin, who were to examine his ship on behalf of the society. But nothing came of this, and Brouncker soon lost interest, primly declaring that 'the matter of navigation being a state concerne was not proper to be managed by the society'.[72]

Petty's nautical endeavours were one of the great excitements at Dublin in the field of harmless entertainment. In 1663 an anonymous poet lampooned the 'genius' in verse as unsuccessful as the latter's double-bottom.

> When first of all this famous model
> Sprung from a mathematick noddle,
> Who honour saw, alltho' dimm sighted,
> And was for fair invention knighted, . . .
> Working in this, now on that matter,
> And compassing both land and water,
> By mathematick and by logick,
> He goes about his famous project.[73]

The Irish sailors being reluctant to man the ship, Petty was forced to dispense burnt wine, stewed prunes, and gingerbread, in an expensive but unsuccessful attempt to make them oblivious to danger.[74] In December 1664 he launched another ship, which was named the *Experiment* by Charles II. It sailed as far as Oporto, but sank on the return journey. After this triple fiasco, although the 'fit of the double-bottom', as Sir Robert Southwell called it, continued to occupy Petty's thoughts, it did not again take material shape until 1684, when another vessel was built with the financial help of some members of the Dublin Society.

Prior to 1683 the only organized bodies in Ireland with scientific connections were the Barber-Surgeons Company and the Dublin College of Physicians. The former, more correctly known as the Guild of St Mary Magdalene, received its first charter from Henry VI in 1446. Its influence is impossible to assess, although it did provide from among its number one member of the Dublin Society – Josias Patterson. It was reformed under James II, who granted a new charter in 1687, which widened its scope to include apothecaries and wig-makers as well as barbers and surgeons. The history of the College of Physicians begins in 1654, when Dr John Stearne, a grand-nephew of Archbishop Ussher and a graduate of Trinity College Dublin and Sidney Sussex College Cambridge, founded a Fraternity of Physicians at Dublin in a house belonging to the university. But already as early as 1619 Dermot O'Meara had written to Lord Deputy St

John, 'There are certainly more persons in Dublin at the present day practising the art of medicine than any other art, yet there are very few of them who have the six qualifications which Hippocrates requires in a medical doctor'.[75] The regulation of the profession was therefore obviously an important and pressing task. In 1626 Peter de Laune, a fellow of the London College of Physicians then practising in Ireland, informed the English body that in answer to a petition signed by himself and four other doctors, the king had agreed to the establishment of an organization at Dublin modelled on Henry VIII's London foundation.[76] The proposed scheme was not however implemented. But already Dublin University had made some provision for a medical fellowship, the holder of which was known as the 'medicus'. The position was first filled by Sir John Temple in 1618, who was succeeded two years later by Thomas Beere. Neither of these men had any formal medical qualifications, and their influence on the progress of medicine in Ireland cannot have been great.

Little is known of Stearne's foundation of 1654, save that it was attached to the university and was most probably not limited to Protestants.[77] In 1662 Stearne, a man of wide literary as well as medical interests, was appointed professor of physic in Trinity College at an annual salary of £60, which was chargeable to the state. Five years later, in August 1667, a royal charter was secured for a College of Physicians, which was to contain not more than fourteen fellows and was to control the practice of medicine within a seven mile radius of Dublin City. The object of the new corporation, whose motto was the topical one of *Ratione et Experientia*, was to stamp out 'the daily abuses of . . . physick in the kingdom by the practice of mountebanks and empirics'.[78] By 1676 the college had secured a small quantity of scientific equipment, and in that year undertook some anatomical dissections for the benefit of the membership.[79] Stearne, the first president, died in 1669, and from then on that officer was appointed by the authorities of Trinity College. Indeed the connection between the two institutions was a close one, the Physicians deciding in 1695 that 'whoever is to be a fellow of this society is first to be admitted Dr of physick in the University of Dublin'.[80] But with the exception mentioned above, the college did not conduct experiments, nor do its members seem to have

C

met regularly for scientific discussion. It was predominantly a professional body regulating the conduct and standards of medical practitioners in Dublin,[81] although even here it was not always successful. As late as the last years of the century the college, having been sent an empiric to examine by the bishop's court, and having judged him 'grossly ignorant', found that it could do little to enforce its opinion.[82] In addition the examinations given to candidates for admission were, until 1716, generally of a medieval character, and the questions disputed were framed in the traditional manner. None the less in 1696 Robert Molesworth could assert that 'I think the Irish doctors better than the English ones.'[83]

Interest in natural philosophy was therefore becoming steadily more widespread after the Restoration, particularly among the Anglo-Irish element. In the few years immediately prior to the foundation of the Dublin Society more and more evidence presents itself of a new awakening in Irish intellectual life. For instance, in 1675 George Tollet, a private teacher of mathematics in Dublin and later a founder member of the society, was importing scientific instruments from England, conducting magnetical experiments, and corresponding with a fellow of the Royal Society.[84] At the same time Robert Wood, an English mathematician elected F.R.S. in 1681, was active in Ireland, from whence he promised Robert Hooke a description of the magnetic variations in 1676.[85] He also subscribed £20 towards Petty's renewed boat-building experiments of 1684.[86] And in 1681 there occurred in Dublin the somewhat improbable event about which Petty wrote to John Aubrey in the July of that year. 'I have taken care,' he wrote, 'that the elephant which was so unfortunately burnt here, might be dissected for so much as the fire left capable of it.'[87]

The physician who anatomized the elephant on Petty's instructions was Dr Allen Mullen, and the pamphlet he published on his findings was to remain the standard work in English on its subject for many years.[88] The macabre happenings described in the pamphlet rivalled Petty's nautical experiments in local popularity, for when the fire had been extinguished, the mob rushed to obtain parts of the animal as souvenirs of the occasion. To prevent this, the manager of the circus in which the elephant had been appearing, 'procured a file of musqueteers to guard him'. Owing to the noisome odour given off by the carcass, Mullen was forced to dissect at once, with the doubtful help of some butchers, whose 'forwardness to cut and slash what came first in their way', made his task a difficult one.[89] Despite these obstacles Mullen was able to perform a dissection at once detailed and informative.

But the most important scientific event at this time concerned the projected map of Ireland, with topographical descriptions, undertaken by William Molyneux as an Irish contribution to Moses Pitt's *English Atlas*. Robert Hooke, who was Pitt's principal scientific collaborator, had insisted that detailed regional descriptions accompany each part of the *Atlas*, and had probably suggested Molyneux as director of the Irish section, having heard of his abilities from John Flamsteed, the Astronomer-Royal and a mutual friend.[90] In the Summer of 1682 Molyneux, in association with some others, published a sheet of queries which were sent around the country to various persons, so that by this means detailed geographical information might be obtained.[91] The actual idea of a natural history of Ireland was neither new nor original. As early as 1654, the work of the Boates being thought of as little more than a beginning, Samuel Hartlib had suggested a similar undertaking to Boyle, proposing that 'it would much further that design if every ingenious head amongst you would take notice of whatsoever worth the observation occureth in any place, that so by little and little we might perfectly come to understand the natural history of all parts in that country'.[92] Petty, with his surveying expertise, was almost certainly involved in Molyneux's scheme, and his influence is noticeable in several of the queries contained in the questionnaire of 1682, one of which asks, 'How each county is inhabited, thickly or thinly?' In 1672 Petty had written the *Political Anatomy of Ireland*, and ten years later was presumably still eager to obtain accurate statistical information for use in any future study. Molyneux's appeal was successful, and a large number of replies were received over a period of three years. Narcissus Marsh, then Provost of Trinity College, also took part in the scheme, and in May 1682 reported to Archbishop Michael Boyle of Armagh, 'We are now (a club of us who meet every week in the college) upon the design of giving an account of Ireland to be printed in the new atlas.'[93] But shortly afterwards Moses Pitt was arrested for debt in London and his grandiose scheme collapsed, only four of the eleven projected volumes having been published. Molyneux described the 'heap of rude materials' which he had gathered together for the venture, and which he hoped 'in time to have shaped and modelled in some sort of order'. Eventually much of it was burned.[94]

The project for a natural history of Ireland reflected a widespread contemporary enthusiasm. The Oxford Society, under the directorship of the topographer Robert Plot, examined particular areas of England, while the short-lived Philosophical Society founded at Boston by Increase Mather (who had studied at Trinity College Dublin in the 1650s), devoted itself to the collection of material for a natural history of New England.[95]

William Molyneux, who is best remembered for his political tract *The Case of Ireland* (Dublin, 1698), may be regarded as the founder of the Dublin Philosophical Society. He was born at Dublin in 1656, and having attended school there, entered Trinity College Dublin in 1671, under the tuition of William Palliser.[96] His career at the university was a successful one, and on going down he was presented with a testimonial, 'drawn up in the strongest terms and in an uncommon form, signifying the high opinion they had conceived of his genius, the probity of his manner, and the remarkable progress he had made in letters.'[97] When he left Trinity in 1675 his father sent him to London to study law, and in the June of that year he entered the Middle Temple.

However he made it not his profession, having a stronger passion for other studies, and a considerable fortune from his father. . . . The bent of his genius lay strongly to mathematical and philosophical studies; . . . even at the university he conceived a great dislike to the scholastick learning then being taught in that place; and young as he was, he fell intirely into Lord Bacon's methods and those prescribed by the Royal Society.[98]

It would seem probable, although there is no direct evidence for this, that during his three years at the Middle Temple Molyneux met several fellows of the Royal Society, and perhaps even attended some of their meetings. What is certain is that when he returned to London in 1680 to seek a cure for his blind wife, he consulted a number of medical fellows including Sir Charles Scarburgh, Walter Needham, and Richard Lower.[99] Molyneux himself mentions how already as an undergraduate he had spent most of his time in reading the *Philosophical Transactions*, and the works of Descartes, Bacon, and Gassendi.[100] It is therefore hardly surprising that when this ardent young Baconian, barely twenty-six years old, discovered, through his activities in connection with Pitt's *Atlas*, what seemed to him a considerable enthusiasm in Ireland for natural philosophy, he should have felt that a more permanent association might flourish in Dublin.[101] That city was then experiencing a rapid growth in population, which by the mid-1680s had risen to about 70,000, a threefold increase since the Restoration.[102] It was, after London, by far the largest town in the British Isles, and supported a considerable number of bookshops and publishers, a sector which underwent a remarkable expansion in the decade between 1680 and 1690.[103] Having seen the Royal Society at close quarters, Molyneux had already held meetings with 'other gentlemen in Dublin' who were concerned with the *Atlas*; and so, he writes, about:

the October of 1683 I began to busy myself in forming a society in this city, agreeable to the design of the Royal Society in London. I should not be so vain as to arrogate this to myself, were there not many of the gentlemen at present [1694] listed in that society, who can testify for me, that I was the first promoter of it, and can witness how diligent I was therein. The first I applied to . . . was . . . Dr St George Ashe, who presently approved of the undertaking, and assisted heartily in the first efforts we made in the work. I first brought together about half a dozen, that met weekly in a private room in a coffee-house, . . . merely to discourse of philosophy, mathematicks, and other polite literature, as things arose *obiter*, without any settled rules or forms. But our company increasing, we were invited by the Rev. Dr Huntington, then Provost of the College, to meet in his lodgings; and there we began to form ourselves in January 1684, and took on us the name of the Dublin Society.[104]

This is the most detailed account of the society's foundation, and although Molyneux may possibly have exaggerated his own rôle in the affair, other sources tend to substantiate it.

By this time Molyneux, without a doubt the most able Irish scientist of his day, was already corresponding regularly with one of the leading fellows of the Royal Society. This was John Flamsteed, the first Astronomer-Royal, who was the recipient of many complaints from Molyneux about the difficulty of conducting scientific experiments in Ireland. In September 1681 he regretted living 'in a kingdom barren of all things . . . [and] wholly destitute of instruments'.[105] But within two years matters had so much improved that in April 1683 Molyneux was complaining of his having to move his large collection of instruments to a more convenient place for astronomical observation.[106] In 1683 William's younger brother Thomas Molyneux left Ireland for Leyden, in order to study medicine in Holland. He interrupted his journey at London, and from there sent several long letters to his brother in Dublin, describing his visits to the Royal Society, and giving short impressions of the fellows. In reply to one of these William wrote to inform Thomas of the new society, which he called a *Conventio Philosophica*, mentioning that its members had already discussed medical problems at their meetings, which were regulated by an *Arbiter Conventionis*, 'at present Dr Willoughby, the name president being yet a little too great for us'.[107] He also claimed that Petty and 'all the virtuosi of this place favour it much', especially Robert Huntington, the Provost of Trinity College. It would seem therefore that the infant society enjoyed the support of at least an important part of the contemporary Dublin intellectual establishment.

Chapter 2

The Members of the Society

The Dublin Philosophical Society, although it had no adminis-
trative links with Trinity College Dublin, was composed in the
main of graduates of that university.[1] The earliest extant
membership list is dated 28 January 1684, on which day the
society met to subscribe to its first set of rules.[2] There are
fourteen names, with Dr Charles Willoughby as director and
William Molyneux holding the combined posts of secretary and
treasurer. Nine of these fourteen original members had studied
at Trinity College, while Huntington, Marsh and Petty, who
were English, had all attended Oxford University. Only Mark
Baggot and George Tollet do not seem to have studied at any
British university. In Baggot's case this is understandable, for as
a Roman Catholic he was debarred from such institutions. The
only Catholic to join the society, he took little part in its proceedings, although quite seriously interested in the science of the
day. His non-attendance at meetings was due largely to his
living in County Carlow. Nevertheless he several times employed
an amanuensis to transcribe some of the works of Galileo and
other writers.[3] After the Williamite Settlement, Baggot, who for
obvious reasons was described by his Protestant neighbours as 'a
virulent Papist', had large parts of his estate confiscated, despite
his close friendship with William King, a fellow member of the
Dublin Society and then Bishop of Derry, to whom he appealed
for help.[4] He still however continued his interest in scientific
pursuits, especially when visiting Dublin at the turn of the
century to obtain restitution for his confiscated property.[5]
George Tollet, a self-educated man, had by 'his own industry . . .
arrived to an eminency in mathematicks, which he [had]
taught in the City of Dublin with credit for many years'.[6] As
early as 1675 he had been in correspondence with the Royal
Society about magnetical experiments, and in 1689 left for
England, where he was appointed one of the Commissioners for

the Navy.[7] He continued to write regularly to William King and acted as his agent in London, where he gained a reputation as 'both an honest and very able man'.[8]

The founder of the society, William Molyneux, was of a wealthy landed family, descended from Sir Thomas Molyneux, who had been Chancellor of the Irish Exchequer under Queen Elizabeth.[9] Through his marriage in 1678 to Lucy, youngest daughter of Sir William Domvile, the Irish Attorney-General, Molyneux was connected with one of the most prominent families in the country. A more considerate landlord than most, in 1690 he reduced the rents of the tenants on his Castle Dillon estate, 'till the poor people could put themselves in a condition of living and paying their landlord'.[10] There is however no evidence to suggest that he improved his property in a scientific manner. Thomas Molyneux, his younger brother, studied medicine at Leyden, then one of the best medical centres in Europe. On his return in 1685 he established a large and flourishing practice in Dublin. There were also two sisters in the family, one of whom married Bishop Dopping of Meath, and the other, Dr John Madden. Dopping was to become a staunch Williamite, whose main intellectual diversion was the study of Eastern languages. John Madden, who had studied medicine at Trinity College, joined the society in 1684, but took little part in its business. The two Molyneuxs came therefore from the higher reaches of the Irish social scale and mixed freely with men of influence and power.

William Petty, born in 1623 and the society's first president, was of humble origins, being the son of 'a meane man somewhere in Sussex'.[11] A child prodigy, he obtained at an early age a number of academic appointments at Oxford, and in 1652 was sent to Ireland as Physician-General to the parliamentary army, thus entering upon a thirty-five-year period of alternating residence in England and Ireland. He was soon working on the Down Survey, in the course of which he managed to obtain for himself several estates, the largest being in County Kerry. Petty impressed most people with his near omniscience, and John Evelyn thought him 'a genius' who 'adventures at nothing which is not demonstration'.[12] Already before the foundation of the society in October 1683, he had met some of its future members, including Tollet, to whom in 1679 he offered the post

of rent collector for his Kerry estates 'on rising wages'.[13] Tollet
however declined. Petty had been a founder fellow of the Royal
Society, and despite his parliamentary background had found
it easy to adjust to the changed circumstances brought about by
the Restoration. Charles II had in fact confirmed his land titles
and knighted him shortly after 1660. His name added prestige
to the infant Dublin Society, and his support provided it with
immediate contacts with contemporary English science.[14]

A strong clerical group is noticeable among the membership
of the Dublin Society during the first period of its existence
between 1683 and 1687. Of the thirty-three persons who joined
before December 1684, no fewer than seven were either present
or prospective Anglican bishops.[15] Narcissus Marsh was already
Bishop of Ferns and Leighlin, and was later to occupy the
metropolitan sees of Cashel, Dublin, and Armagh. Robert
Huntington became Bishop of Raphoe in 1701, having previously
refused Kilmore. St George Ashe was to occupy in succession the
sees of Cloyne, Clogher, and Derry, while Samuel Foley eventually became Bishop of Down and Connor. William King was in
turn Bishop of Derry and Archbishop of Dublin, and William
Palliser was appointed metropolitan at Cashel in 1694, having
already held Cloyne for little over a year. Finally Edward Smyth
succeeded Foley as Bishop of Down and Connor in 1699. As well
as these representatives of the episcopal bench, the society
attracted a number of less exalted, but still important, Irish
clergymen. John Worth held the influential Dublin Deanery
of St Patrick's. John Baynard was Archdeacon of Connor, John
Keogh Prebendary of Termonbarry, and Richard Acton,
although unbeneficed, was, as fellow and Vice-Provost of
Trinity College, an ordained clergyman. Further augmentation
to this group came when Edward Wetenhall, Bishop of Cork and
Ross, joined the society in 1686. This large measure of support
from men who held or were soon to attain positions of power in
the Irish Church, and consequently often in the Irish state,
becomes more significant when it is noted that of the 119
original or charter fellows of the Royal Society in 1663, only two
were later to become bishops.[16] Most of the clerics who joined
the Dublin Society in 1683 and 1684 were young men, almost all
of whom were to obtain advancement in the church. This does
not indicate any violent antagonism against the New Learning

among the Anglican orthodox of Ireland. Indeed the leaders of the Irish Church seem to have been more sympathetic towards and interested in the New Learning than were their English colleagues. This is brought out clearly by the fact that of the seven bishops elected to the Royal Society between 1683 and 1708, six held or were to hold Irish sees, and of these four were members of the Dublin Society.[17] With the single exception of Archdeacon Baynard, who was to become a non-juror under William and Mary, all the clerical members of the society were remarkable for their doctrinal and practical orthodoxy. A short account of their attitude towards Protestant Dissent will illuminate their religious position.

When William King was appointed Bishop of Derry in 1691 he saw his first task to be the reducing of Dissent, an activity in which he soon achieved remarkable success. Like all bishops of the time he strenuously opposed the celebration and legality of Dissenting marriage services. He also insisted that Nonconformist schoolmasters be arrested and put on trial, and vigorously but unsuccessfully opposed the introduction of the Toleration Act of 1719.[18] St George Ashe too found Presbyterian marriages repugnant, and complained bitterly of the Dissenting ministers' 'crowds at communions' in his diocese of Clogher. In 1700 he was putting official requests to the government, asking it to take a stronger line with the Presbyterians, who then formed by far the largest Dissenting group in Ireland.[19] But eleven years later Ashe's views had become a little more moderate, and in 1711 he spoke in parliament against the more extreme forms of physical persecution then being inflicted on the Dissenters.[20] In the same year as Ashe's conciliatory speech, his old colleague in the Dublin Society, Narcissus Marsh, then Archbishop of Armagh and Primate of All Ireland, was personally instituting the prosecution of a Presbyterian minister in Drogheda under the Act of Uniformity. This was soon to become something of a *cause célèbre* because the government intervened to withdraw all legal proceedings.[21] Marsh was famous for his strong opposition to all forms of religion not reconcilable with the tenets of the established church. Open manifestations of Romanism invariably attracted his angry attention, as did the activities of the Dublin Dissenters, whom he warned against the use of public meeting houses.[22] Edward Smyth of Down and Connor found his own position *vis-à-vis* the local Dissenters so exposed, that he wrote to his friend and fellow scientist Bishop King, to ask for advice as to the best means of putting down the widespread practice of Nonconformist marriage.[23] The single exception to this almost complete unanimity of attitude among the Dublin Society clerics was provided by Edward Wetenhall, who favoured a limited form of religious toleration, and who, like Marsh, was a strong believer in the efficacy of Gaelic scriptures as a tool with which to convert the Roman Catholics of Ireland.[24]

A further group of Anglican ecclesiastics joined the society when it was revived in 1693, the most prominent of whom were John Vesey, Archbishop of Tuam, and Edward Walkington, Bishop of Down and Connor.[25] Like his colleagues Vesey was of the opinion that if Presbyterianism were allowed to go unchecked, 'the consequences . . . must be the destruction of the English church in this kingdom'.[26] Walkington, who at one time had enjoyed a reputation as a moderate, found that the assumption of episcopal office in 1695 forced him to petition the Lord Justices 'to put some check on the liberties assumed by the Dissenters'.[27]

Some of the laymen in the Dublin Society were also prominent in what might be called the 'Dissenter Question' in Ireland. Sir Richard Bulkeley, an original member of the society, himself, towards the end of his life, supported an extreme Protestant sect, but died before his actions could involve him in any unpleasant legal proceedings.[28] James Bonnell, who joined the society in November 1693, was a man who, besides applying 'himself with good success to mathematicks and musick', opposed religious intolerance in a manner uncharacteristic of the Ireland of his day.[29] On the other hand one of the most violent opponents of toleration was also a member of the society. This was Sir Richard Cox, who was active in the society during the 1690s, and who in 1695 led the Irish Privy Council against the very limited form of toleration proposed by Lord Deputy Capel. Shortly afterwards, Cox, then a judge of the King's Bench, was dismissed from the council, because, as he put it, 'I was a firm churchman, and stopped a bill for liberty of conscience, by saying I was content every man should have liberty of going to heaven, but I desired nobody might have liberty of coming into government but those who would conform.'[30] In contrast, Petty not only held that,

> Religion's naturall, and good
> For king and state, if understood;
> If not, 'tis but a meere illusion,
> Begetting bloodshed and confusion.[31]

but argued that 'to force men to say they believe what they do not, is vain, absurd, and without honour to God'.[32]

The clerical members of the society were therefore firm Anglicans, and no trace of deep-rooted Puritanism can be found in their doctrinal position. Naturally their religious attitude was in part a political affirmation of loyalty to constituted authority. But this does not in essence affect the question of their orthodoxy. The lay members of the society were by and large of much the same persuasion. It was these men who founded a scientific society, which never had a Puritan bias or even a Puritan element among its membership. Not only did it include no Dissenters (Bulkeley's conversion taking place after it had ceased to meet), but its Anglican members were not on the whole of an especially 'low' doctrinal position. Baggot was actually a Roman Catholic, Baynard was to become a non-juror, Ashe, Foley, and King were what might be loosely described as High Churchmen, while Huntington refused the see of Kilmore in 1692 because of scruples concerning the dismissal of its non-juring incumbent William Sheridan.[33]

The position of the remaining members, and here Petty and William Molyneux with his Lockian belief that 'liberty' is the 'inherent right of all mankind'[34] are fairly typical, might best be described as Latitudinarian. And in this they were heirs to those mid-century religious moderates who had played so important a part in the development of English science.[35] Whatever may have been the position of Increase Mather's Boston Philosophical Society in 1683, described by one writer as a 'Puritan enterprise',[36] the men at Dublin, despite Archbishop Ussher's earlier 'entire affection' for John Preston,[37] seem to have owed little to the types of belief represented by Richard Sibbes, Thomas Goodwin, or even Richard Baxter. Of course the possibilities of the 1680s were not the same as those of the 1640s. But the thesis that British science owed any unique debt to, or even maintained some form of more loosely parallel development with, an identifiably Puritan belief or outlook on life, is not supported by the Irish situation in the late seventeenth century. In any case the controversy on this point, though it has produced a number of valuable studies, is now in danger of foundering upon the rock of semantic definition.[38]

The original initiative for the Dublin Society came from William Molyneux, an Irishman, although some of its most influential members like Petty, Marsh, and Huntington were English. Of the forty persons who were in some way connected (not always as official members) with the society between 1683 and 1687, eleven were English and one was Dutch. Among the membership there was therefore a sizeable group of persons representing a different, though hardly alien, intellectual background from that of the majority. But apart from the Leyden educated Jacobus Sylvius and Patrick Dun, who may have studied at Marischal College Aberdeen and at an (unknown) continental university, only Petty and Willoughby seem to have had personal experience of European education, though of course Thomas Molyneux was at Leyden during the first years of the society's existence.

About 1636 Petty had gone to France to study languages with the Jesuits at Descartes's old school of *La Flèche* and later at Paris, where he became pupil of, and assistant to, Thomas Hobbes, and was admired by that thinker for his 'pregnant geny'.[39] Willoughby, the son of Sir Francis Willoughby, a major-general in the army of Charles I, a member of the Provincial Council of Munster, and in 1636 Governor of Galway, obtained his M.D. at Padua in March 1664, although that university was then no longer the exciting intellectual centre it had once been.[40] On his return he became President of the Irish College of Physicians, and was Treasurer of that body on his election as Director of the Dublin Society. Despite his medical training Willoughby was not an enthusiastic practitioner, maintaining that his 'liberall and universall' education fitted him for a 'superior sphere than the managery of a glyster-pipe; a trade of so much slavery that I never intended to follow otherwise than for want of better employment.'[41] It is clear from this and other evidence that the scientific inspiration for the Dublin Society came almost entirely from England. Some attempts were made in 1686 and 1687 to establish a direct correspondence with continental intellectuals, but the outbreak of the Williamite Revolution prevented their achieving any practical result.[42]

Of the fourteen original members who joined the society in January 1684, two, Mark Baggot and Francis Cuffe, are never mentioned again in either the minutes or any other of the society's official papers. Cuffe, who was married to Honora, the daughter of Michael Boyle, Archbishop of Armagh and Chancellor of Ireland, came from a family well known for its royalist sympathies. His father 'was strongly attached to the royal cause, and contributed strenuously to bring about the Restoration', for which loyalty he received a knighthood in 1660. Cuffe was himself a fine soldier and a 'very fit person to command the Grenadiers'. He held office as Lieutenant of the Ordnance in Ireland from 1692 until his death in 1695, and sat in the Dublin parliament as member for the family seat of Mayo between 1692 and 1694.[43] He rejoined the society after the Williamite Settlement.

John Baynard, Archdeacon of Connor and future non-juror, is only mentioned twice in the minutes of the society, and on both occasions in connection with non-scientific topics. John Keogh, on the other hand, although living in the country, was in frequent correspondence with the society's secretary, especially during the first year of its existence. He came from an old Irish family which had lost its lands in the Cromwellian Confiscations. A poor man, he was helped by his relative John Hudson, Bishop of Elphin, to obtain the prebend of Termonbarry, and in 1673 settled down to a quiet scholar's life near Strokestown in County Roscommon. In March 1684 he wrote to Molyneux enclosing a long and detailed description of that county, presumably as a belated contribution to the Irish part of Pitt's *Atlas*.[44] Keogh's interest in the business of the society declined after about a year, and his last letter of this period is dated June 1684.[45] Prior to this he had expressed great enthusiasm for the aims of the society, and had several times requested information as to its progress. In reply to one of his queries, he had been informed that,

The society goes on very well, and we have the honour of correspondence with some abroad, particularly the Royal Society of London, and that at Oxford. . . . Seeing you are a fellow of the Dublin

Society, tho' you live absent from us, yet I know you do not neglect the designs of our meetings, . . . therefore I hope you will obleidge us now and then with some of your thoughts.[46]

In the same letter Molyneux had praised Keogh for being the sort of scientist favoured by the society, and had told him that as a mathematician 'not willing to take things for granted without full proof and assurance of them', he was held in high esteem by his colleagues in the metropolis. Keogh was much influenced by the contemporary enthusiasm for explaining all phenomena and processes in mathematical terms. He tried for instance to show mathematically 'what dependence the several degrees of beings have on God Almighty', and also wrote a 'Demonstration in Latin verse of the Trinity', for which he received praise and encouragement from Isaac Newton, himself an adept in such matters.[47] But Keogh's contributions to the proceedings of the society were of a varying standard, and their main point of interest lies in his extensive use of Latin. In this he was unique among the members of the society, for by the 1680s Latin had, at least in France and Britain, if not in Germany, lost its earlier predominance as a vehicle for scientific communication. Newton of course still wrote in Latin partly in order to discourage all but the serious from reading his work. In fact he may even have deterred some of those qualified to appreciate his arguments, for as William Molyneux pointed out in 1690, 'there are many ingenious heads, great geometers, and masters of mathematicks, who are not so well skill'd in Latin'.[48]

Narcissus Marsh, the senior clerical member of the society at its foundation, was an Englishman who had been appointed Provost of Trinity College Dublin in 1679 through the influence of the Duke of Ormonde. He was a product of Oxford University, where he had spent the greater part of his life, first as an undergraduate, then as fellow of Exeter College, and finally as Principal of St Alban Hall. One of his passions was music, and when at Oxford 'he had a weekly meeting in his chamber, . . . where masters of musick would come' and play upon various instruments.[49] A few months before the foundation of the society he was appointed Bishop of Ferns and Leighlin, and as such spent a considerable amount of time in his diocese. Despite this handicap he maintained a virtuoso's interest in science, which, together with the study of Gaelic and Oriental languages, was his most frequent intellectual diversion. When Edward Bernard's British catalogue of manuscripts was published in 1697, Marsh's collection, one of the largest in Ireland, contained seventy mathematical, fifty-four medical, and four botanical manuscripts, most of them in Arabic.[50]

In September 1682 Marsh wrote to Robert Boyle from Dublin, regretting his failure to observe the recent comet in any detail, having seen it only twice 'when its head appeared to the naked eye much bigger, and its tail much shorter than that of the last'. He presumed however that the 'virtuosi of London', who were 'always intent' on rarities, had 'not let it escape their accurate observation'.[51] Comets were obviously a special interest, for in the previous year Marsh had corresponded with the English mathematician John Wallis on the subject.[52] A manuscript containing copies of papers and letters on astronomical matters made for him, and now kept in the library of the Royal Irish Academy, shows him to have been a man of keen intellect and wide interests. In the words of his epitaph, 'Studiis Matheseos, et rerum Naturalium donabat, Linguarum, praesertim Orientalium, peritissimus'.[53] In the final analysis however Marsh was not, even in the seventeenth century sense, a professional scientist, and pursued his studies so that he might come to a closer understanding of the divine nature and the origins of the universe, without in any way regarding the discipline as an end in itself.

Jonathan Swift was an undergraduate at Trinity under Marsh and twenty years later recalled his sometime provost in a manner, the unremitting severity of which 'might suggest a reaction against an adolescent awe of apparent saintliness and erudition'.[54]

His disposition to study is the very same with that of an usurer to hoard up money, or of a vicious young fellow to a wench; nothing but avarice and evil concupiscence, to which his constitution has fortunately given a more innocent turn. He is sordid and suspicious in his domestics, without love or hatred; which is but reasonable, since he has neither friend nor enemy. . . . That which relishes best with him, is mixed liquor and mixed company; and he is seldom unprovided with very bad of both.

But Swift could only contrast Marsh's rapid ecclesiastical preferment with his own comparative lack of success, and let parody and a distorted recollection take the place of distinct and possibly embarrassing memories.

Marsh, although not overenthusiastic about living in Ireland, was prepared to make his career in that country. Robert Huntington, on the other hand, was never happy in Dublin. The son of a Somerset curate, Huntington went to Bristol Grammar School and Merton College Oxford, where he took his B.A. in 1658 and soon afterwards was elected to a fellowship. His zeal for oriental studies was so great that in 1671 he took employment with the Levant Company as chaplain to its factory at Aleppo, where he remained for ten years and from whence he sent many botanical specimens to Jacob Bobart the Younger, which are now in the *Hortus Siccus* at Merton College.[55] In 1683 he was offered the provostship of Trinity College Dublin, which he reluctantly accepted. It was not an easy post, and although Marsh had gained 'an eminent degree of applause due to his merit in the government of that ample society',[56] he had, on his elevation to the episcopate, thought himself well rid 'of 340 boys and young men in this lewd and debauch'd town'.[57] Huntington was appointed to succeed Marsh because the fellows had formed themselves into such violent factions, that Lord Deputy Arran thought it essential that someone be sent over from England, and because Bishop Fell of Oxford had recommended him as a 'fit man to bring [the] college into order again'.[58]

As a good Anglican Huntington despised what he considered the pretensions of Rome. But as a scholar he was prepared and even anxious to meet and cooperate with Roman Catholic priests and laymen. While in the East he had maintained 'an epistolary correspondence with the Patriarch of Antioch, the Archbishop of Mount Sinai, the Primate of Cyprus, and many learned Jesuits, Priests, Carmelites, and other religious persons in those parts'.[59] He had liked the Levant, but thought the Irish climate both injurious and unpleasant, and the only facet of Irish life which he found at all congenial was the opportunity it afforded for the study of the Gaelic language. No man, wrote a contemporary biographer, was ever

More intent in promoting and cherishing learning, . . . nor ever any more concerned for the propagation of the Scriptures in Ireland. . . . The Bishop of Ferns and he by consultation often held with divers

D

other great men, . . . by what just and easy method they might remove the dark ignorance of the Irish, at last . . . pitched upon translating the Old Testament into Irish, and . . . they communicated their design to Mr Robert Boyle, that so holy a purpose might be brought to some effect by his assistance.[60]

Eventually a revised version of William Bedell's translation was published at London in 1685, mainly as a result of the efforts of Huntington, Marsh, and Boyle. In 1688 Huntington, with a mixture of fear and relief, fled to England and settled down as Rector of Great Hallingbury in Essex, until in 1701, the year of his death, he returned to Ireland as Bishop of Raphoe. Huntington contributed little to the proceedings of the Dublin Society and had no deep interest in experimental science. The only paper he read at its meetings dealt with the porphyry pillars in Egypt, and on another occasion he presented two bottles of Connaught mineral waters, so 'that experiments may be made on them'.[61] But his membership and support were useful, not only because his position lent academic respectability to the undertaking, but because he had just left Oxford and knew many of the scientists working there. It was he, and not secretary Molyneux, who opened the official correspondence with Robert Plot, the president of the Philosophical Society at Oxford.

St George Ashe, one of the most active members of the society, succeeded Molyneux as secretary in November 1685.[62] His family came originally from England, but at the time of his birth in 1657 his father held estates in County Meath worth about £1000 a year. As these were inherited by the eldest son Thomas, St George decided on an academic career. In 1676 he graduated in arts at Trinity College Dublin, and three years later was elected fellow and tutor. When Jonathan Swift entered the university in 1682 he became one of Ashe's pupils, and it was probably through his tutor's scientific interests that Swift first came into contact with a natural philosophy based on observation and experiment.[63] In 1685 Ashe was appointed Donegal Lecturer and Professor of Mathematics, a post which involved the giving of three lectures during each week of term.[64] Among the dons who joined the Dublin Society,[65] Ashe was certainly the most committed to its aims, and during the group's first period of activity from 1683 to 1687 he read at least twenty-eight papers at its meetings, as well as undertaking a considerable number of public experiments. He was instrumental in procuring telescopes and other equipment for a small observatory established by the college in 1685.[66] During the Williamite Revolution, Ashe, together with seven other members of the society, fled to England, and between 1689 and 1691 held the post of chaplain to Lord Paget, the English ambassador in Vienna. He returned to Ireland in 1692 to become Provost of Trinity College, and was appointed Bishop of Cloyne in 1695, of Clogher in 1697, and of Derry in 1717. Like many scientists of the day Ashe was anything but a specialist, covering the whole gamut of scientific activity, and reporting to the society on the weather, eclipses, experiments of freezing, animal freaks, and mathematical problems. In an age when backbiting and personal abuse were not rare, he seems to have led a charmed existence, for there is none to speak ill of him. On his death in 1718 Joseph Addison grieved that he had 'scarce left behind him his equal in humanity, agreeable conversation, and all kinds of learning'.[67]

Only one man surpassed Ashe in sheer quantity of scientific output within the society. This was Allen Mullen (variously Mullin, Moulin, Molines), whose contributions were, with one or two unimportant exceptions, confined to the medical field. Little is known of his early life save that he was born in the North of Ireland about 1653. Later he became a fellow of the Irish College of Physicians, after having graduated M.B. in 1679 and M.D. in 1684 at Trinity College. When Mullen joined the Dublin Society in 1683 he was already in possession of a large and lucrative general practice among the gentry. At one time he was attending, among others, Sir William Titchborne, Sir Theophilus Jones, and Lord Chief Justice Davies.[68] The most original and important of his contributions to medical science was his discovery of the vascularity of the lens of the eye, which he published as the second part of his *Account of the Elephant* (London, 1682). He visited London in that year and obtained a letter of introduction to Robert Boyle from Provost Marsh, who wrote, 'Sir, the bearer hereof is one Mr Mullan, batchelor in physic of this college, who has been successful in several things that he has undertaken, especially in anatomy, wherein he has good skill; and had an opportunity the last Summer to exercise it on an occasion that rarely occurs, namely in dissecting the elephant which was burnt here in Dublin.[69] Boyle was obviously impressed by the young Irish doctor, whose admission to the Royal Society he arranged in the following year. The two men subsequently undertook joint experiments,[70] and Boyle recommended Mullen to the Earl of Clarendon, who was appointed Lord Lieutenant of Ireland in October 1685. In 1685 Boyle sent Mullen a copy of his recent *Of the Reconcileableness of Specifick Medicines* (London, 1685), and the latter replied with a detailed critique of the work, in which he suggested a number of additional remedies and specifics.[71] These included the tying of threads about certain limbs as a cure for cramp and poultices of nettles as a cure for bleeding. In addition Mullen declared that he had 'known natural balsam produce as considerable effects in coughs, distempers of the stomach, inwards and outward, ulcers, and particularly in fistulas, as any medicine whatever'. In 1686 Mullen was obliged to leave for England as a result of an indelicate love affair. When in London he moved mainly in scientific circles, frequenting Jonathan's Coffee House in Exchange Alley, then a favourite meeting place for fellows of the Royal Society.[72] He also performed a series of zoological dissections with John Clayton (1657–1725), later Dean of Kildare, who had been Rector of Jamestown in Virginia from 1684 to 1686, and was elected a fellow of the Royal Society in 1688.[73] In 1689 Mullen met William O'Brien, Earl of Inchiquin, and in December they together embarked ship for the West Indies, Mullen hoping to improve his fortune by the discovery of valuable minerals in Jamaica. But the joys of anticipation proved too much and he died of the effects of intoxication soon after landing at Barbados.[74]

Samuel Foley, who like Ashe was a fellow and tutor of Trinity College, was born at Clonmel about 1655, the son of a moderately wealthy gentleman. He was sent to the excellent grammar school at Kilkenny, leaving only a year or so before the arrival of Swift, who later remembered 'the confinement ten hours a day, to nouns and verbs, the terror of the rod, the bloddy noses, and broken shins'.[75] At Kilkenny he studied under Edward Jones, a headmaster of Puritan inclinations, whose later career in the church was marred by unusual nepotism and corruption. Foley's sister, Elizabeth, married the physician Christopher Dominick, who joined the Dublin Society in 1684, but took little part in its proceedings, perhaps because he had become a member for no reason other than to please his brother-in-law.[76] William Molyneux's brother-in-law, Dr John Madden may have joined the society for similar reasons. In 1677 Foley accepted a fellowship at Trinity College, despite his belief that the emoluments of the position were by no means commensurate with his duties and responsibilities. In July 1684 he indulged in that activity so endemic among contemporary divines and wrote to Archbishop Sancroft of Canterbury asking for preferment. 'We are told here that the Duke of Ormond intends suddenly for Ireland, and I humbly beg Your Grace that you will now engage him to do something for me. . . . The Archbishop of Dublin has but few things in his disposal, and most of them by our statutes inconsistent with my fellowship.'[77] But the letter did not have the desired effect, and he had to wait some time before the hoped for advancement materialized. Eventually he was created Chancellor of St Patrick's Cathedral in 1688, Dean of Achonry in 1691, and three years later Bishop of Down and Connor. A firm Protestant, he was attainted by the 'Patriot' Parliament of James II. Like Ashe, Foley was a popular figure, and after his death in 1695 was described by his friend John Sterne, Vicar of St Nicholas-Within, as having lived 'fast in the best sense; so fast that he very early came almost at once, to the end of a clergyman, a good Christian, a bishoprick, and heaven'.[78] His contributions to the business of the Dublin Society number six, one of which was published in the *Philosophical Transactions*.[79]

A more bizarre member was Sir Richard Bulkeley, who was born at Dublin about 1661,[80] entered Trinity College in 1677, where he took his B.A. degree three years later. The son of wealthy Sir Richard Bulkeley and Catherine, daughter of John Bysse, the Chief Baron of the Exchequer, he succeeded to his father's baronetcy in 1685. Like Robert Hooke he was a cripple, and being unable to take part in childhood games, passed the time in study, at which pursuit he was so successful, that 'in a few years he acquired a very great measure of learning, and was blessed with so great memory, that his learning and knowledge were therein most securely treasured up – at 16 years of age . . . he had a large stock of human learning, and faculties of soul scarcely equalled; wit, fancy, and apprehension extraordinary;

but a memory almost miraculous'.[81] Bulkeley was only able to attend the early meetings of the society, but maintained a correspondence from his country home at Old Bawn. In 1686 he went to London and became a member of the council of the Royal Society, having been elected a fellow in 1685. He later returned to Ireland and sat in the Dublin parliament as member for Fethard from 1692 until his death in 1710. In 1683 Bulkeley's father had come under suspicion of fanaticism, and was called before Primate Boyle to deny rumours of his regular attendance at conventicles. This he did to the satisfaction of the archbishop, who then proposed to nominate him to the commission of the peace. But Ormonde would not agree, being convinced that he was 'as yet unfitt for it as ever he was'.[82] The younger Bulkeley confirmed these suspicions of his family's orthodoxy, when, during the last years of his life, he espoused the teachings of an obscure French sect, specializing, like so many others, in prophecy and constant miracles. He wrote on their behalf, and presented their leader, one Abraham Whitterow, with large sums of money.[83] His friend George Berkeley described how Bulkeley and the prophet,

distributed a great deal of money and victuals to the poor while they were here [in Dublin], and set a stranger free who had been arrested for forty pounds, which sum they paid. In short Sir Richard was resolved to sell his estate and give all to the poor. But I am told the Chancery opposed him as *non compos*. Whitterow is said to have run away with a young woman. Some clergymen would fain have discoursed him on his mission, but he carefully avoided it.[84]

But despite his later behaviour, Bulkeley was a useful member of the society, to whose affairs he brought an able mind, a large fortune, and an enthusiasm for the experimental philosophy.

So successful was the society during the first year of its existence, that in a period of less than twelve months it was able to attract nineteen new members into its ranks. As none of the fourteen original members had left, there were, by the Christmas of 1684, in all thirty-three official fellows.[85] As Ashe informed his friend Henry Dodwell, 'our society does flourish sufficiently, and is lately increased by the accession of several persons of quality and learning'.[86] But while the number of new members is impressive, few were committed experimenters, and hardly any became seriously involved in the society's business. In their lack of anything more than a conventional interest they differ from the original members, most of whom were active both as scientists and as members of the society. While nineteen new members joined, nine of these were never again mentioned in the society's minutes. Information about some of them is scarce or even non-existent. For example, all that is known of R. Clements is his name, while all that can be said of J. Finglass is that he may be the person of that name who was presented as Rector of Clonmacduffe in Meath in 1671 and listed as Prebendary of St Audeon's at St Patrick's Cathedral about 1689.[87] In other cases little more has come to light. Dr Paul Chamberlain was a medical man practising in Dublin, who specialized in midwifery, performed a post-mortem in 1671, and rented a pew in St Werburgh's Church at £8 a year.[88] The facts available about many of the others in this group are scarcely more substantial or germane. Some of them may have joined the society because they were friendly with, or related to, original members, or perhaps because it had become the smart thing to do. In England the Royal Society was certainly able to attract members for reasons quite unconnected with 'the promotion of natural knowledge', and while the Dublin Society never attained the same social prestige, it may be assumed that any group which included Petty, Molyneux, and Bulkeley, the Provost of Trinity College, the Bishop of Ferns and Leighlin, as well as fashionable Dr Mullen, would have attracted some representatives of Ireland's sophisticated urban *élite*.

Even the remaining ten new members who make some appearance in the minutes cannot, as a body, be admired for their purely marginal enthusiasm. John Stanley, who was born at Waterford in 1663, the son of Sir Thomas Stanley, and who, after having held the offices of Lord Chamberlain of the Household, Commissioner of Stamp Duties, and Commissioner of Customs, was himself created a baronet in 1699, seems to have appeared only once at the society in an active rôle, when he read a paper describing the 'Motion of Water'. In this, exhibiting a very tenuous grasp of contemporary corpuscularianism, he demonstrated how 'the figure of the particles that do compose water are the most unfit for motion', because it can be shown that 'round bodys are the most fit; but the parts of water are generally agreed to be oblong'.[89]

Like Stanley, William Pleydall is mentioned only once, on the occasion of his being elected treasurer of the society.[90] Richard Acton, although born in Cheshire, was a graduate, fellow, and later Vice-Provost of Trinity College Dublin. His sole contribution to the society was a paper on a zoological subject.[91] Henry Ferneley too intervened only once at a meeting in order to give an account 'of a girl about 14 years of age, who lived near him in County Kildare, that was not observed to eat or drink for a twelvemonth'.[92] Like Bulkeley, Keogh, and Baggot, he lived for the most part in the country, but unlike them, did not maintain any correspondence with the society. Ferneley had himself not attended any of the British universities, although he was able to send his son to Trinity College Dublin. Daniel Houlaghan was a medical doctor and presumably gained his degree on the continent, for there is no record of his having studied at any of the home universities. Although not especially active in the society, he did make several contributions to general discussion and also gave a formal account of a 'monstrous kidney' weighing forty ounces, which he had come across in the course of his practice.[93] Sir Robert Redding and Viscount Mountjoy each wrote two pieces which they read to the society. Mountjoy was a close friend of William Molyneux, with whom he went on a continental tour in the Summer of 1685. In that year Molyneux obtained a grant of £100 from the Irish government to enable him to inspect fortifications in Flanders, in the hope that this might help him in the execution of his duties as joint Chief Engineer and Surveyor-General of the King's Buildings and Works in Ireland. After visiting Flanders the two men went to Paris, where, by means of an introduction from Flamsteed, they met Giovanni Cassini and other eminent scientists.[94]

In fact only three of the new members took anything more than a passing interest in the affairs of the society. They were William King, Edward Smyth, and Dr Jacobus Sylvius. King was born at Antrim in 1650, the son of a miller of Presbyterian persuasion. He, however, entered Trinity College Dublin in 1666 and four years later received the degree of bachelor of arts. After obtaining his M.A. in 1673 he competed unsuccessfully for a college fellowship, but despite this was lucky enough to become the *protégé* of John Parker, then Archbishop of Tuam. In 1679 his patron was translated to Dublin, and several months later King was himself collated to the Chancellorship of St Patrick's Cathedral. Shortly afterwards he became involved in a dispute with the Dean, John Worth, who later also joined the society, about the right of the Dean to visit parishes independently of the chapter. It was one of those long litigious quarrels which were a speciality of seventeenth century clerics.[95] Judgement was given against King in 1681. He was created Bishop of Derry (one of the richest sees in the country) in 1691 and Archbishop of Dublin in 1703. As an ecclesiastic he belonged firmly to the 'Irish' party within the church, and his political views were close to those of William Molyneux. King has been accurately described as 'a state Whig, a church Tory, [and] a good bishop',[96] and when John Evelyn met him at Lambeth Palace in 1705 he thought him 'a sharp ready man in politicks, as well as very learned'.[97] King's scientific activity was concentrated mainly in the period from October 1683 to December 1684, and although his name is not on the list of original members, he was certainly attending meetings as early as 22 October 1683.[98] During this time he read seven papers on topics as varied as the acceleration of descending weights, hydraulics, mineral waters, and Denis Papin's recently invented 'Digester'. King maintained a life-long interest in science and scientific research. When already Archbishop of Dublin he joined Samuel (William's son) Molyneux's revived society in 1707, when he once again gave evidence of his particular concern for technology and agricultural studies.

Edward Smyth, who became secretary to the society in November 1686, was, like King and Mullen, a native of Ulster, having been born at Lisburn in 1665. After graduating B.A. in 1681 and M.A. in 1684 from Trinity College Dublin, he was elected to a fellowship there in the latter year. When he joined the society Smyth became its youngest member, being then not yet twenty years old. In 1688 he fled to England, where he was soon able to obtain the post of chaplain to the Levant Company's factory at Smyrna. Having made a considerable fortune in the East, he returned to England and was appointed private chaplain to King William III, whom he attended during the campaigns in the Low Countries. Then, by means of a not uncommon progression, he became Dean of St Patrick's in 1696, Vice-Chancellor of Dublin University in 1697, and two years later

Bishop of Down and Connor. He was twice married, first to a daughter of the Bishop of Kilmore, and then, as if to cement the union of church and state, to Mary, daughter of the third Viscount Massereene. Although appointed Donegal Lecturer in Mathematics at Trinity in 1694, his formal contributions to the Dublin Society, which total seven, deal mainly with problems of natural history. Unlike nearly all the other members of the society he was not universally liked. A contemporary remarked acidly that on his death at Bath in 1720, he left a 'large fortune and plentiful estate to his family – and £10 to the poor'.[99]

Dr Jacobus Sylvius, about whom little is known, was a Dutch physician who had entered Leyden University in 1667 at the age of nineteen.[100] His name is probably a latinized version of a Dutch original, and may have been a pseudonym borrowed from that of the prominent Galenic physician of the same name who had taught Andreas Vesalius at Paris in the early sixteenth century. He is not noted in the *Alumni Dublinensis*, but Samuel Molyneux, in a list of persons educated at Trinity College, notes 'Jacobus Sylvius, Doc. Med. Incorp. July 15, 1684.'[101] His interest was confined to medical matters, and although none of his writings were printed in the *Philosophical Transactions*, he did publish a work on fevers entitled *Novissima Idea de Febribus*, which appeared at Dublin in 1686 and was reprinted several times before the end of the century. The Dublin Grant Book records his dying intestate in 1689.[102]

Several other persons who are not mentioned in the two official membership lists either joined the society or were associated with it in a less formal way. For example, a Mr Patterson attended several meetings during the Spring and early Summer of 1684. He was almost certainly Josias Patterson, a member of the Dublin Corporation of Barber-Surgeons.[103] It is particularly interesting that the physicians, who in London were jealous and scornful of their non-academic brethren, whose association with barbers and periwig makers laid them open to easy abuse, should in Dublin have been willing to cooperate with a surgeon in a scientific society. So low in fact was the general reputation of surgeons at the time that William Petty thought apothecaries a superior and more learned body of men.[104] But in Ireland there was rather less professional friction in this field, and in 1695 John Madden and Thomas Molyneux, both eminent physicians and members of the Dublin Society, were prepared to work with, and draw up testimonials for, one Thomas Proby, a surgeon whose skill they admired.[105] This, together with Patterson's presence in the society, is even more remarkable in the light of the decision of the Governors of Kilmainham Hospital in 1685 that 'one chirurgeon and one assistant was more proper for the use of the old men than to entertayne a phisitian at a large salary',[106] a decision which, on the surface, was hardly designed to smooth relations between the two professions. Patterson read at meetings of the society two accounts of dissections he had performed, and is last mentioned as attending on 7 April 1684, when he 'produced an account of some experiments he had lately made for dissolving the *calculus humanus* by various menstrua'.[107]

Sir Paul Rycaut, secretary to the Lord Lieutenant the Earl of Clarendon, was admitted a member on 1 February 1686, as was Edward Wetenhall, Bishop of Cork and Ross.[108] Rycaut, who came from a strongly Royalist family, had spent about ten years in Turkey as English ambassador to the Porte, and had published important works on the condition of Asia Minor.[109] In October 1685 he was appointed secretary to the new Lord Lieutenant and came over to Dublin in the same month. Rycaut was not popular with the Catholics, who, gaining confidence with a co-religionist on the throne and with Tyrconnell, rather than Clarendon, in virtual control of Ireland, several times accused him of extortion and other financial malpractices, charges which both he and Clarendon frequently and firmly denied. It seems likely that he was admitted into the society because it was hoped that this might encourage the favour and patronage of his master. At the meeting of 25 January 1686 Ashe read an extremely flattering address to the Lord Lieutenant, who 'received their compliment with a great expression of civility and kindness.'[110] Rycaut did not often attend meetings, and although a fellow of the Royal Society, his contributions to general discussion were seldom profound. He dealt mainly with such topics as the 'exquisite poysons' of the Duke of Florence and the sting of the Turkish scorpion.[111]

Edward Wetenhall was, like Rycaut, an Englishman. Both had studied at Cambridge, Wetenhall having entered Trinity College in 1651. They were the only Cambridge men in the

Dublin Society, most of whose English members had been at Oxford. In 1672 Wetenhall came to Dublin to take charge of the Blue-Coat School, and seven years later was appointed Bishop of Cork and Ross, where he distinguished himself as an exemplary pastor. He shared with Marsh and Huntington an enthusiasm for the publication of Protestant religious works in Gaelic, and was one of the few Irish bishops to adopt something approaching a tolerant attitude towards the Dissenters. This may perhaps have been the result of his Cambridge education, for Trinity ranked close behind Emmanuel and Sidney Sussex Colleges as a centre of Calvinist ideas and opinion. Although Wetenhall only became an official member of the society in 1686 he had attended some meetings as early as June 1684, when he had brought messages of goodwill from the Royal Society, of which he was also a fellow.[112]

Dr (later Sir) Patrick Dun, although he did not formally join the society until after the Williamite Revolution, attended meetings and took part in experiments during the Summer of 1684, when he helped William King in certain trials the latter was making concerning the chemical composition of Irish mineral waters.[113] A possible explanation for Dun's comparative neglect of the society in its early years may be found in his dislike of its first Director, Charles Willoughby, against whom he had competed for the post of physician to the Royal Hospital at Kilmainham. Neither, as has already been remarked, was successful, although Dun was eventually to obtain the position in 1692.[114] Only two other persons in addition to those already mentioned enjoyed even a brief association with the society. These were Samuel Walkington, who had been elected a scholar of Trinity College Dublin in 1680, and the distinguished orientalist Dudley Loftus.

As in the Oxford Philosophical Society, the greater part of the business at Dublin was undertaken by a relatively small proportion of the membership. The fourteen original members provided the scientific backbone of the society, for as many as eleven of them can be classified as active in its proceedings. Mr Hill has said of the Royal Society, that the genuine scientists were so anxious to cover up their Puritan pasts, that they flooded the society with 'dilettante aristocrats who hated soiling their hands with experiments'.[115] But those scientists in the

Royal Society who had supported the Commonwealth, men like John Wallis, Jonathan Goddard, William Petty, and John Wilkins, did not find it difficult to accommodate themselves to the changed situation after 1660. Nearly all of them had always been on friendly terms with serious Royalist experimenters like Sir George Ent, Sir Paul Neile, Sir Charles Scarburgh, and Viscount Brouncker. It is at least as important to remember that John Wilkins became Bishop of Chester as that in 1656 he had married Robina, the widowed sister of Oliver Cromwell. To make the suggestion that the Restoration produced no short-term decline in general scientific standards in no way lessens the importance of the achievements of the previous twenty years, and it must be remembered that the foundation of the Royal Society, although the culmination of earlier efforts, was a Restoration and not a Commonwealth event.

It is surely not surprising that the infant Royal Society should have attempted to attract some of the great and wealthy men of the time into its ranks. At this particular moment it so happened that most of these men were Royalists. The group from which the Royal Society had in part evolved, that meeting at Oxford in the 1650s, had operated in the *milieu* of a small academic community. Oxford is not a capital city and was not therefore generally inhabited by those enjoying or seeking the sweets of political power. As a university town it contained a large academic population, and it was from this source that the earlier Philosophical Society had drawn the bulk of its members. After the Restoration London became more than ever the chief centre of the experimental method, and was naturally able to provide a rather different, more varied, background against which the Royal Society might function and grow strong. In any case it is anachronistic to see the Royal Society simply as an exclusive group of experts, or to imagine that it was in its own eyes or those of its contemporaries in some way diminished by its catholicity of membership or of interest. Many prominent natural philosophers of the time, among them Josiah Pullen, Robert Sibbald, Thomas Sydenham, and Robert Morison, never bothered to join, while most of its members, like those of the Dublin Society, saw no sharp contrast between the validity of being interested in Newtonian physics or the effectiveness of sympathetic powder.[116]

Undoubtedly a decline in the quality of scientific work produced in the Royal Society does become evident during the last years of the century. But this was due almost entirely to internal, purely scientific reasons, for on the surface the gradually increasing political stability of the period after the mid-1690s could be regarded as favourable to an intensification of intellectual enquiry.[117] Professor McKie has made a study of the political attitudes of the twelve men who met on 28 November 1660, and of the forty-one others they first invited to join them in the setting up of the Royal Society.[118] Of the twelve, five were confirmed Royalists, three had been Parliamentarians, while the remaining four all seem to have favoured the Restoration. Of the forty-one, thirty-one were Royalists, and only two are known to have supported the Commonwealth with any enthusiasm.

The situation at Dublin was of course different. The society there was founded more than twenty years after the Restoration, and most of the members would have been too young in the 1650s to have been able to adopt political loyalties and religious beliefs. Petty certainly had for a time been a supporter of Cromwell. But his lack of political intensity enabled him to move, without great difficulty, into the new order of 1660. So successfully did he integrate himself into the royalist atmosphere, that he soon received a knighthood and was twice offered a peerage. The only other member with overt Commonwealth affiliations was Dudley Loftus. But he too found this no bar to advancement after 1660. Loftus was on the whole no great believer in the New Learning and was intellectually the least 'progressive' of any of those connected with the society. Huntington, who was older than the average member,[119] had been quite prepared to sign the decree of 1660 at Oxford condemning the proceedings of convocation under the Commonwealth.[120] Not only therefore were most of the members too young to have been actively concerned with the events of the 1640s and 1650s, but even those few who had been so concerned, were none of them convinced or die-hard Puritans.

The most important political upheaval to take place during the existence of the Dublin Society was the Williamite Revolution. The reactions of the more articulate members to this event are therefore of some interest. When James II ascended the throne in February 1685 most Irish Protestants were ready to support his government, believing that he would keep his own religious beliefs a private matter. As Sir John Perceval of Cork noted a year later, 'Here is as great a calmness and serenity . . . as in the most settled times, when the king is best served and most obeyed'.[121] The members of the society, although predominantly Anglicans, did not adhere to that body of opinion which would have had every Catholic dead or banished. There was, for example, never any question of expelling the Catholic Mark Baggot, even when in 1687 the king's real policies were becoming apparent. William King, while agreeing that 'Papists should be debarred all public trust', thought it wrong 'to take away men's estates, liberties, or lives, merely because they differ in estimate of religion.'[122] Less than a month after James II's accession the Protestant clergy of Dublin presented him with an address of loyalty. Among the chief signatories of this document were William King and Dean Worth, both members of the Philosophical Society. In the address they declared that all who belonged to the established church must, 'by the principles [they] have been taught and can't unlearn', be loyal to the crown whatever the monarch's religion.[123] King was at this time a believer in the precepts of passive obedience and non-resistance. He was soon to move away from this position and his new attitude brought with it imprisonment at the hands of the Jacobites in 1689 and again in 1690. But years later he was still trying to obscure the memory of his recommendation of William Sheridan's sermon on St Paul, delivered, at King's own request, at St Werburgh's Church in Dublin during the Lent of 1685. In the preface to the pamphlet in which the sermon was published, King claimed that no single Protestant could be disloyal without renouncing his religion.[124] But unlike Sancroft and Ken in England, who opposed James II only to become non-jurors under William and Mary, King, considering that James had broken his 'royal word', thought himself justified in welcoming the new monarchy. In 1702, looking back on the events of the previous decade, he assured St George Ashe that, 'As for us, . . . we universally loved King William as our deliverer.'[125]

William Molyneux, although he deplored the 'many good turns' his father-in-law Sir William Domvile had been forced 'to do the Irish' when Attorney-General under Charles II, was

prepared to welcome the new Catholic king in 1685.[126] In a letter
to his brother at Leyden in March of that year, he mentions
how there had 'not been in the least grudging in England or
Ireland, so that we may hope, by God's blessing, and the care of
our prince, to live yet an happy people'.[127] But three years later
he and seven other members of the Dublin Society thought
it wise to leave Ireland,[128] for the departure of Clarendon and
the appointment of the Catholic Tyrconnell as Lord Deputy in
February 1687, gave Protestants good reason to fear for their
property, and soon, recalling, with somewhat exaggerated
colouring, the events of 1641, they began also to fear for their
lives. William Petty, one of whose closest friends was the
Catholic merchant John Graunt, and whose apprehensions were
more economic than religious, was still no doubt relieved to hear
from the king in 1686 that there was no question of repealing the
Act of Settlement.[129] He also maintained that no Irish Catholics
should 'be suffered to live in any port', lest they be tempted to
give the ruling Protestant minority an economic 'stab in the
back'.[130] But Petty died in 1687, and so did not live to see the
final extremes to which the king was prepared to go.

The relatively lenient terms granted to the anti-Williamites in
the Treaty of Limerick shocked a number of Protestants,
including Narcissus Marsh, who thought them a betrayal of all
he believed in, while Bishop Dopping of Meath, who was
related to the Molyneuxs, saw no reason why faith should be
kept 'with a people so perfidious as the [native] Irish'.[131] In
common therefore with the majority of Protestants, the members
of the Dublin Society were, in 1685, willing to accept the government of James II. But the events of the monarch's short reign
soon persuaded them that support for Dutch William was not
only God's will, but also the saving of their property and
dominant position in Irish life. While practical politics was a
major preoccupation, few members of the society indulged to any
extent in detailed political theorizing. Beyond a generalized
condemnation of Hobbes, whose De Cive prompted Richard
Acton to deliver a no doubt critical disquisition, little of moment
in this field was discussed at any of the meetings.[132] Lockian
ideas were certainly popular among the members. William
Molyneux's Case of Ireland (Dublin, 1698) owes much to Locke's
influence, while Thomas Molyneux was shocked to find that

the Royal Society hung a portrait of Hobbes in its meeting-room.[133]

Although membership of the Royal Society did not in the seventeenth century indicate any great prominence in the field of science, it is not insignificant, as an indicator of interest if not ability, that of the fourteen original Dublin Society members, seven were, or were to become, fellows of the London body.[134] Seven of the others who joined the society before 1687 also achieved that distinction,[135] as did Thomas Molyneux who might be regarded as a corresponding member. Membership of the Royal Society did carry with it certain advantages, as Ashe discovered when travelling through Germany in 1690, for 'he gained much more respect by the character of being a fellow thereof, than by any deserts he could pretend to, though ... these be extraordinary'.[136] Again, when several members were refugees in London during the Williamite disturbances, their acceptance into the scientific community there was immediate, their names being already well known. Close personal contact between most British scientists was an accepted feature of intellectual life, so that Ashe, Mullen, and William Molyneux, were, within a short time, able to meet Robert Hooke, Sir John Hoskins, Hans Sloane, John Aubrey, Edmond Halley, and Robert Boyle.[137] Without the constant help and encouragement of the London group, the Dublin Society, which so closely followed the concepts and outlook of England, would hardly have survived for more than a few months.

The Dublin Society had among its membership a minority of persons who never took part in its proceedings. There is no evidence that the group as a whole suffered from their inclusion. They did not hamper the work of those who were active. If anything, their subscriptions subsidized the schemes of the serious experimenters. Though no attendance rolls survive, it is probable, although impossible to prove, that several of the silent members attended meetings purely as spectators. Unlike the Royal Society, the Dublin group was not particularly successful in attracting the nobility to its ranks. With a viscount, a baronet, and three knights as members, the society was hardly flooded with dilettante aristocrats. But whereas in London peers were admitted more readily than commoners,[138] their titles excusing their occasional ignorance, in Dublin all men were

E

equal, and no special allowances were made for any particular group. None the less William Molyneux did what he could to attract the nobility, so that the society might become socially acceptable. In November 1685 he sent a paper by Viscount Mountjoy to London with the remark, ' 'tis fit that such a noble person should be incouraged to prosecute these kind of studys, by seeing their indeavours approved of'.[139] The number of peers living in Dublin at this time was comparatively small, although the situation was probably not as bad as that, which, forty years later, prompted Thomas Prior to publish his *List of Absentees of Ireland* (Dublin, 1729). After the Revolution, when the society was revived in 1693, a few additional members of the aristocracy joined, but even then not in overwhelming numbers.[140]

The members of the Dublin Society came from a comparatively wide range of social backgrounds. Some, such as Bulkeley, the two Moyneuxs, Baggot, Ashe, and Willoughby, were products of that part of society where the middling sort of people meet the minor aristocracy. But the society also attracted men of humbler origin who were ascending the social scale along the by then well-worn ladders of church, physic, and civil administration. Most of the clerical members came from undistinguished backgrounds, and some, such as King, abandoned the Nonconformity of their parents. Of those who had not themselves come over from England, almost all were of Anglo-Irish stock. But as far as can be discovered few if any of these were descended from families which had settled in Ireland much before the sixteenth century. Only one was certainly a Roman Catholic. Thus a general picture emerges of rising men from respectable, if not invariably elevated, backgrounds, of a moderate religious persuasion, whose interest in science reflected a broad receptiveness to new ideas both political and intellectual.

Chapter 3

The Society and Dublin University

The account of the composition of the society in Chapter Two has shown that most of the Irish members were graduates of Trinity College Dublin. Of the thirty-three persons who had joined by December 1684, eighteen had studied at Trinity, six were not Irish, and at least one was a Roman Catholic. Therefore about 70% of the Irish Protestant membership had attended Dublin University. These included all the most active and enthusiastic experimenters like the Molyneux brothers, Mullen, Ashe, and Foley. Is it therefore possible to establish any connection, other than one simply of numbers, between active membership and graduation from Trinity College, and were the conditions in that institution likely to produce natural philosophers in the Baconian mould? Before answering these questions a brief survey must be made of the attitude of the English universities towards the New Learning.

The Scientific Revolution as such was not a matter of overnight transformation, and while a slow change in certain areas of intellectual life can be discerned in the sixteenth century, this was confined to a very small group of men. In England particularly institutional advance was slow. While a few continental universities, especially Padua and Leyden, did much to help both the advancement and dissemination of scientific knowledge, Oxford and Cambridge were in general strongholds of conservatism. Even in the second half of the seventeenth century natural philosophy was marginal to the formal teaching of the English universities.[1] There was no lack of educational reformers attempting to improve the situation. But had it not been for the rule of the Commonwealth, even those small curricular changes that were introduced might never have been followed through. However much reformers like John Hall and Noah

Biggs might fulminate against the existing course of studies at the universities, these institutions were, to a remarkable extent, able to insulate themselves from the winds of change. Biggs's strictures lacked nothing in insult. In 1651 he recommended 'a thorough and early plowing up the fallow ground of the universities, that she [sic] may be laboriously rummig'd in her stupendous bulk of blinde learning, and her rubbish cast out, and no longer be a quagmire of pittiful learned idleness.'[2] But he was only echoing John Hall, who, two years earlier, had informed the members of the Long Parliament, that God would punish their 'naturall children with stupidity or ignorance', if they did not take the opportunity to enter 'the paths and mazes of science'. He painted a grim picture of the contemporary Oxbridge don, who, because he knew nothing of chemistry, 'quick or dead anatomies, . . . ocular demonstration of herbes', or the other paraphernalia of the New Learning, allowed himself, 'either to sinke in a quagmire of idlenesse, or to be snatched away in a whirlepool of vice'.[3] But despite the minor academic reforms which followed such criticism, the University of Cambridge presented in 1669 a treatise to the visiting Cosimo de' Medici which condemned the Copernican astronomy.[4]

It was in London, and later in the Dissenting Academies, that science found its most fertile ground. William Godolphin put the matter plainly in a poem written about 1661 concerning the infant Royal Society, in which, referring to Gresham College, he wrote:

> Thy Colledge, Gresham, shall hereafter
> Be the whole world's university;
> Oxford and Cambridge are our laughter
> Their learnings is but pedantry.
> Theise non collegiates do assure us
> Aristotle's an ass to Epicurus.[5]

After the conformity legislation of 1662 many of the best teachers were drained away from the old grammar schools into the new Dissenting Academies, some of which offered a sound grounding in natural philosophy. That established at Newington Green had 'a laboratory, and some not inconsiderable rarities, with an air-pump, thermometer, and all sorts of mathematical instruments', while the books prescribed for students at Sheriffhales Academy included works by Gassendi,

Gunter, Descartes, and Wallis.[6] The Dissenters in Ireland also maintained schools. William King's Presbyterian father had sent him to a County Tyrone school, which in the early 1660s was using Robert Recorde's *Arithmetick* as a textbook. While the 'philosophy school' at Killyleagh was flourishing in 1697, being supported by the general synod of the Presbyterian Church.[7]

While Oxford and Cambridge did little during the early part of the seventeenth century to advance the cause of science, they did at least make some gestures towards the new natural philosophy. For example in 1619 Oxford accepted the bequest of Sir Henry Savile and established chairs of geometry and astronomy. The holders of the latter were actually enjoined to teach the Copernican as well as the Ptolemaic system of the heavens, and as early as 1518 Thomas Linacre had founded lectureships in physic at both Oxford and Cambridge. Certainly by the 1650s, even if the university authorities were still scarcely in the vanguard of scientific advance, the atmosphere prevailing at Oxford in particular did not prevent, and may even have encouraged, the philosophical meetings attended by Boyle, Petty, and others. But few such gestures were made at Dublin, where educational conservatism was even more the vogue than in England.

Several attempts to introduce university studies into Ireland were made before the foundation of Trinity College in the last decade of the sixteenth century. As early as 1312 Pope Clement V issued a bull at the request of Archbishop Lech of Dublin empowering the latter to establish a *studium generale* at Dublin. Nothing however was done until 1320, when Lech's successor, Alexander de Bicknor, appointed four masters for such a university. Although permitted by the bull to erect all the faculties of a *studium generale*, it seems that Bicknor's appointees were to teach only in the two of most immediate concern to the clergy of the diocese – theology and canon law. Again it is clear that Clement, who knew little of Irish affairs, intended the university to be a centre of higher studies for the whole of Ireland, while in reality any such institution, so tied as it was by the terms of the bull to the Archbishop of Dublin, would necessarily be confined almost exclusively to the English settler element. In 1321 Bicknor drew up regulations for the university, which bear a close resemblance to those of contemporary

Oxford. But the university never seems to have had its own buildings, and this, combined with Bicknor's excommunication about 1325, precluded any hope of success. While there is some evidence that the university continued a shadowy existence for another thirty years or so, in 1363 a group of Irish clerks, in a petition addressed to Urban V, remarked on Ireland's lack of a university. The experiment, though modest in conception, had failed.[8]

By the middle of the next century the Irish parliament, in an attempt to 'promote as much the increase of knowledge and good governance as avoidance of riot and misgovernance', recommended the foundation of a university at Drogheda, modelled on, and enjoying the same privileges as, that of Oxford,[9] while thirty-one years later in 1496 a provincial synod at Christ Church under Archbishop Fitzsimon passed a decree requiring clergy to make annual contributions towards the maintenance of a lecturer in theology at the school of St Patrick's.[10] But neither plan left paper for reality.

Behind the English system of education in Ireland a native tradition continued to flourish with varying degrees of success. In 1570 Edmund Campion described a visit to a Gaelic school. The pupils, he noted, were 'learned in their common schooles of leachcraft and law, whereat they begin children, and hold on sixteene or twentie yeares, conning by roate the Aphorismes of Hippocrates and the Civill Institutes.'[11] Such places were not however congenial to the Dublin authorities, and throughout the sixteenth century demand increased for a higher institution modelled along English lines. Already in 1547 Archbishop Browne of Dublin, anxious to see reformed religion established in Ireland, had put forward a plan for the endowment of a university out of the funds of St Patrick's. The proposed foundation was to begin life with four lecturers, who were to teach Greek, Civil Law, Divinity, and, interestingly enough, Physic.[12] In 1579 Walsingham was airing the possibility of a university for Clonfert, while four years later Sir Henry Sidney, perturbed by the number of Irish studying on the continent, produced plans for universities at Limerick and Armagh.[13]

Trinity College was the first tangible outcome of these many proposals. The letters patent granted by Queen Elizabeth gave its members liberty to obtain the degrees of bachelor, master, and doctor, at their 'proper place in all arts and faculties'. This was confirmed in the statutes drawn up by the Ramist William Temple, provost from 1609 to 1627, which also set down the conditions to be fulfilled for a medical degree.[14] Under Temple's rule students in their third year were taught 'physiology', which was however conceived in its traditional sense of an exposition of 'mixed or imperfect bodies, such as meteors; or of perfect bodies, such as metals, plants, and animals'.[15] Even so, as early as 1598 the college register records payment of £40 a year from government sources for the upkeep of a physician, the maintenance of whose post was confirmed in the statutes of 1628 and 1637. Provision was also made from an early date for obtaining the advanced degree of M.D., for which candidates were expected to have attended at least three dissections, cured at least four diseases, and command a thorough knowledge of the Pharmacopoeia. The early holders of the office of 'medical fellow' do not seem to have possessed formal qualifications in the discipline, and perhaps as a result, the first admission even to the degree of M.B. did not take place until 1661. Between then and the end of the century only twenty-eight persons graduated in medicine, of whom fewer than half had been junior members of the college.

Another early genuflection towards natural philosophy can be found in the provision in 1612 of a series of mathematical lectures, for which a Mr Martin, who also discoursed fortnightly on divinity, was paid £8 a year.[16] These seem to have been delivered, how regularly it is not possible to say, until the time of Provost Chappel in the late 1630s.

The earliest statutes of which detailed records survive are those drawn up by William Bedell, provost from 1627 to 1629, who promoted the study of law and physic out of a conviction that it would be a narrow thing to confine Trinity to being merely 'a poor college of divines'.[17] Bedell, a product of Puritan Emmanuel College Cambridge, certainly had Calvinist leanings, while at the same time meriting the title of 'churchman'.[18] More obviously Puritan, the second provost, Walter Travers, had possessed globes and compasses, and had bought and kept books on medicine and alchemy, as well as a *Prognostica finis Mundi*.[19] Were such possessions to indicate even a shadowy interest in the New Learning of the time (and alchemy and chiliastic chronology smack more of Dee than of Gilbert) this was soon crushed by the powerful Archbishop Adam Loftus of Dublin, Travers's predecessor as provost, who, in an oration welcoming the new man, stressed the benefits to be derived from a study of 'good, orthodox, and usefull authors', while decrying the 'reproachfull blotts of innovation and dissension'.[20]

Bedell's statutes show little evidence of concern for the new methods of education then being put forward by advanced thinkers.[21] Nor was the situation significantly altered as a result of the election in 1633 of Archbishop Laud as chancellor of the university, and the appointment in the following year of the Laudian William Chappel as provost. According to Ware, Chappel was 'well versed in the learning of the schoolmen and in casuistical divinity'.[22] With his support, and that of Laud and Wentworth, new statutes were brought into force for the college in 1637.[23] These differ remarkably little from those of Bedell, and it would be a mistake to imagine that the short period of Arminian control saw any marked attempt to alter the curriculum, even though the Irish parliament in 1641 noted that one of the chief complaints made against Chappel was 'that he had discontinued the Hebrew and Mathematical lectures'.[24]

The differences between the two sets of statutes largely concern matters of detail. Those of 1637 recommend more instruction on the controversy with Rome. The dates of terms are changed, and it is specifically noted that no student be forced to abandon the study of theology. Although Chappel is known to have been strict as to matters of clerical dress (the wearing of surplices, etc.), the new statutes continue a requirement of little obvious appeal to Laudians, namely that all resident masters, whether in orders or not, preach a weekly sermon in the college chapel. They also exempt, and this was certainly a useful if minor reform, the fellows in physic and civil law from the general imposition of celibacy.

The details of the course of studies to be followed in every year are carefully defined, and here again Bedell's statutes are closely followed. In order to obtain the primary degree of bachelor of arts, the student had to spend four years at the college. In the first of these logic was taken, the chief texts being the writings of Porphyry and commentaries upon them. In the second year Aristotle's *Organon* was studied, in the third his *Physics*, and in the fourth his *Metaphysics*. Disputations were to be held three times a week by each class. On this matter the new statutes echo the old in their insistence that 'what relates to logic shall be handled logically, that is, syllogistically, not with flourishes of rhetoric'. Mathematics and politics were also provided, but only for the bachelors. These provisions remained in force, with only minor variations, until 1760, and thus directly affected the education of those members of the Dublin Society who had attended the college.

In one respect, however, the college was not so closely tied to tradition. From the foundation it began to buy books for a library, and while the collection remained a small one until the Restoration, a surprisingly large proportion of scientific works was acquired. By the early seventeenth century books were being sought at London. In 1608 Provost Alvey and two colleagues went to England for this purpose, while in the three months October–December 1609 two agents spent £107 6s. od. in London on globes and books.[25]

The surviving contemporary catalogues are however difficult to use, their comprehensiveness and precise terminal dates being uncertain. The earliest (and certainly incomplete) list dates from 1600 and includes a mere thirty-two items.[26] Most are by the expected ancient authorities, Aristotle, Plato, Cicero, Ptolemy, Dioscorides, but two volumes of the great *Historiae Animalium* by the Swiss polygrapher Conrad Gesner are also included. A much more comprehensive catalogue is preserved in the college archives.[27] While it lists a single work published as late as 1670, the great majority (over 95%) of its titles appeared before 1620, which might therefore be offered as the date of near final completion. About 6000 items are noted, and if one excludes the large number of geographical works, approximately 350 concern scientific matters, about two-thirds of them by modern authors. While it is not possible to mention all of these, the following works would hardly have been acquired by a college entirely ignorant of, or uninterested in, the New Learning of the day:

Georgius Agricola, *De Re Metallica* (Basle, 1561).
Ulisse Aldrovandi, *Ornithologiae*, vol. 2 (Bologna, 1600).

Alhazen, *Opticae Thesaurus* (Basle, 1572).

Francis Bacon, *Novum Organum* (London, 1620).

Johannes Bauhin, *De Plantis* (Basle, 1591).

Tycho Brahe, *Astronomiae Instauratae Progymnasmata* (?Frankfurt, 1610), and four other volumes.

Girolamo Cardano, *De Proportionibus* (Basle, 1570), and four other volumes.

Christoph Clavius, *Geometria Practica* (Mainz, 1606), and six other volumes.

Nicolaus Copernicus, *De Revolutionibus* (Basle, 1566). This edition includes the *Narratio Prima* of G. J. Rheticus.

Albrecht Dürer, *Elementa Geometrica* (Paris, 1532), and two other volumes.

Gabrielle Falloppio, *Opera Medica* (Frankfurt, 1584), and one other volume.

Girolamo Fracastoro, *Opera Omnia* (Venice, 1574).

Conrad Gesner, *De Piscibus* (Zurich, 1558), and ten other volumes.

William Gilbert, *De Magnete* (London, 1600).

Johannes Kepler, *Astronomia Nova* (Prague, 1609), and three other volumes.

Giambattista Della Porta, *Magiae Naturalis* (Frankfurt, 1597), and four other volumes.

Johann Müller (Regiomontanus), *De Triangulis* (Basle, 1561), and six other volumes, including an edition of the *Almagest* (Venice, 1496).

Guillaume Rondelet, *De Piscibus* (Lyons, 1554).

Andreas Vesalius, *De Humani Corporis Fabrica* (Basle, 1543).

Franciscus Vieta, *Canon Mathematicus* (Paris, 1579).

Among other modern writers whose works were in the college library by 1620 the most prominent are Thomas Fincke (two volumes), Oronce Fine (two volumes), Paracelsus (six volumes), and Georg von Pürbach (six volumes). Ancient authorities were of course also acquired, and the following are the most important among those whose work has some scientific bias: Archimedes (three volumes), Aristarchos (one volume), Aristotle (twenty-seven volumes), Celsus (three volumes), Dioscorides (four volumes), Euclid (nine volumes), Eutochios (one volume), Galen (four volumes), Hipparchos (one volume), Hippocrates (five volumes), Pappos (four volumes), Ptolemy (fifteen volumes), and Strabo (one volume).

Thus while the library may not have been large, and indeed Sir William Brereton thought little of it in 1637,[28] when one considers the college's endowments, its contents show evidence both of discrimination and a reasonably modern outlook. In 1661 the collection of Archbishop Ussher, consisting of about 10,000 volumes, which had been acquired earlier by the Cromwellian army in Ireland, was presented to the college. It contained a fair number of scientific works published in the seventeenth century, as well as seven volumes by Francis Bacon.[29] Whatever therefore may have been the formal course of studies at Trinity, its members had, by the Restoration period, a comparatively up-to-date, if modest, collection of scientific books at their disposal. Although there were certain restrictions on undergraduate use of the library, fellows were allowed to borrow books, and there is evidence to show that those who joined the Philosophical Society, were, in the 1680s and 1690s, borrowing large numbers of scientific works, the writings of Descartes, Tacquet, Wallis, Oughtred, Wilkins, Hooke, Barrow, and Gassendi being especially popular.[30]

The advent of the Commonwealth produced few significant changes in the college. Many of the existing teachers continued in office so much so, that by the mid-1650s 'sundry godly and well-affected persons in Ireland' were petitioning the lord deputy to rectify 'the want of godly fellows in the college at Dublin for the pious, as well as learned, education of youth'.[31] As a result the Irish Council issued an order in March 1656 commanding the Cromwellian Provost Samuel Winter to exhort the fellows and students 'to a careful walking, becoming the Gospell, and to build up one another in the knowledge and feare of the Lord'.[32] But in addition to such admonitions to piety, the Commonwealth authorities were making some efforts to bring about a new atmosphere of learning at Dublin. In December 1657 Oliver Cromwell himself suggested to his son Henry, then lord deputy, that £2000 a year be used for carrying on a correspondence with scholars at home and abroad, whose abilities 'have made them capable of being in some way or other extraordinary usefull to the publique, and . . . conduceing to the advancement in generall of learning'.[33] Attempts were also being made at this time to establish a second college in the university to be called New College. This plan is mentioned as early as 1650, when a site near St Stephen's Green had been selected for the purpose. The new foundation was to be on 'the broadest basis', but while still being discussed in December 1658, it, like the planned correspondence, was eventually abandoned.[34]

Some real progress was however made at this time when Miles Symner (or Sumner), a major in the parliamentary army, was appointed professor of mathematics in 1652. Symner was a man of some ability and corresponded with a number of prominent English scientists. He was particularly interested in useful learning, and in a letter to Robert Boyle, requested a copy of *A Discours of Husbandrie used in Brabant and Flanders* (London, 1650), which it seems was not available in Ireland.[35] Writing to Samuel Hartlib in 1648 he mentioned Petty's plans for a *Gymnasium Mechanicum*, and declared that he did 'most heartily wish that which my L. Verulam and some others have wished before me, that at least an office of intelligence might be gott up. . . . [But] we may rather wish than hope for the formation and maintenance of such a colledge. . . . In all these studys my scope is for reall and experimentall learning.'[36] He went on to argue that the contemporary universities had little to offer, and that the ancients, who, he felt, still dominated them, had advanced little since the time of Aristotle.

Ten years later Symner was granted a salary of £50 a year by Trinity College, although it is significant that this was lower than the emoluments of the professors of divinity, rhetoric, law, and physic. He had been appointed to his chair chiefly to assist in the training of practitioners for the land survey then being inaugurated under the direction of William Petty. Because of this he lectured on geographical matters and seems to have received information through Ussher from the English mathematician and traveller John Greaves.[37] His salary lapsed at the Restoration, and it was not until the Earl of Donegal founded a mathematical lectureship in 1668 that the college once again had a paid mathematician on its staff.[38] The lectureship and the original chair were united by Provost Marsh in the late 1670s, and Symner, who had continued his scientific studies – Thomas Salusbury, the translator of Galileo thanked him in

1661 for his 'more than ordinary encouragement'[39] – was appointed to the new post. The careers of Petty, Stearne, and Symner certainly suggest that the Commonwealth and its supporters had a beneficial, if hardly revolutionary, effect on Irish intellectual life during the mid-seventeenth century.

Commonwealth educationalists, however, had failed to introduce any fundamental changes into the undergraduate course of studies at Dublin, which also continued to follow traditional lines after the Restoration. Aristotelian logic remained at the centre of teaching. After 1681 Marsh's *Institutiones Logicae* (Dublin, 1681), which shows some evidence of its author's mathematical leanings and was generally known as the 'Provost's *Logic*', was used as an elementary guide. The theology which formed the universal background to contemporary philosophical training was narrowly Anglican and largely controversial. Disputations were still common and were undertaken along traditional syllogistic lines.[40] Jeremy Taylor, Bishop of Down and Connor and vice-chancellor of the university in the years 1660 to 1667, reflected the prevailing atmosphere in an address to the foundation in 1662. 'Spend not your time in that which profits not,' he told his audience,

For your labour and your health, your time and your studies are very valuable, and it is a thousand pitties to see a diligent and a hopefull person spend himself in gathering cockle-shells and little pebbles, in telling sands upon the shores and making garlands of uselesse daisies. Study that which is profitable, that which will make you useful to churches and commonwealths, that which will make you desirable and wise.[41]

This has an old-fashioned ring about it. That it should have come from one of the intellectual ornaments of the Caroline church in Ireland places the achievements of the Dublin Society into a clear and distinct relief.

From 1676 to 1695 the provosts of Trinity, Marsh, Huntington, and Ashe, were all members of the Dublin Society. But with the exception of the last, none of them were really committed or enthusiastic scientists, although Marsh did have some mathematical and astronomical skills. In 1685 Ashe was appointed professor of mathematics in succession to Symner, but the study of that subject was still confined to postgraduate students.[42] The few concessions to modernity made by the college at this time would hardly have been undertaken but for his ceaseless promptings. A remarkable success was achieved in 1685 when he persuaded the college authorities to spend £20 in the purchase of a moderately sized telescope, which was to be the beginning of a university observatory. John Flamsteed was asked to select a suitable instrument, 'seeing 'tis for the promotion of astronomy in this kingdome wherein little has yet been done'.[43] Less than two years later Ashe was writing to the Royal Society as follows:

We have erected an observatory in the colledge, tho' our apparatus of instruments is but small yet; an accurate crop quadrant of 3 feet radius with all the new invented furniture we have, with which by observing the meridian attitudes of the sun, especially at the late solstice, we have exactly enough setled the latitude of this place, not half a minute differing from what is commonly said.[44]

It is not known what became of the observatory. But as it is never mentioned again, it was probably destroyed during the occupation of the college by the soldiers of James II. Again, in 1687 Huntington and the senior fellows agreed to the establishment of a physic and herbal garden 'at the charge of the college'.[45] The war however also interfered with this project and no action was taken until 1710. But these were isolated incidents, and Ashe had every reason to complain in 1686 of how natural philosophy was being 'kept as a minor under the tuition of ambitious and arrogant guardians, buried in cloysters, or the more dark obscurity of affected jargon and unintelligable cant'.[46]

In January 1694 the college, then under Ashe's provostship, celebrated its first centenary, the event being marked by a festive day of decorous jollity, in the course of which poems were read, addresses delivered, sermons preached, and an ode by the then poet laureate, Nahum Tate, himself a Trinity graduate, sung 'by the principal gentlemen of the kingdom'. Set to music by Henry Purcell, it extolled the virtues of the ancients, so that when a few hours later two bachelors of arts held a Latin disputation on the question, 'Whether the sciences and arts are more indebted to the ancients or the moderns', Robert Cashin, the advocate of the latter, faced an audience already conditioned against his argument.[47]

By the beginning of the eighteenth century however the undergraduate course of studies does seem to have included an examination of some modern writers, although Bacon, interestingly enough, was still excluded. In 1703 John Shadwell, a student at the college, wrote to his former schoolmaster, the non-juring divine Laurence Howell of St Mary Axe London,

The course in philosophy was a farrago of conflicting hypotheses drawn from Aristotle, Descartes, Colbert, Epicurus, Gassendi, Malebranche, and Locke. Plato made little show, and Bacon, Digby, and Boyle were absent. The humanities were wholly neglected, although there were some persons illustrious in every point of learning, and amongst them the Provost Dr Browne, Professor of Theology Dr Lloyd, Senior Fellow, and Dr Pratt, Senior Fellow.[48]

The authors mentioned here represent an interesting *mélange* of ancient and modern. Their inclusion in the same sentence shows that Trinity rejected complete adherence to any specific school of thought. The reasonable view that truth is not confined to exclusive philosophies reflects, regardless of how that attitude was actually evolved, considerable maturity of outlook.

Study of these and other authors in the college involved however at this time some practical difficulties. By the first decade of the eighteenth century the library seems to have fallen into a state of disorder, and although the Earl of Pembroke (a patron of the Dublin Society) presented £500 for the purchase of books in 1698, seven years later Thomas Hearne noted that 'the library of Trinity College Dublin . . . is quite neglected and in no order, so that 'tis perfectly useless'.[49] This may have been one of the reasons for the publication in 1707 of an anonymous pamphlet addressed to the Dublin parliament complaining of Ireland's backwardness in the world of learning. This the author attributed mainly to the government's 'want of due encouragement of some of the sciences', particularly medicine and law.[50] The heavy concentration upon the advancement and propagation of Protestantism laid down in the early Trinity statutes had, the pamphlet suggested, been the cause of this comparative neglect. A revision of the statutes was therefore necessary, for 'as long as our university is maimed . . . all that you can make of the college in its present state is but a good divinity school at best'.[51] In June 1709 the Irish House of Commons petitioned the Crown for a grant of £5000 towards a new library for Trinity. This and subsequent amounts were in fact paid and a new building opened in 1732.

It is obvious therefore that those graduates of Trinity College who joined the Dublin Society in the 1680s did so despite, rather than because of, the education they had received. This was certainly the case with William Molyneux, who conceived such a dislike for the purely traditional teaching forced upon him, that, 'young as he was, he fell intirely into Lord Bacon's methods and those prescribed by the Royal Society'.[52] A few of the younger members like Edward Smyth, who were at the college when Marsh and Ashe already taught there, may, by means of private tutorials, have become interested in the New Learning. But to the others the university had given little encouragement.

None the less Trinity College experienced a slow but significant increase in numbers throughout the seventeenth century. Whereas in 1620 its total resident membership had been no more than about ninety, by the time of Marsh's provostship in the late 1670s, this had grown to about 340.[53] In the years 1619–25, the earliest for which detailed figures are available, the average annual number of degrees awarded was 27·5 (14·8 for B.A.s alone), while for the period 1661–81 this had risen to 38·4 (20·3 for B.A.s alone). William Petty drew up a detailed breakdown of college numbers for 1661–81, which shows that in this twenty-one-year period 944 students were matriculated, of whom 208 had been born in England and 112 educated there.[54] In all 426 B.A.s, 245 M.A.s, 6 M.B.s, 6 M.D.s, and 108 other degrees were awarded.

Trinity was of course still small in comparison with the English universities, being about one-tenth the size of Cambridge, which in the years 1661–9 matriculated an average of 300·2 students a year, the comparable figure for Dublin being 33·3.[55] On the other hand Trinity had increased its numbers since the early part of the century, whereas Cambridge had declined. Comparing Cambridge matriculations for the two six-year periods 1620–5 and 1664–9, a reduction of 680 or 26·6% can be noted. While in Dublin, this time using the number of degrees awarded in the same two periods (matriculation data not being available for 1620–25), there was an increase of 20% from 165 to 198.

Three main types of undergraduate were admitted into Trinity at this time: fellow and scholar commoners, who paid high fees, could graduate in three rather than four years, and enjoyed certain other privileges, pensioners, who paid normal fees and formed the bulk of the student body, and sizars, who paid little or nothing, and as a result were required to undertake a variety of menial tasks. The numbers in which these various categories were admitted is noted in the table on p. 68.[56]

From this it will be seen that the average annual number of matriculations between 1661 and 1681 was 44·8, the average proportion of sizars being 15·3%, and of fellow and scholar commoners 16·8%. The growth of the college in the two decades after 1681 can also be noted, and the average annual number of matriculations in the twenty-one-year period 1682–87/1690–1704 (the years 1688 and 1689 being omitted on account of unusually low admissions resultant from contemporary political upheavals), rose to 67·3, while the proportion of sizars (11·7%) fell slightly, and that of fellow and scholar commoners (7·9%) was more than halved.

Now during its first phase of activity the Dublin Society included eighteen Trinity men, all of whom graduated between 1649 and 1681. Nine entered college as fellow or scholar commoners, five as pensioners, three as sizars, while the classification of one is not known. Thus, while allowing that the social composition of the college may not have been the same between 1649 and 1660 as it was between 1661 and 1681,[57] it seems clear that the Dublin Society drew support to an unusual degree from families wealthy enough to matriculate their sons as fellow of scholar commoners.

A further indication of the college's social composition can be found in the occupations of students' fathers given in the Entrance Book. These were recorded with varying diligence, and the precision of the classifications must be treated with reserve. However it will be useful to provide details for three specimen years spanning the period from the Restoration to the end of the century, and to compare these with the occupational backgrounds of the eighteen men who joined the Dublin Society.[58]

F

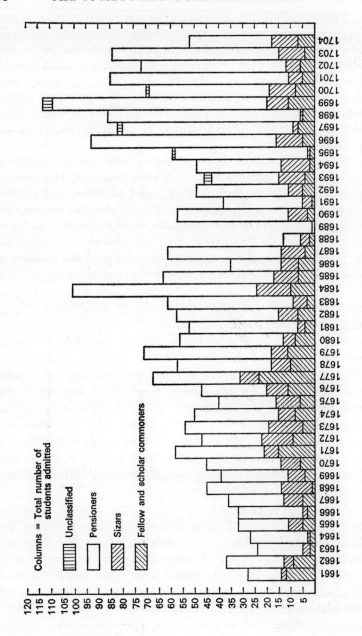

Fathers' occupations	1662	1683	1700	Members of the society
Eques Auratus	1	1		2
Baronet			2	
Eques		1	1	1
Armiger	3	5	10	3
Generosus	5	45	13	4
Episcopus	3			1
Decanus	1			
Clericus			4	
Presbyter	5			
Sacrae Theol. Doctor	1			
Theologus		1		
Senator			2	
Judex			2	
Lictor			1	
Causidicus			1	
Medicinae Doctor	1		1	
Chirurgus			1	
Pharmacopola		1		
Centurio	5			
Chiliarchus			1	
Agricola	2		2	
Colonus			4	
Mercator			2	
Purpuratus		2		
Faber Lignarius			1	
Unclassified	10	5	22	7
TOTALS	37	61	70	18

The table on p. 69 provides confirmation of the earlier figures concerning classes of undergraduate at matriculation, and it can again be seen that the members of the Philosophical Society, were, in so far as their parents' occupations are noted in the Entrance Book, predominantly the offsprings of families firmly entrenched in that part of Irish society where 'gentlemen' and 'esquires' met the knights and baronets. Although it is known that at least Mullen and King (whose parents' occupations are not given in the Entrance Book), came from humble, if respectable backgrounds, few if any of the members seem to have been the sons of those willing to describe themselves as merchants or as professional men, despite the fact that the society itself included no fewer than eight physicians; an indication perhaps that the medical profession at this time was obtaining many of its recruits from untitled landed families. Of course these eighteen men formed only a very small proportion of those who graduated from the college between 1649 and 1681. In fact they represent no more than about 1·4% of all those who obtained B.A.s during this period. And as the society attracted men whose interest in natural philosophy was slender indeed, this figure may be taken as a depressing commentary on the ability of Ireland's only university to arouse among its membership even a passing concern for the scientific revolution taking place outside its walls.

The Royal Society had been founded in 1660 by twelve men meeting at Gresham College, who had decided to ask a further forty-one to join them in the establishment of a scientific club. As in Dublin most of these men had enjoyed an academic education. Twenty-two had been at Oxford, five at Cambridge, and ten others had attended both institutions. This gives a total of thirty-seven or a proportion of 70%.[59] In Dublin over 85% of the founding members had been to Trinity College, to Oxford, or to both. But the Dublin Society, even in its palmiest days, was a great deal smaller than the London group, and a fairer and more revealing comparison can be made with the Philosophical Society at Oxford which dates from the same year as the Irish body. No membership list survives for the Oxford Society, but it is possible to construct one from the signatures to its regulations and from its minutes.[60] The society adopted its rules in March 1684, at a time when it consisted of fifteen members, one more than the Dublin Society had claimed six weeks previously. By Christmas 1684 the Dublin group had grown to a total of thirty-three, while that at Oxford comprised three more than this. But after that date the Oxford Society succeeded in attracting a further fourteen members before its collapse in June 1690, while its Irish counterpart could do no more than augment itself by a further three before its first cessation of business in April 1687. But the achievement of the Oxford Society looks rather less impressive upon closer examination. For instance, on 15 June 1686 six new members were admitted: Edward Tyson, Tancred Robinson, Francis Aston, John Flamsteed, Christopher Pitt, and St George Ashe.[61] While this is certainly an imposing array of talent, none of these men, with the exception of Pitt, ever took any personal part in the proceedings of the society. Ashe of course lived at Dublin and most of the others at London, so that their election involved little more than a form of honorary membership.

The two societies were therefore similar as to size, although in other matters they differed quite substantially. That at Oxford was far more *of* the university, whereas that in Dublin happened to be near a university. Oxford was a very different sort of town, and the *milieu* it afforded was centred almost exclusively upon the colleges, while, although Trinity played an important rôle in the affairs of Dublin City, it did not dominate them. The resident members of the Oxford Society were, without exception, fellows of some college or holders of a post in the university.[62] The meetings were held in the Ashmolean Building, then primarily a scientific institution, which contained a museum on the first floor, a lecture room beneath it, and a chemical laboratory in the basement, as well as a library of scientific books. It was an ideal habitat for a society interested in natural philosophy, which was in the fortunate position of being able to use its facilities without charge. The Dublin Society first met in a coffee-house on Cork Hill, and then for a short time in Provost Huntington's rooms at Trinity.[63] But in neither of these places was it able to undertake anything more than the simplest experiments, and therefore at first confined itself largely to discussion. In the Spring of 1684 William Molyneux was however able to hire a private room in Crow's Nest, an alley near the college, which then became the society's permanent home.[64] Oxford was not a capital city, nor even by the 1680s a centre of political influence. Its Philosophical Society did not include any noblemen or leaders of government. But the Oxford members were more able, for reasons of simple proximity, to visit London, than were the members of the Irish group, and were therefore in more immediate touch with the centre of English natural philosophy. Indeed Elias Ashmole complained of the frequent and lengthy absences of Robert Plot, Keeper of the Ashmolean and sometime president of the society.[65] But while the groups at Oxford and London were both based on a considerable intellectual tradition, that in Ireland was less fortunate. Indeed the mere survival of the idea of a scientific society for a period of twenty-five years from 1683 to 1708 becomes an impressive achievement when placed in the context of the comparative difficulties forced upon such a group in late seventeenth-century Ireland. It was obliged to exist and to work in a country with no real scientific past, suffering from bitter religious and social divisions, and in an almost perpetual state of political tension.

Chapter 4

The Aims, Organization, and Facilities of the Society

I. THE INTELLECTUAL POSITION

None of the members of the Dublin Society was a deeply original thinker in the field of the philosophy of science. They followed current trends in thought as diligently as they did contemporary fashions in experiments and scientific disciplines. Few of the members have left an articulate exposition of their intellectual attitudes, although their very membership is alone proof of an interest, if no more than that, in the New Learning. The Dublin Society, when viewed in a European context, is of little importance in the development of ideas about the rôle of science *vis-à-vis* the contemporary human condition. Its members produced no revolutionary synthesis as regards man and his position in an ever expanding universe, but rather proved to themselves the tenets of a philosophy, which by the 1680s cannot seriously be regarded as new, and which was becoming accepted by an ever increasing number of educated men. The importance of the society lies in its relevance to the Irish situation of the time. That it was not founded until 1683 suggests that Ireland provided infertile ground for the growth of the New Learning. Thus for Ireland the intellectual position of the members is significant, if only to show why that country was then unable to produce anything of real importance in the development of the philosophy of science. The contemporary English scientists with whom the Dublin Society corresponded did not however regard the work of the Irish group with either patronage or contempt, and constantly requested information as to its business and development. The Royal Society included some men of genius who added substantially to scientific knowledge. But these were not representative of the mass of those then interested in natural philosophy. Few men are geniuses, and they are not the whole of an age, even if their contemporaries do little but accept, copy, and duplicate their views and work. The Dublin Society, although among its members were a few men of real brilliance, belonged to the submerged nine-tenths of seventeenth-century science, rather than to the obviously visible and historically almost too well publicized residuum.

It has already been suggested that the outlook of many conservative writers was by no means always in direct conflict with the ideas held by the so-called scientific revolutionaries. Even in practical and theoretical knowledge, as opposed to general philosophical attitudes, the early natural philosophers, especially the alchemists and mathematicians, were often more advanced than was once supposed. But to make this assertion, true as it is, does not take away from the real tension which certainly existed in seventeenth-century Britain, between, on the one hand, those who thought themselves Baconians, and on the other, the representatives of what was regarded by the former as an outdated, false, and useless philosophy. While this tension was frequently brought about by a form of self-induced blindness to the merits of earlier centuries, and while the Moderns were in fact fighting a chimera, to them the struggle was none the less important and the opponent none the less real and identifiable. What men think is happening often influences events, and it is arrogant of the historian to dismiss what to him seem misconceptions as irrelevant to his study. Today the intellectual ambivalence involved in Joseph Glanvill's writing both the *Scepsis Scientifica* and the *Saducismus Triumphatus* is obvious; in Restoration Britain it was not.

Among the more articulate members of the Dublin Society the same need was felt to defend the New Learning against its conservative detractors. This manifested itself in generalized statements which condemned *in toto* the works of Aristotle and his scholastic followers.[1] William Petty, whose views have already been discussed, thought most scientific knowledge brought to light during the Middle Ages to be 'meerly phantasticall'.[2] And this blanket approach was common among those who held similar views. William Molyneux wrote a number of books, two of which are concerned exclusively with scientific subjects. The first was published in 1686 at a time when he was active in the affairs of the Dublin Society. It was entitled *Sciothericum Telescopicum*, and while the actual invention described never became really successful, its Epistle Dedicatory to Henry, Earl of Clarendon, written in April 1686, presents a clear view of Molyneux's ideas on contemporary and earlier science. He emphasized in some detail the superiority of modern learning over that of the past, which:

Consisted rather in disputes, and verbose empty stuff, then in curious discovery of nature's actions. If a man could prove *pro* and *con*, whatever was proposed, and maintain this dispute for two, or three hours, by vain distinctions and idle evasions, he presently gain'd the name of philosopher, tho' all the while he had no manner of notions in his brain answerable to those senseless words he threw out.[3]

In this passage are none of the hesitations found in some earlier writers. But while the New Learning was becoming more and more securely entrenched, and the insult more confidently offered, that final mark of complete self-assurance, namely contempt expressed through indifference, had not yet been attained. Four years later Molyneux was even more certain of his support for the experimental method. He then expressed his views in the Dedication of his most famous scientific work, the *Dioptrica Nova*, to the Royal Society.[4] This book, which greatly benefited from its pre-publication revision by Edmond Halley, was to remain one of the standard works on its subject for many years. The Dedication, written in 1690 while the author was a political refugee at Chester, opens with an eulogy of the Royal Society. Then Molyneux launches into a strong attack on that 'kind of jargon, which [was] call'd philosophy', and which he considered certainly 'the greatest cheat . . . ever imposed on the mind of men', for it was like a 'leprosie deforming its beauty and ruining its strength'. He went on:

But why say I imposed? Men drew it on themselves, and ran their own heads into the noose: and when they had intangled themselves in a thousand ridiculous disputes about empty questions, they vainly thought they had attained the perfection of philosophers; whilst they had no idea in their minds answerable to those noises they made with their tongues; but took more pains to deceive both themselves and others, than is requisite for the propagation of true knowledge.

A common argument employed by the new natural philosophers was that which contrasted the words of the Ancients with the deeds of the Moderns. The Royal Society's motto of *Nullius in Verba* expressed the ideal which its founders hoped would underlie the scientific work of future generations. Petty insisted that the crucial difference between his statistical research and that which had gone before, lay in his exclusive use of 'arguments of sense and . . . such causes as have visible foundations in nature', as opposed to the earlier reliance on 'mutable minds, opinions, appetites, and passions of particular men'.[5] Molyneux too considered that the essential and novel characteristic of the new philosophy was that it realized itself 'in actions, not in words'.[6]

The whole of Molyneux's attitude towards scientific advance is shot through with that stress on experiment which was becoming the hallmark of the modern thinker. For some even the construction of theories had, somewhat unrealistically, attracted to itself a stigma of disrepute. 'But leaving these conjectures,' wrote Molyneux in an article on the Connaught worm in October 1684, 'I come to that which is evident to the senses; and experimental philosophy ought to go no further.'[7] Bishop Marsh, after a perfectly sound and scholarly account of the caterpillar, somewhat nervously concluded that 'all this is conjectures and wants to be confirmed by experiments'.[8] Molyneux himself was utterly convinced that 'liberty of philosophizing', had, by the last quarter of the seventeenth century, been universally acknowledged.[9] The cocoon of practical experimentation, which surrounded the often quaint and scientifically ambivalent activities of the Royal Society, found an enthusiastic response in Dublin. 'But because of *Nullius in Verba*,' remarked one of the members in a piece concerning the apparent magnitude of the sun and moon near the horizon, 'I can assert that I have accurately tried it myself, and have so found it.'[10] The contemporary apotheosis of experiment seemed to exclude all prior theorizing. Molyneux became angry at the 'ingenious men', who ventured 'to offer anything to the learned world . . . before they have made tryals of what they propose'.[11] A few brave spirits still held that 'delight' as well as utility should have a place in scientific endeavour. Samuel Foley introduced a paper on fossils to the members of the Dublin Society in the belief that 'you may be certainly allow'd sometimes without any severe censure to intermix for a few minutes between the scenes of business and seriousness some matters of delight and diversion'.[12] Of course in reality Foley was merely saying what others were doing – albeit somewhat shamefacedly. For the scientific societies were often as credulous as the philosophy they claimed to abhor. When Ashe, in a discourse on the qualities of the air, sweepingly suggested that ancient thought was 'little els than a learned romance, which may amuse and divert, but can never satisfie the mind of man, which is fed only by experiments and demonstration, and not with gay empty speculations and spruce hypotheses',[13] he was uttering no more than a pious hope. Ashe believed in the existence of a new golden age on the grounds that modern science had solved many problems which had 'in vain puzzled the witts of former ages'.[14] Falsely claiming that a situation one desires has actually come into being is a common human delusion, and was not one from which the scientists of the seventeenth century were uniquely exempt.

Molyneux's experience of Trinity College Dublin, and its lack of concern for scientific learning, prompted him to join the ranks of educational reformers. In the *Dioptrica Nova* he censured the universities for hindering the 'advancement of real and useful knowledge', considering it 'full time' that, just as religion had been reformed, so there should be a purge of 'our seminaries of learning from the fopperies and superstition of a false worship'. That Molyneux should in 1690 be urging reform in the universities is a measure of the failure of educationalists like Hartlib, Hall, and Biggs. But in one respect Molyneux showed an appreciation of reality all too rare among those of like view and inclination. For him Aristotle 'was certainly himself a diligent and profound investigator of nature'. This refusal to join in the retrospective witch-hunt of the grand old man of ancient science is evidence of an unusual maturity of outlook. He blamed not Aristotle, but his scholastic successors, who had talked of 'sympathy, antipathy, occult qualities, antiperistesis, and a thousand such other fantastick terms'.[15] Thomas Molyneux also stigmatized the old 'guessing philosophy', which had been the preserve 'of fanciful and credulous men', who had relied 'with as much confidence on their own conjectures, . . . as more wary men on the most convincing testimony'.[16] He derided those who, even as late as 1684, were claiming that 'Hippocrates, Galen, and others of the Ancients knew most, if not all, those discoveries which our modern anatomists have pretended to have been the authors of'. ' 'Tis strange', he wrote, 'to see how far some men are misled, by that blind respect they give to antiquity, and what absurdities they run into, while they would make it omnisient.'[17] For him it was undeniably perverse to claim any large degree of scientific competence for the Ancients, whose learning seemed as nothing when compared with that of his own age.

St George Ashe wrote what is probably the most authoritative statement of the society's aims and philosophical attitude. This important document is in the form of a speech read by him to the Earl of Clarendon, then Lord Lieutenant of Ireland, who attended a meeting of the society in January 1686.[18] A considerable part of the address is taken up with a description of the lowly position natural philosophy had occupied in earlier centuries. Ashe spoke on behalf of the other members and reflected their unflattering opinion of ancient learning. 'Knowledge,' he claimed:

Was of old for the most part only the study of the sullen and the poor, who thought it the gravest peice of science to contemn the use of mankind, and to differ in habit and manners from all others; it was heretofore condemn'd to melancholy retirements, kept as a minor under the tuition of ambitious and arrogant guardians, buried in cloysters, or the more dark obscurity of affected jargon and unintelligable cant; antiquity too was ador'd with such superstitious reverence, as if the beauty of truth, like that of a picture cou'd not be known or perceived but at a distance, as if theire eyes, like the praepostrus animall's, were behind them, and their intellectuall motions retrograde; no wonder then that knowledge did not outgrow the dwarfishness of its pristine stature, and the intellectuall world did continue such a microcosm: for while they were slaves to the dictiates of their forefathers, their discoveries, like water, cou'd never rise higher than the fountains, from whence they were derived.

The uniformity of opinion and phraseology among the defenders of the New Learning is remarkable. Words like 'jargon', 'cant', and 'superstition' were the common stock-in-trade of this kind of polemic. Ashe also joined in the refrain which stressed the tangible nature of the achievements of the new philosophy, which 'instead of words and empty speculations, . . . introduc'd things and experiments'. The static nature of the 'modern' propaganda over a period of a hundred years beginning in 1600, is one of the most noticeable features of the sterile scientific controversy maintained throughout the seventeenth century. By 1700 both sides were using almost precisely the same arguments as they had in 1600, and the means of intellectual communication had become smooth enough to project this sameness not only through time but also through space.

When William and Thomas Molyneux, Petty, and Ashe stressed the deeds, the positive actions, of contemporary science, they soon progressed to a claim of 'usefulness' for their own studies and experiments. Like other exponents of the New Learning, they went to endless pains to demonstrate the practical nature of their work. And while it is possible that, over the long term, scientific knowledge expresses itself in some tangible material way, the researches of the Royal, Oxford, and Dublin Societies added little to man's comfort or prosperity. Even the Académie des Sciences, which was supported by government funds and was expected to produce useful inventions, conspicuously failed to do so.[19]

William Petty for one constantly restated his opinion that all scientific work should be useful. He advised the Royal Society not to waste its time in abstruse theory 'not directly tending to profit and palpable advantages'.[20] In order to set an example for others, he invented a machine designed to increase the speed of writing, a horse-carriage that could not be overturned, and a variety of two-keeled ships.[21] The one feature all these had in common was an utter lack of success or 'usefulness'. But other members of the society held similar views. William Molyneux, in the Epistle Dedicatory to his *Sciothericum Telescopicum*, made large claims for the science of the day, the main task of which he saw to be the improvement of the 'advantage of mankind'. Indeed this phrase runs like a connecting thread through contemporary scientific propaganda. In a letter to the English astronomer Edmond Halley, Molyneux derided that party within the Royal Society which was for rejecting 'all kinds of useful knowledge', save the ranking of birds and insects under their several species. He thought this ludicrous, for it avoided

all study of chemistry, astronomy, mathematics, and mechanics: disciplines particularly conducive to the 'advantage of
mankind'.[22] But while individual scientists undoubtedly made
discoveries which could be adapted to the fulfilment of human
needs, the unique characteristic of the societies, namely
cooperative work, was not an important factor in the development of practical science. Molyneux might claim that it was his
intention 'to increase the convenience of human life, and render
our passage in this world more easy', and that 'these are the
great ends that all philosophical inquiries should tend to',[23] but
the reality of the situation was quite different.

In any case this recurring emphasis on utility is found
predominantly among the propagandists and the lesser men of
science, for it was they who felt most keenly, both the necessity
of justifying their studies to an at worst hostile and at best
indifferent world, and of clinging, at times with something near
desperation, to that Baconian message which stressed the
immediate importance of anthologizing and fact-gathering. The
Dublin Society was sympathetic not only to cooperative
effort – it could hardly have been otherwise – but also to the
weary task of compiling those histories of trades and disciplines,
those mosaics of information, upon which the Baconian 'Inter-
preters of Nature' could exercise their inductive powers.[24] But
such beliefs find an altogether more muted expression in the
attitudes of a Galileo or a Newton 'wrestling with the profound
and complex problems of a strange new conceptual world'.[25]

Perhaps the single most important motive underlying late
seventeenth-century British science was the hope that the study
of natural phenomena would at once glorify and illuminate the
works of the Creator. Science was still inexorably bound up with
religion, and men like Boyle and Newton spent as much time in
theological study as they did in research and experiment. The
New Learning posed a number of problems for a theology based
largely on Scripture, particularly the Old Testament. But that
there was no essential conflict between science and religion in
late seventeenth century Britain, is borne out by the ease with
which so many orthodox divines were able to take part in the
work of the societies at London, Oxford, and Dublin. Many
religious beliefs were scrutinized. The whole question of
miracles and prophecy was examined, while at the same time a

Christian attitude towards the possibility of a plurality of worlds was being evolved. But no such specific problems were discussed at the Dublin Society, the members of which confined themselves to general statements about their belief in the efficacy of natural philosophy as an aid and a prop to sound religion. In his diary Narcissus Marsh intertwined remarks on the study of algebra with affirmations, albeit fairly conventional ones, of his Christian faith. In January 1691 he wrote, 'I united a difficult knot in algebra, for which I praise the Almighty,' and on 7 February he noted how, 'after great study, I had a good invention in conical sections, for which God's holy name be praised.' Lastly, the entry for 18 May 1691 reads, 'Thy name be praised O Lord for all thy mercies, this evening I invented a way to find out the moon's distance from the centre of the earth without the help of its parallax.'[26] Marsh would probably have agreed with Henry Power, who claimed that 'nature itself is nothing else but the art of God. . . . To find the various turnings, and mysterious process of this divine art . . . must needs be the proper office of . . . the experimental and mechanical philosopher.'[27] Petty also shared this concern for the religious implications of natural philosophy, and prayed that he might invent new machines and implements for the greater glory of God 'and the good of the world'.[28] He wrote scientific treatises in the hope that they might teach man to be humble, and 'check the insolent sceptisismes which do now pester the world'.[29] But perhaps the most audacious of his many plans was a scheme to discover a series of basic principles of devotion, which would be acceptable to rational men, while at the same time providing a statement of belief common to all Christians.[30] This was to be based on the principles of contemporary science, which he considered universal.

To use science and the methods of science to solve problems not directly connected with natural philosophy was a favourite pursuit among late seventeenth-century science-theologians. The Reverend John Keogh (a member of the Dublin Society), for example, used mathematics to show 'what dependence the several degrees of beings have on God Almighty'.[31] He in turn may have been encouraged to do this by William Molyneux, who in 1680 had translated the *Meditations* of Descartes, so that an English-speaking public might see demonstrated mathematically 'what was once commonly asserted without proof, . . . *viz.* that God is the fountain and original of truth'.[32] Not only were scientific modes of reasoning used to verify the tenets of Christianity, but the wisdom of God was sought within nature, and Christianity was justified by the supposed symmetry and ordered design of creation. As Bishop Sprat put it, 'The invisible things of God are manifested by the visible,' and as the scientist can, 'by the help of experiments', bring to light a whole new range of creatures and processes, it becomes obvious that his task must be the Miltonic one of asserting eternal providence and justifying the ways of God to men.[33] The 'argument from design' became one of the central features of British apologetic theology in the late seventeenth and eighteenth centuries. Already in 1688 William Molyneux was drawing the conclusions later discussed at such length in the works of William Derham, Nehemiah Grew, and John Ray. Writing to Flamsteed, he referred to the astronomical operation of the sesquialteral ratio as 'beyond exception the strongest argument that can be drawn from the frame of this universe for the proof of God, to see one law so fixed and inviolable amongst those vast and distant chori, who certainly could not therefore be put into this posture and motion by chance, but by an omnipotent intelligent Being.'[34] Molyneux saw the creation as 'this most beautiful, orderly, and admirable event', and attacked those like Descartes who rejected 'final causes in natural philosophy', which above all provided 'occasion of admiring and adoring the divine wisdom'.[35] Science for Molyneux only had meaning and interest in so far as it tended 'to illustrate the creation and set forth the infinite power of the Creator'.[36] But while fully accepting the necessity of an interest in final causes, he believed these to some extent unknowable, and therefore urged scientists to concentrate in the first instance on a study and understanding of 'the properties and affections' by which they might find tangible order in things;[37] while William King, in his famous book *De Origine Mali* of 1702 and in his sermon of 1709 on divine foreknowledge, makes it clear that his deity 'is only to be known analogically, and is practically an unknown God far, far away'.[38]

Like his brother, Thomas Molyneux, who specifically regarded his science as a 'physico-theological notion',[39] argued the existence of God out of a study of the physical world. He esteemed the Giant's Causeway in Northern Ireland 'one of the greatest wonders nature or the First Cause of all things has produced'.[40] The implication that in some sense 'nature' and the 'First Cause' are interchangeable smacks strongly of a form of pantheism. The search for meaning in all things, the obvious extension of such an approach, led the Irish scientists, as it did others, towards a belief that every phenomenon had a use or purpose. In other words, a rational creator, the greatest scientist of all, would and must reflect himself in a rational universe. As one of the Dublin Society's correspondents asked, when discussing a 'serpent stone' or fossil, 'As God Almighty in nature hath caused so rare and strange a piece (since he never made anything in vain) whether there may not be some strange virtue in it, that man has not yet found, which might be worth consideration?'[41] Again it was felt that God would not create any animal or vegetable simply to see it become extinct, for if nature had a theological meaning, that meaning must be as eternal as its first cause. And in consequence Thomas Molyneux argued that no 'species of living creature' had died out since the beginning of the world, and suggested that this belief was grounded 'on so good a principle of providence taking care in general of all animal productions, that it deserves our assent'.[42]

Although there were important differences of interpretation among the various science-theologians, their language and style of argument were remarkably similar. Certainly little echo can be found, either among the Dublin Society's members or opponents, of that strand of Calvinism, which Mr Skinner thinks 'still spoke of a providential God who moved in a mysterious way his wonders to perform', and was 'still crucial to religious life in seventeenth-century England'. For Molyneux's and King's assertions of the comparative unknowability of God were the products of a very different aspect of Protestantism, and the design argument *was* the dominant one among the Irish philosophers, who showed small fear of criticism, either from Professor Merton's 'orthodox, dogmatic theologians', or from the representatives of Mr Skinner's 'strand of Calvinism'.[43] William Molyneux's view of the sesquialteral ratio echoes Newton, who declared that, 'This most beautiful system of the sun, planets, and comets, could only proceed from the

G

counsel and dominion of an intelligent and powerful Being.'[44] Boyle in turn employed the same phrases when he insisted that any study of the universe must induce man, 'as a rational creature, to conclude, that this vast, beautiful, orderly, and (in a word) many ways admirable system of things, that we call the world, was framed by an author supremely powerful, wise, and good'.[45] Beginning with the publication in 1691 of John Ray's *The Wisdom of God Manifested in the Works of Creation*, a flood of literature defending Christianity by reference to scientific discovery was produced in Britain and on the continent. Purpose was now seen in everything, and whatever was, was good, was meant to be, and existed for man's comfort or edification. Destructive natural phenomena like volcanoes were squeezed into the system, on the grounds that in general they reminded man of the majesty of God, and in this particular case possibly provided chimneys for the fire burning within the earth. Disease existed in order to reconcile man with physical death, and human suffering was explained by reference to a just and didactic God. Nature was even achieving a voice of its own quite apart from that of its creator, and Samuel Foley was not alone in stressing *its*, rather than the Almighty's 'infinite prudence' and rational organization.[46] Although the Dublin Society had ceased to meet before the final futility had been attained, some of its members, not surprisingly, shared and believed in the early, and more moderate, stages of this confused and in the end destructive philosophy.

II. THE ORGANIZATION, FACILITIES, AND PATRONAGE OF THE SOCIETY

During the first four months of its existence the Dublin Society had no fixed regulations, discussing problems as they arose, 'without any settled rules or forms'.[47] But as the number of members increased, it became plain that some more precise organization would be necessary. About Christmas 1683 therefore, a committee of three was set up, to draft a set of rules for the better ordering of the society's affairs. It consisted of William Molyneux, Petty, and Willoughby, and presented its findings on 7 January 1684.[48] The committee recommended that the group be officially known as 'The Dublin Society for the

Improving of Naturall Knowledge, Mathematicks, and Mechanicks',[49] a title, the provenance of which is obvious. There was to be a rector, who would hold office for a year and could appoint a deputy. The rector was to preside at all meetings and make sure that 'there be noe interruption, cavills, heat or confusion'. He might call for new discourses, but should above all vigorously 'promote experimentall philosophy, medicin, [and] mechanicks'. The annual election of officers was to take place on All Saints' Day, and the method of election to be modelled on that of the Royal Society. For the time being, and in order to simplify matters, the positions of secretary and treasurer were to be combined in one person, who was required to keep three books, one of admissions and benefactions, another of minutes, papers, and letters (the only one that has survived), and the third an account book. The secretary, it was proposed, would have a clerk to assist him. A council of five was to be established, which alone would have authority to change the rules. On admission each member should pay two cobbs (about eight shillings and six pence), and thereafter one shilling a week. But as no account books have survived, it is impossible to assess the society's financial position, although if the Royal Society was at all typical, this cannot have been very secure. By November 1684 the society had however so increased in numbers that it became necessary to divide the offices of secretary and treasurer between two individuals. William Molyneux described the election of that year in a letter to his brother.

We met in the morning about ten, where we had printed catalogues of all our fellows. Every one present (which I think were about eighteen) took a catalogue and marked with a P., S., and T., those he would have stand for president, secretary, and treasurer. Then all delivered up their papers to the old secretary, who publicly counted in an unmarked catalogue who had marks on their names for being officers; so he that had most marks stood. This is the method practised in the Royal Society, and takes off the odium of a man being proposed and refused, as likewise no one knows who proposes and refuses. Sir William Petty and Dr Willoughby had equal marks for president; but upon a second election Sir William carried it by four votes, so he stood. . . . They continue me secretary and Mr Plowdall [*sic*] treasurer.[50]

The earliest rules of an English scientific group are those of the first Oxford Society, which are dated 23 October 1651.[51] These are very similar to those later adopted at Dublin, save that they include provision for a fine of 2s. 6d. on any member failing to produce a promised experiment punctually. In 1660 the group which was to become the Royal Society adopted a declaration stating, among other things, that it would meet weekly and that each member would pay 1s. at every meeting. It also passed a rule 'that no person shall be admitted into the society without scrutiny, excepting only as are of the degree of barons or above'.[52] The Dublin Society could not afford, and had no reason to be, so socially exclusive, for in 1683 the need to present a royalist front was no longer so acute as it had been twenty years earlier. The Oxford Philosophical Society of 1683 stipulated that no member of the university could join unless he were at least of the rank of M.A. or LL.B.[53] Although Dublin did not demand this, its academic members all had identical or equivalent degrees.

When Petty was elected president of the Dublin Society in November 1684 he drew up a new series of 'advertisements, . . . containing some proposals for modelling . . . our future progress'. These were 'so well approved of, that they were readily submitted to by the whole company'.[54] Petty's revised rules are of some importance, for they reflect contemporary ideas on advancing natural philosophy through cooperative work and personal discussion. Experiments, Petty declared, must form the main business of the society, which should prefer them 'to the best discourses, letters, and books they can make or read, even concerning experiments'. But this advice was not followed, and the society always spent more time in listening to accounts of work performed elsewhere or in private, than it did in undertaking experiments during meetings. True to the tenets of the new philosophy the members agreed that they would never rely on the evidence of isolated observations, but only on 'the comparison of many'. Petty was obviously deeply influenced by the growing emphasis on the quantitative side of scientific research, an emphasis which he himself applied to economic study, and urged the members to 'provide themselves with rules of number, weight, and measure; not only how to measure plus or minus of the qualities and schemes of matter;

but to measure and compute such qualities and schemes in their exact proportions with scales and tables with which they are to provide themselves'. Having seen what had happened in the Royal Society, he insisted that none of the Dublin fellows should 'pester the society with useless and troublesome members for the lucre of their pecuniary contribution'. So useful did Samuel Pepys, then president of the Royal Society, consider Petty's advertisements, that only a month after their compilation, he desired a copy 'for his own use'.[55] The rules of the societies at Dublin and Oxford are alike in all important respects, although some minor divergencies do occur. For example, in Oxford there was provision made for an official styled 'Director of Experiments', whose duties were to enquire 'into the desiderata of severall arts and sciences; [and] in offering things to be tryed'. There was no equivalent post in the Irish group. Again, an Oxford member had to pay only 20s. a year, while at Dublin the annual charge was 52s. over and above the entrance payment of 8s. 6d. None of the three societies limited its membership to any particular number, although the Dublin Society may have planned to do so during the early months of its existence. Anthony Wood noted somewhat cryptically in 1684, 'Newsletter, Aug. 22 F., that a Royall Society is about to be erected at Dublin to consist of 26 persons only.'[56] There is however no other evidence to support this assertion. The differences in organization were therefore slight, and do not vitiate the fact that the two smaller groups were of remarkably similar constitution and design.

The Dublin Society did however indulge in activities which at Oxford and London would have been regarded as beyond the scope of a scientific organization. In 1663 Robert Hooke had reflected the consensus of opinion within the Royal Society, when he had stated that its task was 'to improve the knowledge of naturall things', without any 'meddling with divinity, metaphysics, moralls, politicks, grammar, rhetoric, or logick'.[57] This restriction had been taken over from the Philosophical Society which had met at Oxford under the Commonwealth and had purposely avoided, as the royalist Sprat put it, 'the passions and madness of that dismal age', so that it could concentrate exclusively on the study of natural philosophy.[58] This, according to Joseph Addison writing some years later, was just as well, for the scientists might easily have 'set their country in a flame', had they 'engaged in politics with the same parts and application' they had devoted 'to the disquisitions of natural knowledge'.[59] The Dublin Society was however at first less narrow in its interests. At a meeting in December 1683, for example, 'upon occasion of some former discourse, Mr Archdeacon Baynard proved at large that monarchy is the most natural government'.[60] Although the paper has unfortunately not survived, Baynard's use of the word 'natural' may well indicate a rejection of Hobbes's belief in the independence and virtual equality of men in a state of nature, and adherence rather to the arguments presented on that point in Sir Robert Filmer's *Patriarcha*, which had appeared posthumously in 1680. A few years later Baynard carried his beliefs to their logical conclusion by refusing to take the oath of loyalty to William III.

Besides excursions into politics, some members of the society set themselves the task of establishing Christianity on a scientific basis, hoping thereby to make it stronger and more convincing than before. Huntington describes how in December 1683,

Several of the number meet at five upon Sunday nights (as the whole company does on Mondays) to discourse theologically, of God suppose, and his attributes, and how to establish religion, and confute atheism, by reason, evidence, and demonstration: And when this work shall be done (for all are not arguments, that some men call so) the way to the Scriptures and Christianity will be plain and easy; and the end is, that men might walk therein.[61]

These meetings lapsed in 1684, but were revived towards the end of that year under the direction of William Palliser, then a fellow of Trinity College, and later Bishop of Cloyne and Archbishop of Cashel.[62] This circle was still in being as late as June 1685, when Ashe told his friend Henry Dodwell how 'Mr Acton has taken great pains with good success in clearing natural theology after a plainer and more demonstrative method than is yet extant', and how the group was then particularly concerned with the 'controversies betwixt us and the Papists'.[63] By the following month, however, most of the members of the theological meeting had left for their homes in the country, and although Ashe and the few who remained were 'resolved to prosecute the study of the Fathers and controversial divinity',[64] nothing more is heard of this appendage to the society proper.

Subsequently the society concentrated more exclusively on scientific and quasi-scientific matters. But the activities of the theologians do explain the presence in the society of a number of men, such as Finglass and Palliser, who seem to have had small interest in the New Learning, which was after all the main concern of the majority of the members.

One of the first tasks Petty set the society was 'that they provide themselves with correspondents in several places'.[65] William Molyneux had, since 1681, been writing regularly to John Flamsteed, and in the late 1670s had taken part in an exchange of letters with Edmund Borlase, mainly on historical matters.[66] But what Petty wanted was an official correspondence with the two scientific groups in England. Accordingly Robert Huntington was chosen to write the first letter to the Royal Society, because, having just come over from England, he was on friendly terms with several of the London fellows. He suggested to Robert Plot that the Dublin group should send its letters and papers to the Royal Society, which would then transmit them to Oxford.[67] He also mentioned that the Dublin members would 'never grudge to defray all manner of charges' incurred, and had 'raised a fund of which to do it'. On receipt of Huntington's letter, the Royal Society at once instructed its secretary Francis Aston to reply in the most favourable terms.[68] Aston therefore wrote to Molyneux as follows. 'I am to congratulate your new establishment of a society of honourable and learned persons; for the improvement of natural knowledge; and to assure you of all our assistance in your good work, which this place is able to give you, Dr Plot has proposed my writing to you but once a fortnight, which if I have health, I will not fail of.'[69] In the same month the secretary of the Oxford Society William Musgrave also wrote to Molyneux and sent him the minutes of the Oxford group.[70] From that time until April 1687 a regular correspondence took place between the three societies, which proved of inestimable value to the Irish body. In addition, the private exchange of letters between, for example, Molyneux and Flamsteed, and Bulkeley and Lister, helped to keep the society well informed as to the latest philosophical developments in England. Flamsteed in particular wished the society well and urged Molyneux to be optimistic about the future. 'Since your society commences with such happy circumstances, as an increasing trade, a city daily growing, and a country improving as fast, and has the happiness of several ingenious persons . . . settling in it, I see no reason why you should not promise yourselves as fair a progress as any society in being and further fame.'[71] Petty of course conducted an extensive correspondence, and was in close touch with Sir Robert Southwell, later president of the Royal Society. In March 1685 he told Southwell that 'our Dublin Society is pretty well thriven. They have already as much contribution as they need spend. Their number is above 30, whereof the greater part are very sufficient men.'[72]

One of the features of scientific societies and academies at this time was the publication of learned journals, in which papers concerning natural philosophy were printed. The earliest of these was the French *Journal des Sçavants*, first published in 1665. It was soon followed by a large number of imitators, the most important of which were the *Philosophical Transactions* (1665), the *Miscellanea* of the Collegium Naturae Curiorsorum (1670), the Leipzig *Acta Eruditorum* (1682), and Pierre Bayle's *Nouvelles de la République des Lettres* (1684). Already as an undergraduate Molyneux had been reading the *Philosophical Transactions*,[73] and when in 1683 these resumed publication after a lapse of some twelve months, he reminded Flamsteed that 'we forreiners suffer'd much for want of them, for we were thereby kept ignorant of what was doing abroad in the ingenious world'.[74] The *Transactions* were regarded in Dublin as an important link with English and continental science, for they contained much detailed information which could not easily be transmitted by letter. They did however take a long time to reach Ireland, even though the society had appointed Moses Pitt as its London agent for the purchase of scientific literature. Molyneux frequently complained of Pitt's inefficiency, for if the journals failed to arrived punctually, they were of reduced interest, 'for it is the novelty of many things therein that please'.[75] In 1687 arrangements were made for a Dublin bookseller, William Norman, to stock the *Transactions* at his Dame Street shop, where in July of that year he found it worth while to keep thirty-seven copies of the publication.[76] Most of the active members bought the *Transactions*, and some, including Molyneux, Dun, and King, also ordered the *Acta Eruditorum*.[77]

Direct links with the continent were few, the chief being the correspondence between William and Thomas Molyneux. Thomas sent to Ireland descriptions of Dutch scientists and of any notable events met with. In 1684 he visited Christiaan Huygens at The Hague, and was shown a spring balance and other instruments.[78] Thomas also kept the society informed as to the latest scientific books published in Holland and Germany. His opinion of German authors was not high, and he claimed that their books were 'made up of little else than meer cotations out of others'.[79] While in Holland Thomas discussed the Irish society with several Dutch scientists, and his brother mentions in a letter to him how, 'the tidings that our name is in the journals of Amsterdam, was very pleasing to me', and how 'our city and nation may be herein somewhat beholden to us, for I believe the name Dublin has hardly ever before been printed or heard of amongst foreigners on a learned account'.[80]

Fitful attempts were also made to establish a correspondence with continental intellectuals. Already as early as March 1684, Ismael Boulliau, the French astronomer, had heard of the Dublin group, and had been told that news of its activities would be conveyed to him by the secretary of the Royal Society.[81] In September 1685 Huntington wrote to Sir William Trumbull, shortly before the latter's departure for Paris as British envoy-extraordinary, asking him to contact learned men with a view to an exchange of ideas. 'And now,' remarked Huntington, 'laugh on at our Hibernian learning, or else help us to more. Really in France it flourishes if anywhere; and if we become the better for it, we shall gladly acknowledge to whom we stand indebted.'[82] Earlier in the same year Thomas Molyneux at Leyden was writing to Pierre Bayle, that one-man clearing-house for new ideas, describing his experiments on bodies floating in a menstruum.[83] This lead was followed up by Jacobus Sylvius, who in September 1686 informed Bayle of his research into the nature of fevers, the conclusions of which he had recently published at Dublin under the title *Novissima Idea de Febribus*.[84] Shortly afterwards Bayle published in his *Nouvelles de la République des Lettres* an account by Sylvius of a 'horny girl' examined by the Dublin Society.[85] In December 1686 the society itself instructed its then secretary, Edward Smyth, to write to Bayle. This he did, assuring Bayle that science in Ireland was in need of foreign assistance, and offering to commence a regular correspondence. 'Primam adhuc agimus infantiam, et si quos edere contigit feliciores vagitus, nos nostraq' tuis permultum debere praeconiis grato animo omnes agnoscimus; et bene viximus, quibus aliquid tanti nominis viro dignum concipere licuit, et qui perficiendo pares eramus.'[86] Bayle replied in January 1687. He complimented the 'illustrious' Dublin Society on its work, and agreed that scientific knowledge should obtain the widest possible circulation throughout Europe.[87] But the cessation of the society's meetings three months later seems to have ended the correspondence, which, had it continued, might have established an important direct link between the Irish scientists and their continental colleagues, many of whom were well known to Bayle. Already the work of the members of the Dublin Society was being printed in continental journals, and the situation seemed ripe for a mutually beneficial exchange of ideas.[88] The political upheavals of James II's reign however brought these promises to an early grave.

The facilities enjoyed by the Oxford Society meeting in the Ashmolean Building have already been described. Even the earlier Oxford group had kept an extensive 'elaboratory' in John Wilkins's rooms at Wadham College. This had included an automaton, shadow dials, perspectives, a 'way-wiser' or pedometer, a thermometer, a large loadstone, and a 'balance on a demie circle'.[89] The Royal Society met at Gresham College, which also afforded considerable advantages in the field of instruments and other equipment. The London group also owned the great Norfolcian Library, which had been presented to it in 1666 by Henry Howard, later sixth Duke of Norfolk. The resources at Dublin were modest in comparison. In December 1683, Huntington, whose prejudices against Ireland must be kept in mind, complained to Plot that,

Here, alas, we are destitute of all such helps and advantages; scarce a place to put our heads in a room big enough to hold us. We have indeed chambers and lodgings such as they are, but you must not measure them according to your proportions: they are suited to a narrow capacity, fit for Hibernian learning, which (your English wits say) may be contained in a very little space.[90]

In the same letter he also remarked that the Dublin group had no 'materials to work upon', save for those which they could obtain from England. He appealed to the Royal Society to 'free us from Egyptian bondage, that we man't be slaves'. What Huntington was saying in purple prose, Molyneux corroborated in a lower key. As early as September 1681 he had regretted that, 'living here in a kingdom barren of all things, but especially of the ingenious artificers, I am wholly destitute of instruments I can rely on'.[91] Even after the founding of the society, Molyneux had no high opinion of his birthplace as a centre for philosophical studies. 'This city,' he told Flamsteed, 'is not yet sufficiently replenished with men that way inclined. Men here are most incumbent on their gains, and in making their fortunes, and have not time or mony to spend in the pursuit of philosophy.'[92] To Molyneux, Ireland was that 'corner of the world half buried', and he rightly regarded himself as one of the pioneers of Irish science. Ashe too, with oratorical exaggeration, referred to Ireland as a country where 'not long since a mathematician and a conjurer were aequivalent terms, and a telescope and quandrant were things as unknown as a frog or toad'.[93] Although the members of the Dublin Society were willing to make their country seem even more backward than it was, in order to impress strangers with the difficulty of their situation, they were basing their arguments on solid fact. In 1683 Ireland had little to offer the natural philosopher.

These practical obstacles were not however entirely insurmountable. In April 1684 the society found permanent quarters in a house at Crow's Nest off Dame Street, where its rooms were situated above the apothecary's shop of Robert Witherall, who in 1693 became master of the Dublin Barber-Surgeons Company.[94] There they erected an herbal garden and a well-equipped laboratory.[95] Soon they also owned a museum or repository in imitation of that at Gresham College, and Molyneux, who had heard unflattering things from his brother as to the condition of Dutch science, seemed more optimistic than before, pointing out that, 'ignorant as we are in this place, God be thanked we know what a baroscope is'.[96] Although the society had some instruments of its own, the members probably used Molyneux's personal collection, which, by 1684, had become quite large. Ten years later he was to remark, 'as to my instruments, I had formerly some large astronomical ones, but these I parted with intending to procure better. . . . The instruments which I retain . . . are chiefly dioptrical, such as glasses for telescopes of all lengths, from one to thirty feet, microscopes of all kinds, prisms, magick lanterns, micrometers, pendulums, clocks, etc.'[97] After his son Samuel died in 1728, about 200 lots of instruments were auctioned out of the estate, each consisting of not less than three separate items. Many of these had been inherited, and the following had probably belonged to William, who had purchased new instruments in the last years of his life: 'A quadrant, spirit-levels, cones, microscopes, a helioscope, telescopes, a theodolite, compasses, ring-dials, an air-pump, barometers, loadstones, a camera obscura, an instrument for reducing pictures to miniature size, and a set of surveying chains.'[98] In 1685 William Molyneux visited the London instrument-maker, Richard Whitehead, who built for him a telescope after a special design,[99] and from 1685 the small observatory at Trinity College was also used by the academic members of the society, who achieved considerable notoriety among the undergraduates for their scientific interests.[100]

Records survive for the libraries of only two members of the Dublin Society, namely William Molyneux and Charles Willoughby. The former was an inveterate bibliophile, and having a large fortune, was well able to indulge his enthusiasm. When he heard that Edmond Halley had brought some copies of the second part of the astronomer Johannes Hevelius's *Machinae Coelestis* to England, he immediately wrote to Flamsteed, declaring himself willing to pay any price for a new or second-hand copy.[101] His brother was also ordered to buy books at auctions in Holland, and on one occasion 'laid out . . . a good sum of mony, and amongst other things bought Kepler *De Motu Stellae* and one of his *Rudolphine Tables*, both bound together for 6 shls. and six pence'.[102] When Molyneux died in 1698 his library consisted of about 2000 volumes, of which the vast majority dealt with scientific subjects.[103] Its composition reflects the interest of a serious, highly literate, and wealthy scientist, whose main concern was for astronomy and optics. The works of Boyle, Descartes, Gassendi, Grew, Hooke,

Newton, Wilkins, and Willis were prominent, and the collection also included a large number of books dealing with the methods and philosophy of science in general. Here Bacon, represented by about fifty volumes, quite naturally takes pride of place. While among the many propaganda pamphlets and treatises are to be found the works of Joseph Glanvill, Thomas Sprat's *History of the Royal Society* (London, 1667), Ralph Cudworth's *True Intellectual System of the Universe* (London, 1678), and that rambling piece, Nathaniel Fairfax's *Treatise of the Bulk and Selvedge of the World* (London, 1674).[104] Indeed the library was exactly what might have been expected of Molyneux, and despite its size, provides evidence of a fair degree of discrimination.[105]

Charles Willoughby's library, although smaller, displayed very much the same sort of interests.[106] As a physician, Willoughby's main concern was medicine, and he owned a large number of books by eminent seventeenth century medical men like Francis Glisson, William Harvey, Thomas Sydenham, and Thomas Willis, as well as the more traditional works of Galen and the iatrochemical writings of Glauber. The first director of the society was a good linguist, and bought books and journals in no less than six languages, ranging from Hebrew to Dutch. All the obvious authors – Bacon, Boyle, Descartes, Galileo, Hooke, Kepler, Newton, and Sprat – were included, and the composition of the collection confirms the view that the active members of the society, while seldom of more than moderate ability, were remarkably well informed as to contemporary scientific developments in Europe. These two libraries were at the disposal of the membership as a whole, and Willoughby lent a number of books to his friends, who were usually also fellow members.[107] But the collecting of scientific books was not confined to members of the Philosophical Society. On the death of Mr Thomas Scudamore in 1698, for example, his library of some 4000 items was put up for auction, and was advertised as containing 'the most valuable' works on 'physick, philosophy, cosmography, history, mathematicks, philology, and chronology etc., in Hebrew, Greek, Latin, and other tongues'.[108]

As a body the Dublin Society was not prosperous enough to be able to employ a large staff of scientific assistants and full-time secretaries. At the foot of the minutes for 3 March 1684 occurs a short note to the effect that, 'Nicholas Hudson, our operator, attended first on us'.[109] But this person is not mentioned again, and his employment was probably of short duration. The Oxford Society had its Director of Experiments, while at London there was a staff of clerks, librarians, and operators. In 1676 the Royal Society was actually paying Robert Hooke, its Curator of Experiments, £40 a year, and employed Harry Hunt as his assistant at an annual salary of £20. Both amounts were however often in arrears. The Dublin Society also hired an amanuensis to copy out the minutes, but he did not attend meetings, and was probably paid on a piece-rate system. In some draft minutes Molyneux noted that, 'Mr Samuel Davis began to write for us, Mar. 15, '84'.[110] Beyond this nothing is known of the activities of these scribes. In 1685 the society did however appoint Joseph Ray of College Green as its official printer. But the only item he was to produce in this capacity was a double-sheet of 'Cheap, Vulgar, and Mean Experiments', devised for scientists by Sir William Petty.[111]

From its foundation the Royal Society enjoyed the favour of Charles II, who, while withholding financial aid, gave it his blessing and lent his personal prestige to the undertaking. The Dublin Society also received some encouragement from the men of state in Ireland, who may have been induced to give their support by the example of their royal master in England. William Molyneux was on friendly terms with the Duke of Ormonde, who, until 1685, held the office of Lord Lieutenant of Ireland. He owed the friendship to the Franciscan Peter Walsh, who had spoken highly to the duke of Molyneux's learning and character.[112] When Ormonde came to Dublin he sought out Molyneux, and being at once impressed by the latter's abilities, appointed him to the post of joint Chief Engineer and Surveyor-General of the King's Buildings and Works in Ireland. On several occasions Ormonde joined the Dublin Society in gunnery experiments with a mortar-piece in a field outside the capital. And Molyneux noted how, 'Hereby I had the opportunity to be known to His Lordship, who was pleased to give me his discourse on various subjects for a great while; and I am told that he does not speak ill of me ever since.'[113] Ormonde may well have been persuaded to take an interest in the society by his principal secretary, Sir Cyril

Wyche. Wyche had been born at Constantinople in 1632, and had the, for an Englishman, rare distinction of being the godson of the orthodox patriarch of that city. He had studied at Christ Church, Oxford, and already in the 1670s was secretary to the Earl of Essex, then Lord Lieutenant of Ireland. His appointment under Essex did not however necessitate his leaving London, and he acted as president of the Royal Society in 1683 and 1684, having been elected a fellow in 1663. He continued to hold office as principal secretary under Ormonde, who thought him 'an honest gentleman and a good Protestant'.[114] In 1684 he was obliged to come over to Ireland to help his master deal with the already confused political situation in that country. By October he was attending dinners given by the Dublin Society, which he formally joined during the following month.[115]

An even more substantial patron was the Earl of Clarendon, who succeeded Ormonde as Lord Lieutenant in October 1685. James II appointed Clarendon, his brother-in-law, in the hope that the new viceroy would both reduce Protestant fears and give discreet relief to the Roman Catholics. But Clarendon could not compete with the intrigues of Tyrconnell and Sunderland, and his governorship was no more than an interlude between Ormonde and Tyrconnell, between the old world and the short-lived new. Not long after his arrival in Ireland he attended a meeting of the Dublin Society, and was presented with a congratulatory address by St George Ashe, which he received 'with a great expression of civility and kindness'.[116] Ashe's speech was typical of the hyperbolical public utterances of the day. After a short survey of the Irish scientific scene, he dedicated the society's 'studies and endeavours . . . to render (if possible) the great names of Hyde and Clarendon more illustrious and renown'd'.[117] Subsequently Clarendon did all he could to help the society, and a week later his secretary, Sir Paul Rycaut, joined as an ordinary member.[118] In April 1686 Clarendon urged the members to form themselves into a corporate body and procure a charter modelled on that of the Royal Society.[119] Although a fund was started for this purpose, Bulkeley, for reasons which are not clear, opposed the plan, even though he recognized Clarendon as 'extremely' a 'friend' of the society. By June he had persuaded enough members to reject the idea of a charter, so that, as he told his friend Martin Lister, it began 'to fall of itself'.[120]

When Clarendon was dismissed in January 1687 the society recorded the following motion.

Ordered by the society: that in gratitude to His Excellency the Lord Lieutenant, who has beene so particularly kind to us, the society wait upon him before his resigning the government, and give him the complement of a speeche as an acknowledgement of his kindness. Appointed for the making a speech Mr Edw. Smyth; and that wee may also pray the protection of the succeeding governor, His Excellency the Lord Deputy; ordered that wee addresse to him after the same manner.[121]

But Lord Deputy Tyrconnell had other things on his mind, and Molyneux was later to blame him for the collapse of the society and for the destruction of 'all other good things' in Ireland.[122]

The members of the Dublin Society maintained an intellectual attitude which was in general similar to that displayed by the Royal Society. They rarely theorized in detail about the uses of natural philosophy, or its rôle in the world at large, being content to regard themselves as, in the final analysis, dutiful followers of Bacon. They claimed for themselves a divinely-orientated and utilitarian science, but like their English counterparts, failed, without realizing it, to practise what they preached. Despite the pioneering nature of the venture, the Dublin Society was without great difficulty able to collect the equipment then essential for the successful pursuit of science in the modern manner. This, and the creation in Ireland of an atmosphere at least partially receptive to the contemporary natural philosophy, were the Dublin Society's most remarkable achievements.

Chapter 5
The Work of the Society

This chapter is devoted to a study of the scientific and other work undertaken by the Dublin Society, or by its members experimenting individually outside its meetings and business, chiefly, but not exclusively, in the period 1683 to 1687. Instead of presenting a long and probably indigestible account of these activities in the form of a continuous narrative, the chapter has been divided into a number of main and subsidiary headings. The three main sections are, I Science, II Technology, and III Humanities. Natural Philosophy in the seventeenth century was of course far less stratified than such an approach might imply, and consequently some of the headings are more precise than were the subjects with which they deal. Whenever the present study leads to any general conclusions, these are given at once. They are not grouped anaemically by themselves. It should be pointed out that the writer is not a scientist, and that this chapter does not contain any scientific evaluation in depth of the work performed by the society. Instead it is hoped that a general picture will emerge of the nature and peculiarities of Irish science during the last twenty years of the seventeenth century.

PART I SCIENCE

i. Chemistry

Chemistry in the seventeenth century suffered more than most sciences from the fact that a magical provenance still denied it complete philosophical respectability. Its alchemical antecedents and connections, influential as late as the mid-eighteenth century, made it for some a suspect learning, and although the work of Robert Boyle stimulated interest, chemistry was not yet recognized as the intellectual equal of say astronomy or mathematics. Paracelsus, with his alchemical preoccupations, had

H

defined it as 'an intention, imagination, and studying, or considering how or whereby the species of metals are transmuted from one degree and nature into another'. The iatrochemical aspects of Paracelsus's thought achieved widespread currency during the early seventeenth century, and in 1610 Jean Beguin insisted that the chemist's chief task was the discovery of 'safe and grateful medicaments'.[1] But in England chemistry, despite the work of men like Robert Fludd, did not become an integral part of the new philosophy until the time of Boyle. Indeed it is perhaps not even useful to talk of anything called 'chemistry' at this early stage, for in England at least the subject did not adopt even the outlines of its modern characteristics until about the time of the Restoration. Boyle was, of course, among other things, especially concerned to point out that chemistry was not merely ancillary to medicine, but had an importance quite apart from its purely utilitarian applications – an argument different from that often thought necessary in the justification of many other sciences, where utility was frequently stressed to the virtual exclusion of other criteria of value.

The members of the Dublin Society showed considerable enthusiasm for chemistry, and often discussed at their meetings problems common to most contemporary scientists. Both Sir Richard Bulkeley and Allen Mullen read papers dealing with the nature of digestion, which they explained in terms of an acid–alkali reaction.[2] Similar theories had been pioneered by Van Helmont, and later developed by his follower Franciscus Sylvius of Leyden. Both had maintained that, as all secretions in the stomach appeared to be either acid or alkaline, and as these seemed always to react effervescently, the process of fermentation, then synonymous with digestion, must be an acid–alkali reaction. Here the Dublin Society was simply examining older theories, which had already proved of considerable interest to both the Royal and Oxford Societies. Bulkeley, for example, acknowledged his indebtedness to 'Dr Grew's experiments of that kind',[3] while William Musgrave, the Oxford secretary, performed, in August 1684, a series of experiments which led him to assert that the 'great worke of digestion proceeds from a volatile alcali'.[4] The acid–alkali theory became so popular partly because chemical investigation of internal secretions (such as saliva, bile, pancreatic juice), led experimenters, in this case relying as much on taste as on anything else, to assert that all such secretions were either acid or alkaline, and partly because their claims that acids and alkalis always react effervescently seemed to obtain support from the experimental use of salt of tartar (potassium carbonate), the commonest alkali of the time, which gives off carbon dioxide when an acid is added to it.

Some of the medical members of the society were, naturally enough, interested in the development of iatrochemistry, and Charles Willoughby's library included several volumes dealing with the subject, as well as a large number of pharmacopeias.[5] Willoughby himself however seems to have preferred the traditional herbal remedies. When writing to William King, then Bishop of Derry, who had requested medical advice for one of his flock, he recommended, as a cure for rickets, 'A drying dyet, forbearing flesh and living on dryed and preserved fruits, raisins, almonds, sweetmeats, hartshorne and ivorie, with the roots of filipendula and scrofula.'[6] At the same time Allen Mullen was perfecting a new cure for gout, which eventually earned him a large financial reward.[7] The remedy, of which no analysis has survived, may have been chemical in composition, but could well have been similar to that proposed by Thomas Wells of Oxford, who thought beer in which mustard seed had been steeped an efficacious specific for those suffering from the disease.[8] In the Spring of 1684 the Dublin Society built a laboratory designed by Mullen in a room over the apothecary's shop of Robert Witherall, which was to be used chiefly for chemical experiments. By choosing to meet near an apothecary's premises, the society was following a tradition well established in English science, for during the late 1650s both Boyle and Petty had lodged with an apothecary at Oxford, 'because of the convenience of inspecting drugs and the like'.[9]

Besides experimenting with a set purpose in mind, such as the discovery of particular medicines, the members of the society indulged in more general chemical operations. At a meeting in July 1685 Mullen performed some experiments, in the course of which he mixed together a variety of substances, ranging from river-water to spirit of wine (alcohol) and from urine to syrup of violets, in order to note the resultant reactions.[10] This series of experiments is interesting because it shows the way in which scientific trends were transmitted from one country to another. A similar group of observations had been made by John Ballard at a meeting of the Oxford Society in May 1685.[11] The minutes for that month, had, as usual, been sent to Ireland, and had arrived there well before the beginning of July.[12] Ballard himself had undertaken the experiments as a result of a letter received from the Royal Society,[13] which in turn had culled them from a book written by the German chemist Johann Kunckel.[14] In this case Ballard's researches had merely reactivated a problem previously discussed at Dublin, where Kunckel's theory had already been examined, particularly in relation to a quarrel between him and another German scientist called Voight, as to whether spirit of wine is acid or alkaline. Kunckel held that as spirit of wine turns green when mixed with syrup of violets, it must be an alkali. The Royal Society had received a copy of his book shortly after its publication in 1684, and soon became involved in the controversy. It referred the matter to Boyle, who rather archly maintained 'that the society had not been used to judge in these cases: that they were now making experiments, and were not come so far as to frame systems'.[15] The first news of the argument to reach Dublin came in a letter from Francis Aston, the Royal Society's secretary, dated 8 November 1684, which was read at a meeting held about a fortnight later.[16] Little immediate interest was shown, and it was not until the following March that 'an epitome of the controversy between Kunckel and Voight was committed to Dr Sylvius and Dr Mullen'.[17] They eventually reported in the Summer of 1685, and their conclusions were quite different from those reached at Oxford.[18] Mullen confirmed that spirit of wine turns green when mixed with syrup of violets, as Kunckel claimed, even though Ballard was unable to obtain a similar coloration, his mixture turning bright red. Mullen thus succeeded in 'verifying' the erroneous Kunckelian theory, even though Samuel Demaistres, at a meeting of the Royal Society, had already proved that spirit of wine was not an alkali.[19]

The Irish Winter of 1683-4 was unusually severe, and the Dublin Society busied itself with trials and observations connected with freezing. In February Ashe reported a number of experiments he had been prompted to make after reading

Boyle's *New Experiments and Observations Touching Cold* (London, 1665, 2nd ed., 1683).[20] Ashe made little attempt to draw any general conclusions from his research regarding the nature of cold (although like Boyle he seems to have believed it the result of more or less rapid motion), but merely provided descriptions of what happened to various substances when exposed to low temperatures. The list of materials used provides evidence of little more than that lowest (if essential) common denominator of seventeenth century science, an unlimited curiosity. They included 'St Patrick's Well, pumpwater, water with about one 20th part of salt dissolved in it, which is above the proportion said to be in seawater, ale, milk, clarett, anniseed water, urine, and syrup of gillyflowers.'[21] Ashe noted what proportion of each liquid froze, how many came to contain air bubbles, and how many lost their taste. Like Boyle he was puzzled by the great force exerted by water when freezing, but whereas Boyle tried to discover explanations, and even to define the nature of coldness,[22] Ashe simply recorded the phenomenon. The Oxford Society had also taken advantage of the frosty weather, and Demaistres had performed similar experiments with a somewhat smaller, though equally eclectic, range of substances.[23] Ashe was a typical virtuoso, in that his interests were too catholic to enable him to devote himself to any one major activity. While experimenting during the same Winter, he could not, for example, resist the temptation of making artificial snow, 'by beating the whites of eggs or any other substance into a froth which exposed to the cold air, soon turned into flakes of snow, not to be distinguished from the natural'.[24]

The more practical side of chemistry was not neglected by the society, and at a meeting in January 1686, Ashe gave an account of a new solid fuel he had invented.[25] This consisted of a mixture of clay and coal dust, which he claimed would make a 'better and more lasting fuel than coal'. Trials were also made to discover the properties of mineral waters, and Petty drew up a list of thirty-two standard tests for this purpose.[26] Among the questions requiring solution were, he suggested, 'How much common water will extinguish its taste?' and 'Whether it will hinder or promote the curdling of milk and fermentation of liquors?' Petty was always ready to use any experience for scientific purposes, and, even before joining the society, had, on a journey to his Kerry estates, made a special detour to Edenderry, so that he might examine the mineral waters to be found there.[27] Later both King and Huntington presented bottles of mineral waters to the society for experimental purposes.[28]

Like its Dublin counterpart, the Oxford Society devoted a considerable amount of time to chemical studies. In March 1685 Robert Plot, then its president, drew up 'a catalogue of the arcana and desiderata in chymistry'.[29] When news of this reached Dublin a request was made for a copy to be transmitted to Ireland.[30] The catalogue, a mixture of good sense and alchemical lore, gives clear evidence of the confused nature of seventeenth century chemistry. It shows that neither of the societies was as yet entirely sceptical as to the possibility of the transmutation of metals, and that Plot himself counted among the proper activities of the contemporary natural philosopher, the making of 'a universall medicine'. Plot was essentially a topographer, and more able experimenters, like the Molyneux brothers, were probably not overenthusiastic about his catalogue. It would however be wrong to exaggerate the backwardness of Plot's views. Alchemical ideas died hard, and as late as 1782, James Price, F.R.S., a respected chemist, announced that he had invented a white powder capable of converting fifty times it own weight of mercury into silver.[31]

In all ten papers dealing either exclusively or predominantly with chemistry were read at the meetings of the Dublin Society between 1683 and 1687. Some of its medical activities also had important chemical implications. As the number of papers produced by the society in this period was 159, those on chemistry constituted 6·3% of the total. In the years 1684 to 1687 some 6·2% of the articles printed in the *Philosophical Transactions*, which reflected the interests of the Royal Society in particular, were devoted to chemical problems and experiments.[32] The two figures are remarkably similar, and show how close was the thematic connection between English and Irish science.

ii. Anatomy and Medicine

Medicine was probably the only branch of science in the seventeenth century which was prosecuted by professional specialists, although of course many discoveries were made, and experiments carried out, by persons with no formal medical training. Between 1683 and 1687 eight physicians and one surgeon joined the Dublin Society, about a quarter of whose membership therefore earned its livelihood by the practice of physic. Nor were the doctors modest as to their professional expertise. Charles Willoughby, who had spent some years at Padua, was convinced that British practitioners were 'the most learned and best studied men in the world',[33] while Thomas Molyneux examined the physiology of insects 'from an inclination, common to those of my profession, to make inquiries into things natural'.[34]

Of the papers read to the society during its first period of business, forty-four dealt with medical matters, and over half of these were the work of Allen Mullen. The greater part of the medical experiments were undertaken privately, being merely described at meetings by the members concerned. The most common types of communication were accounts of dissections, vivisections, experimental injections, and reports by physicians on the diseases of their patients. But the largest single group among the society's medical dissertations was concerned with human and animal oddities. In fact, so eager were members to examine freaks of every kind, that on one occasion they tried to purchase the corpse of a young double-headed girl, only to find, to their evident disappointment, that 'the parties who had the property in this monster, would not sell it'.[35] A week later however they were given 'a male child with two compleat heads, one somewhat bigger than the other'.[36] It was considered so unusual that a special drawing was made for transmission to the Oxford Society.[37] This was executed by Edwin Sandys, one of the most prominent Irish artists of the time, who also made a sketch of a 'monstrous kitlin',[38] and acted as the society's unofficial draughtsman. The list of monsters, or 'errors of nature', as Molyneux preferred to call them,[39] examined by the society is long and varied. Besides those already mentioned, there was a double-headed calf, a monstrous fish, and a large number of deformed cats. Mullen wrote a detailed description of the dissection of such a 'double cat', which was later published, with diagrams by Sandys, in the *Philosophical Transactions*.[40] He concluded the animal to have been born dead, for the lungs were 'compact and free from air'. The main point of interest lay in whether or not the cat had twice as many organs as a normal animal. In this case there was one head, but two necks, only one stomach, but two livers and two hearts. Mullen's anatomical examinations were always thorough and often extremely detailed. They compare well with the best English observations by contemporaries such as Hooke and Willis.

Other freaks brought into the society, or described to it, include a 'monstrous chicken with two bills' and a girl with 'horns' growing on her body.[41] These interests may now seem rather extreme, but in the seventeenth century they were part of every scientific society's stock-in-trade. The study of hermaphroditism in particular took up a great deal of time in most European academies. In 1667 Henry Oldenburg was tantalizing the inquisitive Robert Boyle with promises that at the next meeting of the Royal Society he would give 'a good account of a pretty hermaphrodite, now in London, which was lately visited by Dr Allen and myself'.[42] Eighteen years later Willoughby informed the Dublin Society of 'one especially (that passed for such) which he saw in Dublin'.[43] These unfortunate people, together with dwarfs, giants, and deformed children, were often forced, in order to keep themselves alive, to tour the countryside as part of some quack's 'medical exhibition'. Pregnancy, and the whole problem of birth, provided another wide field for speculation, and misshapen babies were often blamed on what might today be called psychosomatic disturbance, but then ranked as the 'power of the imagination'. Indeed two strikingly similar conclusions were reached about monstrous births at London and Dublin. In England the *Philosophical Transactions* recorded the birth of an ape-like child to a woman, and explained the phenomenon by reason of the mother having seen a monkey when already five months advanced in pregnancy.[44] In Dublin Ashe related 'the history of a gentlewoman in town, who upon sight of a natural, brought forth exactly such another, not only resembling it in features, and particularly in the red eyes, like those of a ferret, but also imitating all its awkward gestures'.[45] Only a few months later Ashe was claiming that the chief difference between the old philosophy and the new was that, while the exponents of the former could find pleasure only in 'irregularities and monsters', the true scientists devoted themselves to 'the delight of knowing and studying' nature's 'most beautifull works'.[46] It is therefore perhaps surprising that the Dublin Society did not concern itself with the most popular of all seventeenth century 'freaks', namely the monstrous foetus, towards the study of which many, particularly German, academies devoted an inordinate amount of time.[47] In this respect the Oxford Society was more in the mainstream of continental medical trends, evincing considerable interest in the foeti of hybrids preserved and exhibited by the Earl of Abingdon.[48]

This concentration on the anatomy of human and animal monsters clearly reflects the ambivalent nature of contemporary science in general. Certainly it cannot be argued that as a body the academies of Europe were primarily interested in the discovery of abstract immutable natural laws. The Dublin Society's inclinations were often towards the curious and fantastic and its spirit only intermittently sceptical and critical. Nor was Ireland unique in this respect. The two English societies and many of those on the continent exhibited similar traits. Of course the study of freaks, often of considerable intrinsic importance, also led to more general work in the field of comparative anatomy, a study of increasing popularity since its use by Harvey in the discovery of the circulation of the blood. Circulation is easily seen, with the aid of a microscope, in frogs and newts, and it was Marcello Malpighi's observations of blood passing from the arteries to the veins by way of capillary vessels in the lungs of a frog, which had clinched Harvey's argument. This demonstration became a favourite one among the scientists of the period, for it provided striking evidence of the minute marvels of the Lord. And the fact that as late as 1672 a French University approved a thesis which concluded the circular motion of the blood to be impossible, shows that constant reiteration of Harvey's theory could still be thought necessary.[49] At Dublin in May 1684:

Mr Molyneux opened before the company a water-newt, which he takes to be a *salamandra aquatica*. In the body of this animal there are two long *sacculi aerei*, on which the blood vessels are curiously ramified: to these blood vessels, applying a microscope, he showed the circulation of the blood *ad oculum*, as plainly as water running in a river and more rapidly than any common stream. Likewise the pulsation of the heart was very manifest.[50]

In the following month Molyneux wrote to Nehemiah Grew describing the observation, which, despite its lack of originality, proved of considerable interest to the Royal Society. Martin Lister claimed 'the same to be visible in frogs, and some snails at some times, even through their shells'.[51] And although bad eyesight prevented Petty from following the demonstration in detail, he none the less thought it 'a very useful discovery'.[52] In October 1685 the Oxford Society received a letter from George Middleton of Aberdeen 'concerning the circulation of the blood, easily seen in the *lacerta aquatica* by reason of its transparentnesse'.[53] But when the Dublin Society was informed, it was quick to point out its own precedence in this particular field of medical research.

Experiments with living animals were commonplace, especially in the study of phenomena like respiration and muscle contraction. Robert Hooke was the first English scientist to perform the subsequently popular experiment, in which, using an ordinary bellows, air was pumped into a dog's lungs, which could then be deflated at will.[54] By these means it was possible to keep the animal alive for a considerable time, even after its stomach and thorax had been fully opened. The experiment however prompted Hooke to remark, in a manner uncharacteristic of his age, that 'I shall hardly be induced to . . . further trials of this kind, because of the torture of the creature'.[55] Mullen was not restrained by such humane scruples, and in May 1684 embarked on a series of analogous experiments. These were performed before the whole society, and involved the cutting off of large parts of a dog's lungs, pumping them full of concentrated opium, and studying the results. After a few weeks Mullen, to his evident surprise, was able to report the animal's complete recovery.[56]

Allen Mullen was for his time an intelligent and informed physician, and most of his experiments were the result of advanced medical thinking. He made good use of animals to test his theories in both the physiological and surgical branches of medicine. He had, for instance, heard of a man suffering from a severe pain in the thorax, who asserted that if only a small part of one of his lungs were removed, recovery would follow.

But the physicians attending him were afraid to undertake so radical an operation and the man died. Mullen's interest was aroused by the story, and he tried similar surgery on a dog, which soon recovered its health. Six months later he killed and dissected the animal and found that the wound had almost entirely disappeared.[57] Another useful experiment was his attempt to measure the precise quantity of blood in a human being. This he did by draining the blood from various animals, including a dog, a lamb, a sheep, a rabbit, and a duck, and then calculating its weight in relation to the total weight of the animal in question. Then, striking an average, he estimated that a man weighing 160 pounds would contain about 128 ounces of blood.[58] The general premise on which the observation and conclusion were based is sound enough, but Mullen did not know that some blood remains in a corpse even after a seemingly complete drainage and, because of this, his estimate is too low.

As usual the Oxford Society was working its way through experiments similar to those being undertaken by the Irish physicians. In March 1684 Mullen had injected 18 ounces of water into a dog's thorax.[59] When news of this reached Oxford, William Musgrave recalled how some time previously he had done exactly the same and had injected warm water into every available part of a greyhound bitch's body.[60] These experiments seem to have had little specific purpose, and were undertaken in a spirit of indiscriminate scientific enthusiasm. But while in its medical studies the society was mainly concerned with animal physiology and pathology, its members were not entirely uninterested in the pattern of human diseases. The society's obvious preference for accounts of dissections and vivisections, which could be regarded as 'experiments', probably inhibited Mullen and his colleagues from discussing at any length the more mundane matters of everyday medicine. Mullen's patients belonged chiefly to the upper classes, and he was therefore perhaps reluctant to describe in detail the often embarrassing ailments of prominent persons in church and state.[61] However in November 1686 he did discuss a case 'which offered in his practice', and which deserves quotation in full, for it is typical of seventeenth century Irish medical reporting.

Having had a patient reduc'd to extreme weakness which caus'd his fainting every minute, so that nature being quite spent he was now utterly despaired of. He in the extremity of his weakness voided instead of stoole a greate number of little bladders of an orbicular figure, fil'd with substance of very different consistencys: in some there was a thick ropy liquor in others a pellucid. Some contain'd a hard substance of a consistency like a greene plum and some harder: they were of very different colors and bignesses some nigh as big as a pidgeon's egg. Of these came from him in three days in which he was senseless at least five hundred. At last came out a large bladder in shape and bigness resembling that of an ox: after this he recover'd to admiration and is now an healthy man.[62]

As was often the case the patient here recovered without the direct help of the physician. That they also recovered after the often terrible and always frightening attentions of the contemporary doctors, who usually used bleeding, dosing, and enemas (the three great pillars of the physic of the time), in varying proportions for all complaints, argues well for the strength of the seventeenth-century constitution.

In an age when Boyle could recommend powdered mechoacan root worn about the neck as a specific against cramp,[63] it is often difficult to distinguish between the methods of the quack and those of the genuine practitioner. Mullen at least was sceptical when he examined the herb *Tithymalus Hibernicus*, commonly called mackenboy, which was reputed to act as a purgative when carried on the person. At a meeting of the society in March 1687 'this fabulous story, which has long prevail'd, he prov'd false, by carrying its root for three days in his pocket, without any alteration of that sort'.[64] Already thirty-five years before an anonymous pamphlet entitled *An Interrogatory relating more particularly to the Husbandry and Naturall History of Ireland* (London, 1652) had asked whether the supposed properties of the herb were in fact nothing more than a fable, while Petty, in his *Political Anatomy of Ireland* (London, 1691), written about 1672, had declared the story erroneous and untrue.[65]

Traffic in arcana and secret remedies was not at this time, nor until much later, thought improper, and most physicians regarded certain prescriptions and nostrums of their own as legitimate sources of profit. One of the most famous was 'Goddard's Drops', compounded by the extremely respectable Dr Jonathan Goddard, F.R.S., which included ingredients as efficacious as viper's flesh, human bones, and spirit of harts-horn. The Dublin Society was not on the whole very active in this field, although on one occasion Ashe did recommend new beer as a cure for smallpox. As Mullen's tests with mackenboy show, the society delighted in disproving old wives' tales of long currency. It was again Mullen who pointed out, after observation, that, contrary to popular belief, toads could live quite happily in Ireland, even over long periods.[66] This sort of thing was considered important by contemporary natural philosophers, and the Royal Society went out of its way to prove that a spider could not be enchanted by 'a circle of unicorns horn or Irish earth laid round about it'.[67] But the frantic search for rational explanations of confusing phenomena often resulted in new superstitions replacing the old. Martin Lister, for example, claimed that the so-called fairy-rings were in fact made by moles 'running round after one another underground in a circle, at the time of their coupling', an explanation which met with the acclaim of the fellows of the Royal Society.[68]

Dentistry also took up the time of the Dublin Society. In March 1686 Charles Allen, although not a member, personally presented a copy of his book *The Operator for the Teeth* to the assembled company, and received its 'hearty thanks' for the gift.[69] The pamphlet is an excellent work combining good sense with considerable scientific knowledge. Allen advocated frequent cleaning of the teeth, and recommended 'oyl of camphire' for toothache, admitting, with unusual candour, that his 'remedies do not take effect always'.[70] He described some false teeth he had constructed from the incisors of dogs and other animals, and was the first dentist to use the phrase 'tooth enamel'. The second part of the pamphlet is concerned with the beating of the pulse and indicates a wide reading among natural philosophers both ancient and modern, including Descartes, Gassendi, Lower, and Willis. Allen regarded himself as a specialist and dentistry as a science in its own right. Conscious of the pioneering nature of his work he told those who could not understand it that they had better 'go and comment upon Job, or paraphrase some psalms, than meddle with physical matters'.[71]

Despite the value of much of this work the society added little to general medical knowledge. Perhaps the most important advance made by any of its members was Mullen's discovery of the vascularity of the lens of the eye, which he published in the second part of his *Account of the Elephant* (London, 1682). As was so often the case in the seventeenth century, he had been led to the discovery as a result of his study of comparative anatomy. Mullen, undoubtedly the most gifted physician in the society, was also the first to note certain small but important channels in the ear.[72]

The Dublin Society, while hardly involved in scientific work of a revolutionary kind, was, as has been shown, well abreast of contemporary medical developments, and was certainly no less advanced in this respect than its sister society at Oxford. Meetings were few during which medical matters were not discussed, and more than a quarter (27%) of the papers read by members were concerned with medical problems, as compared with 24·6% of the articles in the *Philosophical Transactions* between 1684 and 1687.[73]

iii. Astronomy

In the sixteenth and early seventeenth centuries astronomy achieved a temporary dominance over other scientific disciplines, for the work of Copernicus, Kepler, Galileo, and Tycho Brahe posed general philosophical problems largely in astronomical terms. Their research and its implications brought about some of the first decisive breaks with traditional methods, a process which, because of its bearing on religious belief and established attitudes, led almost inevitably to conflict and dispute. But after the death of Galileo interest in the subject, while of course it remained considerable, became less pronounced, and English scientists began to show an increasing concern for physiology and the organic sciences in general.[74] Towards the end of the seventeenth century however there was a revival in England of astronomical studies, which received royal approval when Charles II founded the observatory at Greenwich and appointed John Flamsteed as the first Astronomer-Royal. Soon, under the influence of men like Newton and Halley, astronomy, in line with many of the other sciences, was to become more and more abstract and mathematical.

The Dublin Society shared in this revival, although its members were at first hampered by lack of adequate instruments. Already in 1681 William Molyneux was complaining of the absence in Dublin of 'ingenious artificers'.[75] This is perhaps a little surprising. Certainly Dublin could not then provide a market large enough to support exceptionally skilled instrument makers. But there were in the city a large number of clock and watch makers, some of whom must have been capable of producing basic scientific equipment. In the period 1660 to 1680 at least seventeen watch- and clock-makers were active in Dublin, and their number was to increase during the last twenty years of the century.[76] None the less in 1681 Molyneux began, with Flamsteed's help, to place orders with London craftsmen. In December, when he himself was already using two telescopes, respectively sixteen and thirty feet in length, he promised to send twelve pounds for 'one of those small quadrants of 2 foot radius with telescopicall sight'.[77] Two years later the situation had so much improved that he had 'a fair prospect of having within a while a pretty convenient place for observation'.[78] Thus even before the foundation of the society, Molyneux was making astronomical observations, and through his correspondence with one of England's ablest astronomers, was keeping in touch with the latest scientific developments. Molyneux clearly regarded Flamsteed with a mixture of awe and admiration. Even discounting the fulsome conventions of the day, his estimate of the Astronomer-Royal as 'our English Copernicus, Titho, Kepler', implied a high measure of praise.[79] When Trinity College decided to buy a telescope Flamsteed was asked for advice, 'seeing 'tis for the promotion of astonomy in this kingdome, wherein little has yet been done'.[80] This was certainly true, for besides Molyneux and the Dublin Society, there were at this time no more than a handful of serious astronomers in Ireland. The most important of these were Henry Osborne and Robert Wood. Osborne lived on his estate in County Meath, where, among other instruments, he had a quadrant with telescopic sights, a micrometer, and a telescope.[81] Molyneux thought him 'a most devoted man to astronomy, very judicious and modest'.[82] He sent Osborne's observations of the solar eclipse of July 1684 to the secretary of the Royal Society, who published them in the *Philosophical Transactions*,[83] and the second part of the *Dioptrica Nova* is dedicated to 'My esteemed friend Henry Osborne of Dardys-Town in the County of

Meath'. Wood, who had come to Ireland about 1683 after his dismissal from the mastership of the mathematical boys at Christ's Hospital London on account of his unwillingness to teach rudimentary courses, was also known to Molyneux.[84] An able mathematician and astronomer, Wood died in 1685. The year before his death he joined eight members of the Dublin Society in subscribing twenty pounds towards the cost of one of Petty's double-bottomed boats and, while never a member, was certainly on friendly terms with those who had joined the society.[85]

Although Molyneux's interests were typically varied, astronomy and optics were the subjects to which he devoted most of his energy. He found so many astronomical instruments inaccurate that in 1685 he commissioned the London craftsman Richard Whitehead to construct a telescopic dial after his own design.[86] This was very large, and consisted of an octagonal horizontal sundial, on which was fitted a swinging telescope for more accurate observation. Although he wrote his book *Sciothericum Telescopicum* in order to popularize the invention, it never came into widespread use. A description of the dial also appeared in the *Philosophical Transactions*, and John Wallis, the English mathematician, declared that he had 'not been better satisfied with any' he had 'seen on that subject',[87] while the authorities of Trinity College Cambridge thought it a useful instrument, and in 1703 purchased one for their already well-equipped observatory.[88] It was again Molyneux who suggested that the Dublin Society should undertake a number of joint observations, particularly of solar and lunar eclipses, with the Oxford and London groups. The first of these took place about July 1684 under the joint direction of Ashe and Molyneux. The minutes give the following account. 'The day being much overcast hindered them from taking anything accurately, but towards the middle of the eclipse, they had a short view of the sun, as much as to estimate that about eight digits were covered. At the ending also they had a faint view thereof, and assigned its end at H3.56Min. p.m.'[89] The same eclipse was noted by members of the Oxford Society. They gave its end as 25 minutes 14 seconds later than at Dublin,[90] the difference being due partly to their more easterly situation, but mainly to the irregularity of contemporary chronometers. Most subsequent eclipses were observed jointly at Oxford, Dublin, and Green-wich.

One of the liveliest scientific controversies of the time concerned the benefits or otherwise to be derived from the use of telescopic sights. Johannes Hevelius, one of the most respected of European astronomers, had, in his *Annus Climactericus* (Danzig, 1685) repeated earlier assertions of the superiority of plain sights in telescopes. The book was reviewed for the *Philosophical Transactions* by John Wallis, who, a better mathe-matician than astronomer, supported Hevelius's dubious views.[91] Flamsteed explained this in a personal way, claiming that Wallis agreed with Hevelius merely to spite Hooke, who had criticized the continental astronomer and was the leading (and rabid) English supporter of telescopic sights.[92] Francis Aston, the editor of the *Transactions*, thought the review un-satisfactory and commissioned Molyneux to write a new one, which was to be translated into Latin, so that a copy might be sent to Hevelius, who had no English. Molyneux accepted and expressed the view that while Hevelius was certainly a great scientist, indeed 'he alone by his own labours and charges has done more towards the advancement of astronomy than the joynt forces of all ages',[93] telescopic sights were unquestionably superior to plain. E. F. MacPike considers Molyneux's account of the controversy 'certainly fairer than that by Wallis, and the treatment more scientific'.[94] Despite his criticisms, Molyneux was obviously unhappy about Hooke's overdramatic attack on Hevelius. A believer in polite conventions in scientific com-munication, he censured Hooke for desiring 'not the instruction of him or the world, but merely the correction or beating of the author'.[95] Hooke in turn took offence at Molyneux's calling his *Animadversions on the First Part of [Hevelius's] Machina Coelestis* (London, 1674) a pamphlet rather than a book, only to be informed that in Ireland this was the term properly applied to 'small stich'd volumes'.[96]

Molyneux also wrote several other astronomical pieces, dealing with such topics as the problem of the apparent magnitude of the sun near the horizon being greater than at its zenith.[97] This article prompted Halley, who had previously been puzzled by the phenomenon, to look further into the matter and to ask his friend Wallis for information about the

I

young Irish astronomer.[98] This was to lead to a fruitful collaboration between the two men, and Halley helped Molyneux to revise the text of the *Dioptrica Nova* before publication.

Besides using the telescope in the orthodox manner, Molyneux modified it so that it might be employed in the viewing of miniature pictures and etchings. He described this strange instrument in a paper read to the Dublin Society, in which he claimed that it would 'represent the small face of a curious piece of miniature with all the advantage imaginable, as big if not bigger than life.'[99] But despite Molyneux's enthusiasm, the other members of the society, with the exception of Ashe, never became greatly interested in astronomy. Nearly all discussion on the subject was initiated by Molyneux, and all difficulties arising from it referred to him. Those others who were at all interested were generally feeble practitioners, as Flamsteed discovered when George Tollet and Edward Smyth, then on a visit to Greenwich, offered to assist him during observation.[100] At the Oxford Society, on the other hand, astronomical work was carried out by a larger group, and it was common practice for as many as four or five members to cooperate in the observation of an eclipse or a comet.[101]

The impetus behind Molyneux's intense interest in the heavens was the belief that from a study of the universe he could convince himself, beyond all possibility of doubt, of the existence of a supreme being. He esteemed the advances made by contemporary astronomy chiefly because out of them could be taken 'considerable hints towards the establishment of a rational system of the world'.[102] And the 'rational system' thus sought was not godless, but one in which a philosophical creator expressed himself within logical and perhaps eventually understandable terms of reference. For the mathematical laws by which the universe seemed increasingly to be governed, were for Molyneux, as for others, almost certainly the expression of a God whose actions were more and more to be comprehended in a rational, and less and less in an arbitrary, manner.

About 6·3% of the Dublin Society's papers dealt with astronomy. The figure for the *Philosophical Transactions* between 1684 and 1687 is 11·3%. But this was exceptionally high, and fell to 2·6% in the period 1694–6.[103]

iv. Mathematics

As a result partly of the work and achievements of sixteenth century astronomers, and partly of internal progress, mathematics had, by the middle of the seventeenth century, attained a position central and indispensable to the continuation of scientific advance and to its concomitant philosophy of progress. It helped to systematize ideas which the scientists could not otherwise have hoped to state in terms at once so precise and so immutable. As Professor Hall has put it, 'In this ideal world of abstraction, without resistance or friction, in which bodies were perfectly smooth and planes infinite, where gravity was always a strictly perpendicular force and projectiles described the most exquisitely exact parabolas, the principles of Euclidean geometry held absolutely.'[104] In the early seventeenth century English mathematics found possibly its most congenial home among the technologists, a tradition later maintained in the Royal Society by men like Hooke and Wren. In addition there were a number of natural philosophers more interested in pure mathematics, of whom John Wallis, Isaac Barrow, Isaac Newton, and Viscount Brouncker were among the most prominent. As a discipline mathematics impinges on nearly all other scientific studies, and often acts as a common denominator between them. But in the seventeenth century the relevance of mathematics to medicine, and even to chemistry, was only slowly becoming understood. Geometry was still dominant, although algebra, especially in the latter half of the century, was becoming more and more important, partly as a result of contemporary improvements in notation. None the less the only algebraic paper read to the Dublin Society was that produced by Samuel Walkington in the Autumn of 1683. It has not survived, although its title, 'On the Algebraical Way of Proceeding in Demonstrations Mathematicall',[105] indicates the general nature of its contents, while its isolation is evidence of how little the subject was being studied by the Irish scientists of the time. The overall standard of the society's mathematical work was fairly elementary as to content and vague as to method. Most papers were diffuse and seldom dealt with problems of real weight. But Ashe wrote an able piece 'Concerning the Evidence of Mathematical Demonstration and the reason thereof above other Sciences',[106] as well as attempting to discover a method for squaring the circle or at least proving the feasibility of such an undertaking.

The problems involved in squaring the circle, in themselves as old as Archimedes, still occupied the minds of seventeenth century mathematicians. Only a year before Ashe's effort, Robert Hooke had, with equal lack of success, pursued the same mathematical chimera.[107] Ashe's paper was really a historical epitome shot through with rather pious hopes for the future.[108] He conceded that all prospects of a successful extension of the Archimedean method had come to an end with the work of Willebrord Snell, whose *Cyclometricus* (Leyden, 1621) he had read, and realized the importance of Christiaan Huygens's *De Circuli Magnitudine* of 1654, in which π was calculated with even greater accuracy than had been attained by Ludolph van Ceulen, and which 'laid down rules how to find right lines equall to any peripheries or arches given, with the most insensible difference, and likewise a very short method of calculation to discover the falsity of pretended quadratures'.[109] The most interesting feature of this paper lies not so much in its conclusions, which are basically commonplace, but in the breadth of reading which had gone into its composition. Ashe was not unique in this respect among the members of the Dublin Society, and it will be useful to list the authors discussed, most of whom had clearly been studied with some care.

Ancient

Apollonios of Perga
Archimedes
Hipparchos of Nicaea
Hippocrates of Chios
Menelaos of Alexandria
Pappos of Alexandria
Ptolemy

Modern

Christoph Clavius (1537–1612)
Ludoph van Ceulen (1540–1610)
Claude Comiers (d. 1693)
René Descartes (1596–1650)

Jean-Charles de la Faille (1597–1652)
Paul Guldin (1577–1643)
Christiaan Huygens (1629–95)
Georg Joachim Von Lauchen (Rheticus) (1514–76)
Gottfried Wilhelm Leibniz (1646–1716)
Adriaan Metius (1571–1635)
Johann Müller (Regiomontanus) (1436–76)
Bartholomäus Pitiscus (1561–1613)
Grégoire de St Vincent (1584–1667)
Joseph Scaliger (1540–1609)
Christian Severin (Longomontanus) (1562–1647)
René François de Sluse (1622–85)
André Tacquet (1611–60)
Evangelista Torricelli (1608–47)

Not a single Englishman is mentioned in the paper, and the most surprising omission is perhaps that of Franciscus Vieta (1540–1603), whose remarkable *Canon Mathematicus* of 1579 represents an important breakthrough as regards the calculation of π. Ashe concluded his piece with the eminently sensible remark, 'Since we can perform all the reall uses which may be expected from the solution of these celebrated problems, and that so many other parts of usefull philosophy do yet want improvement, that it's scarce worth the while to throw away time upon such barren notionall speculations.' The Oxford Society requested a copy of the article, which, when it arrived, was given to John Caswell for detailed examination.[110] His report is unfortunately no longer extant.

Ashe's attitude towards mathematics in general is best seen in another paper presented in April 1684, in which he tried to demonstrate a number of Euclidean propositions independently, 'without any precedent lemmas'.[111] Here the preamble is particularly interesting, for in it Ashe argued that mathematics was superior to other branches of learning because of the certainty of its methods of procedure and its easy exposure of paralogisms. This he ascribed to the fact that quantity, the object with which it is conversant, is a tangible obvious thing, and that consequently the 'ideas we form thereof are clear and distinct, and daily represented to us in most familiar instances, because it makes use of terms which are proper, adaequate, and unchangeable'. It was the immutability of mathematical laws, eschewing as they seemed to do, 'all trifling in words and rhetoricall schemes, all conjectures, authority, prejudices, and passion', which appealed to men who saw science as perhaps one of the few fixed points of reference in a changing world. William Petty's statistical researches, for example, were underpinned by such a belief. Like Ashe he saw in what might rather naively be called the 'value-free' nature of numbers a uniquely objective means of analysis. Already in 1674 he had called for a quantitative approach to mechanical philosophy. 'Apply your mathematicks to matter', he told his colleagues in the Royal Society, for only by the rules of number might natural philosophy, and especially matter theory, free itself from the confusion of qualities and words.[112] Mathematics in effect was becoming the archetype of strict and objective modes of reasoning.

William Molyneux did not neglect mathematics, and talked to the society on a variety of subjects, in particular the geometrical implications arising from the theory of concentric circles.[113] But for him this was merely incidental to his work in astronomy and optics, although he was naturally forced to employ mathematical methods in the study of other sciences, conceding that 'there is no part of philosophy wherein the mathematicks are not deeply ingredient'.[114] The problems posed by the volution of concentric circles were also discussed by Petty, who had, with his usual ingenuity, 'produced an instrument in wood . . . for explaining the difficulty'.[115] George Tollet was by profession a teacher of mathematics, and most of his contributions to the society were in some way connected with that discipline. His chief interest lay in the field of applied mathematics, and his papers 'On Gunnery' and 'On the Weight of Iron Shot'[116] are models of their kind. After the society had ceased to meet he went to England, where he obtained a position with the Commission for the Revenue and later acted as William King's unofficial London agent. While in England he became interested in the mathematics of averages and chance, a study of widespread popularity at the time. Samuel Pepys, for example, spent long hours in calculating gambling odds, and it was he who first approached Tollet for help in solving the following problem.

Presuming:

A Has 6 dice in a box with which he is to fling a six.

B Has in another box 12 dice with which he is to fling two sixes.

C Has in another box 18 dice with which he is to fling three sixes.

Whether B and C have not as easy a task as A at even luck?[117]

So concerned was Pepys to establish the correct solution, for he was anxious to use it as the basis of wagers, that Newton was also asked to submit his views. After some technical misunderstandings, both he and Tollet agreed that A would have an advantage over B, who in turn would be more favourably placed than C.[118] Another member of the Dublin Society wrote an article for the *Philosophical Transactions* entitled 'An Arithmetical Paradox concerning the Chances of Lotteries'.[119] This was the Honourable Francis Robartes, son of the Earl of Radnor, who joined the society in 1693, and whom Molyneux thought 'a most excellent mathematician, and admirably accomplished otherwise'.[120] About the turn of the century an unusually large number of mathematical books on gambling were being published in England. The most important of these was Abraham de Moivre's *The Doctrine of Chances* (London, 1718), which was a revised version of an earlier French edition. In the preface de Moivre thanked Robartes for his encouragement while preparing the book, and for having suggested solutions to a number of difficult problems.

But pure mathematics constituted a small part of the Dublin Society's business, and only nine papers, or 5·7% of the total, dealt with that subject. This was not however unusual. The Oxford Society did not display a greater interest, while in the period 1684–7 only 3·5% of the articles in the *Philosophical Transactions* fell into this category.[121]

About this time, largely as a result of Newton's work, mathematics was becoming estranged from, and beginning to be regarded as in some way superior to, the other sciences. This development has been noticed by writers like Margaret 'Espinasse, who suggests that 'a hiatus became apparent between the lofty Newtonian sciences and the humble non-mathematical sciences, and these began to lose' prestige.[122] It is certainly true that Newton, by the very magnitude of his achievement, tended to assume the position of a new Aristotle. Many regarded him as having pronounced final judgement on a wide range of physical problems, and this attitude was paradoxically the prime cause of the comparative decline of the natural sciences during the early eighteenth century.

As has already been suggested, the Dublin philosophers shared the view which stressed the pre-eminence of mathematics over other branches of scientific learning. Molyneux felt that, while searching for shells and insects was not in itself unimportant, without mathematics 'nothing solid or usefull in philosophy' could be attained.[123] While Edward Smyth saw mathematics both as 'the direct path to knowledge', and the most satisfyingly logical of all the sciences. Its language he thought universal and its results at once useful and precise.[124] It is plain therefore that Irish science to a large extent shared contemporary beliefs as to the primacy of mathematics. It also shared in the subsequent comparative decline in natural philosophy. Between 1708 and 1731 no institutional scientific activity took place in Ireland, and even the foundation of the Royal Dublin Society in the latter year was to some extent a reaction against Newtonianism.[125] Its stress on the directly 'useful' sciences like agriculture was to establish a trend later adopted in both England and Ireland with the foundation of the short-lived Dublin Physico-Historical Society in 1744 and of the Royal Society of Arts at London in 1754.

Before concluding this section one other paper read to the Dublin Society by Samuel Foley should be mentioned. The title explains its contents: 'Computatio Universalis seu Logica Rerum, Being an Essay attempting in the Geometrical Method to Demonstrate an Universal Standard whereby one may judge the real Value of Everything in the World'.[126] This piece was part of a larger *genre*, and was an attempt to apply mathematical rules and procedures to judgements on moral and philosophical matters. As such it owed an obvious debt to Descartes's 'Universal Mathematical Science' and to Hobbes's suggestion in *De Cive* that, had moral philosophers more closely followed the methodology of the geometrician, 'the strength of avarice and ambition, which is sustained by the erroneous opinions of the vulgar, as touching the nature of right and wrong, would presently faint and languish'.[127] Foley wrote in order, as he put it, to assist man 'to procure as much happiness as is procurable', and despite the question-begging nature of the axioms postulated, his piece to some extent foreshadowed certain aspects of English utilitarian thought. He began by defining terms like 'wisdom', 'a fool', 'pleasure', and 'displeasure', and then listed various happinesses enjoyed and sought by men (women are ignored) at particular periods in life. Between the ages of 25 and 36 these are 'recreations, courtship, and pleasures suitable', while between 49 and 65 man was largely bent on the pursuit of riches and power. The method followed is not of course strictly mathematical, being rather an attempt to apply the logic of geometry to human affairs by postulating axioms and propositions, and from them developing solutions. Foley even claimed to have discovered a way in which to measure time in terms of money, and in fact came close to enunciating what economists have since called the law of diminishing marginal utility. But his procedure was often arbitrary and confused and does not permit the making of any large claims for his anticipation of later economic thought.

Although the 'Computatio' aroused the fleeting interest of the Oxford Society,[128] it was not published in the usually catholic *Philosophical Transactions*. Mathematics never found a congenial home in the scientific societies, probably because it was then in the main a solitary pursuit, deriving little benefit from cooperative modes of procedure. By becoming more and more complex it excluded itself from the studies of the amateur, who was to find the organic and technological sciences more suited both to his tastes and abilities. The Dublin Society was, even in the contemporary context, an amateur group, and only its medical members were able to give professional attention to scientific affairs. The concentrated application required for the study of late seventeenth century mathematics was beyond the capabilities of even its most gifted members.

v. Physics

By the time of the Dublin Society's foundation it is no longer correct to speak of physics as a single coherent discipline. This most pervasive of subjects was already beginning to split into a variety of smaller more specialized sciences. Among the most important of these were the study of acoustics, dynamics, heat, optics, magnetism, mechanics, and statics. No natural philosopher of any competence was able entirely to avoid these topics. Newton, whose achievements reach out into the allied disciplines of astronomy and mathematics, made his greatest impact on the scientific world in the decade of the Dublin Society's foundation. Although much of his finest research, such as that on the compound nature of light, had been virtually completed during the immediate post-Restoration period, he had published little, so that the appearance in 1687 of the *Philosophiae Naturalis Principia Mathematica* came as something of a surprise to all but the best informed sections of scientific opinion. Newton's relative isolation at Cambridge, and his often strained relations with the Royal Society, had not helped in making his views widely known. Although the publication of the *Principia* coincided with the first collapse of the Dublin Society, some of its members were quick to realize the momentous implications of the book's theories.

In itself a difficult book, the *Principia*'s use of Latin was, already at this time, a further deterrent to potential readers. William Molyneux had originally intended to write his *Dioptrica Nova* in that language, but had decided that there were 'many ingenious heads, great geometers, and masters in mathematicks, who are not so well skill'd in Latin'.[129] The first news of the *Principia* arrived at Dublin in the Spring of 1687 when Molyneux received a section of the book from Edmond Halley, who, having financed the venture, thought 'it to be the utmost effort of the human capacity'.[130] A year later Molyneux had 'not yet had time to settle to it seriously', because, as he remarked, 'I find I must rub up all the little notions I have of conicks and the doctrine of ratio, which are half slipt out of my head, before I venture upon it.'[131] Despite his considerable expertise, Molyneux found it difficult to understand some parts of the book. In a letter to Flamsteed he remarked, 'I question after all, whether I shall be able to master it, for I perceive it is a piece that requires great application, or else it is invincible. Neither do I know any mathematical head in this place that has thoroughly considered the whole.'[132] Sir William Petty lived just long enough to read the *Principia*, and at once concluded it a great work. He also realized that some would not share his opinion. 'Poor Mr Newton,' he wrote, 'I have not met with one person that put an extraordinary value on his book. . . . I would give £500 to have been the author of it; and £200 that Charles [his son] understood it.'[133] From one so notoriously careful in financial matters, this was praise indeed.

In 1697 when a second edition was mooted, Molyneux hoped for some 'elucidations upon those sublime thoughts therein contained', and while he despaired of Newton himself undertaking such a task, felt that 'perhaps some other mathematician' might do so.[134] Molyneux did not have long to wait. John Keill's *Introductio ad Veram Physicam* appeared at Oxford in 1702 and Humphrey Ditton's *General Treatise on the Laws of Nature and Motion . . . Being Part of the great Mr Newton's Principles* at London in 1705. Within a relatively short time Newton's influence began to concentrate English scientific interest on the physical disciplines. But the Dublin Society's first and most fruitful period of work was already over before this trend had fully permeated British natural philosophy, and despite the example of earlier work by men like Galileo, Descartes, and Hooke, it devoted relatively little of its time to the study of physics. The arguments concerning Descartes's mechanistic view of the universe were never paralleled in Ireland, even though Molyneux had, as a young man, translated the French philosopher's *Meditations* into English. Nor did any of Newton's early published work excite much comment in Ireland, although in 1682 Molyneux had thought highly of the researches into the nature of colours, and particularly the prismatic experiments.[135] From the evidence available it would seem that William Molyneux was the only Irish natural philosopher of the time to be fully aware of the latest English and continental developments in general physics and astronomy.

One aspect of physics did however capture the attention of the Dublin Society. This was the study of magnetism, which had been widespread in England ever since the publication in 1600 of William Gilbert's *De Magnete*. It was regarded as a 'useful' science largely because of its relevance to the development of a modern system of navigation. The Royal Society had at one time even thought it important enough to warrant the appointment of a curator of magnetics.[136] Unfortunately no detailed records survive of the Dublin Society's magnetical research, although at least six experiments involving loadstones were undertaken in the period February to July 1684. The Oxford Society has left lengthy descriptions of its work in this field, which was probably very similar to that performed at Dublin. For example, in November 1683 the Oxford group experimented with calcined iron ore, which, being applied to a magnet, was found 'to draw the needle'.[137] It was all rather elementary, and rarely progressed much beyond holding a loadstone under a sheet of paper on which a pin had been placed, and then noting the strength of the attraction.[138]

The earliest article by a member of the Dublin Society to be printed in the *Philosophical Transactions* was entitled 'An Introductory Essay to the Doctrine of Sounds, Containing some Proposals for the Improvement of Acousticks', and was written by Narcissus Marsh.[139] While Galileo and Mersenne had done important work in the field, acoustics was not a particularly widely studied science in the seventeenth century. But although the Oxford Society thought Marsh's article of 'great consequence',[140] it contains few original conclusions, being remarkable chiefly because of its author's coining of three terms which have since become well established in scientific nomenclature. He used the word diacoustics to describe the study of refracted sound, catacoustics for that of reflected sound, and most important of all, was the first scientist to write of a microphone. The paper itself is mainly concerned with drawing parallels between acoustics and optics, and applying, with varying success, the methods of the latter to the elucidation of the former. This use of scientific analogy was common at the time, and Robert Hooke reversed Marsh's procedure when he drew on acoustics for his optical studies.

The somewhat conventional conclusion reached by Marsh at the end of his long article was that if the 'rude and unartificial' stentoro-phonecon could be improved 'according to the rules of art', a significant and useful development would have taken place in the field of otacoustics or aid to hearing. The projection of sound was however of obvious interest to the society, for it is recorded in the minutes for 7 July 1684 that 'Mr Ashe having in his possession one of Sir Samuel Morland's speaking trumpets, it was moved by Sir Wm. Petty that a striking watch may be put into it, and tryed how much further than ordinary it would transmit its sound'.[141] In fiction at least Marsh's wishes had already been more than met. Thomas Shadwell, in his play of 1676, *The Virtuoso*, reported Sir Nicholas Gimcrack as having developed a 'stentrophonical tube', which could transmit sound 'eight miles about', and as being in a position to improve it even further, 'for there's no stop in art'.[142]

Another member of the society seriously concerned with the study of acoustics was Francis Robartes, who approached the subject through a description of the trumpet and of another musical instrument called the trumpet-marine.[143] The latter seems to have been a monochord, whose notes were excited by bowing and selected by touching the strings at points dividing them into aliquot parts. Robartes exhibited the observed notes of the trumpet, sixteen in number, on a musical stave, and asked why the 7th, 11th, 13th, and 14th notes, being out of tune, should require flattening. He demonstrated the reason by referring to the stringed instrument and calculating the lengths of the vibrating sections of the string required to give the 'trumpet notes' he was considering. In this way he showed why the intervals, today called the harmonic seventh, eleventh, thirteenth, and fourteenth, were 'out of tune, and the rest exactly in tune'. This paper, which is of some importance in the development of musical theory, was an extension and elaboration of an earlier article by John Wallis on the trembling of consonant strings, 'A New Musical Discovery'.[144] Contemporary musical theory was often studied as a branch of mathematics, and Robartes's piece shows the usefulness of such an approach. Later Swift was to satirize these musico-mathematical notions in *Gulliver's Travels* when he described the Laputans cutting their food into hautboys and fiddles and discussing feminine beauty 'by words of art drawn from music'.[145]

Physics in all its forms played a relatively minor rôle in the Dublin Society's first period of experimentation. Only 7% of the papers read at meetings dealt with the subject, as compared with over 13% of the articles printed in the *Philosophical Transactions* between 1684 and 1687. In this case however the proportion of articles in the *Transactions* is not an accurate reflection of the activities of the Royal Society itself.[146]

Apart from what has already been discussed, there remain

only a few isolated incidents to show that the study of physics
(excluding magnetism) was not entirely neglected at Dublin.
John Stanley's confused paper on the motion of water has been
mentioned earlier. Its eclectic borrowings from Boyle's corpuscularianism and Cartesian mechanical theory shows
evidence of some reading if little thought. Also, in February
1684 William King 'proposed some quarys relating to the
acceleration of descending weights and force of percussion
particularly a given weight A being in one scale and a weight
B being given, 'tis required to determine the height from whence
B falling shall raise A'.[147] King was also concerned with the
problems involved in raising water by hydraulic engines. In
June 1684 he described to the society thirteen different machines
which could be used for this purpose, including those developed
by Sir Kenelm Digby, Sir Samuel Morland, and John Wilkins.[148] King showed an excellent knowledge of the technical
difficulties involved. His purpose in presenting the paper,
which dealt with practice rather than theory, was to encourage
Irish farmers to drain their land and Irish local authorities to
improve the hygienic amenities of their towns. As a result of
this address Petty informed the society of 'an hydraulic engine
he had contrived to be moved by fire, and the unsuccessfulness
thereof'.[149] While some two years later the society returned to
the subject when it discussed Denis Papin's new engine for
raising water, of which it had been informed by the Oxford
Society.[150]

William Molyneux considered the study of optics one of his
major preoccupations. His *Dioptrica Nova* of 1692 was to become
a standard work. But already in December 1683 he had presented to the society a paper on double vision, in which he attacked
with great force, Gassendi's argument 'that we see but with one
eye at once one and the same point of an object, . . . whilst the
other is idle and does nothing'.[151] Against this Molyneux argued
that although we do see objects in two places, 'that is not taken
notice of by us'. Three years later he produced another piece
concerning a problem raised in the *Journal des Sçavants* of September 1685.[152] The French writer had asked why, seeing that
perspectives of one convex glass make objects appear upright,
which those of two convex glasses invert, and again those of
three rectify, those of four, which seemingly ought to invert, do

in fact make objects appear upright. Molyneux's reply was very simple. He argued that by dividing a telescope into four rather than two convex glasses, the problem had been made unnecessarily difficult.[153] In reality one convex glass in a telescope inverts; the second (that is, the first eye-glass) does nothing towards erection or reversing, but simply represents the image as it is in the distinct base of the object glass (that is, inverted); the third erects or restores what was before inverted; the fourth represents the image as it receives it from the distinct base of the third, namely erect. The *Dioptrica Nova* was therefore the culmination of earlier studies and observations. The book was written while its author was a political refugee at Chester during the Williamite Revolution. It 'mett with the best reception and has been allowed by all judges to put that subject in the clearest light'.[154] But without the pre-publication revisions of Edmond Halley, the *Dioptrica* would hardly have attained the high standard of accuracy it did. Halley also allowed Molyneux to print for the first time his famous theorem for finding the foci of optic glasses, which was included as an appendix. But the book's appearance ended the eleven-year friendship between Molyneux and Flamsteed, because the latter took offence over the printing of solutions he had put forward as answers to the 10th, 16th, and 18th propositions, after, rather than before, those postulated by the author himself. As a result, Flamsteed, once 'our English Copernicus', became, in Molyneux's eyes, 'a man of so much ill-nature and irreligion how ingenious and learned whatever'.[155] The Irishman had reason for his bad temper, for Flamsteed had made it his business to inform the learned world of Molyneux's supposed incompetence. Sir Littleton Powys, for example, in a letter to Samuel Pepys, mentioned how 'an ingenious friend of mine in discourse yesterday evening did happen to mention Mr Molyneux's *Dioptrica Nova* with great commendation; whereupon I said that in a letter formerly sent to me by Mr Flamsteed he had enumerated several gross errors in that book which are not meer errata of the press'.[156]

Despite the growing interest in scientific affairs during the late seventeenth century there were still a number of important books, especially those by continental authors, which were hard to obtain in England or out of print. Thomas Salusbury's translation of Galileo's *Dialogues concerning the Two Chief World*

Systems published in a volume entitled *Mathematical Collections and Translations* (London, 1661), had, twenty years after its appearance, become almost impossible to acquire, a situation which prompted Molyneux to translate the dialogues of the third and fourth days into English for the use of the society. His claim that 'I had not look'd into an Italian grammar, or other Italian author over three days before I undertook this work',[157] would, if true, indicate a remarkable achievement, for the translation is accurate enough. Molyneux also englished Evangelista Torricelli's important *De Motu Gravium Naturalitur Descendentium et Projectorum* (Florence, 1644).[158] With these translations he put at the disposal of the Dublin Society two of the most important works on the physical sciences published in the first half of the seventeenth century. The comparative lack of response on the part of the members is difficult to explain, although the Oxford Society presented a similar picture. Some reasons for this neglect may however be found by means of an examination of why the members indulged in scientific activities. In Chapter 4 some of the motives behind the members' interest in natural philosophy have been discussed. A close study of the minutes shows that spectacular, if occasionally trivial, experiments were the most popular and the most often repeated. At the time chemistry and medicine could provide these more readily than physics or mathematics, although some disciplines such as optics, and more particularly microscopy, were exceptions to this rule. The microscope was at the time thought perhaps the greatest wonder of all and was therefore the most usual point of departure for the satirists of the New Learning. On the other hand, dropping lead weights or rolling metal balls down narrow planks had little direct appeal to the virtuosi, when compared with obviously impressive and gaudy chemical experiments or human and animal dissections.

The most notable and damaging defect from which the Dublin Society suffered was of course the lack of any really first-rate mathematician among the membership. Ashe, Molyneux, and Tollet were all competent, but in an age when the 'book of nature – or at least of physics – was written in mathematical characters',[159] competence alone was not enough. Thus while the less serious element in the society neglected physics on account of its superficially drab and unspectacular nature, the more earnest members were debarred from such study by their lack of advanced mathematical ability.

vi. Meteorology

It was Robert Hooke, 'our first meteorologist',[160] who, in the latter half of the seventeenth century, developed the study of weather into a separate and distinct science in its own right. Consequently when it caught the attention of some of the members of the Dublin Society, meteorology was still a comparative newcomer to the field of rationalized natural philosophy. Most of the work in this science took place in the years 1685 and 1686 when Ashe kept a regular diary of the weather at Dublin. But prior to this William Molyneux had already been active in the improvement of instruments for measuring meteorological phenomena. Hooke had listed three instruments he considered essential 'for making a history of the weather', namely a wind-gauge, a thermometer, and a hygroscope.[161] Molyneux was particularly interested in the hygroscope, which is used to indicate the moisture of the air. While Hooke's version had been based simply on the reactions to variations in humidity of a wild oat beard, Molyneux preferred to use a special type of cord sensitive to changes in air moisture. He developed his improved instrument early in 1685 and sent a detailed description, accompanied by an illustrative plate, to the Royal Society. The article was printed in the *Philosophical Transactions* and the invention labelled the 'Dublin Hygroscope'.[162] It was constructed by suspending from a whipcord a metal ball having a horizontal point, which traversed a graduated scale as the cord wound and unwound with variations in humidity. This model was in turn improved by Marsh's substitution of a lute-string for the somewhat fragile whipcord.[163]

The earliest letters sent by Francis Aston, the Royal Society's secretary, to the Dublin group, contained a considerable amount of meteorological information, including several descriptions of Martin Lister's observations on the behaviour of mercury in glass tubes during storms and similar disturbances.[164] The problems involved in obtaining a true and accurate measurement of wind force were also widely acknowledged, and as a contribution to their eventual solution Richard

K

Bulkeley invented yet another 'improved' anemometer.[165] Its success or otherwise is not recorded.

In May 1684 Molyneux began to keep a diary of the weather at Dublin 'according to Dr Lister's ingenious and compendious method'.[166] Robert Plot of the Oxford Society embarked on a similar venture about the same time.[167] But as early as March a long discussion had taken place at a meeting of the Dublin Society

concerning the keeping a diary of the weather, which was looked upon by Sir William Petty as very difficult to perform, so as to make it useful and instructive without a great apparatus of barometers, thermometers, hygroscopes, instruments for telling the point of the wind, the quantity of rain that falls, the times of the sun's shining and being overcast. As to the common thermometers of spirits and hygroscopes of oat beards, wooden planks, etc., hitherto invented, it was objected, that they lose their quality by keeping; and that they are not constant standards; and if we have new ones every year, we can make no estimate of the weather by them, in relation to what was observed by others last year.[168]

In 1685 Ashe replaced Molyneux as the society's meteorological observer, presumably having overcome most of these initial difficulties. Some years previously the Royal Society had designed a standard printed form on which to enter monthly weather information. The Dublin Society had duplicates printed in Ireland, and these were used by Ashe. Unfortunately only that for May 1684 has survived.[169] On it is recorded the barometer reading, the position and strength of the wind, and the 'state of the weather' for each day of the month. To give an example, the description for 12 May reads: 'Mercury, 29.7; Wind, S.W. Breeze all day; State of the Weather, Morning clear sunshine, about 10 overcast, and so continued all day. Slight rain in the night.'

Merely noting the nature of weather conditions over a short period did not in itself yield any immediately useful or important results. This the Dublin Society realized and therefore began to use its statistics in the study of comparative meteorology. Recordings for various years were compared, an activity which, not surprisingly, resulted in 'some remarkable differences'.[170] Molyneux also noted the variations observed 'on comparing the hystory of the weather at Oxford and

Dublin'.[171] In meteorology, as in other sciences, the Dublin
Society tried hard to maintain an attitude of informed scepticism, as when Ashe demonstrated how 'what Dr Garden affirms,
that when the wind turns to the north, N.E., or N.W., the
mercury also rises, was not . . . true'.[172]

While the Oxford Society was making early, if unsuccessful,
attempts at weather forecasting,[173] the Dublin group confined
its attentions to a study of causes. Of obvious interest was the
deplorable Irish climate. In October 1686, Ashe, after presenting his monthly diary, 'descended to the weather we have
here at Dublin, and endeavoured to assign those causes, which
seem to render the situation unwholesome'. After stressing the
importance of air to all forms of life and claiming that it was
'the allowed vehicle of health and sickness', he gave a short
account of research to date.[174] Much of this he thought useless,
because, in contradiction to the central tenets of natural
philosophy, it was based on 'gay empty speculations or spruce
hypotheses', rather than on 'experiment and demonstration'.
None the less, in Ashe's view the invention of the thermometer,
a discovery somewhat dubiously attributed to the Rosicrucian
philosopher Robert Fludd, was obviously of prime importance,
although he recognized its contemporary defects, in particular
its making 'the liquor play at such distances, and the divisions
so many, that the least variety of heat or cold' could not
accurately be measured. He then went on to describe the
modern hygroscopes (including of course Molyneux's) and
baroscopes, and to discuss their advantages and the possibility
of their improvement. Finally Ashe discussed the necessity of
collecting meteorological data over long periods, so that general
theories could be established as to trends and forecasting. He
compared figures from Oxford with those he himself had produced at Dublin, and concluded that the weather in the latter
place was less wholesome, largely because of Dublin's being
situated so near the Wicklow Mountains, which attracted
clouds, and consequently rain, and kept 'the air and smoak
pent up stagnant over us, preventing the motion and agitation,
which is necessary to preserve it pure and defaecated'. In
addition he argued that the proximity of the sea produced too
great an element of 'saline steams' in the air, which were both
injurious to health and to the preservation of metals. Ashe was

not of course able to suggest remedies for this condition, although he did make the practical suggestion that, as Dublin experiences predominantly westerly winds, all noisome manufactures should be situated on the east coast. In general however the paper indicates that the Dublin Society was at this time more concerned with the preliminary task of collecting information than with drawing any immediately useful implications, say for agriculture or navigation, from the vague corpus of material at hand. In meteorology, therefore, as in other sciences, it was felt that only experiment and a prolonged collection of data would enable the natural philosopher to produce really useful conclusions or frame really valid general theories.

In the years 1685 and 1686 Ashe compiled not less than eight monthly weather diaries and also contributed three general papers on meteorology to the transactions of the society. This constituted nearly two-fifths of his scientific writings in the period 1683–7. When it is further noted that of the meteorological matter submitted almost three-quarters was Ashe's work, the beginnings of a primitive scientific specialization can be recognized. Among the other members only Bulkeley, Molyneux, and Petty took an active interest in the study of meteorology. This trend towards what might be called a 'generalized' specialization was one of the most important aspects of the development of scientific organization at this time. While it was of course nothing new for natural philosophers to have personal interests, by the late seventeenth century an element of enforced specialization becomes apparent. As a result the majority of scientists could claim reasonable competence only within a restricted range of subjects, with the implied limits being imposed as it were from without, rather than emanating from the individual's own inclinations and predilections. The growing complexity of contemporary natural philosophy made it increasingly difficult to attain real command over any sizeable part of the scientific spectrum. Although men of outstanding brilliance like Boyle, Hooke, and Newton, were able to move with skill and dexterity among the various disciplines, these cannot be regarded as in any way typical of their age. Indeed this aspect of the history of science provides evidence of how errors of interpretation can arise if enquiry is limited to a few men of supreme genius. It is a paradox that the generality of seventeenth-century practitioners were, at least in their enforced reliance on a degree of specialization, more 'advanced' and 'modern' than their intellectually more gifted colleagues. Thus methodological change in scientific studies sometimes proceeds from the submerged majority of moderately competent and usually forgotten practitioners. It can be argued that their very mediocrity compelled them to abandon the universality of previous centuries earlier than their more able colleagues, and that this passive action is of little historical consequence. But historical movement is the result of a series of chain reactions, and the mere abandonment of previous methods, and here it is irrelevant whether this was voluntary or enforced, added another powerful catalyst to the forces working for scientific change and development, a development in which the occasional mighty eminence should not be allowed entirely to distract attention from the more humble, yet none the less significant lowlands and plains. This embryonic form of specialization was admittedly of the broadest sort, and the trend which was to produce a larger and larger number of smaller and smaller intellectual circles, was only beginning to emerge. Nor was science alone in this. About the same time the study of history was undergoing a similar process. The first English medievalist proper, William Dugdale, who began to publish in 1655, can be compared with the earlier William Camden, who would have regarded so rigid a division as unseemly and false. Professor Douglas has described a development parallel to that taking place in the world of science. He writes:

After the Restoration . . . it became clear that a stricter discipline was necessary. Much of the older universality of interest was to remain, but some limitations now began to impose themselves upon individual curiosity, though not on individual effort. History was becoming circumscribed as a separate study, and even within historical scholarship some distinctions were beginning to be made.[175]

As a group the Dublin Society did of course exhibit an interest in most aspects of scientific investigation. For example, when Halley wrote to Ashe in March 1686 thanking him on behalf of the Royal Society for information sent over from

Ireland, he included in his acknowledgements a veritable rag-bag of news: 'Your method of demonstrating the most knotty propositions in Euclid, your new invented dyall, your experiments of injections of liquors into animals, and the account of your mathematical girle.'[176] As individuals however the members of the society were participating in the general move towards a greater limitation of personal interest and competence.

vii. Geology

In common with meteorology, geology was only promoted to the status of a separate and distinct study during the latter half of the seventeenth century. The term itself was not actually used in its modern sense until 1657, when the Danish naturalist M. P. Escholt called his book on minerals the *Geologia Norvegica*. This was translated into English by Daniel Collins in 1663. The theological difficulties posed by the Copernican revolution in astronomy had by then been largely resolved, while in physics Newton's scheme, by its very brilliance and satisfying symmetry, was soon seemingly to preclude religious doubt. But in the field of geology the first faint murmurings were to be heard of ideas which, two hundred years later, were to provide a cradle for the Darwinian theory of natural selection. Of course the very concept of the Great Chain of Being, so widely propounded in the late seventeenth and the eighteenth centuries, contained pointers and hints towards an evolutionary explanation of life. Petty, for example, was a firm believer in a version of this theory, and postulated two distinct scales of being, the first ascending from man to God, the second descending from man to the lower animals. This division was not peculiar to him, although the exact position of various species on the scale was a matter of fierce dispute. Petty, after discussing the claims of various beasts and insects, including apes, elephants, parrots, and bees, to seniority in the scale, eventually decided that the elephant ranked highest and closest to man. But his arguments were based more on supposed intellectual qualities than on external physical appearance.[177]

The nature of fossils posed many problems which perplexed the seventeenth century natural philosophers, even though Leonardo da Vinci had already suggested a connection between them and the study of geological processes. Robert Hooke, in this matter a man of advanced views, proposed the obvious difficulty when he wrote, 'It seems, I say, contrary to that great wisdom of nature, that these prettily shap'd bodies should have all those curious figures and contrivances (which many of them are adorn'd and contriv'd with) . . . for no higher end then onely to exhibit such a form.'[178] He thought it quite possible for the earth to have undergone great changes over a long period of time, through the action of water, earthquakes, and slow crustal movements. More daringly still he suggested that several species of animal had become extinct, as a result of 'alterations of the climate, soil, and nourishment', thus running counter to most Chain of Being theories.[179] Certainly Thomas Molyneux at Dublin was at one time firmly convinced that the concern which 'providence' must and did show for 'all animal productions', precluded the possibility of species becoming extinct.[180] But even Hooke was not of course an evolutionist, and while his views were in advance of orthodox contemporary belief, it would be wrong to exaggerate the modernity of his general outlook.

The Dublin Society, although none of its members ever really committed themselves as to the nature and origin of fossils, followed contemporary controversies in some detail. It also evinced an interest in the mineralogical problems posed by the petrifying qualities of Lough Neagh in Ulster. Consequently while William Molyneux and Edward Smyth examined petrified wood from the lough, Samuel Foley read a paper in June 1684, in which he epitomized the various views regarding the origin of fossil remains.[181] Although the minutes claim that Foley advanced 'some observations and thoughts of his own', the paper consists mainly of an impartial summary of existing theories. After deciding that 'the main question is what these stones are', Foley proceeded to discuss the opinion of, among others, Nicholas Steno, John Ray, and Robert Hooke, which was 'that these stones were originally the shells and bones of liveing fishes and other animals bred in the sea'. This was however denied by Martin Lister, who, in an article in the *Philosophical Transactions*, had, following the arguments of the German Jesuit Athanasius Kircher, decided that a 'plastick vertue' within the earth had produced stones in the shape of marine creatures.[182] Lister was well known in Ireland, having corresponded with Bulkeley and Sir Robert Redding, another member of the Dublin Society, who, in September 1684, had sent him a box of rare stones and ores found in Ireland.[183] Foley, by implication opposed to Lister, paraphrased the latter's answer to Hooke's question about the 'wisdom of nature' as follows: ' 'Tis not so inconsistent with the wisdom and goodness of the supreme nature to beautify the world with these varieties which have so much use for ought we know as tulips and some other curious flowers.' This argument contrasting man's lack of knowledge with the almighty's omniscience, was, and continued to be, a favourite device of the theologically conservative apologist. But the attitude that sees direct intervention in all as yet unfathomed natural phenomena is sadly prone to collapse with every new discovery. None the less Lister's views had more staying power than their force merited, and continued, until well into the nineteenth century, to provide a last refuge for men reluctant to accept change, although over the years these were to become increasingly the products of what might best be called the scientific underworld.

Interest in palaeontology was often coupled with antiquarianism, and occasional notes in the minutes of the Dublin Society show that its members collected formed stones more often out of fascination for their curious shapes than for strictly scientific reasons. In May 1685, for instance, Ashe presented to the society a 'formed stone most exactly resembling a cock', having already 'produced a pretty figurate stone, found in the chapel yard of the college'.[184] But while the fossil controversy did not always engender equal passion and heat, some naturalists like John Ray suffered great anguish because of the seemingly conclusive evidence pointing towards the animal origin of fossil remains. He knew, and the pathos of his position as priest-scientist is obvious, that acceptance of this evidence would involve 'such a train of consequences, as seem to shock the Scripture-History of the novity of the world; at least they overthrow the opinion generally received, and not without good reason, among divines and philosophers, that since the first creation there have been no species of animals or vegetables lost, no new ones produced'.[185] Thomas Molyneux, on the other hand, although an antiquary and geologist of some ability, was bored by this particular dispute. In 1698 he expressed the hope that Edward Lhuyd's forthcoming *Lithophylacii Britannici Ichnographia* (London, 1699) would finally 'determine the pusling controversy about figured stones'.[186] Lhuyd, who was in touch with members of the Dublin Society in the 1690s, and who toured Ireland extensively for both geological and philological purposes, was however to disappoint Molyneux's hopes. His book was certainly a remarkable achievement, containing as it does descriptions of some 1600 British fossils, but its argument that fossils were produced by the germination of small organisms spread by the air and by water was more ingenious than accurate.

The Philosophical Society at Oxford also concerned itself with palaeontology, Plot and Lhuyd in particular presenting numerous reports of their work in the field. Both maintained erroneous theories, as did one of the society's rural correspondents, a Dr Hatly of Maidstone, who tried to convince the membership that 'these petrifactions are *lapides sui generis* and not made in animal molds'.[187]

Another subject which provided an endless source of speculation at Dublin was the nature and origin of the Giant's Causeway in County Antrim. But as this belongs more properly to the society's activities in the 1690s, and therefore to Chapter Seven of this work, only a short account will be given here. Lhuyd considered the causeway 'one of the noblest curiosities this age hath discoverd in the mineral kingdom',[188] and it certainly gave the Irish scientists something unusual, if not unique, about which to inform their English colleagues. Thomas Molyneux, who thought Ireland on the whole lacking in 'natural rarities', considered it 'very extraordinary', and unlike some of his fellows, firmly believed it to be of natural origin.[189] In 1694 two short descriptions of the causeway, one by Sir Richard Bulkeley and the other by Samuel Foley, appeared in the *Philosophical Transactions*.[190] Bulkeley's account, in the form of a letter to his friend Martin Lister, was based almost entirely on hearsay, and scarcely measured up to Baconian standards of personal observation. Foley's piece, which the Royal Society thought 'very accurately handled',[191] was more scientific, and mentioned most of the causeway's important features with reasonable precision. So enthusiastic did the Royal Society become about the subject that in 1697 William Molyneux despatched an octagonal pillar taken from the causeway to Gresham College, where it was included in the society's museum.[192] This gift was made in return for the London group's offer to 'bestow on the Dublin Society such duplicates or rarities as can be spared out of the repository'.[193] The pillar, or 'joynt' as it was called, was followed three months later by a detailed description of the causeway by Thomas Molyneux. This was also printed in the *Transactions* and included a large and accurate sketch headed, 'A true prospect of the Giant's Causeway near Pengore Head, . . . taken from the north west by Edwin Sandys in 1696 at the expense of the Dublin Society.'[194] Molyneux's exhaustive treatment closed the matter for the next ten years.

It follows, that while the Dublin Society maintained a desultory interest in the general field of geology, in comparison with other disciplines it constituted but a small part of the society's proceedings. Although occasionally a formed stone was produced at meetings and a general discussion undertaken, only one of the 159 papers presented during the period 1683 to 1687 dealt with the subject. London however was only marginally more active, and only 3·9% of the articles printed in the *Philosophical Transactions* between 1684 and 1687 were concerned with geology or allied sciences.[195]

viii. *Zoology and Botany*

The most important of the remaining sciences studied by the Dublin Society were zoology and botany. In common with many other disciplines at the time, zoology possessed few really well-defined limits. This makes it difficult to isolate the strictly zoological part of the society's transactions. Several papers and discussions closely concerned with non-human animal structure and life have already been described, but while comparative anatomy may have important zoological implications, the end in view is usually medical. Allen Mullen, for example, conducted a series of experiments connected with the structure of the ear. In these he compared the human organ with those of several animals in the hope of discovering more about the former through a study of the latter. The aims behind Molyneux's oft-repeated observations on the water-newt were medical and were intended to demonstrate the circulation of the blood. On the other hand Marsh's knowledge of insects, and particularly of caterpillars, was zoologically up to the mark. He was acquainted with the researches of Johann Goedart, of whose major work Martin Lister had published an English translation in 1682.[196] Marsh tried to discover some reliable and logical method of insect classification – one of the perennial problems of contemporary zoology – and his proposals were not without merit, for they incorporated the suggestion of classification by follicles and aurelias.

Although Richard Acton read an account of the scoter duck to the society in July 1685,[197] this is now lost, and only one paper dealing with animals in a scientific manner remains extant. This, the work of Thomas Molyneux, was presented to the society on 24 March 1684 and describes the anatomy of a bat dissected by him in September 1682.[198] It is written in Latin and was probably prepared as part of Molyneux's study for the degree of M.B., which he was awarded in 1683. The contents are uncontroversial, but considering that the piece was the work of a twenty-one-year-old student, its careful and accurate treatment is remarkable. Molyneux found himself in agreement with the great ornithologist Francis Willughby, who, in opposition to the traditionalist classification of Ulisse Aldrovandi, had declined to include the bat under the general heading of 'birds'. The paper itself had probably been inspired by the publication at Amsterdam in 1681 of Gerard Blasius's *Anatome Animalium Terrestrium Variorum*, which included (p. 165) a discussion of the bat with which Molyneux could find no fault. But his account failed to create more than a passing interest in zoology at Dublin. And this reflected the situation at the Royal Society, where that subject, despite the work of Willughby and Ray, was largely neglected.[199]

The state of botanical studies at Dublin was, quantitatively speaking, at almost as low an ebb as that of zoology. Only two contributions are of more than passing interest. The first of these, on the anatomy of the common garden bean, achieved a high standard of observation and description. Presented by Samuel Foley in 1684, it is one of the outstanding papers read to the society during the first months of its existence.[200] Careful use of the microscope enabled Foley to augment Nehemiah

Grew's work on the same vegetable.[201] In particular Foley noticed the peculiar superficies on the bean's outer coat, which led him to conclude that these were designed, not only to protect the seed, but also to allow the percolation of necessary nourishment. He confirmed Grew's opinion as to the permeability of the small aperture at the thick end of the vegetable, and provided a much more detailed account than had Grew of the bean's various coats and layers. Foley ended his paper with a description of the interior parts of the bean, namely (using Grew's terminology), the cuticula, the radicle, the plume, the seminal root, and the parenchyma.

In comparison with Foley's excellent contribution, Edward Smyth's views on the germination of poppies, presented to the society in May 1686, are not especially impressive.[202] Admittedly, the study of plant reproduction was still in its infancy, and it was not until Rudolph Camerarius published his *De Sexu Plantarum Epistola* in 1694 that the sexuality of plants began to be understood. Smyth had observed a field in Donegal, in which, after the ground had been turned over, a large number of poppies had sprung up, having never grown within ten miles of the place before. To explain this seemingly baffling phenomenon he propounded the theory that 'the minute parts of the earth, or perhaps any other impregnated matter disposed into the shape of the seed of a vegetable, and endow'd with the same qualities, . . . may by the heat of the sun be animated into a vegetable'. The possibility of spontaneous generation in the animal world had, of course, already been disproved by Francesco Redi's experiments of 1668, and twenty years later informed opinion had largely accepted his views. Certainly Smyth's ideas ran directly counter to the opinions of those who felt that without the quashing of the spontaneous generation myth science could never finally detach itself from magic and necromancy.

PART II TECHNOLOGY

ix. Navigation and Shipping

The seventeenth-century stress on utility is nowhere better demonstrated than in the contemporary concern for the problem of marine transport. This was one of the most important areas of practical research in England and included not only the study of building techniques, but also the study of navigation and other skills connected with the sailing of ships. Petty, who believed in the necessity of a strong navy, had set the Royal Society along the path of maritime enquiry, and later when in Ireland continued to urge craftsmen and scientists to combine in the building of swifter and more efficient vessels. In May 1684 he proposed the construction of his fourth and last double-bottom at a yard in Ring's End, Dublin.

The society as a body was not directly concerned with Petty's plan, but some of its members were financially involved in the scheme. The minutes for 13 October 1684 record that 'We had no meeting of the society, but there was a meeting about the building of the sluice vessel'.[203] Already in April Petty had gathered together a group of fourteen subscribers who were each to contribute £20 towards construction costs, which were estimated at about £400 in all.[204] The subscribers, of whom eight were members of the society,[205] provided the money because they were convinced that double-bottomed shipping would 'be for the general good and benefit of mankind'. Petty, in order to demonstrate the sound design of the proposed vessel, employed the modern technique of first experimenting with scale models in a test tank, and these were considered 'very extraordinary beyond the common built'.[206] According to Molyneux he had a 'vast apparatus' of these Lilliputian models,[207] and even before the foundation of the society had demonstrated a toy navy: 'He has a fleet of ships in little modells of about one and a half and two foot long, of all kinds, more than the King of France, and with these in a great broad trough of water he performs wonders.'[208]

At first two vessels were to be constructed, one of fifteen the other of a hundred tons. But as usual lack of money proved an insurmountable obstacle to such grandiose plans, and from the beginning there were protracted disputes about cost and workmanship which ended only when some of the original partners disassociated themselves from the enterprise. At last, after a second round of subscriptions in September, a ship named the *St Michael the Archangel* was launched. Petty, although one of the ablest experimenters of his time, had little luck and less success in his maritime undertakings. His three attempts in the early 1660s had all been at least partial failures while that of 1684 was a total loss. Molyneux informed the Royal Society, which had asked for news, that 'even before the wind shee does nothing, soe that the whole designe is blown up'.[209] This fourth fiasco finally persuaded Petty to stop wasting his money, although he was to spend his remaining years in theorizing and 'diging for truth in this matter'.[210] Earlier in the same year Samuel Folcy had read a paper on 'the sailing of ships with oblique winds'.[211] In it he attempted to demonstrate 'from the most ordinary and common principles of mechanics', how a ship should sail with a side wind. With the help of diagrams he calculated a mathematically correct course taking water resistance into consideration.

The measurement and recording of the movement of tides was of obvious concern to seamen. Molyneux became interested in the problems involved on receiving a request from Flamsteed for information about the tides at Dublin. As he knew comparatively little about the subject he consulted 'a gentleman belonging to our Custom House', whose answers to Flamsteed's queries did not however prove satisfactory.[212] Eventually in 1686, to still the Englishman's incessant demands, Molyneux published a short paper in the *Philosophical Transactions* giving the times of high water at various places in Dublin and comparative figures for a number of English ports.[213] In London several fellows of the Royal Society, including Sir John Hoskins, John Aubrey, and Richard Waller, were also interested in tides.[214] Molyneux, however, unlike for example the genteel Evelyn, had no reservations about approaching craftsmen and labourers when he wanted expert information. In 1687 he had several long conversations with 'an old experimented seaman, who ply'd on the coast between Chester and Dublin these forty years', and who happened to be 'an excellent and profound mathematician'.[215] A few years later he even gave the sailor, whose name was Glover, a copy of his *Dioptrica Nova*.[216]

In the course of a tour of the continent in 1685 Molyneux had also studied the state of inland navigation, and on his return to Ireland reported to the society on the manner of crossing the Rhine at Cologne and Utrecht.[217] At the former place he had been particularly interested to observe a double-bottomed boat, 'on which stand men, horses, or other carriages transported.

The platform will hold some troops of horse. This kind of double vessel has been used here some hundreds of years (as I am told) and therefore the fancy is not so new, as some would have thought it.'

In the early years of the seventeenth century a close and fruitful association had been maintained between many of the best English scientists and sea-captains and other naval personnel. This connection weakened after the Restoration, although men like Boyle and Flamsteed frequently consulted with London craftsmen and Robert Hooke relied heavily on the help and advice of Tompion the clockmaker. But it was the societies which continued to hanker for a natural philosophy of utility, while the leaders of scientific movement in Britain were in general adopting an increasingly abstract science, which, while not strictly opposed to arguments of use, regarded these as simply irrelevant to philosophical advance.

The difficulties involved in obtaining an accurate measurement of longitude at sea constituted one of the most pressing problems facing utilitarian science in the seventeenth century. The chief obstacle to a solution was the lack of a really exact timepiece and none was invented until the middle of the next century. The discovery of Jupiter's satellites enabled the astronomer to observe their eclipses and thence calculate longitude with reasonable accuracy. But even when using the new reflecting telescope, which was much smaller than the earlier refracting instrument, this method was useless on board ship, because the piece's polished speculum became tarnished when exposed to sea air and salt water.[218]

From its inception the Royal Society had concerned itself with this problem, and at Dublin, too, various suggestions were made in an attempt to find a solution. In May 1685 Jonathan Aland, a prominent citizen of Waterford, appeared at a meeting and read a paper in which he claimed to have discovered an accurate method of calculating longitude at sea.[219] This involved measuring the distance from the moon to the sun, its latitude from the ecliptic, and its distance from certain of the other planets. Once this medley of information had been gathered together, a complicated and pointless calculation followed. The result was nonsense. Even the usually charitable Molyneux was moved to call Aland's scheme that of 'a man perfectly ignorant of mathematics and astronomy'.[220] Aland was not however to be discouraged, and his friend the astrologer John Whalley announced in an almanac for 1686 his 'absolute familiar easy discovery of the true (though long sought for) longitude or meridian distance of places', which, it was claimed, had been 'approved by the honourable Society and University of Dublin'.[221] To clear the air and to encourage serious experimenters, George Tollet reviewed for the society the progress hitherto made in the matter.[222] But nobody responded to the challenge.

In the same year as Aland's unfortunate appearance the society acted as arbitrator between two disputing parties, who differed as to the nature of the lines of longitude and latitude. The men involved, Dr Samuel Haworth and John Ker, chose as their respective champions before the society William Hearne and George Tollet. The latter argued that the lines of longitude run north and south, while Hearne, for reasons which became more complex the longer he discussed them, maintained that they run east and west. Hearne was the son of John Hearne a London instrument maker, who, in a broadsheet entitled *Longitude Unvailed and Laid Open to the View of All Men* (London, 1678), had announced, 'I have a way of making a globe, that shall endure the weather, if it be set in a garden, which I taught my sons to make, and my eldest son hath made several in Dublin, of 16, 18, and 22 inches diameter, with all the great and necessary circles put thereon, by which, with the help of a wire of about a foot and a half long, [the longitude] may be known.'[223] The elder Hearne's views were orthodox; those of his son bizarre. Not unnaturally the Dublin Society favoured Tollet's judgement of the matter.[224] Hearne, not satisfied with the decision, published a pamphlet addressed to 'the Royal Societies of London and Paris, and to the professors of the mathematicks in the City of London', in which he set forth his opinions.[225] Arguing almost exclusively from ancient authorities, he complained of the treatment he had received in Dublin and asked the world's vindication. Now it would seem reasonable to suppose that the world greeted the request with discriminating silence. But in fact the Royal and Oxford Societies debated the matter with generous deliberation. Although both condemned Hearne,[226] the fact that three scientific groups should have concerned themselves at such length with so puerile a dispute shows how quick and easy was the journey from the sublime to the ridiculous and how ready were the societies to embark on it.

x. Land Transport

The members of the Dublin Society coupled an interest in navigation and sea transport with a study of land communications. The rise of the turnpike system and new and extensive road building in England provided scientists with stimulating incentives to turn their attentions to the improvement of internal transport. Once again Petty, the great exponent of 'the advancement of all mechanical arts and manufactures',[227] initiated this particular line of enquiry. He put forward the view that 'carriage by carts and wagons is cheaper than on horses' backs, and this cheaper than by men'.[228] It followed therefore that considerable economic benefits would derive from the production of a really well-designed cart. Petty's interest in land carriage had been aroused by a letter from a Mr Clignet, a Dutchman living at Limerick, who was trying to develop an early independent four-wheel suspension system for horse-drawn vehicles.[229] Clignet claimed that his invention would cost no more than an ordinary coach, but would not reveal his design until a patent had been obtained.[230] He maintained that his carriage could withstand a $3\frac{1}{2}$ foot difference in alignment between the wheels on either side, and that, in case of danger, the horse might easily be disengaged by the operation of a single lever. Petty, Molyneux, and Bulkeley were all 'so well satisfied by the usefullness of the invention', that they each ordered and paid for a carriage at 'six or eight pounds a piece'.[231]

On hearing of Clignet's work Petty drew up a list of questions and observations on transport, and, as in his trials with the double-bottom, 'produced an engine for trying the experiments relating to land carriages'.[232] This was a solid parallelepiped about 5 inches thick, which could be mounted on various types of miniature wheel and then used as a scale model for testing and improving the design of larger coaches. In July 1684, after many experiments, including studies of the effects of friction, of the size of wheels in relation to the whole, and of motion on various surfaces, a full-sized carriage was built at a cost of ten pounds.[233] The claims made by Petty for this inven-

L

tion were large. Indeed, not only would it not overturn, but it could carry two persons, with thirty pounds of baggage, over thirty Irish miles in a day. The coach, it was suggested, could be adapted to city use, in which case it could be drawn by 'one man with one in it, and that with less pains than one of the sedan bearers does undergo.'

The failure of the carriage ever to come into widespread use rather vitiates Petty's grandiose recommendations. But his efforts had aroused some interest in Oxford, where, in August 1684, Joshua Walker started a discussion concerning the causes of the dishing of cart wheels and later wrote an article on the advantages to be derived from the use of large wheels, which was sent to Dublin.[234] In London it was believed that if the Irish experiments could 'be brought to any certainty', the invention would undoubtedly prove 'very useful'.[235] During the following year, at a meeting of the Royal Society, Robert Hooke read a paper 'concerning the different ways of carriage' there are upon land and water.[236] But not content with this, he took up the remainder of the society's time by discussing an extremely long article by Simon Stevin on the 'sailing chariot', a vehicle similar to the modern land yacht, from which the practical advantages to be derived seem minimal.[237]

The extent of Petty's failure is evidenced in Richard Bulkeley's work on the construction of a similar type of coach only a year after the former's supposed masterpiece. Bulkeley was the epitome of the contemporary virtuoso, and in fact the production of new chariots became, during the late seventeenth century, something of a gentleman's sport.[238] Bulkeley sent his findings to London where they were published in the *Philosophical Transactions* for 1685.[239] And in the Royal Society's archives is a copy of a long letter he wrote to Ashe on the subject which opens with the rather testy remark that as 'philosophical registers do not disdain to record the number of stitches which go to the making of a doublet', an account of a new carriage might be of interest.[240] Not satisfied however with the advocacy of the written word, Bulkeley hurried to London, where, in October, he described his invention at a meeting of the Royal Society. John Evelyn, in unusually light-hearted mood, attended the gathering, and his account of Bulkeley's performance merits quotation.

Sir Ri: Bulkeley, described to us a model of a charriot he had invented, which it was not possible to overthrow, in whatsoever uneven way it was drawn: giving us a stupendious relation, of what it had perform'd in that kind; for ease, expedition, and safty: There was onely these inconveniencies yet to be remedied; . . . it was ready to fire every 10 miles, and being plac'd and playing on no fewer than 10 rollers, made so prodigious noise, as was intolerable: These particulars the virtuosi were desir'd to excogitate the remedies, to render the engine of extraordinary use.[241]

Bulkeley, who was inspired with an almost religious zeal for the propagation of his calash had, only a week before been at Oxford, where he had also spoken enthusiastically of the invention.[242] A year later he told Martin Lister that he had travelled from Kilkenny to his house outside Dublin in twelve hours, 'with the greatest ease, both to the horse and myself'.[243] But he admitted that the brass rollers wore away too quickly and that the invention had reached a crucial point in its development. The difficulties were to prove insurmountable, so that in 1706 Robert Molesworth was left to complain that 'I never in my life went in any gentleman's coach and four that I was not in continual agony for fear of my neck'.[244]

The study of land transport is unusual in that it was one of the few fields in which the first important stimulus came from Ireland. There had of course, been earlier attempts to develop improved carriages, but the activities of the Dublin Society were the first to generate this particular burst of interest among the three societies in finding a solution to the problems of transport on land.

xi. Military Technology

Military technology, besides having a certain mathematical fascination, was interesting to members of the Dublin Society because memories of the rebellion of 1641, by then elevated to the status of Protestant myth, were highly coloured and vivid. In addition many, including Petty and Molyneux, were convinced that ballistics was among the branches of mechanical science worthy of study,[245] and in fact most of the work undertaken at Dublin was of a predominantly theoretical nature. William Molyneux had, however, as early as 1682 built a mortar piece of his own design, so that he might test current theories regarding the flight of projectiles. Molyneux had probably inherited an interest in gunnery from his father, Samuel Molyneux Senior who, at the siege of New Ross in 1643 had distinguished himself as master of ordnance and who approached the subject in a robustly practical manner. In the introduction to his small work entitled *Practical Problems concerning the Doctrin of Projects* he had remarked, 'I have abstracted these [propositions] in this method and volum, merly for the help of the practick gunner in the feild, who I suppose skill'd in arithmetick and plain trigonometry.'[246] It is certainly significant that, for all the down-to-earth nature of his views, Samuel Molyneux should have taken the 'practick gunner's' knowledge of mathematics so for granted. His son had, however, also read Galileo and Torricelli on the subject, but had found their conclusions not entirely satisfactory. Despite this he translated some of Torricelli's writings on the 'motion of heavy bodys naturaly falling' into English and presented them to his father as a birthday gift.[247] Galileo, turning away from the old Oresmic impetus theory, had demonstrated the parabolic trajectory of a projectile. But notwithstanding the work of Mersenne in France, Robert Anderson in England, and most importantly of the Dutchman Christiaan Huygens, no contemporary scientist was ever able to calculate a trajectory correctly and this did not become possible until the development of the differential and integral calculuses.

Molyneux had, however, realized that air resistance must at all points be taken into consideration, and while it is true that Galileo had not disregarded its effect on a projectile, he had believed it to be constant throughout flight and had therefore neglected it after an initial adjustment. But air resistance, especially over long distances, is not always equal, and this led Molyneux to claim that 'a bullet does not fly in a true parabola, . . . but a parabola is the nearest sort of known curve to the one in which it flys'.[248] But even air resistance could hardly, he felt, retard a bomb by more than forty feet over a two-mile flight.[249] Casting techniques and gunpowder mixtures being what they were in the seventeenth century, Molyneux found it impossible to construct an accurate mortar and could 'hardly make shotts anything nigh each other'.[250]

As with the land and sea transport experiments, the Dublin

Society used models to observe and elucidate the laws of projectiles. In 1684 Molyneux 'explained a contrivance of his own for demonstrating to the eye the figure wherein projects do move'.[251] In its use of what today would be termed controlled laboratory trials, the Dublin Society seems to have been more experienced than either of the groups at London or Oxford.

Another member with military inclinations was George Tollet, who was especially interested in 'calculating the angles of elevation and suppression of a piece to shoot up or down hill or to and from a height'.[252] This was a particularly vexing problem and had puzzled gunners for a long time. It had been discussed at some length in a recent book by the French architect and mathematician François Blondel entitled *L'Art de Jetter les Bombes* (Paris, 1683). Tollet thought the work of small merit and considered Blondel's rules 'to be neither short, clear, or certain, nor his calculus accurate'.[253] He himself delivered a paper to the society in which he discussed the problem, 'The greatest random of a piece, the horizontal distance of an object, and the height or descent from the horizontal line being given, to find the two elevations or the elevation and depression of a piece to strike the given object.'[254] But perhaps the greatest difficulty encountered by contemporary artillery was caused by the unreliability of seventeenth-century gunpowder. To alleviate this Molyneux undertook a series of contolled experiments in a pistol barrel designed to show which mixture would give the best results.[255] Small arms as well as ordnance were studied by the society and Viscount Mountjoy often demonstrated the workings of the then still novel air-gun, which was approved of by all.[256]

It is unlikely that any of these experiments proved of practical use during the Williamite Revolution. But they show, once again, how completely the Dublin Society was in step with its English counterparts, for the Royal Society was also devoting its time to an examination of a new type of air-gun invented by Denis Papin.[257] Even from its earliest days the London group had been interested in the study of military technology and had examined problems such as the exact trajectory and velocity of a bullet in flight.[258] But despite these efforts, the Royal Society, like the Dublin and Oxford groups, was never able to develop a really effective weapon of war.

xii. *Textiles and Agriculture*

In general the Philosophical Society of 1683 to 1687 showed small interest in those subjects which, after 1731, were to be pursued with such enthusiasm by the Royal Dublin Society. Improvements in agriculture and industry were of marginal moment to the former, while the latter's very name of 'The Dublin Society, for improving Husbandry, Manufactures, and other Useful Arts' is redolent of a Protestant 'patriotism' which scarcely existed before 1700 and which was in part inspired by the publication in 1698 of William Molyneux's *Case of Ireland*. Only incidentally did the Philosophical Society touch on these matters, as when William King, after having given a report on the chemical properties of Clonus Water, mentioned 'that the sediment of these waters, with oak leaves yield a good black die to cloth'.[259] The production of a fast black dye was, and still is, one of the outstanding problems of the textile finishing industry, and realizing this the society 'ordered that some experiments should be tried to help our dying black'. But these instructions do not seem to have been carried out. Later in the same year Mountjoy proposed 'that the bleaching or whitening of linen cloth, as practised in this country, should be taken into consideration and enquired into, that a matter of that consequence to this nation, especially to the northern parts thereof, should be advanced as much as possible'.[260] But the Irish virtuosi had not yet been conditioned to thinking along these lines and the scheme came to nothing.

Husbandry, later the chief study of the Royal Dublin Society, was to a large extent neglected by the members of the earlier group. Apart from William King, only Sir Richard Bulkeley, a sort of seventeenth-century Turnip Townshend, evinced any real interest in Irish agricultural improvement. At a meeting in July 1686 he presented a paper on farm economics by Martin Lister, which, the minutes note, was 'an essay so new and ingenious, and which promises so usefully', that it 'was received with the joynt applause of the whole society, every man resolving to recommend it to the trial of his friends in the country'.[261] It is easy to discern here the beginnings of that eighteenth century outlook later typified by such men as Thomas Prior and Samuel Madden.

King concerned himself with the more specialized problem of land drainage which was of course of particular relevance to the Irish situation. His article on the subject was published in the *Philosophical Transactions*, and F. V. Emery thinks it 'a reasoned paper, based on . . . observation'.[262] It is certainly a good example of seventeenth century practical research at its best. After listing the disadvantages occasioned by the excessive amount of bogland in Ireland, King went on to describe the various types of bog, such as red bogs, quaking bogs, and turloughs, and mentioned their peculiar properties and characteristics. King's economic views, which were refreshingly intelligent, led him to suggest that 'an act of parliament should be made . . . that who did not in such a time, make some progress in draining their bogs, should part with them to others that would'. In addition the advice given on the technical problems of land reclamation were sensible and to the point. He described the different trenches to be dug, their length and size, and the times of year most suitable for such work. The paper, an excellent piece of controlled thinking on a particular problem, shows King to have been not only a politician and churchman of intelligence and perspicacity but an able, if infrequent, natural philosopher.

In 1693 two short essays by Bulkeley appeared in the *Philosophical Transactions*. One dealt with the growing of maize and the other with the 'propagation of elms by seed'.[263] In the former Bulkeley described tests made by him to discover the advantages of one type of maize over another. His account, with its precise observations and comparisons, discussed a careful series of agricultural experiments conducted in a scientific manner. John Ray, the great English naturalist, thought it 'a commendable essay', although he doubted whether maize would prove a crop suitable to Ireland.[264] The second paper was based, according to its author, on the views of 'a poor meer Irish labourer (who having worked many years under a head gardiner in a gentleman's garden, has got a genius of planting)', and included a simple description of how to grow elm trees from seed.

Thus, while agricultural matters constituted but a minor part of the society's business, the beginnings of eighteenth century 'patriot' enthusiasm for improvement were already present. In the last period of the Philosophical Society's existence during 1707 and 1708 William King, then Archbishop of Dublin, once again gave evidence of his concern for Irish agriculture, a concern which sprang not only from scientific sources but also from a deep political conviction which was shared by Molyneux, Prior, Berkeley, and Swift.

PART III HUMANITIES

English science in the 1680s was still to some extent operating under the influence of Bacon, who had tended to believe something approaching ultimate knowledge an attainable goal. If only a vast number of facts could be gathered and digested, it would, so the argument ran, become possible to construct a peculiarly durable scientific analysis. But so as not to waste time, a catalogue should be drawn up listing all the facts already known and understood. The early society at Oxford, had, for example, considered its first task to be the gathering 'together such things as are already discovered and to make a booke with a generall index of them, then to have a collection of those which are still inquirenda and according to our opportunityes to make inquisitive experiments'.[265] Petty too had given a similar undertaking to the students of his proposed *Gymnasium Mechanicum* of 1648, while the Royal Society had initiated histories of various trades and crafts.[266] As late as 1684, at a meeting of the Dublin Society, 'there was a paper produced, containing a catalogue of the discoveries of this and the last age'.[267] Indeed, so optimistic had some natural philosophers become that the editor of the *Philosophical Transactions* felt it necessary to warn that, despite the many discoveries already made, much remained to be done, enough at least, he thought, 'for the age of the world'.[268]

The study of antiquities was the most important of the nonscientific activities pursued by the members of the Dublin Society, although philology was not neglected. In an age when the world of ideas was expanding, the need for a common universal language, in which it would be possible to express scientific concepts with accuracy and precision, was widely acknowledged. The most famous of these artificial languages was John Wilkins's 'Real Character' devised in 1668, in which symbols represented ideas rather than sounds.[269] And in 1665 the Royal Society had set up a committee 'to improve the English tongue, ... particularly for philosophical purposes'.[270] There were thus two movements working for the linguistic improvement of scientific communication, one attempting to discover a new alphabet of universal application, the other trying to purify the English language itself. Professor da Costa Andrade is however mistaken when he suggests that interest in the matter ceased after Wilkins's death in 1672, for twelve years later the Dublin Society was still working on the problem.

In December 1684 the society received a letter from John Keogh in which he gave notice of 'various curiosities he had under consideration, and some of them finished, as a philosophical character'.[271] The society obviously thought the matter of some importance and 'much discourse passed about various attempts that way'. Although no sample of the character survives, it was probably based on principles similar to those evolved by Wilkins. Keogh worked on it for a year and in September 1685 St George Ashe, then secretary to the society, promised to send a specimen to London 'if it be thought worth the while'.[272] His failure to do so three months later when Keogh at last presented 'a large discourse' on the subject, would seem to indicate the society's poor opinion of the final product. No more is heard of the philosophical character, and Keogh's absence from Dublin – he was Church of Ireland clergyman at Strokestown in Roscommon – probably deprived the scheme of its most energetic advocate.

Politics was also regarded as a proper area for study by the society, which at its earliest meetings heard Archdeacon Baynard prove 'at large that monarchy is the most natural government'.[273] Some months later the same member gave his views on university education, but these have unfortunately been lost.[274] While there were also occasional excursions into egyptology, travel, and folklore,[275] the society concentrated most of its efforts in the humanities into the study of Irish antiquities. Study is perhaps the wrong word, for at first there was nothing systematic about the society's approach to Ireland's past, which took the form of short, undisciplined, but enthusiastic, bursts of activity. Descriptions of archaeological discoveries were read by Mullen and Smyth, while the former 'also produced a stone, said to be an elf-dart, but [which] was agreed to be nothing but the head of an arrow of the antients'.[276] Ashe informed the society of 'a very antient Irish inscription taken off a large stone cross', having previously presented 'ten pieces of old British coin, found in the middle of a rock',[277] while one of Mullen's correspondents from Dontrilegue in County Cork sent the society an account of several urns found on his estate, which he conjectured had been there 'ever since the Romans'.[278]

It was, however, only after the Williamite Revolution that a real and intensive study was undertaken of Irish antiquities. One of the leaders of this movement was Thomas Molyneux, who, through his friendship with Roderic O'Flaherty and the Welsh scholar Edward Lhuyd, laid the foundations for an organized scientific interest in Ireland's more distant past. The establishment of the Royal Irish Academy in the last quarter of the eighteenth century institutionalized a discipline which for the Dublin Society had been a small if fascinating sideline.

Before concluding, a few oddities of a general nature should be mentioned which confirm the very general character of the society's interests. In March 1685 the society was twice visited by an itinerant German, who performed a variety of tricks before the assembled membership. On 23 March he began by shooting bullets at pieces of paper, and then, 'rubbing his hands in juice of onion and urine, . . . suffered molten lead to fall on them lightly without injury'.[279] But the members soon tired of the magician's prestidigitation, and at his second and last appearance the secretary noted that 'the rest of our time was taken up by some mountebank tricks of the German's'.[280] This sort of thing seems to have been a German speciality, for Viscount Mountjoy, writing to the society in 1686 from Nürnberg, described how 'an ordinary workman showed him a piece of common cold iron which, without fire or any other help but his hammer, he in half a minute made red-hot, so that it burnt wood'.[281] But this particular 'trick' had serious implications. Boyle, for one, was interested in the problem, a study of which led to a consideration of the relationship between the mechanical philosophy and the production of qualities.[282]

The wandering mountebank was of course a feature of seventeenth- and eighteenth-century life. Some earned their living by the strangest of means. For example, one Irish puff broadsheet gave 'a wonderful account of the grand devourer of butter-milk', one Cormock McMahon, who 'slits a hot potatoe and puts his tongue into it, and, while his tongue is parboiling, sings the Irish cry to admiration'.[283] Professor Oliver Ferguson hints that the German conjurer at the Dublin Society may have given Swift the idea for his pamphlet of 1721 entitled *The Wonder of All the Wonders that ever the World Wondered At*.[284] This describes the marvels of another (fictitious) German called John Emanuel Schoitz. But there is no direct evidence to support this view which must remain purely conjectural.

Besides manual dexterity, feats of memory were regarded with great admiration at the time, especially when they were concerned with mental arithmetic. In 1671 John Wallis, then suffering from insomnia, had passed a night in extracting the square root of a fifty-two digit number, dictating the answer (a number of twenty-seven digits) to his clerk in the morning. An account of this achievement was included in the *Philosophical Transactions* for 1685.[285] When the news first reached Dublin the society 'was informed that one of their members had by the help of memory easily extracted the root of a number of fourteen places, going in an arithmetical progression of odd numbers, as 1, 3, 5, 7, etc., and could have proceeded with equal facility'.[286] The member in question was probably George Tollet, who in the following year brought a pupil of his, a girl of eleven, to a meeting of the society, 'at which she astounded all with her precocious mathematical ability'.[287] She too was able to extract the square root of a number of twenty digits by memory and attended in all six meetings to prove her knowledge of algebra, mechanics, chronology, geography, and astronomy. On 19 April 1686 she 'showed her skill in practical music upon the fiddle, which was accompanied with a consort of excellent music'.[288] The Countess of Clarendon, wife of the lord lieutenant, attended one of her performances and desscribed the scene in a letter to that voracious student of the curious John Evelyn. 'She did answer to all the most hard questions in geometry, and had such a crowd about her, that one could hardly breathe in the room; then the best musicians in this place joined with her in playing the composure of the last opera in France, her part was upon the violin, which she performed admirably; it was as fine music as ever I heard.'[289] The members of the Dublin Society and their friends obviously enjoyed themselves even when engaged in the onerous task of the 'advancement of learning'.

It is obvious from this account that no large claims of originality can be made for the scientific and other researches of the Dublin Society. Men like Molyneux, Mullen, and Petty would have been distinguished in any company, but most of the others were of no more than average ability. The sort of work they undertook was closely modelled on that of contemporary English cooperative science, and the lack of anything but sporadic contacts with the continent proved a grave disadvantage. Nevertheless a comparatively large section of the membership was surprisingly well informed as to the latest scientific developments of the time, and was by no means uncritical in its reactions. Although naturally enough the society was not exempt from much contemporary credulity, many new theories were tested and the foundations laid for a more lasting concern in Ireland for all branches of scientific learning. In this respect the Dublin Philosophical Society and its members were the first heralds of that remarkable renaissance in Irish political and intellectual life which took place in the latter half of the eighteenth century. Having themselves found no tradition on which to build, they established one. Their achievement was that they provided a context in which others might work to greater advantage.

Chapter 6

Attacks and Lampoons on the Society and its Members

It has already been pointed out that even in the last quarter of the seventeenth century there still existed a sizeable residue of opposition to the New Learning. The dispute was not simply one between two clearly antagonistic parties labelled Ancients and Moderns, but like most great conflicts of thought shifted and twisted along the intellectual keyboard. Although loyalties were seldom precisely obvious, or positions well defined, a certain pattern of attitudes does become apparent. Some of the opponents of the new natural philosophy have been discussed in Chapter 1, and it would have been strange had Dublin science not antagonized similarly inclined conservative intellectuals. England had its Butler and Shadwell, wits who pushed contemporary scientific extravagances to even greater extremes, and its Stubbe, who saw a threat to sound religion under every microscope. Irish science, far smaller in scale than that of England, provoked a less widespread opposition. The fiercest critic of the Dublin Society was one of its own original members, Dudley Loftus. None of his writings on this matter have been published, and he was not, as Stubbe was, a professional baiter of things and men scientific. However, what he has left in manuscript shows him to have been the equal in vituperation of his English counterpart, and almost as confused in his opinions and assertions. R. F. Jones has maintained that Stubbe's writings 'reveal little else than contradictions'.[1] Loftus's are, if anything, even more tortuous and diffuse.

Dudley Loftus was born in 1619 the son of Sir Adam Loftus. He graduated B.A. from Trinity College Dublin in 1638 and then, on the advice of Primate Ussher, went to Oxford, where he studied at University College for two years, proceeding M.A. in 1640. On his return to Ireland he sat in the House of

Commons as member for Naas (1642–8) and then for Kildare
and Wicklow (1659), holding several offices under the Commonwealth, including those of deputy judge-advocate, chief
engrosser of the exchequer, and master in chancery. He was,
however, able to ride the storm of the Restoration without
difficulty, being confirmed in most of his positions and in
addition being appointed a judge of the Prerogative Court and
vicar-general for Ireland.[2] Indeed so attentive was he to the
necessity of standing well with constituted authority that he
dedicated his *History of the Twofold Invention of the Cross* (Dublin,
1686), to Mary of Modena, the Catholic consort of James II.
Loftus was active in politics after the Restoration, although in
1673 his gift for compromise seems temporarily to have broken
down for he was then suspended from the post of master in
chancery 'for his leading the resistance to the rules lately made
by the lord lieutenant and council for the better regulating of
the corporation of Dublin'.[3] His main interest was, however,
the study of oriental languages, of which he is said to have
learned twenty in as many years.[4] His chief purpose in translating eastern manuscripts was that it should 'appear that
Protestants of the Church of England dare print antient entire
oriental commentaries on the N[ew] T[estament] in confidence
and full assurance of having thereby the explicit suffrages of the
oriental churches to maintain their tenets against the Church of
Rome'.[5] In other words he was part of an important group of
writers who sought to justify Anglican doctrine by recourse to
historical precedent, a *modus operandi* much favoured in the
seventeenth century. It is odd that it should have been Loftus
with his Commonwealth connections who provided the most
scornful Irish opposition to the New Learning. His views were,
however, not quite as simple as this, for he did on occasion
express modified admiration for some aspects of science, and
even of the new philosophy, while deploring the exemplar of
that movement flourishing in Dublin. Loftus was not a dedicated puritan and his career after 1659 shows him to have been
a fine trimmer, attacking beliefs he had once supported.
Although his learning in languages and the law was held in
high esteem by his contemporaries, his personal reputation was
that of an irascible and difficult individual. Ware records that
'he was accounted an improvident and unwise man; and his

many levities and want of conduct gave the world too much reason to think so.'[6] His strictures on the Dublin Society certainly show him to have been a writer with a ready pen, as bitter as he was long-winded.

At first the Dublin Society was not as relatively narrow in its interests as it was later to become. For example, in the period from its foundation in October 1683 until the first rules were adopted in January 1684, several topics, not in any way connected with natural philosophy, were discussed. On 22 October Loftus himself 'discoursed concerning Père Simon's *Histoire Critique*'[7] – his only contribution to the society – while a small group met 'upon Sunday nights (as the whole company . . . on Mondays) to discourse theologically, of God suppose, and his attributes, and how to establish religion, and confute atheism, by reason, evidence, and demonstration'.[8] And Loftus may well have belonged to this group which evidently considered natural philosophy a secondary interest. It was not, of course, unusual for contemporary scientists to be deeply involved in religious matters, although the medieval concept of a predominantly teleological view of the universe was becoming less popular. It has been said of Robert Boyle that 'for him, religion itself belonged to the life of reason and nature itself was part of revelation',[9] and it was certainly the occult rather than the divine which was being ejected from contemporary attitudes towards the world and its creation. What was unusual about the theological meeting was that it should have taken place under the aegis of a philosophical society, when those in England strictly forbade such discussion.

Perhaps as a result of friction as to what should be the proper subject matter of the society, a minor purge of members seems to have taken place about Christmas 1683. The particular occasion for this dispute was the drafting of the first set of rules by a committee of three (Molyneux, Petty, and Willoughby) and their presentation for adoption on 7 January 1684. These rules, which have been discussed in Chapter 4, reflect a shift of interest away from general learning and towards a more scientific emphasis in the business of the society. Petty and Molyneux were certainly the chief movers in the matter, and their more precise and restricted view of the society's work, however ineffectual it was to prove in the long run, aroused the anger of Loftus, who at once committed his disagreement to paper.[10]

There are in all, eight articles by Loftus dealing with the Dublin Society and its members. After Christmas 1683 the society held three meetings for which no minutes have survived, and it was probably at one of these that Loftus delivered the piece entitled 'Dudley Loftus his speech at a meeting of the society'.[11] His main point of contention here was that a small clique had succeeded in appropriating the offices of the society. In his view the new rules seemed 'rather to improve particular interests than advance the generous ends of this society or to serve the honour of ourselves or the successes of our endeavours in the advancement of learning'. In this passage Loftus was arguing only against a group which, in his opinion, was impeding the grand Baconian design of the 'advancement of learning'. Elsewhere he maintained a quite different and opposite point of view and criticized the New Learning as such. The proposed rules made provision for subsidies to be given by the society to deserving experimenters. This generous proposal infuriated Loftus, who, while admitting that 'money be as necessary to maintain tryals and experiments as oyl is to maintain the lamp', was singularly reluctant to part with any of his own.[12] Here a somewhat more precise attitude becomes apparent, although Loftus still inveighed only against the wilder reaches of contemporary science when he asserted his refusal to support financially anyone who was 'att expenses of money in finding out a means to snuff the moone when she seemed to him to burn dim'.

This was, however, merely the first and mildest of a series of attacks, most of them based on a mixture of intellectual opposition and sheer personal pique. One of the pieces began, 'The Society of the mechanicks of fresh philosophers of Dublin is various in its names and titles, (being sometimes called a society of usefull learning, sometimes a shop of useless subtelties, but most commonly termed the Petty–Mulleneuxan meeting). It is variable in its constitutions and no less changeable in its resolutions.'[13] But like so many contemporary opponents of the New Learning Loftus often contradicted himself. He claimed the new philosophy to be false, and then attacked the Dublin Society for not promoting that philosophy more vigorously. The

conclusion that can be drawn from his writings is that he was
not so much what might loosely be termed an Ancient, as an
angry man looking for a stick with which to beat those who had
insulted him. He dissected at some length the characters of
three unnamed members of the society, two of whom were most
probably Petty and Molyneux. One of these, Petty perhaps, was
described as going about the town 'like an Armenian pedlar'
vending 'threadbare experiments of others for new ones of his
owne, as a courtezan her virginity and a popish priest his first
mass'.[14] This was no more than personal abuse. But more
serious still, in Loftus's opinion, was the fact that this man
ventured 'to censure Primate Usher and Bishop Prideux for
want of learning'.[15] When others disputed scholastically and
according to traditional modes, the new philosopher, declared
Loftus, condemned the undertaking as of no value. Another
member was criticized for being 'so much glorified in his own
conceit, that he lifts up his eyes to heaven, as if he needs no
more of terrain glory, or perhaps it is as much in admiration of
himself as out of hypocrisy'.

Elsewhere however, one approaches a more genuine distrust
of the New Learning in general, as when Loftus upbraided the
members for hindering 'true and sublime', while maintaining
'sterile and useless learning', and for being skilled in little more
than 'a nimble kind of windage'.[16] Most of their experiments,
he believed, had proved to be like 'blanchers and citrinations in
chemistry, which will not abide trial'. Yet, he went on, 'by an
unmanlike kind of learning they would maintain them to be
true by votes, which are more their friends than reason, and
therefore prefer the drawn arguments of votes before the topics
of Aristotle'. Then, having shown that he knew a thing or two
about alchemy, Loftus referred disparagingly to those 'Italian
empirics' lauded by the society, and to the fact that it, in his
view vainly, sought to aspire to the condition of the Royal
Society, comparing it, in a figure of speech common to seventeenth century controversialists, with the pygmy who seeks to
'bear the armour of a giant'. And in addition, he declared, the
society was intent on reducing Dublin University to nothing
more than 'a brabbling shop of vain jangling'.

In a letter to an unknown correspondent, written in January
1684, Loftus repeated his charges, and added that he felt con-

M

vinced the society would soon come to an end.[17] 'The Society,' he remarked, 'is now mounted to its *non plus ultra*, some of them thinking themselves as able as so many Atlases to sustain the world, whilst they are not able out of the revenue of their experiments to maintain the charge of their . . . slender society.' Loftus was, however, reluctantly willing to concede that science might, for the layman at least, be a harmless pursuit. But he urged the clerical members to abandon such nonsense, quoting Luther's critic Albert Krantz, 'Fryar, Fryar, goe into the cloister and follow thy beads'.[18]

It can be seen how difficult it is to assess with any precision the exact tendency of Loftus's views, which shoot rather haphazardly in various directions. What does seem clear is that Loftus, who saw as his main task in life the giving 'testimony of antiquity in favour of the doctrine and discipline of the Church of England',[19] found himself unable to further this cause by means of membership of a more or less exclusively scientific society. Although a catalogue of his library does not include any works by contemporary opponents of the new natural philosophy, the provenance of at least some of his arguments is obvious.[20] Like Meric Casaubon, but without his perspicuous style, Loftus tried to show that none of the inventions so lauded by the scientists of the day was really new at all. In particular he referred to Petty's ship-building activities, claiming that these double-bottomed craft were 'mentioned by Athenaeus, who lived many ages before the birth of any mechanick now alive'.[21] His arguments were not new, and put crudely, would run something like this. Modern science is useless, and in any case use is not the sole, or even the most important, criterion in such matters. Even conceding that a particular thing may be useful it was undoubtedly first invented by the ancient Greeks. Besides, science is dangerous to sound religion, being either part of a Roman Catholic or an atheist plot against the established church. The confusion of such views is readily appreciated.

It would however be wrong to imagine that all the abuse came from one side. Joseph Glanvill could indulge in equally vicious invective in defence of the Royal Society and the New Learning, which suffered from the rashness of their supporters almost more than from the vituperation of their abusers. When Bishop Wilkins declared that 'the creation of a glorious angel did not cost Him [God] more than that of a despicable fly',[22] he merely antagonized many who still had an open mind with a remark that was scarcely the result of careful experiment. Loftus's attacks on Irish science were therefore, both as regards content and manner, closely connected with a much wider European debate.

One point of factual interest mentioned by Loftus is his claim that the society lost most of its original members as a result of the adoption of the first rules.[23] No other source supports this assertion. He went so far as to say that the Petty–Molyneux faction 'finished two parts of their business in provoking . . . two-thirds of the society to depart from them', adding optimistically that 'at their next meeting they will accomplish . . . a totall dissolution'.[24] However, of the members mentioned in the minutes prior to this dispute, only two seem to have left the society after January 1684. One of these was Loftus himself, while Samuel Walkington's resignation is purely conjectural. Thus unless there had been a large group of members who had taken no part in the society's proceedings before January 1684, and are therefore not mentioned in the minutes, this claim cannot possibly be true. Loftus in fine was making the wish father of the fact.

The only reference to these attacks was made in the address delivered by St George Ashe to the Earl of Clarendon in January 1686. 'Thus, my Lord,' remarked Ashe, 'tho our designe seems very fair and usefull, at least to give offence to no one, yet in our Cradle, like Hercules, we have suffer'd persecution, and been fircely oppos'd by a Loud and Numerous; tho (God be thanked) an impudent sort of adversaries, the Railleurs and the witts.'[25] This speech was therefore at least in part a belated reply to the strictures of Loftus and others. Ashe was particularly scornful of that attitude which surrounded antiquity 'with such superstitious reverence, as if the beauty of truth, like that of a picture, cou'd not be known or perceived but at a distance'. He was quite ready to admit that much of the work of the Dublin Society might seem useless, but insisted that 'many Loads of unprofitable earth shou'd be thrown by, before we come at a vain [sic] of gold'. Ashe not only criticized the upholders of the old scholastic view, but also those virtuosi interested only in the bizarre and unusual. The true philosopher, he felt, should study the natural world by means of its most rounded and beautiful works. An excessive interest in the vagaries of nature was certainly the hallmark of the scientific societies, and one from which Ashe himself was by no means exempt.

While Loftus might be classed among the 'railleurs', there were others poking fun at the Dublin Society who would more properly fall under Ashe's heading of 'witts'. In the Tripos speech delivered at Trinity College Dublin in July 1688 by John Jones, for which he was temporarily deprived of his degree, several members of the society were ridiculed, both for their interest in science and for less specific reasons. One of the items in this production is an imaginary dialogue between 'Sainty' Ashe and Samuel Foley, in which the conversation runs along the by then well-worn lines of Shadwell's *The Virtuoso*.[26] The two men are depicted in a discussion concerning an imminent eclipse of the sun and are drawn in the heavy satire of the time. Foley, for example, declares, 'I cut my hair by the stars; and will tell the physiognomy and sex of my child, before my wife's brought to bed.'[27] Ashe follows this by asserting his belief that during the eclipse 'we are all like to be in the dark'. Richard Acton, another member of the society, is the subject of an 'Heroick Poem', in which his seemingly chaste life is commented upon with amazement, and he is labelled 'a mortal enemy of punning', and consequently a kill-joy.[28] Jones discusses at some length an imaginary lady who had donated all her money to found a new university, in which 'several officers are yet wanting, as divinity professors, preachers, physicians, lecturers, surgeons, historians, chymists, civilians, register, linguist, and many others, all of which are to be supplied by that colossus of learning Mr Foley'. Dr Charles Gwithers, who was to join the society after the Revolution, is mentioned as presenting to this fictitious institution, as a contribution to a fund for poor fellows, the 'generous gift' of 'an old glister-pipe'.[29]

These juvenile lampoons are quite different in kind to the ponderously learned views of Dr Loftus. Jonathan Swift, whose tutor as an undergraduate had been Ashe, also commented on the society, which probably provided his first contact with the kind of science he was later to satirize so savagely in 'A Voyage to Laputa'. Among poems attributed to him are several which mention members of the society, including Thomas Molyneux, Sir Patrick Dun, and Ralph Howard. In one of these entitled 'Mad Mullinix and Timothy' Molyneux is supposed to be giving advice to a young man.

> Your conversation to refine,
> I'll take you to some friends of mine;
> Choice spirits, who employ their parts,
> To mend the world by useful arts.
> Some cleaning hollow tubes, to spy
> Direct the zenith of the sky.[30]

In another of his less inspired moments Swift wrote a piece called 'A Dialogue in the Castilian Language'.[31] The *dramatis personae* include Ashe, Thomas Molyneux, and Lord Pembroke, the lord lieutenant, the action taking place at Dublin Castle in the autumn of 1707. At one point Lord Pembroke asks Ralph Howard: 'Doctor, I did not see you at the society last meeting.' But the remark is *apropos* of nothing, and the rest of the vignette consists of a long series of those tortuous puns with which Swift was prone to scrub his wit.

By this time however the situation in Ireland had changed, and at the opening of the first scientific laboratory at Trinity College Dublin in 1711, one of the fellows, William Thompson, was ordered to recite original Latin verse in praise of science. Referring to medicine and pharmacy Thompson declaimed:

> Hinc medicina viget, varias hinc pharmaca sumunt
> Virtutes, vultuque novo natura superbit.[32]

Although the building was opened with considerable pomp, it was both primitive and long overdue. Even if other evidence were lacking, the fact that Dublin University had no proper laboratory until 1711 would alone be enough to indicate how scientifically backward were Ireland's educational facilities during the late seventeenth and early eighteenth centuries.

These attacks were however the last significant effort on the part of the Ancients. For despite Stubbe's assertions to the contrary, opponents of the New Learning were rapidly becoming fewer and less influential. By the beginning of the eighteenth century only die-hard literary conservatives like Swift still felt the struggle worth a continuance.

Chapter 7

Dublin Science 1688–1708

I. INTERLUDE

The unrest in Ireland which eventually followed the accession of James II to the throne affected not only the political life of that kingdom but brought a sudden halt to the work of the Dublin Society. The last recorded meeting took place on 11 April 1687, and although informal sessions may have been held throughout the following months, Ashe informed William Musgrave in the middle of July that 'the jealousy, suspition, and prospect of troubles in this kingdome have such unhappy influence on our philosophical endeavours, that little of late worth communicating has been done among us'.[1] But at Oxford and London the situation was soon to follow a similar course, and early in 1691 Plot, in a letter to Edward Lhuyd, deplored the fact that the two English societies were quite asleep.[2] Soon the threat of open war in Ireland became so serious, that a number of members, all but one of whom were Protestants, fled to England, where they remained until the Williamite Settlement had been finally imposed. The Molyneux brothers went to Chester, where they both maintained their interest in natural philosophy and where William began to write his *Dioptrica Nova*. While in London Ashe and Mullen moved in scientific circles, and already in 1689 were frequenting Jonathan's Coffee House, which had become a meeting place for fellows of the Royal Society.[3]

Ashe soon obtained employment as chaplain to Lord Paget, the English ambassador at Vienna, and remained in that city for eighteen months. Already in the Spring of 1686 he had travelled through France, having obtained a recommendation from the Earl of Clarendon to the ambassador at Paris, Sir William Trumbull, who knew a number of French scientists.[4] While in Austria Ashe tried to continue his scientific work and succeeded in maintaining a correspondence with the Royal Society, of which he was by then a fellow. In July 1690 he wrote, 'You can scarce imagine how very ignorant a place this Vienna is among the numerous crowd of priests and other religious here, and notwithstanding their famous and antient university, there is not one mathematician to be found; and shou'd I fix any telescope, I should fear being seized by the inquisition as a conjurer.'⁵ Ashe was obviously suspicious of the popish Austrians, and had found Augsburg and Nürnberg, which he had visited on his journey south, more congenial cities in which to pursue his scientific inclinations. As well as writing to the Royal Society he was in communication with Molyneux at Chester, whom he informed of the 'mighty acquaintance' he had made in Germany on account of his fellowship of the Royal Society, which was there held in high esteem.⁶ While at Nürnberg he had met the two German astronomers Johann Philipp von Wurzelbau (1651–1725) and Georg Christoph Eimmart (1638–1705).⁷ The latter had shown him his observatory, which, reported Ashe, 'is upon a bastion of the city, conveniently enough placed, and contains 4 or 5 quadrants, though none with telescopic sights, a large horizontal circle with a most exact meridian line, and a perpendicular, an arch of 118 degrees, whose radius is 16 Norick feet'. He also corresponded with Johann Sturm (1635–1703), the professor of mathematics at Altdorf University, who sent him an account 'of a strange phenomenon in the heavens', and after his arrival at Vienna began an exchange of letters with the great Italian bibliophile Antonio Magliabechi (1633–1714) of Florence, who told him of recent philosophical developments in Italy. In return Ashe kept Magliabechi informed as to intellectual affairs in England and especially the appearance of new books there. On 18 March 1691 (N.S.) for example, he sent to Florence news he had received from London concerning the publication of Anthony Wood's *Athenae Oxonienses*, 2 vols. (London, 1691–2), Robert Boyle's *Medicina Hydrostatica* (London, 1690), *Vinetum Angliae: A New and Easy Way to make Wine* [London, ?1690] by D. S., and Thomas Tryon's *Pythagoras his Mystick Philosophy reviv'd* (London, 1691). Magliabechi thought Ashe's bibliographical information important enough to transmit to Leibniz, with whom he corresponded.⁸ Ashe eventually returned to Ireland, and in 1692 was appointed Provost of Trinity College Dublin at the early age of thirty-four.

Not long after his appointment Ashe preached a sermon at the college as part of the celebrations marking its centenary. He took the opportunity, not only to place Trinity firmly within the context of the revolutionary settlement, but also to reaffirm his own interest in the natural sciences. The physical universe is equated with the 'great body politick', and, in a strange mixture of modern thought and traditional analogy, Ashe justifies the study of science as exhibiting both the power of God and 'the friendly correspondence between the higher and the lower world'. Reason takes its place beside revelation as the great source of divine truth, for ''tis certain our church and religion can never be safer than amidst the consequences of a rational learned age, and all the various improvements of knowledge, since they aim not at the captivity but freedom of men's minds'. Commonplace rhapsodies on the usefulness of science to 'trade, commerce, navigation, the culture of lands, and the advancement of mechanicks', are followed by eulogies of Archimedes, Galileo, and Bacon. Science is represented as the one constant in a world of other disciplines merely 'conjectural and litigious', for only in mathematical demonstration do 'Peripatetick and Cartesian, Catholick and Heretic . . . all agree'. Ashe ends with a plea for cooperative work by university scholars, for 'no part of knowledge seems insuperable to the just endeavours of a well regulated society, united in common studies and the prosecution of the same useful ends'.[9] The work and concerns of the Philosophical Society shine through the sermon at every point, and Ashe's concept of the ideal university is drawn largely from his experiences of the previous decade. His appointment as provost marks a growing acceptance on the part of the college of the necessity of new methods and a new approach, a change of heart for which the propaganda of the Philosophical Society must at least in part have been responsible.

By 1692 most of the members of the society had returned to Dublin, although Huntington remained in England as rector of Great Hallingbury near Bishop's Stortford, and Smyth left Europe to take appointment as chaplain to one of the Levant Company's factories in the East. William Molyneux had returned in 1690, and although the society was not to meet again until the Spring of 1693, was almost at once involved in scientific enquiry. In 1692 his major work, the *Dioptrica Nova*, was published at London, and copies were presented to many of the author's friends and colleagues, including Flamsteed, Halley, Hooke, and Newton.[10] After reading the book Charles Willoughby wrote to Bishop King, then in Derry directing the affairs of his diocese, saying that nothing had ever given him so much pleasure as this proof of Molyneux's abilities. He found it 'the fullest of dioptricall learning of any peece I have yet seen on that subject', and praised the author for having been 'very industrious and truly . . . exact'.[11]

The book, which embodies all of Molyneux's optical research, was the best synthesis then available. In it Molyneux tried to demonstrate the essential unity of all sciences and their general dependence on the creator, whose nature they both reflected and in part helped to explain. Discussing the movement of the planets, he wrote:

And from hence we may justly fall into the deepest admiration, that one and the same law of motion should be observed in bodies so vastly distant from each other, and which seem to have no dependence or correspondence with each other. This does most evidently demonstrate that they were all at first put in motion by one and the same unerring hand, even the infinite power and wisdom of God, which has fixed this order amongst them all, and has established a law, which they cannot transgress. Chance or dull matter could never produce such an harmonious regularity in the motion of bodies so vastly distant. This plainly shews a design and intention in the first mover.[12]

In Holland Christiaan Huygens was shown a copy of the *Dioptrica* by a young German friend, J. G. Steigerthal, and at once made lengthy extracts from a book which both complimented his abilities and complemented his own *Traité de la Lumière* of 1690. He told the Swiss mathematician Nicholas Faccio of Duillier, who had settled in England in 1687, 'Je trouve qu'il explique mieux les effects des télescopes que jusqu'icy personne n'a fait,' and urged Rotterdam publishers to produce a Latin edition, which however they failed to do.[13] Similarly in Germany, Sturm, who had seen a review of the

Dioptrica in the *Acta Eruditorum*, wrote to his friend Ashe to express admiration for the book's accuracy and originality.[14]

If the *Dioptrica* ended Molyneux's friendship with Flamsteed, it was the cause of a new and fruitful association with John Locke. In the Epistle Dedicatory Molyneux had written, 'To none do we owe, for a greater advancement in this part of philosophy [logic], than to the incomparable Mr Locke, who, in his *Essay of Human Understanding*, hath rectified more mistakes . . . than are to be met with in all the volumes of the ancients.' He had left a copy of the book in London to be given to Locke when he came to town. The philosopher was flattered, and wrote a letter thanking Molyneux for his gift. 'Sir, you have made great advances of friendship towards me, and you see they are not lost upon me.'[15] This was the first letter in what was to become a lengthy correspondence between the two fellows of the Royal Society, which ended only with Molyneux's death in 1698.

It was Locke who first popularized Molyneux's famous problem concerning the relationship between experience and reason, which was to provide endless speculative possibilities for the philosophers of the eighteenth century. It has generally been held that the problem was originally suggested by Molyneux in a letter to Locke dated 2 March 1693,[16] but a note in Molyneux's hand among the Locke Papers dated 7 July 1688 contains an earlier and somewhat different statement of the matter. It runs,

A man, being born blind, and having a globe and a cube, nigh of the same bigness, committed into his hands, and being taught or told, which is called the globe, and which the cube, so as easily to distinguish them by his touch or feeling; Then, both being taken from him, and laid on a table, let us suppose his sight restored to him; whether he could, by his sight, and before he touch them, know which is the globe and which the cube? Or whether he could know by his sight, before he stretched out his hand, whether he could not reach them, tho they were removed 20 or 1000 feet from him.[17]

Superficially simple, the problem is of great theoretical interest, for on various levels it touches on both the physiological and the psychological nature of vision and perception. Molyneux, in the *Dioptrica Nova*, where the actual problem is not discussed, was largely concerned with a geometrical explanation of vision. In this he echoed the earlier work of Descartes and Malebranche. But so exclusively geometrical an approach left almost untouched the nature of the psychological construction undertaken by the mind upon the physical data presented to it. That such construction took place was simply taken for granted. Molyneux's theories, as set out in the *Dioptrica*, did not therefore either offer any serious obstacles to the geometrization of the external world, or raise any real and inconvenient doubts as to the existence of such a world or the validity of our knowledge of it.[18] Vague doubts did indeed trouble Molyneux, especially concerning the case of inverted images, but these were summarily resolved by the suggestion that the representations of images in the retina are perceived 'by the sensitive soul (whatever it be) the manner of whose actions and passions, He alone knows who created and preserves it, whose ways are past finding out, and by us unsearchable. But of this moral truth we may be assured, that he that made the eye shall see'.[19]

Locke was so interested in the problem that he printed its revised version of 1693 in the second and subsequent editions of *An Essay Concerning Human Understanding*.[20] Molyneux himself had merely posited that the man should be debarred from touching the cube and the globe, while Locke, intent on showing how much we 'may be beholding to experience, improvement, and acquired notions', imposed the additional condition that the man should identify the objects at first sight. Both Locke and Molyneux answered the problem in the negative, thus confirming the essentially empirical nature of their philosophy. Berkeley did the same, but for more extreme reasons. He extended the argument by suggesting that we cannot see bodies in space until we have touched some of them while we look, and he used the problem to demonstrate the heterogeneity of sight and touch.[21]

The first affirmative reply came from Edward Synge, a future Archbishop of Tuam, author of *The Gentleman's Religion* (1693), and at the time vicar of Christ Church, Cork. In 1695 he wrote a letter to a friend, which Molyneux forwarded to Locke, in which, adopting arguments later used by Leibniz, he suggested that 'upon sight of the globe and cube, there be grounds enough for such a person clearly to perceive the agreement, and the difference, between his pre-conceived ideas, and newly conceived images of those figures', so that he might therefore 'know which is the globe, and which the cube, without touching them'.[22] Like Leibniz, who argued that in the globe there 'are no points distinguished by the side of the globe itself, all there being level and without angles, while in the cube there are eight points distinguished from all the others',[23] Synge believed that such data provided sufficient grounds upon which reason might construct a proper judgement.

Molyneux's problem continued to be discussed in England and on the continent throughout the eighteenth century by philosophers as different as the Newtonian James Jurin, Etienne Condillac, Diderot, and Voltaire. In addition several tests were undertaken in an attempt to provide an experimental solution. At least forty-eight are recorded as having taken place between 1695 and 1813, the most famous being that on a thirteen-year-old boy described by Cheselden in 1728.[24] The results however, were always inconclusive, for as R. L. Gregory remarks, 'the difficulty is essentially that the adult, with his great store of knowledge from the other senses, and reports from sighted people, is very different from the infant who starts with no knowledge from experience'.[25] Even in fiction the problem exercised its fascination, being mentioned in a somewhat transmuted fashion both in Swift's *Gulliver's Travels* (1726) and Fielding's *Tom Jones* (1749).[26]

The friendship between Locke and Molyneux was a close one. Soon after the beginning of their correspondence the former asked for 'advice and assistance about a second edition of my *Essay*'.[27] Molyneux, in turn, was so enthusiastic about the work that he recommended it to many of his friends, including 'the reverend provost of our university, Dr Ashe, a most learned and ingenious man, . . . he is so wonderfully pleased and satisfied, that he has ordered it to be read by the bachelors in the college, and strictly examines them in their progress therein'.[28] The correspondence dealt mainly with philosophical and political matters and seldom touched on the natural sciences. In its warmth and friendliness however, it has no equal among Molyneux's personal writings. There was of course a vast difference between the ages of the two men, Locke being over sixty, while Molyneux had just passed his thirty-sixth birthday. And perhaps because of this one can discern an element of hero-worship in the Irishman's feelings, as when he wrote to Locke, 'You are so tender in differing from any man, that you have captivated me beyond resistance.'[29] Indeed so great was his enthusiasm, that his son Samuel, born in 1689, was carefully educated along the lines laid down in *Some Thoughts Concerning Education* (London, 1693).[30] But by that time the Dublin Society had, with a greatly increased membership, already resumed its meetings.

II. THE SOCIETY REVIVED

In April 1693 the society met for the first time since the Revolution, initially with sixteen members, but before the end of the year with forty-nine.[31] The Oxford Society did not however experience a similar revival, and as late as March 1694 Robert Plot was unsuccessfully urging Arthur Charlett, the Master of University College, to 'cordially set about it'.[32] However, the institutional records for this period of the Dublin Society's existence are few. They consist of only about a dozen letters and the minutes of four meetings, although a reasonable number of papers has survived.

On 26 April 1693 Marsh, Ashe, Willoughby, Sir Cyril Wyche, and William Molyneux met in the provost's lodgings at Trinity College, and resolved that 'notice be given to the antient members of the society now residing in and about Dublin of the reviving of the society'.[33] Wyche, who as principal secretary to Ormonde had been a member for a short time in 1684 and 1685, had just arrived in Ireland as one of the lords deputy. Shortly after leaving England he had received a letter from Huntington, then rector of Great Hallingbury, urging him to work for 'the improvmts. of learning, ingenuity, and religion' in Ireland, and rejoicing 'exceedingly that Trinity College (the growing nursery of these three)', was so likely to flourish under his patronage.[34] Wyche, as an ex-president of the Royal Society, took the advice to heart and became one of the most active members of the reconstituted Dublin group.

At the first meeting three new members, John Vesey, Archbishop of Tuam, Hon. Francis Robartes, and Sir Richard Cox, were admitted, and a week later Cox read a long paper on the

County of Derry, 'part of an entire geographical description of
the whole kingdom . . . designed to be perfected by him'.[35] Cox
was already known to the society, having in 1685 contributed
a description of County Cork to Molyneux's abortive natural
history of Ireland. In November 1685 he had sent further information to Molyneux and had asked that copies of Petty's maps
and Ware's *De Antiquitatibus* be sent to him. 'I'le give,' he had
remarked, 'any price if it be bought, or any security for their
returne, if it be lent.'[36] From his youth he had been interested
in history and antiquities, and at the age of fourteen had spent
his time reading the popular *Microcosmus* of the Laudian
propagandist Peter Heylyn, which relied heavily on arguments
from analogy, as well as other works 'in rhetorique, logick, and
part of phisick'.[37] By 1685 he had made, as he told Molyneux,
'a rough collection of the affairs of Ireland from the English
conquest 1170 to 1641', and four years later published his
Hibernia Anglicana (London, 1689), which, dedicated in the
most fulsome terms to William and Mary, shows how entirely
contrary were Cox's political opinions to those of Protestant
'patriots' like Molyneux and Prior. At the time of his joining
the society Cox was one of the justices of the king's bench, and
was later, as Lord Chancellor of Ireland, to distinguish himself
as a virulent opponent of Nonconformity.[38]

The membership of the revived society was, as has already
been remarked, considerably larger than that of its predecessor.
Of the forty-nine persons who had joined by the end of 1693,
only thirteen had belonged to the pre-revolutionary group.
Socially the members of 1693 came from the highest reaches of
contemporary Irish life. The society had obviously become
well known and popular in Dublin, and managed to attract
two archbishops, five bishops, a dean, the Provost of Trinity
College, and five fellows of that institution, as well as three
peers, the son of an earl, a baronet, four knights, seven physicians, and three judges. An especially interesting member was
the merchant Bartholomew Vanhomrigh, an alderman of
Dublin since 1687 and lord mayor in 1697, who was of course
the father of Esther, Swift's 'Vanessa'. His membership is
perhaps evidence of a growing interest in the society's affairs
among Dublin's mercantile class.

The inaugural meeting of the society opened with public

prayers led by Marsh, who declaimed, 'O Lord, grant that in studying Thy works, we may also study to promote Thy glory (which is the true end of all our studies) and prosper, O Lord, our undertakings, for Thy name's sake.'[39] But, not content with purely supernatural aid, the members ordered their new secretary, Dr Owen Lloyd, fellow of Trinity College, to renew the connection with the Royal Society. Accordingly, in June 1693 he wrote to Richard Waller, 'We are as yet, but very young, and therefore cannot hope to make any suitable returne for what you send us, but must have a little time to settle after the disorder the warr has put everything into here. Mr Robartes is chosen pra'sident, and our number increases by new elections.'[40]

The early meetings seem to have been largely concerned with problems of topography, Cox presenting a full description of Ireland on 10 May, 'after which some papers were read relating to the perle fishing' in County Antrim.[41] A week before, Wyche had communicated extracts from Varro's *De Lingua Latina*, in order to explain the 'antient Roman way of numbering'.[42] By July communications with the Royal Society had been fully restored, and the Dublin group was once again in receipt of the *Philosophical Transactions*. The lack of minutes for this period makes it difficult to establish the precise date on which the society ceased to function. However, the last credible reference to it in the present tense can be found in a letter of Bulkeley's addressed to Martin Lister and dated 13 April 1697,[43] which year must therefore be taken as its *terminus ad quem*. In all, nineteen papers have survived for this period of the society's existence, although a number of others are mentioned in correspondence with England. Of these nineteen, five concern the Giant's Causeway, four deal with zoology, four with medicine, three with mathematics, and a similar number might be classed as miscellaneous natural history.

The most important contribution was undoubtedly that of Thomas Molyneux, who presented seven papers to the society. The nearest to his professional interests concerned the cutting of an ivory bodkin out of the bladder of a young woman who had swallowed the weapon by accident.[44] The operation, a difficult one, was performed by a Dublin surgeon named Thomas Proby, and just as the society of 1683–7 had been prepared to accept a surgeon among its numbers, so Molyneux, a qualified physician, was willing, unlike many of his English colleagues, to work professionally with a surgeon. The operation itself was unusual, for after having unsuccessfully adopted the traditional technique of using a catheter to withdraw urine, followed by forceps to dislodge the obstruction, Proby moved to more radical measures. He made an incision about an inch and a half long on the outside of the right *musculus rectus* until he reached the bladder. Then he cut the bladder with a small curved bistoury and slipped out the bodkin with his fingers. After a month the wound had healed and the patient recovered. This sophisticated and successful operation was witnessed by Molyneux, who sent an account of it to the Royal Society.

Another of Molyneux's papers was sent to London in March 1694 by the society's secretary Owen Lloyd. This was an historical account of 'the late general coughs and colds' in Ireland, and was printed in the *Philosophical Transactions*.[45] Molyneux's aim in preparing the piece had been to provide observations of how the distemper in question affected men's bodies, 'rather than to raise wild and fruitless speculations in reasoning about it, which being conjectures in all likelihood must fall short of the truth'. Adopting therefore the high ideals of the New Learning, he had decided that, 'passing by all hypotheses', he would 'set down nothing that was not confirmed . . . by wary and repeated observation'. Molyneux traced the beginnings of the epidemic to November 1693, when the weather, which had been unnaturally warm, suddenly moved to the opposite extreme, 'whereupon rheums of all kinds, such as violent coughs that chiefly affected in the night, great defluxion of thin rheum at the nose and eyes, immoderate discharge of the saliva by spitting, hoarseness in the voice, . . . seized great numbers of all sorts of people in Dublin'. The paper went on to describe various physical symptoms of those affected, such as headaches, loss of appetite, emission of 'foul turbid urine, with a brick coloured sediment at the bottom', as also the length of time the illness took to work itself out, which varied from eight to twenty-one days. In gauging the high-water mark of the disease Molyneux used both observations drawn from his own and his colleagues' practices and more general evidence, such as the amount of coughing to be heard in church on Sundays. In addition he traced its geographical movement from France and Flanders to England, and from thence to Ireland, and compared it with the universal fever of 1688, which had affected animals as well as humans. The paper made no attempt to discover the causes of the disease, but contented itself with general descriptions. None the less it was one of the first Irish reports on public health and in its careful concern for detail had few contemporary equals.

The other articles by Molyneux, with the exception of that on the Giant's Causeway, are of less moment. One dealt with a hitherto undescribed *scolopendra marina*,[46] and was sent to the Royal Society by Locke, who also transmitted a piece on the swarms of insects then infesting the province of Connaught.[47] These insects Molyneux identified as the *scarabeus arboreus* mentioned in Thomas Moffett's *Insectorum sive Minimorum Animalium Theatrum* (London, 1634), and this led him into a general disquisition upon the Old Testament's descriptions of similar beetles, especially in Leviticus XI, 22 and Joel I, 4 and II, 25. This historico-theological approach is even more evident in Molyneux's last contribution to the proceedings of the revived society. This concerned 'the large horns frequently found underground in Ireland', and foreshadowed its author's subsequent interest in archaeology.[48] Already in June 1694 he had informed the society of 'an extraordinary head of a large beast of the stag kind, being from tip to tip 10 foot'.[49] The subsequent paper expanded the discussion, and in it Molyneux concluded that the horns in question, of which there is an illustration in the *Philosophical Transactions*, belonged to an animal related to the American moose. He was now forced to admit that this beast was extinct, a view which ran counter to prevailing theories (earlier espoused by Molyneux) which suggested that the creator could not have fashioned any living creature only to allow it to die out entirely. Molyneux rejected the 'short and ready way' of solving the dilemma presented by those who claimed that 'this like all other animals might have been destroyed from off the face of this country by that flood recorded in Holy Scripture'. In any case he did not believe that the deluge had been universal, and instead ascribed the reasons for extinction either to 'a certain ill constitution of air in some of the past seasons long since the flood, which might occasion an epidemic distemper', or to the animal's being excessively

N

hunted 'and killed like other venison as well for the sake of food as mastery and diversion'. The article is a curious mixture of scientific information, historical surmise, and theological daring. The books and authors mentioned in it indicate some of the sources of this strange eclecticism. They include Gerhard Vossius's *De Theologia Gentili et Physiologia Christiana*, 2 vols. (Amsterdam, 1641), Francesco Redi's *Experimenta circa res diversas naturales* (Amsterdam, 1675), Robert Plot's *Natural History of Staffordshire* (Oxford, 1686), Johann Scheffer's *Lapponia* (Frankfurt, 1673), John Josselyn's *New-Englands Rarities Discovered* (London, 1672), Jan van Laet's *L'Histoire de Nouveau Monde* (Leyden, 1640: Originally published in Dutch, Leyden, 1625), Olaus Worm's *Museum Wormianum* (Leyden, 1655), and Walter Charleton's *Onomasticon Zoicon* (London, 1668).

The paper was sent to London, where it 'was read before the Royall Society and kindly received by them', upon which Molyneux wrote to Hans Sloane to ask whether the English scientists could add anything to his account. For, as he put it, by 'reely communicating any other particulars relating to this argument, you'l highly obleidge me, and give me further encouragement to spend what leasure hours I can command from the attendance on my troublesome profession in prosecuting enquirys about the history of nature'.[50]

Perhaps the strangest paper submitted to the society at this time was one concerning physiognomy written by Molyneux's medical colleague Charles Gwithers. Early in 1694, Gwithers, a fellow of the Dublin College of Physicians, its anatomist since 1693, and according to the bookseller John Dunton a man 'of great integrity, learning, and sound judgement',[51] had produced at the society 'the penis of a man blown up and dried, . . . cut transversly so as to show the several cells of the *corpora nervosa*, which appeared very plain'.[52] His interest in physiognomy had been aroused by the excessive claims made for that art by those who regarded it 'as a great truth handed down by infallible antiquity'.[53] While rejecting such an approach, Gwithers refused to go to the opposite extreme, maintaining that its study could lead the sober enquirer to viable conclusions regarding human nature. The article, which was printed in the *Philosophical Transactions* and attracted the particular attention of that enthusiastic student of the bizarre, John Evelyn,[54] did however fall down in its promised citation of persuasive 'concrete examples'. These, while colourful, were hardly conclusive. 'We see,' wrote Gwithers:

great drinkers with eyes generally set towards the nose, the aducent muscles being often employed to let them see their loved liquor in the glass, in the time of drinking; . . . Lascivious persons are remarkable for the *oculorum mobilis petulantis*, as Petronius calls it. From this also we may solve the Quakers' expecting face waiting the pretended spirit, and the melancholy face of the sectaries.

In short, Gwither's piece was a worthy successor to some of the writings produced by the earlier society, and particularly to Foley's rather extravagant *Computatio Universalis*.

The remaining papers were all competent examples of observation or analysis, but little more. William Molyneux's essay on surveying was obviously written under the influence of Petty's publications,[55] while Robartes's account of lotteries reflected current enthusiasm for the mathematics of chance.[56] Robartes also contributed a paper 'concerning the distance of fixed stars,' which was read at a meeting of the Royal Society as well as being presented at Dublin.[57] From the Levant Edward Smyth sent to London articles on a 'strange kind of earth' found near Smyrna and on the 'use of opium among the Turks'.[58] The latter contains some nice observation, but it is not certain whether either of these pieces ever reached the Irish scientists.

The society was at this time particularly anxious to establish a museum of rarities, its earlier repository having presumably been destroyed or neglected. Ashe therefore wrote to the president of the Royal Society, Sir Robert Southwell, asking for any 'natural curiosities' of which the Gresham College collection possessed duplicates, and offering to make 'suitable returns' when the occasion arose.[59] Three days later Bulkeley informed Lister that the Dublin Society was dispatching to London 'some transparent stones found in the County of Clare, of an amethystine water', and that his colleagues were prepared to pay up to £8 in order to increase their collection of minerals, shells, and fossils.[60] The Royal Society agreed to these proposals, and in 1695 Owen Lloyd thanked Sloane for 'the valuable present of your own duplicates', adding that 'when nothing else can keep us together, the memory of this favour, with what we receiv'd from the illustrious society, will be able to do it'.[61] In addition the Dublin Society was at this time considering the employment of an official operator of experiments, and Bulkeley made an approach to Denis Papin's brother, whom he offered an annual salary of £20.[62] What became of this is not however known.

Although the revived Dublin Society concerned itself with a wide variety of subjects, one topic occupied its attentions more than any other. This was the Giant's Causeway in County Antrim, Ireland's most outstanding natural rarity. In 1694 Samuel Foley produced for the society a short description of the causeway, in which he listed its main characteristics, its extent, and composition. This was published in the *Philosophical Transactions*, together with a series of rather crude illustrations by one Christopher Cole, who lived in the north of Ireland.[63] At the same time Foley provided answers to a series of nine questions concerning the causeway posed by Sir Richard Bulkeley.[64] The latter had particularly wanted to know the shape of the basalt pillars of which the causeway is composed. To this query Foley replied, 'The pillars are composed of stones which stand upon one another, some half a foot, others a foot, others a foot and a half, and two foot thick; which are most either pentagons or hexagons, all of them irregular. We saw no squares, and but a few heptagons.' Foley's account was accompanied by an analysis prepared by Thomas Molyneux, who concerned himself especially with the causeway's origins.[65] These were then still obscure, and Molyneux found it necessary to dispel the illusions of those who maintained that it was 'rather the workmanship of art and men's hands than an original production of nature.' He also found certain similarities between the causeway's formation and a description given by the sixteenth century German mineralogist Johann Kenntmann of another basalt structure three miles outside Dresden.[66]

In 1697 William Molyneux sent to the Royal Society a joint removed from the causeway itself, as well as a more exact 'prospect of the place taken on the spot by an hand which we sent on purpose for that end the last Summer'.[67] Interest in the causeway continued, however, and in the following year Thomas Molyneux wrote the last of this series of descriptions, which he sent to Martin Lister in England.[68] In it he added little of substance to what had gone before, although, as a detailed account, this piece superseded all its predecessors. But by 1698 the Dublin Society had almost certainly ceased to meet, and for the next nine years its members were to pursue their scientific interests in a less organized and more isolated manner.

III. MEMBERS WITHOUT A SOCIETY

The ending of regular meetings by the Dublin Society about the middle of 1697 seriously affected the scientific output of its members. William Molyneux, the moving spirit behind Irish natural philosophy, was becoming so deeply involved in political affairs that he no longer had time for scientific research. He had been elected to sit as a university member in the parliament that had first met at Dublin in 1692, and in the Winter of that year had been appointed, on the recommendation of his fellow member Sir Richard Cox, one of the commissioners of the forfeitures in Ireland. He had however declined this highly paid post worth £400 a year, 'chiefly on account of the ill reputation of the other commissioners named'.[69] At this time Molyneux seems to have occupied a central position in Irish politics, and his appointment as a commissioner would indicate that he had played at least a neutral rôle in the Commons' discussion on their right to originate money bills. Although he had declined one post, he accepted appointment to the Commission for Stating the Accounts of the Army in Ireland, and between 1690 and 1695 received over £1000 for the often onerous work attached to such office.[70]

From Molyneux's correspondence with Locke it is evident that during the mid-1690s he was investigating the effect of recent English legislation on the Irish linen and woollen industries, and as a result was moving slowly towards a 'patriot' position in Irish political life. Despite these preoccupations, he was still anxious to continue his scientific work, but, as he told Sloane in November 1697, 'this place affords little curiositys, and my troublesome circumstances afford little leisure to prosecute them as I would. However, now and then I can steal an hour or two; and when I can, 'tis dedicated to your service.'[71] To show that he had not entirely abandoned scientific interests, Molyneux sent to Sloane a critique of Jean de Hautefeuille's *Moyen de Diminuer la Longuer des Lunettes d'Aproche, sans Diminuer leur Efet* (Paris, 1697), which had recently been occupying the time of the Royal Society.[72] He found the work inadequate, remarking that,

perhaps the author may excuse himselfe for not making tryal of what he offers by the same reason that I give for not examining his proposal by experiment, *vizt.* want of proper glasses. But they that know Paris and Dublin will be more apt to excuse me than him in this particular. Here we cannot obtain glasses on all occasions, Paris affords artists of all sorts in this business.

He also busied himself with trying to persuade the Royal Society to engage someone to popularize and simplify Newton's *Principia* for readers 'not so wel versed in abstruse mathematics',[73] thus anticipating the subsequent flood of publications in that field.

For Molyneux however the most important event of these years was the publication of his book *The Case of Ireland's being Bound by Acts of Parliament in England Stated* (Dublin, 1698). In this work, which was dedicated to William III, he attempted to prove that Ireland was a separate kingdom and not a conquered country, and that if the English parliament was to have the right to legislate for Ireland, Irish members must be allowed to sit at Westminster. After the usual historical introduction, Molyneux analysed a number of legal cases sympathetic to his argument. Basing his views on those of Grotius, Pufendorf, and above all, Locke, he asserted that 'all men are by nature in a state of equality, in respect of jurisdiction or dominion', and that this, combined with Anglo-Saxon historical development, led him to condemn the view that 'Ireland should be bound by acts of parliament made in England' as quite simply 'against reason'.[74] Molyneux admitted to Locke that it was 'a nice subject', but wrote, 'I have treated it with that caution and submission, that I cannot justly give any offence.'[75] In this he was much mistaken, for the English House of Commons voted it 'of dangerous tendency to the crown and people of England, by denying the authority of the king and parliament of England to bind the kingdom and people of Ireland'.[76] Opinion in Ireland was sharply divided, and even among the ranks of the Dublin Society there were supporters and opponents of Molyneux's views. Bishop King of Derry, whose dispute with the Irish Society of London had originally prompted the tract, could not 'see why Mr Mollyneux's booke, being written by a private gentleman, without consulting anybody that I can find, can justify a publick resolution to the detriment of a kingdom'.[77] Sir Richard Cox, on the other hand, thought 'the doctrine was false, and unseasonably published, and would have ill consequences'.[78] But another of Molyneux's close friends, St George Ashe, was in full agreement with his arguments, and praised him for having the courage to maintain them in public.[79]

Although *The Case of Ireland* is in size little more than a pamphlet, its long-term influence is difficult to overestimate. It provided one of the first public and articulate expressions of that peculiar 'patriot' movement, which, loyal to the crown, although inexorably opposed to the unenlightened policies of successive English governments, was neither separatist nor fundamentally anti-British, and which was to achieve a striking, if diffuse, exposition in the writings of Jonathan Swift.

In October 1698, when the dispute was at its height, William Molyneux died at Dublin. He was only forty-two years old, and had never enjoyed good health. His death was caused by the aggravation of a kidney complaint from which he had suffered all his life. Locke, when he heard the news, wrote to Thomas Molyneux, 'I have lost, in your brother, not only an ingenious and learned acquaintance, that all the world esteemed; but an intimate and sincere friend, whom I truly loved, and by whom I was truly loved: and what a loss that is, those only can be sensible who know how valuable, and how scarce, a true friend is, and how far to be preferred to all other sorts of treasure.'[80] In his will Molyneux had, with his own hand, inserted a bequest of five pounds to Locke as a token of his esteem, and had made similar provision for Ashe and Smyth.[81]

William Molyneux had always been the most active member of the Dublin Society, and despite his many other commitments, had been the ablest and probably the most energetic Irish scientist of his day. His early death 'was heartily lamented by all lovers of learning',[82] who had good cause for grief, for it had removed from the contemporary Irish scientific scene the catalyst which for so long had provoked others into playing an active part in the 'advancement of learning'. A noticeable decline becomes apparent almost immediately after his death. In 1698 four papers by ex-members of the society appeared in the *Philosophical Transactions*; throughout the period from 1699 to 1706 only three such articles, all of them by Thomas Molyneux, were so published.

William King maintained an interest in natural philosophy for a few years, but his situation in Derry isolated him from instruments, books, and like-minded friends. He occasionally wrote to Mark Baggot in Dublin, asking him to buy, among other things, a portable barometer, Kersey's *Algebra*, and De la Hire's *Conicks*.[83] Baggot had as a Catholic been expelled from his estates and was living in Dublin so that he might petition their restitution. King, while convinced that 'Papists should be debarred all public trust', thought it wrong 'to take away men's estates, liberties, or lives, merely because they differ in estimate of religion'.[84] He gave Baggot what help he could. But the granting in 1705 of permission to carry sword, gun, and pistols, can hardly be regarded as adequate compensation for the loss of the extensive Baggot lands in County Carlow.[85]

Sir Richard Bulkeley, on the other hand, had recently inherited a large fortune, and was eager to promote learning in Ireland. In 1699 he was prepared to give an annual sum of £420 towards the establishment of a new university to be built near Dunlavan. He hoped that discipline would be 'most strict' in the new foundation, believing it 'to be the life of a society that consists of subordinate ranks'.[86] The scheme came to nothing, and although Bulkeley maintained a desultory connection with the Royal Society,[87] he was soon devoting his fortune to the cause of an obscure French religious sect led by one Abraham Whitterow who specialized in prophecy and the more obviously physical manifestations of the almighty.[88] Bulkeley wanted to sell his estate and give the proceeds to Whitterow, but was prevented by the Chancery Court's declaring him *non compos*.[89]

St George Ashe, like King, was trying to conduct scientific

research in a part of the country hardly suited to such an undertaking. When, early in 1701, King had promised to call at Clogher on his way back from Dublin, Ashe at once wrote asking him not to forget to bring with him the 'latest mercuries, both French and English, and other new books'.[90] Almost exactly a year later Ashe was in London, where he met his old friends George Tollet and Edmond Halley, 'and they had among them a deal of learned chat'.[91] Nor did Archbishop Marsh entirely abandon his earlier interests; a notebook of his contains a number of mathematical problems dating from 1703 and including 'What force is sufficient to cast a body from the earth, perpendicularly upward, so as it never may returne again?' and 'What number besides 1, has 1 for its cube?'[92]

Thomas Molyneux was however alone in keeping up a regular correspondence with the Royal Society. In April 1699 Sloane asked him to send to London any 'account you hear or meet with that is curious', and three years later presented Molyneux with a copy of Luigi Ferdinando Marsigli's *Danubialis Operis Prodromus* (Nürnberg, 1700) as well as the *Philosophical Transactions* for recent years.[93] Molyneux's interests at this time were however becoming more and more divorced from that sort of science which had been the main concern of the Dublin Society. The two papers which he wrote in response to Sloane's requests deal respectively with giants and with 'the ancient Greek or Roman lyre'.[94] The former harks back to his earlier discussion of the large antlers found in Ireland, and its combination of sceptical intent and 'curious' content, bears all the marks of a well-filled, if inadequately organized, imagination, while the latter is an exercise in semantics rather than in natural philosophy.

The one really important scientific event of this period was the tour of Ireland made by the great Welsh naturalist and antiquary Edward Lhuyd. Lhuyd had already been to Ireland for a short visit in the late 1680s, when he had met William and Thomas Molyneux, and had talked with them 'about a natural history of Ireland'.[95] But at the time he had only remained in Dublin for a few weeks, and the project had come to nothing. Subsequently Thomas Molyneux, while in exile at Chester in 1689, had written to him on botanical matters and especially the recent publication of John Ray's *Fasiculus Stirpium Britanni-*

carum (London, 1688).[96] Lhuyd had been trained as a botanist by Robert Plot, but had later allowed his interests to spread over a far wider field. As a geologist he supported a rather peculiar fossil theory, believing that 'formed stones' grow in the earth out of seeds dispersed by vapours from the sea.[97] An extremely poor man, Lhuyd had hoped that the virtuosi at Dublin, on whose behalf Owen Lloyd had invited his 'correspondence in all chapters of natural history',[98] would pay him to come to Ireland. For, as he told Martin Lister, his own commitments in the matter had been made 'onely on supposition that the provost of the college at Dublin, Sir R. Bulkeley, Dr Mollineux, etc., would invite me to it and ensure me present maintenance for travelling, with what further encouragement would seem requisit'.[99] Eventually he proposed the sum of sixty pounds to cover the expenses of the undertaking, but William Molyneux quickly informed him that it would be impossible to raise so large an amount of money in Ireland.[100]

After this initial rebuff Lhuyd temporarily abandoned his Irish plans and turned instead to his native Wales. In 1695 he issued an appeal for money to enable him to write the natural history of that country in imitation of Plot's descriptions of Oxfordshire and Staffordshire. But the appeal was only partially successful and work on the project slow and uneven.[101] Despairing of any real progress in Wales, and in order to escape the angry demands of exasperated creditors, Lhuyd decided in 1698 to go to Ireland some time in the following year. He therefore sent printed sheets of queries to Thomas Molyneux, with the request that they be distributed to persons with a knowledge of natural history.[102] Molyneux promised to do this, but regretted that 'there is scarce any one here that has any insighte into that pleasant and useful parte' of learning, and that, although at one time he himself had hoped to undertake 'such sort of inquiryes', the 'constant attendance on the business' of his profession, left him little time for other studies.[103]

Eventually Lhuyd, together with two student assistants from Oxford, crossed over to Ireland in August 1699.[104] After spending three days in Dublin, where he met Thomas Molyneux and Ashe, he started for the Giant's Causeway by way of Tara, New Grange, Armagh, and Lisburn, in which last he encountered another ex-member of the society, Edward Smyth, who, some months earlier, had been elevated to the see of Down and Connor. Late in 1699 he went to Scotland for a few months, but returned for a longer stay the following January, having brought with him two books by the noted Scottish antiquary Sir Robert Sibbald, whom he had met and who had given him the volumes as presents for the Irish virtuosi.[105] Lhuyd's pre-occupations on this tour were almost equally divided between archaeological, botanical, geological, and philological matters, and a long letter to Thomas Molyneux includes descriptions of New Grange, which he thought 'a place for sacrifice used by the old Irish', the famous Celtic crosses at Monasterboice, and of large numbers of plants and minerals, some of them new to contemporary science.[106]

While in Ireland Lhuyd made a point of visiting any Gaelic scholar he could find. In May he travelled to Longford and called on 'one Teague O'Roddy . . . an excellent Irish anti-quary' and recorded how that gentleman received him 'civilly, and has promised his solution to some queries I left with him'.[107] O'Roddy was already known to the Dublin Society, having written a description of County Leitrim for William Moly-neux's ill-fated contribution to the *English Atlas* of 1683.[108] According to himself he had a vast collection of 'Irish books of philosophy, physicke, poetry, genealogys, mathematicke, in-vasions, law, romance, etc., . . . as ancient as any in Ireland'.[109] But Lhuyd found nothing remarkable among these much-vaunted treasures. Shortly before leaving Ireland he went to Galway in order to meet Roderic O'Flaherty, probably the last of the great Gaelic scholars, who fourteen years earlier had published his *Ogygia seu Rerum Hibernicarum Chronologia* (London, 1685), which treated of the history of Ireland from the earliest times to 1684, and included chrono-genealogical catalogues of the kings of England, Scotland, and Ireland to the reign of Charles II. Although Thomas Molyneux claimed with some justice that O'Flaherty 'busied himself little in real anti-quities, . . . but chiefly' spent his time 'in the inquiry into . . . fabulous history',[110] Lhuyd found him so knowledgeable that he maintained a correspondence with Galway until shortly before his death. O'Flaherty was at this time extremely poor, and as he could not afford to send letters direct to Oxford, he addressed them to Molyneux at Dublin, who then forwarded them at his own expense. Between 1702 and 1708 O'Flaherty wrote at least thirty letters to Lhuyd, whose replies have not however been preserved.[111]

Little of scientific importance was undertaken in the years immediately following Lhuyd's departure from Ireland in the Spring of 1700. Many of those who had been members of the Dublin Society were now dispersed throughout the country, and thus found it impossible to produce any work of a cooperative nature. William Molyneux, Foley, Mullen, and Willoughby were dead; Tollet and Huntington in England; Smyth at Lisburn; Ashe at Clogher; and after 1702 Marsh spent some periods of time at Armagh. King, too, until 1703, was often in Derry. Only Thomas Molyneux preserved links with the Royal Society. He continued to subscribe to the *Philosophical Transactions* and sent occasional reports to Lhuyd on his botanical and antiquarian researches. He tried to further Lhuyd's interest in Celtic philology, and in 1702 offered to lend him Marsh's manuscript copy of Richard Plunket's Irish–Latin Dictionary, while admitting that 'there is not any of the youth in our college, that I can hear of, that understands writing the Irish character'.[112] None the less he himself was 'every day more convinced that the Irish tongue is but a dialect or corruption of the old British'. Molyneux was however by then an isolated figure, and the overall situation was not to change until 1707, when his nephew Samuel refounded the Dublin Society for the second and last time.

IV. THE SOCIETY OF SAMUEL MOLYNEUX

William Molyneux had begun a family tradition, and his interest in natural philosophy was inherited by his only son. Samuel Molyneux was born in 1689, and because of his father's early death was adopted and educated by his uncle, by then already a fashionable and wealthy Dublin physician. He entered Trinity College in 1705 at the age of sixteen, and took his B.A. degree three years later. While at the university Molyneux had the good fortune to receive private tuition from George Berkeley, who had recently been elected a fellow and was soon to become a close friend. In 1707 Berkeley dedicated his *Miscellanea Mathematica* to 'Egregio adolescenti D. Samueli

Molyneux, in Academia Dubliniensi sociorum commensali, filio viri clarissimi Gulielmi Molyneux, paucis abhinc annis acerbo, tam patriae quam rei literariae, fato denati.'[113] He praised his pupil for studying sound philosophy and mathematics, and predicted that these intellectual abilities would certainly make him 'one of the great ornaments of the rising age'.

About this time, although still only a fellow commoner, Molyneux became convinced of the necessity of refounding the Dublin Society. He was already deeply interested in natural philosophy and was beginning to buy instruments with which to conduct experiments in physics, chemistry, and physiology. He had of course inherited a large collection of laboratory apparatus from his father, but had found a number of important items lacking. Accordingly in January 1707 he wrote to Francis Hawksbee, the noted London instrument maker, ordering an air-pump of the 'largest and best sort', and describing in detail the various special modifications that were to be made before the engine was despatched to Dublin.[114] It arrived during the following month at a cost of £26 8s. od., together with a letter from Hawksbee regretting his inability to adapt the instrument for use in the giving of 'anatomical injections'. This, he said, would require a separate machine costing not less than £6.[115]

About this time Molyneux was also concerned with the publication by Awnsham Churchill of his father's correspondence with Locke. Churchill wrote to him in March 1707 requesting permission to copy any letters in Molyneux's possession.[116] He was soon in receipt of the originals, and the volume in question eventually appeared under the title *Some Familiar Letters between Mr Locke and Several of his Friends* (London, 1708). As a result of these communications, Molyneux began to use Churchill as his London agent and ordered from him books not readily available in Ireland. In December 1707, for example, he asked for information about 'the many new and good books that are expected from the press', and especially Flamsteed's *Historia Coelestis*, which had begun printing in 1706 but was not to appear until 1712, and the impending reissue of John Harris's *Lexicon Technicum* (2d ed., London, 1708), while he actually ordered a copy of Newton's recent *Arithmetica Universalis* (Cambridge, 1707).[117] It was through Churchill that

Molyneux first contacted the English scientist William Derham in the Summer of 1707.[118] He had read Derham's account of a 'pyramidal appearance in the heavens' published in the *Philosophical Transactions*, and having noted the same phenomenon in Dublin, communicated his observations to Derham.[119] He also enclosed an account of the sun spots seen in Ireland in 1704 and a description of the lunar eclipse of 6 April 1707. Derham replied two months later, thanking Molyneux for his interest and asking him to commence regular meteorological observations in Ireland similar to those then being undertaken by fellows of the Royal Society.[120] To this request, Molyneux, who owned a barometer made by the London craftsman John Patrick, readily acceded.[121]

It was in a letter to Derham that Molyneux first announced the renewal of the meetings of the Dublin Society. In September 1707 he wrote:

I presume you must be acquainted with the ingenious Mr Francis Robarts, I believe the news of the revival of the Philosophical Society of Dublin, of which he was once president when in Ireland, will not be unacceptable to him. There has been already four or five meetings, at one of which I had the honour of giving the company a very acceptable entertainment in reading your ingenious letter.[122]

Molyneux was soon writing to the men who had belonged to the earlier societies, asking for their help and encouragement in the advancement of his scientific plans. Ashe wrote from Clogher congratulating Molyneux on having been chosen secretary, and assuring him that he would inherit 'every one' of his 'father's valuable qualities'.[123] Molyneux had in fact reprinted his father's queries for a natural history of Ireland, and had sent some to Ashe with the request that they be distributed among those 'whose leisure and knowledge make them very capable of giving answers'.[124]

While no membership list as such survives for this period of the society's activity, it is certain that the group never became large and was probably restricted to no more than about twenty persons. On 12 November 1707 a council of ten was chosen to regulate the society's affairs.[125] The new president was the Earl of Pembroke, then Lord Lieutenant of Ireland, who, as Molyneux noted, honoured them 'with his presence and protection'.[126] Pembroke, a friend of Swift, was a generous patron of learning, and had already given £500 to Trinity College for the purchase of books.[127] The two vice-presidents (a new office) were Marsh, then Archbishop of Armagh, and King, then Archbishop of Dublin. Besides Molyneux himself, the other officers included his uncle, who acted as curator, Samuel Dopping, the son of Bishop Dopping of Meath and hence Molyneux's cousin, who was appointed treasurer, and Peter Browne, Provost of Trinity College and later author of *The Procedure, Extent, and Limits of Human Understanding* (London, 1728), in which he criticized Locke and Berkeley and argued that man can have no direct knowledge of the nature of divine attributes, though he may have an analogical comprehension of them through revelation. A recently graduated member of the college, John Hawkins, the son of a clergyman, was also a member of the council, as were the eminent Dublin physician, Bryan Robinson, who was later, in his *Treatise of the Animal Economy* (Dublin, 1732), to show some knowledge of the nature of oxygen, and Captain Thomas Burgh, the Irish surveyor-general and architect of the new library at Trinity College begun in 1712. Not the least remarkable aspect of the new society was that men so eminent in public life were prepared to join undergraduates like Molyneux in the task of advancing the study of natural philosophy.

In his rôle as secretary Molyneux was soon writing to all who might be of use to the society. Like his father he was particularly interested in the natural history of his native land, and Ashe was not the only person to receive copies of the society's printed queries. Walter Atkin, Molyneux's old teacher at the university and in 1707 rector of Roxborough near Youghal, was approached in this manner, on account, as Molyneux put it, of 'the pleasure I gratefully remember you to have taken in instructing me in these natural studies while we were together'.[128] Atkin, who possessed an antiquarian turn of mind, sent back to Dublin descriptions of two tombs found near Midleton and his thoughts 'of timber dug up out of boggy moorish ground', which he believed rendered obsolete John Woodward's theory of a universal deluge as set out in *An Essay towards a Natural History of the Earth* (London, 1695, 2nd ed., 1702).[129] Other reports of natural curiosities reached the society from Keogh, a former member, who described a giant's tooth and the rare plants grown in the greenhouses of Sir Arthur Shane near Athlone, and from Archbishop King's former agent in Derry, Charles Norman, whose chief interest was the barnacle found in northern waters and its method of breeding.[130]

The most extensive correspondence of this period is however that between Molyneux and Roderic O'Flaherty. The latter was not of course a scientist, and his letters are concerned chiefly with 'natural curiosities' and his own somewhat dubious historical theories. O'Flaherty devoted much of his time to angling for financial support from the society, which however proved reluctant to part with its funds. Given sufficient encouragement, he could, so Molyneux was informed, extend the work of 'Primate Usher and Sir Ja. Ware, who grounded their dictates delivered to public view on the authentic monuments of their country'. Already he had embarked on the collection of material for a critique of Sir George Mackenzie's objections to the *Ogygia* with the aim of destroying 'romantic stories' as well as 'Dr Stillingfleet's assertions of no Irish letters before St Patrick, no ancient monuments or records'.[131] This work was not, however, to be published during O'Flaherty's lifetime, and eventually appeared as the *Ogygia Vindicated* in 1775. O'Flaherty's influence was not beneficial to a society trying to dispel superstition and establish a rational science. His views were essentially unscientific and unsympathetic even to those of Irish philosophers unwilling entirely to exile the mysterious from the study of human and natural phenomena. 'It is a fault incident to human nature', he once told Molyneux, 'to dote on the curiosities of natural causes and secular science and to be idiots and simpletons in acquiring the supernatural end, whereunto we are created'.[132] In truth, O'Flaherty, then seventy-nine years old, was no longer interested in young men and their ambitions, being more concerned with the possibility of having some of his confiscated lands restored and with obtaining minor government appointments for his many relatives. He declared himself completely destitute, and when Molyneux visited Galway in 1709 he found O'Flaherty 'in a miserable condition', without money, books, health, or even food.[133]

More germane to the real interests of the society was the

renewal of the correspondence with the Royal Society. Already in August 1707 Thomas Molyneux had told Sloane that he was dining regularly with Ashe and Smyth, and that Lord Pembroke, 'a man of great curiosity, reading and judgement', had attended some of their meetings.[134] On hearing of the Irish group's revival, the Royal Society ordered Sloane to respond in the most favourable terms and to ask Samuel Molyneux for copies of papers read at meetings in Dublin. He did so, and promised to send, 'by the first opportunity, the *Transactions* for the last two years', and to defray all postal charges between the two capitals.[135]

Although no minutes have survived for Samuel Molyneux's society, a few of the papers read by its members are still extant. Most of them reflect the tenor of Molyneux's correspondence with O'Flaherty, in that they are concerned largely with the curious and bizarre and exhibit little in the way of scientific discrimination. Ashe reported on 'an odd hare's tooth', a correspondent from the country, Samuel Waring, 'on a strange thunder and lightening', and Thomas Molyneux on 'a petrified honeycomb'.[136] Some pieces do however stand out as sentinels of what might have been had the society survived longer than it did. William King's discussion of the manner of manuring land with sea shells as practised in the north-west of Ireland was a real contribution to agricultural knowledge.[137] He described the methods employed and the results obtained, and concluded that 'some thousands of acres have been improved by the shells, and that which formerly was not worth a groat per acre is now worth four shillings'. In addition Thomas Burgh discussed a proposal for improving Dublin harbour, then still improperly dredged and subject to great tidal variations,[138] while Thomas Molyneux communicated a study of coal mining in Ireland and a description of an engine 'to force water out of a quarrie or the like'.[139]

The most interesting paper was however submitted by the society's most distinguished member, George Berkeley. It is entitled 'Of Infinites', and was delivered at a meeting in November 1707.[140] In it Berkeley was concerned with maintaining a distinction between the concepts of 'infinity' and 'infinite', thus denying the arguments of George Cheyne and Joseph Raphson, who both claimed that it was possible to divide a finite line into infinitesimal parts.[141] To him it was

o

'evidently impossible there should be any such thing, for every line, how minute soever, is still divisible into parts less than itself; therefore there can be no such thing as a line *quavis data minor* or infinitely small'. Dr A. A. Luce, the authority on Berkeley, considers this paper 'to touch the heart' of Berkeley's philosophy, largely because it is 'vitally connected with the massive argument for immaterialism' so central to his beliefs.[142] Berkeley's other contribution to the society's business is a good, accurate, and straightforward description of the famous cave near Dunmore.[143] This had actually been written early in 1706, when Thomas Molyneux had sent a copy to the Royal Society, with the recommendation that its author 'for his years is remarkably curious and a great lover of raritys of all sorts both in art and nature'.[144] But the Royal Society's secretary did not think it worthy of inclusion in the *Philosophical Transactions*.

Archaeology was not completely neglected by the members of the third society, and in November 1707 Thomas Molyneux read a letter he had received from 'a French gentleman in Connaught', who described some urns found by Mr Oliver St George 'entre son château de Hedfort et Schull'.[145] A week later Molyneux was himself informing the society of 'a large stately stone-cross, standing at Munster-Boys near Drog-hedagh', which he thought 'the most antient remain we have of the Christian religion now extant in Ireland'.[146] Thomas Molyneux had always been a competent antiquary, but now his enthusiasm for archaeology became so intense that little time was left for scientific experimentation. Already at Leyden in 1684 he had met a Norwegian scholar who had persuaded him that many of the early Christian remains in Ireland were of Scandinavian origin.[147] Molyneux adopted this theory, and became one of the founders of that eighteenth-century school of archaeology which saw a Viking behind every ruined fortress and every ancient ornament in Ireland. In 1707 he noted 'an old Danish trumpet of bras' near Carrickfergus,[148] and some years later synthesized his ideas in a *Discourse Concerning the Danish Mounts, Forts, and Towers in Ireland* (Dublin, 1726). Molyneux was convinced that he was dispelling ignorance and bringing a sceptical and scientific mind to bear on the study of Irish archaeology. In fact his scepticism made him condemn all traditional views whether false or not. Teague O'Roddy was scornful of Molyneux's theories, which he labelled 'a mere vulgar error. For these forts . . . were entrenchments made by the Irish about their houses'.[149] Here again then is a case in which the attitudes engendered by the new philosophy indiscriminately pushed aside the merits, as well as the falsehoods, of what its proponents thought an out-dated and foolish learning. Scepticism had in some ways become the new superstition.

Not long after Thomas Molyneux's misdirected excursions into archaeology the society began to decline. In August 1708 his nephew told O'Flaherty that no meetings had been held for some time and that he saw little chance of their resuming.[150] The third Dublin Society had lasted for less than a year. It was not a good time for cooperative scientific study. The Royal Society was entering a long period of comparative mediocrity. The Oxford Society had been dead since 1690, and when the German traveller Zacharias von Uffenbach visited the laboratories at Oxford in 1710 he found the equipment broken and everything covered in filth.[151] But the main cause of the Dublin Society's decline lay in Samuel Molyneux's having temporarily lost interest in natural philosophy. In March 1709 he wrote to his cousin Giles Domvile, who had recently abandoned the law in order to study science, 'You will be much surprised when I tell you that of late the tables also are turned with me too. Mathematicks are thrown aside and systems of politicks and government now take place where the whyms of philosophy were of late settled. . . . You will hardly believe so great change can be produc'd in me, and I can hardly believe I ever could have been of another taste.'[152] A few months later Molyneux left Dublin and devoted the next two years to the improvement of the family estate at Castle Dillon. He still kept up a correspondence with Berkeley on metaphysical questions, and especially on the nature of imagination in relation to the existence of material things; Molyneux repeating the arguments of Descartes, while Berkeley still supported Locke's views on the matter.[153]

In 1712 Molyneux left Ireland for London, where he was to spend the remaining years of his life. Shortly after his arrival he visited Francis Hawksbee to watch demonstrations of airpumps and other devices, and then went on to a glass-grinder called Wilson, who sold sets of microscopes for three pounds, which Molyneux considered 'not by any means dear'.[154] In

February 1713 he travelled to Greenwich, where Flamsteed, the quarrel with his father forgotten, showed him the observatory and its rarities.[155] Not long after, Molyneux went to Oxford, where he found, as Uffenbach had done, that the laboratories were in a poor condition and all the instruments broken, with the exception of 'a pretty good quadrant'.[156] A few months later he was sent on a political mission to Hanover by the Duke of Marlborough, and, owing to the deaths of both Queen Anne and the Electress Sophia, was able to accompany George I back to England. In 1715 he became a member of parliament for a west country constituency and was appointed private secretary to the Prince of Wales. Elected a fellow of the Royal Society in 1712 he soon regained his enthusiasm for the study of natural philosophy.

In 1725 Molyneux met the astronomer James Bradley and joined him in a series of observations designed to discover the parallax of fixed stars.[157] For this purpose a special telescope was built at Molyneux's house near Kew by George Graham the London watchmaker. It had glasses fixed in a tube made of strong tin-plate very carefully soldered together, which moved on a horizontal axis at the top of the instrument. The attempt was of course, a failure, for no instrument of the time was capable of performing the task in question. However the two men were able to make measurements on the aberrations of stars, and on that basis calculated that light took 8 minutes 12 seconds to travel from the sun to the earth, the resulting velocity of 318,000 kilometres per second being a remarkably good result.[158] Although Molyneux became a Lord Commissioner of the Admiralty, he still maintained a spasmodic interest in astronomy. Shortly before his death he wrote articles on 'The method of grinding and polishing glasses for telescopes' and on the casting of metals for reflecting instruments.[159] He was particularly anxious that a standard telescope be invented, which could be built by even the most ordinary craftsman, and eventually constructed a prototype, which was presented to King John V of Portugal when on a visit to London.[160]

*   *   *

Samuel Molyneux died at London in 1728 and with him the spirit of the Philosophical Society and the virtuoso scientists who had supported it. Three years later the Royal Dublin Society was founded, and although Thomas Molyneux was among its earliest members, it was inspired by a new and different attitude towards natural philosophy, being set firmly and exclusively on the rocks of utility and technology. Pure science of the kind that had constituted much of the business of the Philosophical Society made little headway during the first half of the eighteenth century, and comparative domestic stability seemed unable to produce scientists of a quality equal to those who had grown out of internal war and rebellion. Pure scientists were obsessed with the necessity of codifying Newtonian ideas. It was at once the age of thin elegance and of Squire Western. The virtuoso was dead.

But the work of the Philosophical Society had established in Ireland the beginnings of a scientific tradition. Its intimate connection with English natural philosophy reflected an increasingly close relationship between the intellectual lives of the two countries. Men like William Molyneux and Ashe, Mullen, and King, drew inspiration directly from English sources. Their influence led the Dublin group to adopt modes of procedure and areas of interest common to the two English scientific societies. Dublin shared with London characteristics of both credulity and scepticism. Like the fellows of the Royal Society the Irish philosophers formed themselves, not into a closely organized and rigorously rational scientific society, but into something more like a club for gentlemen of means and intelligence. In their breadth of interest, based as much on an eclectic curiosity as on the more strictly formulated and abstract speculation of men like Newton, they were typical of the mass of contemporary scientists both in England and on the continent. They produced justifications for their work drawn from writers like Bacon which often bore small relation to reality. They were in religious outlook closely bound to the dominant school within the Anglican Church and exhibited few theological unorthodoxies, whether puritan or otherwise. But when all is said and done, when all possible criticisms of their often dilettante and sometimes naïve proceedings have been made, it must be allowed that their work introduced into Ireland a spirit of sceptical enquiry such as that country had not hitherto experienced.

Appendix A

Whereas there is an accurate Account and Description of Ireland designed to be made Publick in the *English Atlas* undertaken by *Moses Pitt* of *London,* and in Order thereto, some Gentlemen in *Dublin* have agreed to meet weekly for reviewing such an Account, as shall from time to time come from under the Pen of Mr *William Molyneux,* as also to bring in some Materials to the said Description; This is earnestly to entreat all Persons that they would be pleased freely to communicate their Answers to these following Quaeries, or any of them, Directing them to Mr *William Molyneux* nigh *Ormonds Gate* in *Dublin,* or to any other of their Acquaintance in *Dublin* that may Communicate to them the said Mr *Molyneux,* not forgetting to specifie in their Letters the place of their Habitation that they may be again written to if Occasion requires.

Quaeries to which Answers are Desired for the Illustration of that part of the *English Atlas* relating to Ireland.

1 The nature of the Soyl of the County, or place, and the Chief Product thereof.

2 What Plants, Animals, Fruits, Mettals, or other Natural Productions there are peculiar to the Place, and how Order'd?

3 What Springs, and Rivers, or Loughs, with the various Properties thereof, as whether Medicinal, how replenish'd with Fish, whether Navigable, Rapid, or Slow, etc.

4 What Curiosities of Art, or Nature, or Antiquity are or have bin found there?

5 What Ports for Shipping, and their Description, and what Moon causes High Water?

6 What great Battels have been there fought, or any other Memorable Action, or Accident?

7 What peculiar Customs, Manners, or Dispositions the Inhabitants of each County, or Town have among them?

8 How each County is Inhabited, thickly or thinly?

9 What Places give, or formerly have given Title to any

Noble-Man; as also what Antient Seats of Noble Families
are to be met with?

10 What Towns of Note in the County, and especially Towns
Corporate?

11 The names of such Towns both Antique and Modern,
English and *Irish*, and why so called?

12 The Magistracy of Towns Corporate, and when Incorporated, and by whom built, with their return of Parliament Men?

13 Trade of the Town, with the number of Houses, and Inhabitants, and manner of Buildings.

14 What Publick, or Antique Buildings?

15 What Synods have been held there, what Monasteries,
Cathedral, or other Churches are or have been there, and
from what Saint named?

16 In what Bishoprick each County or any part thereof is?

This Paper may be had *Gratis* at the Shop of Mr *Dudley Davis*
Bookseller over against the *Rose Tavern* in *Castle Street, Dublin*;
Where is to be sold The Antient Usage in bearing Ensigns of
Honour as are called Arms, with a Catalogue of the Present
Nobility and Baronets of *England, Scotland*, and *Ireland* By Sir
William Dugdale Knight, Garter Principle King at Arms. And
by *Moses Pitt* at the *Angel* in St *Pauls* Church-yard *London*.

It's Desired that Answers to these Queries may be given as to
any other Country whatsoever.

Appendix B

1 That they chiefly apply themselves to the making of experiments, and prefer the same to the best discourses, letters and books they can make or read, even concerning experiments.

2 That they do not contemn and neglect common, trivial, and cheap experiments and observations; not contenting themselves without such, as may surprise and astonish the vulgar.

3 That they provide themselves with rules of number, weight and measure; not only how to measure the plus and minus of the qualities and schemes of matter; but to measure and compute such qualities and schemes in their exact proportions with scales and tables with which they are to provide themselves.

4 That they divide and analyze matters into their intergral parts, and comput the proportion which one part bears to another.

5 That they be ready with instruments and other apparatus to make such observations as do rarely offer themselves and do depend upon taking opportunitie.

6 That they provide themselves with correspondents in several places, and make such observations as do depend upon the comparison of many experiments, and not upon single and solitary remarks.

7 That they be ready to entertain strangers and persons of quality.

8 That they carefully compute their ability to defray the charge of ordinary experiments, forty times per annum, out of their weekly contributions, and to procure the assistance of benefactors for what shall be extraordinary, and not pester the society with useless and troublesome members for the lucre of their pecuniary contribution.

9 That whoever makes experiments at the public charge do first ask leave for the same.

10 That the secretary do neither write nor receive any letters

on the public account of the society, but what he communicateth to the society.

11 That persons (though not of the society) may be assisted by the society to make experiments at their charge upon leave granted.

12 That for want of experiments, there shall be a review and a rehersal of experiments formerly made.

13 That the president at the presenting meeting shall order what experiments shall be tried at the following meeting, that accordingly a fit apparatus may be tried for it.

Appendix C

Dr St George Ashe, Provost of the Colledge
Dr John Baxton
Lord Blessington
Mr James Bonnell
Sir Rich. Bulkeley Bt.
John Bulkeley
Captain Wm. Bourke
Mr Carre
Mr Justice Coote
Sir Rich. Cox
Francis Cuffe
Wm. Duncomb
Patr. Dun M.D.
Nem. Donelay
Jo. Evelyn [Junior]
Dr Sim. Digby, Lord Bishop of Elphin
Henry Fernly
Charles Gwithers M.D.
Sir Jo. Hely, Chief Baron of the Exchequer
R. Howard
Lord Bishop of Kildare [William Moreton]
Sir Jo. Ivory
Dr Wm. King, Lord Bishop of Derry
Earl of Longford
Mr Owen Lloyd
Dr Narc. Marsh, Lord Archbishop of Cashel
Jo. Madden M.D.
Tho. Molyneux M.D.
Wm. Molyneux
Dr Wm. Pallisar, Lord Bishop of Cloyne
Mr Petty
Mr Benjamin Pratt
Mr Hen. Price, Dean of Cashel
Mr Hen. Prescott
Edw. Pearce

Mr Rich. Reader
Francis Robarts
Bennet Scroggs D.D.
Mr John Robarts
Arth. Shane
Lord Shelbourn
Mr Rob
Geo. Tollet
Bartholemew van Homrigh
Dr Jo. Vesey, Lord Archbishop of Tuam
Edw. Walkington
Charles Willoughby M.D.
Dr Edw. Wetenhall, Lord Bishop of Cork
Sir Cyrill Wych, One of the Lords Justice of Ireland: President

Appendix D

A COMPARISON OF THE WORK OF THE SOCIETIES
AT DUBLIN, OXFORD, AND LONDON, 1684–6

In this appendix a numerative comparison is made of the type of work performed in 1684, 1685, and 1686, at the meetings of the Royal, Oxford, and Dublin Societies. It is based on the minutes of the three societies, which have been studied from the following sources:

The Royal Society: Thomas Birch, *The History of the Royal Society*, 4 vols. (London, 1756–7), IV, 244–516.

The Oxford Society: R. T. Gunther, *Early Science in Oxford*, 14 vols. (Oxford, 1923–45), IV, 29–196.

The Dublin Society: B.M. Add. MS 4811, ff. 160–80v, and R.S. MS Early Letters, S.1.135.

Each mention in the minutes of a particular subject (e.g. geology, agriculture, etc.), is counted as one unit. For the years in question the units for each of the fifteen particular and three general headings used have been added together, and then expressed in the form of a percentage of the total work for each year. All figures given are therefore percentages. Thus in the year 1684, 10·2% of the Dublin Society's activities were devoted to mathematics, the comparable figures for the Royal and Oxford Societies being 5·2% and 2·8% respectively. In addition, the Subject column has been divided into three main sections. The first (reading from the top of the page downwards) is confined to what might broadly be called science, the second to technology, and the third to subjects which cannot be included under either of these headings. Each main section is separately totalled. The average figure for each society over the whole of the three year period is also given. Some of the subject headings are necessarily broad in scope, although a separate heading for magnetical work has been included because of the relatively large amount of time devoted to this topic by all three groups. Any reference in the minutes which deals with two or more of the listed subjects has provided one unit for each of the headings involved.

SUBJECTS	1684 Dublin	1684 Oxford	1684 London	1685 Dublin	1685 Oxford	1685 London
Medicine	20·5	14·1	14·3	26·5	26·2	19·8
Chemistry	14·9	18·8	14·8	12·5	11·4	16·9
Biological Sciences	3·9	12·5	12·3	10·2	16·2	15·7
Physics	5·0	3·8	8·0	2·4	3·8	4·5
Magnetism	4·0	6·0	8·6	0·0	1·8	1·3
Mathematics	10·2	2·8	5·2	1·5	6·2	4·8
Astronomy	7·0	5·3	4·4	3·1	3·3	4·4
Meteorology	5·0	10·9	7·2	9·3	6·2	6·1
Geography	1·9	4·1	1·3	0·0	0·0	3·2
Geology	4·5	5·5	6·1	3·1	1·8	5·2
Others	1·3	0·0	0·6	0·8	1·3	1·6
TOTALS	78·2	83·8	82·8	69·4	78·2	83·5
Land Transport	3·2	1·0	2·0	2·4	1·8	2·3
Navigation	2·6	2·3	4·4	2·4	2·5	2·6
Military Technology	2·0	0·0	1·5	7·0	1·8	1·9
Agriculture	0·7	1·4	0·6	2·4	1·3	0·7
Others	6·3	5·5	3·5	7·8	6·2	4·4
TOTALS	14·8	10·2	12·0	22·0	13·6	11·9
Philology	0·7	0·0	0·0	0·8	1·3	0·7
Other Miscellaneous	6·3	6·0	5·2	7·8	6·9	3·9
TOTALS	7·0	6·0	5·2	8·6	8·2	4·6

SUBJECTS	1686 Dublin	1686 Oxford	1686 London	Average Dublin	Average Oxford	Average London
Medicine	21·9	28·1	13·6	23·0	22·8	15·9
Chemistry	4·6	5·8	12·8	10·7	12·0	14·8
Biological Sciences	4·6	10·7	11·7	6·2	13·1	13·2
Physics	4·9	5·8	7·1	4·1	4·5	6·5
Magnetism	2·0	0·0	1·2	2·0	2·6	3·7
Mathematics	10·3	6·8	3·7	7·3	5·3	4·7
Astronomy	8·0	6·8	5·9	6·0	5·2	4·9
Meteorology	13·7	6·8	8·5	9·3	8·0	7·3
Geography	4·9	2·9	2·4	2·3	2·3	2·3
Geology	1·2	4·8	6·6	3·0	4·0	5·9
Others	2·4	0·0	1·1	1·5	0·4	1·1
TOTALS	78·5	78·5	74·6	75·4	80·2	80·3
Land Transport	1·2	0·0	0·0	2·3	0·9	1·5
Navigation	5·9	1·0	5·7	3·6	1·9	4·2
Military Technology	2·3	1·0	5·9	3·8	0·9	3·1
Agriculture	1·2	2·0	0·0	1·3	1·6	0·4
Others	7·1	6·8	5·9	6·9	6·2	4·6
TOTALS	17·7	10·8	17·5	17·9	11·5	13·8
Philology	0·0	1·0	1·6	0·6	0·8	0·8
Other Miscellaneous	3·8	9·7	6·3	6·1	7·5	5·1
TOTALS	3·8	10·7	7·9	6·7	8·3	5·9

The method used in the above table has obvious limitations. For example, a lengthy description of a series of complex chemical experiments provides only one chemical unit, while a two line account of a simple mathematical problem equally counts as one mathematical unit. Again, the measure is merely a quantitative one, and does not differentiate between work of a high and of a low quality, and at times the divisions adopted imply a greater degree of subject definition than was in fact the case. The results obtained are therefore crude, and should be treated with extreme caution.

The immediate conclusion suggested is that the three societies shared the same sort of interests, and this supports the view set out in Chapter 5. The figures for individual years do sometimes differ fairly substantially, but those for the whole of the three year period are, by and large, remarkably similar. Medicine is one of the few exceptions, and it is surprising that the Royal Society, which had a proportionately larger medical membership than the Irish group, should have devoted less of its time to that subject. But as regards the biological sciences London was ahead of Dublin, and in the seventeenth century these were really quasi-medical disciplines. If therefore the average figures for medicine and biology at London and Dublin are added together, the difference between the totals is a mere o·1%.

Robert K. Merton has made a study of the minutes of the Royal Society for the year 1686, and has concluded that 57·3% of the activities of that society were devoted to work 'related to socio-economic needs'.[1] Now my Royal Society figure for technological research for 1686 is 17·5%. This, I feel, is more indicative of the real situation as regards 'useful' work. Merton has presumably included in this category anything with even the vaguest practical implications, whereas I have tried to confine it to work with a direct and obvious technological bias. I would therefore suggest that the societies' oft-repeated declarations of an ingenuous Baconianism must be treated with more reserve than has sometimes been the case.

Appendix E

The only scientific societies to achieve any sort of permanence in the British Isles during the late seventeenth century were the groups at London, Oxford, and Dublin. It is surprising that Cambridge, the home of Barrow and Newton, did not produce a group similar to that which flourished seventy miles to the south-west at Oxford. An attempt to found 'a philosophick meeting' was made at Cambridge about 1684, and among those involved were the Platonist Henry More and Charles Montagu, the future Earl of Halifax.[1] Newton had also been approached, but, as he told Francis Aston, 'that which chiefly dasht the buisiness was the want of persons willing to try experiments'.[2] He himself was only prepared to take part in a scientific meeting on the understanding that it would not interfere with his other work, an attitude hardly conducive to the success of the project. Perhaps if John Wilkins had not been deprived of the mastership of Trinity College in 1660, Cambridge might have shown greater enthusiasm for the establishment of a philosophical society twenty years later. As it was the scheme came to nothing.

In 1670 a proposal to place on a firmer basis 'a philosophical correspondence already begun in the County of Somerset, upon encouragement given from the Royal Society', was made in a short anonymous pamphlet published in London.[3] The headquarters were to be at Bristol, but persons living in any part of the county were to be allowed to take part. But the Bristol Society existed only in print, and the difficulties of carrying on such an undertaking throughout a large and mostly rural area obviously proved too great.

The most serious attempts to establish additional scientific societies were made in Scotland. In July 1684 the Dublin group learned from William Musgrave that 'we have now great hopes of a society in Scotland; 'tis our desire that learning may be advanc't by a joynt force'.[4] The Oxford Society was already in regular correspondence with members of King's College,

Aberdeen, and of the Colleges of St Salvator and St Leonard in the University of St Andrews.

Dr George Middleton, Principal of King's College, was certain that at Aberdeen there were many willing 'to apply themselves to the enquiries of nature' and 'to joyne ... in some settled way of corresponding together'.[5] The Oxford Society was asked to help by giving encouragement and detailed advice concerning the constitution and organization of a scientific society. Dr George Garden, also of Aberdeen, was convinced that 'There is certainly nothing could more tend to the promoting of our knowledge in the history of nature than the setling of many such societies throughout the learned world, and their maintaining of a mutuall correspondence, which is free of all the impossibilities of the L. Verulam's one great colledge, and may answer all its designs'.[6]

From St Andrews, where a short-lived university observatory had been established in 1670, the Provost of St Salvator's, Dr Skene, expressed the feelings of his college, when he declared that they all supported 'the real and experimental philosophie', and were eager to start a society.[7] Like William Molyneux, however, he felt that, while the new science deserved full support, this should be done 'without disparaging Aristotle, to whom ... the world ows very much for what he did toward the advancment of learning'. At St Leonard's College a correspondent described how 'solemne dispute in devine and philosophick arguments, goe on every moneth very briskly'.[8] By 1705 a regular meeting was taking place in Edinburgh, at which scientific affairs were discussed and plans drawn up for a library, a museum, and a botanical garden.[9] It does not however seem to have continued for very long.

P

Bibliography

A. GUIDES TO SOURCES

Abbott, T. K., *Catalogue of the Manuscripts in the Library of Trinity College Dublin*, Dublin, 1900.

Alden, J., *Bibliographica Hibernica: Additions and Corrections to Wing*, Charlottesville, 1955.

British Museum, Catalogues of the Sloane and Lansdowne Collections and of Additions to the Manuscripts.

Church, A., *The Royal Society: Some Account of the Classified Papers in the Archives*, Oxford, 1907. Contains an index to the manuscript catalogue of the Classified Papers kept in the Library of the Royal Society.

Dix, E. R. McC., *Catalogue of Early Dublin Printed Books 1601–1700*, 5 Parts, Dublin, 1897–1912.

Eager, A. R., *A Guide to Irish Bibliographical Material, Being a Bibliography of Irish Bibliographies and some Sources of Information*, London, 1964.

Halliwell, J. O., *A Catalogue of the Miscellaneous Manuscripts preserved in the Library of the Royal Society*, London, 1840. Contains W. E. Shukard's catalogue of the Royal Society's collection of Early Letters.

Hayes, R. J., *Manuscript Sources for the History of Irish Civilization*, 11 vols., Boston, 1965.

Hunt, R. W., *A Summary Catalogue of the Western Manuscripts in the Bodleian*

Library at Oxford which have not hitherto been catalogued in the Quarto Series, 7 vols., Oxford, 1922–53.

Labrousse, E., *Inventaire Critique de la Correspondance de Pierre Bayle*, Paris, 1961.

Public Record Office of Ireland, *Fifty-Seventh Report of the Deputy Keeper of the Public Records and Keeper of the State Papers in Ireland*, Dublin, 1936.

Royal Irish Academy, 'Catalogues of the Haliday Pamphlets and Tracts' (Manuscript).

Scott, J. R. and White, N. J. D., *Catalogue of the Manuscripts remaining in Marsh's Library Dublin*, Dublin, 1913.

Southampton Public Libraries Committee, *A Catalogue of the Pitt Collection*, Southampton, 1964.

Wing, D., *Short-Title Catalogue of Books printed in England, Scotland, Ireland, Wales, and British America and of English Books printed in other Countries 1641–1700*, 3 vols., New York, 1945.

B. ORIGINAL SOURCES

i. Manuscript Material

DENMARK

Copenhagen

Kongelige Bibliotek

MS Thott. 1208 b-c 4°, Letters from members of the Dublin Society to Pierre Bayle.

ENGLAND

Calne, Wiltshire

Bowood House

Lansdowne MSS. Box labelled 'Royal Society etc.' Contains Petty's statistical table of students at Trinity College Dublin, 1661–81.

Cambridge

Trinity College Library

MS R.4.45. Papers and Letters of the Oxford Society, including letters etc. from Dublin. A companion volume to Bodl. MSS Ashmole 1810–1813, and mostly printed in R. T. Gunther, *Early Science in Oxford*, IV and XII.

University Library

Add. MS 711. Commonplace Book of Anthony Dopping.

London

British Museum

Sloane MS 360. Contains an anonymous satirical poem on Petty's Double-Bottom, c. 1663.

Sloane MS 427. Contains a letter from Miles Symner to Samuel Hartlib.

Sloane MS 1008. Contains letters from William Molyneux to Edmund Borlase.

Sloane MS 1786. Contains a testimonial for Thomas Proby the Surgeon signed by John Madden and Thomas Molyneux, c. 1695.

Sloane MS 3329. Contains a paper on Dublin Harbour read to the Dublin Society by Thomas Burgh in 1707.

Sloane MSS 4036–41, 4044, and 4062. Contain letters from members of the Dublin Society to Hans Sloane.

Add. MS 4223. Contains a short anonymous account of the life of William Molyneux, c. 1730.

Add. MS 4811. Minute and Register Book of the Dublin Society, 1684–93.

Add. MS 4812. Register Book of the Dublin Society, 1707–8.

Add. MS 38856. Contains an unaddressed unsigned letter from Dudley Loftus concerning the Dublin Society, 1684, copy of an item in King's Inns Dublin MS No. 33.

Lansdowne MS 1228. Contains some papers relating to William Petty, 1683–4.

W. Molyneux. *Dioptrica Nova*. London, 1692. Pressmark 537.k.17. Includes important manuscript notes by William Molyneux.

Royal Society Library

Copy Journal Books, vols. 1 to 10. The minutes of the Royal Society, 1660–1710. Those for 1660–87 are printed, with reasonable accuracy, in T. Birch, *History of the Royal Society*.

Early Letters. A collection of letters to the Royal Society in 38 guard-books, including some thirty from members of the Dublin Society.

Classified Papers. A collection of papers in 39 guardbooks, including many by members of the Dublin Society.

Copy Record Books. Contain copies of papers sent to the Royal Society, including some by members of the Dublin Society not in the Classified Papers.

Copy Letter Books. Contain copies of letters to the Royal Society, including some from members of the Dublin Society not in the Early Letters.

Boyle Letters. A collection of letters to, and copies of letters from, Robert Boyle.

Oxford

Bodleian Library

MSS Ashmole 1810–13. Minutes, etc., of the Oxford Society, including letters, papers, and other documents from the Dublin Society. Much of this material is printed in R. T. Gunther, *Early Science in Oxford*, IV and XII.

MSS Ashmole 1816, 1817a, and 1820a. Contain letters and papers by Thomas and William Molyneux, Roderic O'Flaherty, and others.

MSS Bradley 38, 39, and 44. Contain letters and papers by Samuel Molyneux.

MSS Lister 3 and 35–7. Contain letters from Richard Bulkeley to Martin Lister.

MSS Locke c 16 and 18. Contain letters to Locke and an early version of the Molyneux Problem.

MS English Letters c 29. Contains letters from St George Ashe to Henry Dodwell.

Southampton

Civic Centre Archives

MS D/M 1/1. The William Molyneux–John Flamsteed correspondence, 1681–90. Unbound letters loosely inserted in a blank volume.

MS D/M 1/2. Letter Book of Samuel Molyneux.

MS D/M 1/3. Fragment of another letter book of Samuel Molyneux.

MS D/M 2/1. Rent Roll of the Molyneux estate at Castle Dillon, c. 1693.

MS D/M 3/1. Account Book of Samuel Molyneux.

MS D/M 4/15. Translations of the Third and Fourth Dialogues of Galileo by William Molyneux.

MS D/M 4/16. Fair copy of MS D/M 4/15.

FRANCE

Bibliothèque Nationale

Fonds Français MS 13050. Contains an unsigned letter in French dated 27 March 1684 to the astronomer Ismael Boulliau mentioning the Dublin Society.

IRELAND

Dublin

King's Inns Library

MS No. 33. Contains copies of articles and letters on the Dublin Society by Dudley Loftus, 1684.

Marsh's Library

MS Z2.2.3. Copy of Narcissus Marsh's Diary.

MS Z2.2.3B. Typescript of MS Z2.2.3.

MSS Z3.1.10 and Z4.2.8(8). Scientific manuscripts transcribed for Mark Baggot.

MS Z4.5.14. Contains a short list of books owned by Dudley Loftus.

Public Record Office of Ireland

Wyche Papers, Lot 158. Letters to Sir Cyril Wyche.

Royal College of Physicians of Ireland

Minute Book, vol. 1. Early minutes of the college.

Royal Irish Academy

MS 12/D/34. A commonplace book containing notes and papers by Narcissus Marsh.

MS 12/W/22. Contains letters by John Keogh, Edward Lhuyd, William Molyneux, and Teague O'Roddy. Originally Phillipps MS 6686.

Trinity College Library

MS D.1.2. Catalogue of the college library compiled c. 1604–20.

MS D.1.3. Catalogue of Archbishop Ussher's library presented to Trinity College, compiled c. 1660.

MS E.4.9. Catalogue of Charles Willoughby's library.

MS F.4.24. Contains a list of members of the Dublin Society in 1693.

MSS I.1.2–3 and I.4.12–19a. The papers of William and Samuel Molyneux. These include draft minutes, letters, papers, and drawings relating to the Dublin Society.

MSS R.2.20–21. College library loan books for 1680s and 1690s.

Lyon MSS. Letters to William King, not bound, but arranged chronologically in boxes.

King Correspondence. Letter Books containing copies of letters by William King.

MS College Entrance Book 1637–1725. This is kept in the Muniment Room of the college.

ITALY

Florence

Biblioteca Nazionale Centrale

MS Cl. VIII Ser. I Tom. I. Contains seven letters from St George Ashe to Antonio Magliabechi, 1690–1.

ii. Printed and Calendared Material

de Beer, E. S. (ed.), *The Diary of John Evelyn*, 6 vols., Oxford, 1955.

Berkeley, E. and D. S. (ed.), *The Reverend John Clayton: A Parson with a Scientific Mind, His Scientific Writings and other Related Papers*, Charlottesville, 1965.

Bernard, J. P., Birch, T., and Lockman, J. (ed.), *A General Dictionary Historical and Critical in which a new and accurate Translation of that of the celebrated Mr Bayle, with the Corrections and Observations printed in the late Edition at Paris, is included*, 10 vols., London, 1734–41. Vol. 8 contains a number of letters from William Molyneux to John Flamsteed which are not in Southampton MS D/M 1/1.

Birch, T. (ed.), *The History of the Royal Society of London for Improving of Natural Knowledge, from its first Rise*, 4 vols., London, 1756–7. Contains the minutes of the Royal Society from 1660 to 1687.

Birch, T. (ed.), *The Works of the Honourable Robert Boyle*, 6 vols., London, 1772.

Bolton, R. (ed.), *A Translation of the Charter and Statutes of Trinity-College, Dublin*, Dublin, 1760.

Caulfield, R. (ed.), *The Autobiography of the Rt Hon Sir Richard Cox*, London and Cork, 1860.

Clark, A. (ed.), *The Life and Times of Anthony à Wood*, 5 vols., Oxford, 1891–1900.

Davis, H. (ed.), *The Prose Works of Jonathan Swift*, 14 vols., Oxford, 1939–68.

Desmaizeaux, P. (ed.), *Lettres de M. Bayle, publiées sur les Originaux*, 3 vols., Amsterdam, 1729.

Deutsche Akademie der Wissenschaften zu Berlin, *Gottfried Wilhelm Leibniz saemtliche Schriften und Briefe*, Erste Reihe (Allgemeiner politischer und historischer Briefwechsel), VI, Berlin, 1957, and VII, Berlin, 1964.

Doble, C. E., Rannie, D. W., and Salter, H. E. (ed.), *Remarks and Collections of Thomas Hearne*, 11 vols., Oxford, 1885–1921.

Dublin University Magazine, XVIII (1841). Contains long extracts from the correspondence between Thomas and William Molyneux while the former was in England and Holland, the originals of which have been lost.

Elrington, C. R. (ed.), *The Whole Works of the Most Reverend James Ussher D.D.*, 17 vols., Dublin, 1864.

Gilbert, J. T. and Lady Gilbert (ed.), *Calendar of Ancient Records of Dublin*, 19 vols., Dublin, 1889–1944.

Gunther, R. T. (ed.), *Early Science in Oxford*, 14 vols., Oxford, 1923–45. Volume 4 contains the minutes and volume 12 the correspondence of the Oxford Society.

Gunther, R. T. (ed.), *Further Correspondence of John Ray*, London, 1928.

Hall, A. R. and M. B. (ed.), *The Correspondence of Henry Oldenburg*, 6 vols. to date, Madison, 1965–.

Harris, W. (ed.), *The Whole Works of Sir James Ware*, 2 vols., Dublin, 1739–46.

Historical Manuscripts Commission

Eleventh Report, Appendix III (1887), Corporation of Southampton.
Fourteenth Report, Appendix II (1894), Portland MSS.
Calendar of Ormonde MSS, Old and New Series, 11 vols., 1895–1920.
Reports on Various Collections, VIII (1913), Clements MSS.
Calendar of Egmont MSS, 3 vols., 1920–23.
Calendar of Downshire MSS, 3 vols., 1924–38.

Hull, C. H. (ed.), *The Economic Writings of Sir William Petty*, 2 vols., Cambridge, 1899.

Irish Manuscripts Commission

Analecta Hibernica, I (1930) and II (1931), Rawlinson MSS.
McNeill, C. (ed.), *Calendar of the Tanner Letters*, Dublin, 1943.
Pender, S. (ed.), *Council Books of the Corporation of Waterford 1662–1700*, Dublin, 1964.

King, C. S. (ed.), *A Great Archbishop of Dublin: William King D.D. 1650–1729*, London, 1908.

Lansdowne, Marquis of (ed.), *The Petty Papers*, 2 vols., London, 1927.

Lansdowne, Marquis of (ed.), *The Petty–Southwell Correspondence*, London, 1928.

Lansdowne, Marquis of (ed.), *The Double-Bottom or Twin-Hulled Ship of Sir William Petty*, Oxford, 1931.

Lascelles, R. (ed.), *Liber Munerum Publicorum Hiberniae ab An. 1152 usque ad 1827*, 5 parts, London, 1824–30.

The Works of John Locke, 10 vols., 11th ed., London, 1812.

Luce, A. A. and Jessop, T. E. (ed.), *The Works of George Berkeley Bishop of Cloyne*, 9 vols., London, 1948–57.

MacPike, E. F. (ed.), *The Correspondence and Papers of Edmond Halley*, Oxford, 1932.

Molyneux, C., *An Account of the Family and Descendants of Sir Thomas Molyneux Kt.*, Evesham, 1820. Contains an autobiography written by William Molyneux in 1694, the original of which has been lost.

Rigaud, S. P. (ed.), *The Miscellaneous Works and Correspondence of the Reverend James Bradley*, Oxford, 1832.

Singer, S. W. (ed.), *The Correspondence of Henry Hyde, Earl of Clarendon*, 2 vols., London, 1828.

Smith, A. (ed.), 'Journey to Connaught by Thomas [sic] Molyneux, 1709', *Miscellany of the Irish Archaeological Society*, I (1846).

Smith, R., *A Compleat System of Opticks*, 2 vols., Cambridge, 1738. Contains some pieces by Samuel Molyneux, the originals of which have been lost.

Société Hollandaise des Sciences, *Œuvres Complètes de Christiaan Huygens*, 22 vols., The Hague, 1888–1950.

Spedding, J., Ellis, R. L., and Heath, D. D. (ed.), *The Works of Francis Bacon*, 7 vols., London, 1857–9.

Tanner, J. R. (ed.), *Private Correspondence and Miscellaneous Papers of Samuel Pepys*, 2 vols., London, 1926.

Todd, J. H. (ed.), 'Autograph Letter of Thady O'Roddy', *Miscellany of the Irish Archaeological Society*, I (1846).

Turnbull, H. W. and Scott, J. F. (ed.), *The Correspondence of Isaac Newton*, 4 vols. to date, Cambridge, 1959–.

Williams, H. (ed.), *The Poems of Jonathan Swift*, 2nd edn., 3 vols., Oxford, 1958.

Williams, H. (ed.), *The Correspondence of Jonathan Swift*, 5 vols., Oxford, 1963–5.

Willoughby, C., 'Observations on the Bills of Mortality and Increase of People in Dublin, 1690', *Proceedings of the Royal Irish Academy*, VI (1856).

C. CONTEMPORARY AND NEARLY CONTEMPORARY WORKS

i. Books

Anonymous, *Some Proposals humbly offered to the Consideration of the Parliament, for the Advancement of Learning*, Dublin, 1707.

Anonymous, *A Catalogue of the Library of the Honble. Samuel Molyneux Deceas'd ... Consisting of many Valuable and Rare Books in Several Languages ... With Several Curious Manuscripts, and all his Mathematical, Optical, and Mechanical Instruments*. London, 1730.

Allen, C., *The Operator for the Teeth, shewing how to Preserve the Teeth and Gums from all Accidents they are subject to*, Dublin, 1686.

Ashe, St G., *A Sermon Preached in Trinity-College Chappell before the University of Dublin January the 9th 1693-4, Being the first Secular Day since its Foundation by Queen Elizabeth*, Dublin, 1694.

Bernard, E., *Catalogi Librorum Manuscriptorum Angliae et Hiberniae*, Oxford, 1697.

Biggs, N., *Mataeotechnia Medicinae Praxews, . . . With an humble Motion for the Reformation of the Universities*, London 1651.

Boate, G., *Irelands Naturall History*, London, 1652.

Boate, G., and Molyneux, T., *A Natural History of Ireland in Three Parts*, Dublin, 1726. This contains, (*a*) A reprint of Boate's *Irelands Naturall History*, (*b*) A selection of papers concerning Ireland taken from the *Philosophical Transactions*, (*c*) T. Molyneux's *Discourse Concerning the Danish Mounts*.

Boyle, R., *Some Considerations touching the Usefulnesse of Experimental Naturall Philosophy*, Oxford, 1663.

Boyle, R., *New Experiments and Observations touching Cold*, 2d edn., London, 1683.

Grew, N., *Museum Regalis Societatis, or a Catalogue and Description of the Natural and Artificial Rarities belonging to the Royal Society*, London, 1681.

Grew, N., *The Anatomy of Plants*, London, 1682.

Hall, J., *An Humble Motion to the Parliament of England Concerning the Advancement of Learning and Reformation of the Universities*, London, 1649.

Hamilton, W., *The Life and Character of James Bonnell Esq.*, Dublin, 1703.

Hearne, W., *An Answer to two Arguments produced by the Learned the Society of the City of Dublin, as their Judgements upon a Thesis relating to the Line of Latitude and the Line of Longitude upon the Terrestrial Globe*, Dublin, 1685.

Hooke, R., *Micrographia: Or some Physiological Descriptions of Minute Bodies made by Magnifying Glasses with Observations and Inquiries thereupon*, London, 1665.

Locke, J., *An Essay concerning Human Understanding*, 2d edn., London, 1694.

Molyneux, S. (Senior), *Practical Problems concerning the Doctrin of Projects*. The only known copy at Trinity College Dublin lacks the title-page.

Molyneux, W. (Trans.), *Six Metaphysical Meditations wherein it is proved that there is a God*, London, 1680. Translated from the Latin of Descartes, with an introduction.

Molyneux, W., *Sciothericum Telescopicum: Or a new Contrivance of adapting a Telescope to an Horizontal Dial for observing the Moment of Time by Day or Night*, Dublin, 1686.

Molyneux, W., *Dioptrica Nova: A Treatise of Dioptricks in Two Parts*, London, 1692.

Molyneux, W., *The Case of Ireland's being bound by Acts of Parliament in England Stated*, Dublin, 1698.

M[ullen], A., *An Anatomical Account of the Elephant accidentally burnt in Dublin on Fryday June 17 in the year 1681: . . . Together with a Relation of new Anatomical Observations in the Eyes of Animals*, London, 1682.

Osborne, H., *A More Exact Way to Delineate the Plot of any Spacious Parcel of*

Land as Baronies, Parishes, and Townlands, as also of Rivers, Harbours, and Loughs, etc., Dublin, 1654.

Parker, S., *A Free and Impartial Censure of the Platonick Philosophie, Being a Letter written to his much Honoured Friend Mr N.B.*, Oxford, 1666.

Petty, W., *The Advice of W.P. to Mr Samuel Hartlib for the Advancement of some particular Parts of Learning*, London, 1648.

Petty, W., *A Declaration concerning the newly invented Art of Double Writing*, London, 1648.

Petty, W., *The Discourse made before the Royal Society the 26 of November 1674 Concerning the Use of Duplicate Proportion*, London, 1674.

Petty, W., *Political Arithmetick*, London, 1690.

Salusbury, T., *Mathematical Collections and Translations*, London, 1661.

Smith, T., *Admodum Reverendi et Doctissimi Viri D. Roberti Huntingtoni*, London, 1704. An English translation of the biographical part of this work can be found in the *Gentleman's Magazine* for 1825.

Sprat, T., *The History of the Royal Society of London*, London, 1667. There is an excellent modern edition of this work with critical apparatus by J. I. Cope and H. W. Jones. St Louis, 1958.

Stubbe, H., *Campanella Revived: Or an Enquiry into the History of the Royal Society*, London, 1670.

Taylor, J., *Via Intelligentiae: A Sermon preached to the University of Dublin, shewing by what Means the Scholars shall become most Learned and most Useful*, London, 1662.

Wallis, J., *A Defense of the Royal Society and the Philosophical Transactions, particularly those of July 1670, in answer to the Cavils of Dr William Holder*, London, 1678.

Whalley, J., *Vox Urani*, Dublin, 1685.

Whalley, J., *Syderus Nuncius*, Dublin, 1686.

Whalley, J., *Mercurius Hibernicus*, Dublin, 1692.

Whalley, J., *Ptolemy's Quadripartite: Or Four Books concerning the Influence of the Stars*, Dublin, 1701.

Whitterow, A., *Warnings of the Eternal Spirit spoken by Abraham Withro, with a Preface by Sir R. Bulkeley*, London, 1709.

ii. Articles by Members of the Dublin Society printed in the Philosophical Transactions *(Short titles only)*

Anonymous

An Extract of the Journal of the Society at Dublin; giving an Account of a Periodical Evacuation of Blood, XV (1685), 989–90.

Ashe, St George

A New and Easy Way of Demonstrating some Propositions in Euclid, XIV (1684), 672–6.

Observations of the Solar Eclipse 2 July 1684 (with William Molyneux), XIV (1684), 749.

Concerning a Girl in Ireland who had several Horns growing on her Body, XV (1685), 1202–4.

On the Extraordinary Effect of the Power of Imagination, XVI (1686), 334.

An Account of an extraordinary Meteor, XIX (1696), 223–4.
On the Effects of the Imagination and the Virtues of Mackenboy, XX
    (1698), 293–4.

Bulkeley, Sir Richard

Concerning a new Sort of Calash, XV (1685), 1028–9.
Concerning the Giant's Causeway, XVII (1693), 708–10.
Concerning the Improvement to be made by Maize, XVII (1693), 938–40.
Concerning the Propagation of Elms by Seed, XVII (1693), 971.

Foley, Samuel

An Account of the Giant's Causeway, XVIII (1694), 170–82. (Written in
    conjunction with Sir Richard Bulkeley and Thomas Molyneux.)

Gwithers, Charles

Discourse of Physiognomy, XVIII (1694), 118–20.

Huntington, Robert

Concerning the Porphyry Pillars in Egypt, XIV (1684), 624–9.

King, William

Of the Bogs and Loughs of Ireland, XV (1685), 948–60.
An Account of the Manner of manuring Land with Sea Shells, XXVI
    (1708), 59–64.

Marsh, Narcissus

An Introductory Essay to the Doctrine of Sounds, XIV (1684), 472–88.

Molyneux, Samuel

A Relation of the strange Effects of Thunder and Lightning, XXVI (1708),
    36–40.

Molyneux, Sir Thomas

Concerning a prodigious *Os Frontis* in the Medicine School at Leyden, XV
    (1685), 880–1.
An Account of a Stone of an extraordinary Bigness spontaneously voided
    through the Urethra by a Woman, XVII (1693), 817–24.
An Historical Account of the late general Coughs and Colds: With some
    Observations on other Epidemic Distempers, XVIII (1694), 105–11.
An Account of a not yet described *Scolopendra Marina*, XIX (1697), 405–12.
Concerning the large Horns frequently found under ground in Ireland, XIX
    (1697), 489–512.
Concerning Swarms of Insects that of late years have much infested some
    Parts of the Province of Connaught, XIX (1697), 741–56.
Some additional Remarks on the extracting the Stone of the Bladder out of
    those of the Female Sex, XX (1698), 11–15.
Some additional Observations on the Giant's Causeway in Ireland, XX
    (1698), 209–23.

A Supplement to the Account of the *Scolopendra Marina*, XXI (1699), 127–9.
A Relation of the cutting an Ivory Bodkin out of the Bladder of a young Woman in Dublin, XXII (1700), 455–9. (Describes the operation performed by Thomas Proby.)
An Essay concerning Giants, XXII (1700), 487–508.
Some Thoughts concerning the ancient Greek and Roman Lyre, and an Explanation of an obscure Passage in one of Horace's Odes, XXIII (1702), 1267–78.

Molyneux, William

Concerning Lough Neagh and its petrifying Qualities, XIV (1684), 552–4.
An Ingenious Retraction of a Part of the Above [concerning Lough Neagh], XIV (1684), 820.
An Account of the Connaught Worm, XV (1685), 876–9.
Concerning a new Hygroscope, XV (1685), 1032–5.
Concerning the Circulation of Blood as seen by the Help of a Microscope in the *Lacerta Aquatica*, XV (1685), 1236–8.
A Discourse on why Bodies dissolved in Menstrua specifically lighter than themselves, swim therein, XVI (1686), 88–93. (See, Some Reflections on this paper by Sir Thomas Molyneux, XVI (1687), 93.)
Why four convex Glasses in a Telescope show Objects erect, XVI (1686), 169–72.
An Account of the Course of the Tides in the Port of Dublin, XVI (1686), 192–3.
Eclipsis Lunae Observata Dublinii Novembris 19, 1686, XVI (1686), 236–7.
Concerning the apparent Magnitude of the Sun and Moon or the apparent Distance of two Stars when nigh the Horizon, XVI (1687), 314–23.
Concerning the Parallax of fixed Stars, XVII (1693), 844–9.
A Demonstration of an Error committed by common Surveyors in comparing the Surveys taken at long Intervals arising from the Variation of the magnetic Needle, XIX (1697), 625–31.
An Account of a moving Bog in Ireland, XIX (1697), 714–16.

Mullen, Allen

Discourse on the Dissection of a monstrous Double Cat, XV (1685), 1135–9.
A Conjecture at the Quantity of Blood in Men, together with an Estimate of the Celerity of its Circulation, XVI (1687), 433–4.
An Account of an Experiment of the Injection of Mercury into the Blood and its ill Effects on the Lungs, XVII (1691), 486–8.
Some Experiments on a black shining Sand brought from Virginia, XVII (1693), 624–6.
Anatomical Observations in the Heads of Fowl, XVII (1693), 711–16.

Petty, Sir William

Experiments to be made relating to Land Carriage, XIV (1684), 666–7.
Some Queries whereby to examine Mineral Waters, XIV (1684), 802–3.
A Miscellaneous Catalogue of mean, cheap, vulgar, and simple Experi-

ments, XV (1685), 849–53. Also published as a separate pamphlet by Joseph Ray, 'Printer to the Dublin Society', of which a copy can be found in Bodl. MS Ashmole 1813, ff. 356–7.

An Extract of two Essays in Political Arithmetic, XVI (1686), 152.

A further Assertion of the Proposition concerning the Magnitude, etc., of London, XVI (1686), 237–40.

What a complete Treatise of Navigation should contain, XVII (1693), 657–9.

Redding, Sir Robert

Concerning Pearl Fishing in the North of Ireland, XVII (1693), 659–64.

Robartes, Francis

A Discourse concerning the musical Notes of the Trumpet and Trumpet-Marine, XVII (1692), 559–63.

An arithmetical Paradox concerning the Chances of Lotteries, XVII (1693), 677–81.

Concerning the Distance of fixed Stars, XVIII (1694), 101–3.

Smyth, Edward

Concerning Lough Neagh, XV (1685), 1108–12.

On a kind of Earth found near Smyrna, XIX (1696), 228–30.

Concerning the Use of Opium among the Turks, XIX (1696), 288–90.

   iii. Articles by Members of the Dublin Society printed in other Journals

Ashe, St George

Account of the horny Girl, *Acta Eruditorum Lipsiae*, (1686).

Molyneux, Sir Thomas

An Essay on Bodies dissolved in a Menstruum, *Nouvelles de la République des Lettres*, II (1684).

Further Reflections on the Same, *Nouvelles de la République des Lettres*, III (1685).

Molyneux, William

The Circulation of the Blood in the Water Newt, *Journal des Sçavans* (15 April 1683).

Solution of a Dioptric Problem, *Bibliothèque Universelle et Historique*, III (1686).

An Account of the Connaught Worm, *Acta Eruditorum Lipsiae*, (1686).

An Account of the Hygroscope, *Acta Eruditorum Lipsiae*, (1686).

Sylvius, Jacobus

An Account of the horny Girl, *Nouvelles de la République des Lettres*, VII (1686).

D. MODERN WORKS

Armytage, W. H. G. 'The Royal Society and the Apothecaries 1660–1722', *Notes and Records of the Royal Society*, XI (1954).

Badcock, A. W. 'Physical Optics at the Royal Society 1660–1800', *British Journal for the History of Science*, I (1962).

Barrett, J., *An Essay on the Earlier Part of the Life of Swift* . . . *to which are subjoined Several Pieces ascribed to Swift*, London, 1808.

Beall, O. T., 'Cotton Mather's early *Curiosa Americana* and the Boston Philosophical Society of 1683', *William and Mary Quarterly*, 3rd Series, XVIII (1961).

Beckett, J. C., 'William King's Administration of the Diocese of Derry 1691–1703', *Irish Historical Studies*, IV (1944).

Beckett, J. C., *Protestant Dissent in Ireland 1687–1780*, London, 1948.

Berry, H. F., 'The Ancient Corporation of Barber-Surgeons or Guild of St Mary Magdalene, Dublin', *Journal of the Royal Society of Antiquaries of Ireland*, XXXIII (1903).

Bluhm, R. K., 'Remarks on the Royal Society's Finances,' *Notes and Records*, XIII (1958).

Boas, M., *Robert Boyle and Seventeenth Century Chemistry*, Cambridge, 1958.

Brooks, E. St J., 'Henry Nicholson: First Lecturer in Botany and the earliest Physic Garden', *Hermathena*, LXXXIV (1954).

Bryant, A., *Samuel Pepys: The Years of Peril*, Cambridge, 1935.

Burtchaell, G. D. and Sadlier, T. V., *Alumni Dublinenses: A Register of Students, Graduates, Professors, and Provosts of Trinity College in the University of Dublin*, 2d edn., Dublin, 1935.

Butlin, R. A., 'The Population of Dublin in the late Seventeenth Century', *Irish Geography*, V (1965).

Cameron, H. C., 'The Last Alchemist', *Notes and Records*, IX (1951).

Campbell, J. L., 'The Tour of Edward Lhuyd in Ireland in 1699 and 1700', *Celtica*, V (1960).

Carter, P. W., 'Edward Lhuyd the Scientist', *Transactions of the Honourable Society of Cymmrodorion*, (1962).

Clark, G., *A History of the Royal College of Physicians of London*, 2 vols., Oxford, 1964–6.

Clokie, H. N., *An Account of the Herbaria of the Department of Botany in the University of Oxford*, Oxford, 1964.

Corcoran, T., *State Policy in Irish Education A.D. 1536 to 1816*, Dublin, 1916.

Corcoran, T., *Education Systems in Ireland from the Close of the Middle Ages*, Dublin, 1928.

Cotton, H., *Fasti Ecclesiae Hibernicae*, 6 vols., Dublin, 1845–78.

Curtis, M., *Oxford and Cambridge in Transition 1558–1642*, Oxford, 1959.

Da Costa Andrade, E. N., 'The Real Character of Bishop Wilkins', *Annals of Science*, I (1936).

Davis, J. W., 'The Molyneux Problem', *Journal of the History of Ideas*, XXI (1960).

Dewhurst, K., 'The Genesis of State Medicine in Ireland', *Irish Journal of Medical Science*, No. 368 (1956).

Dewhurst, K., *Dr Thomas Sydenham 1624–1689*, London, 1966.

Dictionary of National Biography.

Dix, E. R. McC., 'A Dublin Almanack of 1612', *Proceedings of the Royal Irish Academy*, Section C, XXX (1913).

Doolin, W., 'Dublin's Surgeon-Anatomists', *Annals of the Royal College of Surgeons of England*, VIII (1951).

Ehrenpreis, I., *Swift: The Man, His Works, and the Age*, 2 vols. to date, London, 1962–.

Emery, F. V., 'Irish Geography in the Seventeenth Century', *Irish Geography*, III (1958).

'Espinasse, M., *Robert Hooke*, London, 1956.

'Espinasse, M., 'The Decline and Fall of Restoration Science', *Past and Present*, No. 14 (1958).

Evans, E., *Historical and Bibliographical Account of Almanacks, Directories etc. etc. published in Ireland from the Sixteenth Century*, Dublin, 1897.

Fennell, G., *A List of Irish Watch and Clock Makers*, Dublin, 1963.

Ferguson, O. W., *Jonathan Swift and Ireland*, Urbana, Ill., 1962.

Feuer, L. S., *The Scientific Intellectual*, New York, 1963.

Fisch, H., 'The Scientist as Priest: A Note on Robert Boyle's Natural Theology', *Isis*, XLIV (1953).

Fitzmaurice, Lord E., *The Life of Sir William Petty 1623–87 . . . chiefly derived from Private Documents, hitherto unpublished*, London, 1895.

Fleetwood, J., *History of Medicine in Ireland*, Dublin, 1951.

Fraser, A. M., 'The Molyneux Family', *Dublin Historical Record*, XVI (1960).

Gillispie, C. C., 'Physick and Philosophy: A Study of the Influence of the College of Physicians of London upon the Foundation of the Royal Society', *Journal of Modern History*, XIX (1947).

Goblet, Y. M., *La Transformation de la Géographie politique de l'Irlande au XVIIᵉ Siècle*, 2 vols., Paris, 1930.

Graham, E. C., *Optics and Vision: The Background of the Metaphysics of Berkeley*, [Columbia Ph.D.]. Printed, 1929.

Gregory, R. L., *Eye and Brain: The Psychology of Seeing*, London, 1966.

Gwynn, A., 'The Medieval University of St Patrick's, Dublin', *Studies*, XXVII (1938).

Hall, A. R., *Ballistics in the Seventeenth Century*, Cambridge, 1952.

Hall, A. R., *The Scientific Revolution 1500–1800*, 2d edn., London, 1962.

Hall, A. R., *From Galileo to Newton 1630–1720*, London, 1963.

Hall, A. R. and M. B., 'The Intellectual Origins of the Royal Society – London and Oxford', *Notes and Records*, XXIII (1968).

Hartley, H. (ed.), *The Royal Society its Origins and Founders*, London, 1960.

Herity, M., 'From Lhuyd to Coffey: New Information from unpublished Descriptions of the Boyne Valley Tombs', *Studia Hibernica*, No. 7 (1967).

Hill, C., *The Century of Revolution 1603–1714*, London, 1961.

Hill, C., *Intellectual Origins of the English Revolution*, Oxford, 1965.

Hill, C., 'The Intellectual Origins of the Royal Society – London or Oxford?', *Notes and Records*, XXIII (1968).

Hoppen, K. T., 'Queries for a Seventeenth Century Natural History of Ireland', *The Irish Book*, II (1963).

Hoppen, K. T., 'The Royal Society and Ireland: William Molyneux F.R.S.', *Notes and Records*, XVIII (1963).

Hoppen, K. T., 'The Dublin Philosophical Society and the New Learning in Ireland', *Irish Historical Studies*, XIV (1964).

Hoppen, K. T., 'Sir William Petty 1623–87', *History Today*, XV (1965).

Hoppen, K. T., 'The Royal Society and Ireland II', *Notes and Records*, XX (1965).

Houghton, W. E., 'The English Virtuoso in the Seventeenth Century', *Journal of the History of Ideas*, III (1942).

Johnson, F. R., 'Gresham College: Precursor of the Royal Society', *Journal of the History of Ideas*, I (1940).

Johnston, S. P., and Lunham, T. A., 'On a Manuscript Description of the City and County of Cork . . . written by Sir Richard Cox', *Journal of the Royal Society of Antiquaries of Ireland*, XXXII (1902).

Jones, R. F., and Others, *The Seventeenth Century: Studies in the History of English Thought and Literature from Bacon to Pope*, Stanford, 1951.

Jones, R. F., *Ancients and Moderns: A Study of the Rise of the Scientific Movement in Seventeenth Century England*, 2d edn., St Louis, 1961.

Kargon, R., 'William Petty's Mechanical Philosophy', *Isis*, LVI (1965).

Kearney, H. F., 'Puritanism, Capitalism, and the Scientific Revolution', *Past and Present*, No. 28 (1964).

Kearney, H. F., 'Puritanism and Science: Problems of Definition', *Past and Present*, No. 31 (1965).

Kirkpatrick, T. P. C., 'Charles Willoughby M.D.', *Proceedings of the Royal Irish Academy*, Section C, XXXVI (1923).

Kirkpatrick, T. P. C., 'The *Novissima Idea de Febribus* of Jacobus Sylvius', *Irish Journal of Medical Science*, No. 96 (1933).

Kirkpatrick, T. P. C., 'A Short History of the Medical School, Trinity College Dublin', *Hermathena*, LVIII (1941).

Knox, S. J., *Walter Travers: Paragon of Elizabethan Puritanism*, London, 1962.

Le Fanu, W. R., 'Two Irish Doctors in England in the Seventeenth Century', *Irish Journal of Medical Science*, No. 463 (1964).

Lodge, J., *The Peerage of Ireland*, revised by M. Archdall, 7 vols., Dublin, 1789.

Logan, P., 'Dermot and Edmund O'Meara: Father and Son', *Journal of the Irish Medical Association*, XLIII (1958).

Lynam, E., *The Mapmaker's Art: Essays on the History of Maps*, London, 1953.

Lyons, H., *The Royal Society 1660–1940: A History of its Administration under its Charters*, Cambridge, 1944.

MacLean, K., *John Locke and English Literature of the Eighteenth Century*, New Haven, 1936.

MacLysaght, E., *Irish Life in the Seventeenth Century*, 2d edn., Cork, 1950.

MacPike, E. F., *Hevelius, Flamsteed, and Halley: Three contemporary Astronomers and their mutual Relations*, London, 1937.

Mahaffy, J. P., *An Epoch in Irish History: Trinity College, Dublin, its Foundation and early Fortunes, 1591–1660*, London, 1903.

Mahaffy, J. P., 'The Library of Trinity College, Dublin: The Growth of a Legend', *Hermathena*, XII (1903).

Mant, R., *History of the Church of Ireland*, 2 vols., London, 1840.

Maxwell, C., *A History of Trinity College Dublin 1591–1892*, Dublin, 1946.

Merton, R. K., 'Science, Technology, and Society in Seventeenth Century England', *Osiris*, IV (1938).

Morison, S. E., *The Intellectual Life of Colonial New England*, 2d edn., New York, 1956.

Mullinger, J. B., *The University of Cambridge*, 3 vols., Cambridge, 1873–1911.

Murphy, H. L., *A History of Trinity College Dublin from its Foundation to 1702*, Dublin, 1951.

Murray, R. H., *Revolutionary Ireland and its Settlement*, London, 1911.

Nicolson, M., *Newton Demands the Muse*, Princeton, 1946.

Nicolson, M., *Science and Imagination*, Ithaca, N.Y., 1956.

Nicolson, M., *Pepys' Diary and the New Science*, Charlottesville, 1965.

O'Kelley, F., *Irish Book-Sale Catalogues before 1801*, Dublin, 1953. Publications of the Bibliographical Society of Ireland, VI, No. 3.

O'Sullivan, W., 'Ussher as a Collector of Manuscripts', *Hermathena*, LXXXVIII (1956).

Oulton, J. E. L., 'The Study of Divinity in Trinity College Dublin since the Foundation', *Hermathena*, LVIII (1941).

Park, D., 'Locke and Berkeley on the Molyneux Problem', *Journal of the History of Ideas*, XXX (1969).

Parker, I., *Dissenting Academies in England*, Cambridge, 1914.

Price, D. J., 'The early Observatory Instruments of Trinity College Cambridge', *Annals of Science*, VIII (1952).

Purver, M., *The Royal Society: Concept and Creation*, London, 1967.

Rabb, T. K., 'Puritanism and the Rise of Experimental Science in England', *Journal of World History*, VII (1962).

Rattansi, P. M., 'The Intellectual Origins of the Royal Society', *Notes and Records*, XXIII (1968).

The Record of the Royal Society, 4th edn., London, 1940.

Schneer, C., 'The Rise of Historical Geology in the Seventeenth Century', *Isis*, XLV (1954).

von Senden, M., *Space and Sight: The Perception of Space and Shape in the Congenitally Blind before and after Operation*, London, 1960.

Shapiro, B. J., 'Latitudinarianism and Science', *Past and Present*, No. 40 (1968).

Simms, J. G., *The Williamite Confiscation in Ireland*, London, 1956.

Simms, J. G., *The Treaty of Limerick*, Dundalk, 1961.

Simms, J. G., 'Dublin in 1685', *Irish Historical Studies*, XIV (1965).

Skinner, Q., 'Thomas Hobbes and the Nature of the early Royal Society', *Historical Journal*, XII (1969).

Smyly, J. G., 'The Old Library [of Trinity College Dublin]: Extracts from the Particular Book', *Hermathena*, XLIX (1935).

Stokes, G. T., *Some Worthies of the Irish Church*, London, 1900.

Stubbs, J. W., *The History of the University of Dublin*, Dublin and London, 1889.
Stubbs, J. W., *Archbishop Adam Loftus and the Foundation of Trinity College Dublin*, Dublin and London, 1892.
Syfret, R.H., 'The Origins of the Royal Society', *Notes and Records*, V (1948).
Syfret, R. H., 'Some Early Critics of the Royal Society', *Notes and Records*, VIII (1950).
Taton, R. (ed.), *The Beginnings of Modern Science 1450–1800*, London, 1964.
Taylor, E. G. R., *The Mathematical Practitioners of Tudor and Stuart England*, Cambridge, 1954.
Taylor, E. G. R., *The Haven-Finding Art*, London, 1956.
Taylor, F. S., 'An Early Satirical Poem on the Royal Society', *Notes and Records*, V (1947).
Thorndike, L., *A History of Magic and Experimental Science*, 8 vols., New York, 1929–58.
Toulmin, S., and Goodfield, J., *The Fabric of the Heavens*, London, 1961.
Turbayne, C. M., 'Berkeley and Molyneux on Retinal Images', *Journal of the History of Ideas*, XVI (1955).
Turnbull, G. H., *Hartlib, Dury, and Comenius*, Liverpool, 1947.
Urwick, W., *The Early History of Trinity College Dublin 1591–1660*, London, 1892.
Watson, F., *The Beginnings of the Teaching of Modern Subjects in England*, London, 1909.
Weld, C. R., *A History of the Royal Society with Memoirs of the Presidents*, 2 vols., London, 1848.
Westfall, R. S., *Science and Religion in Seventeenth Century England*, New Haven, 1958.
Widdess, J. D. H., *A History of the Royal College of Physicians of Ireland 1654–1962*, Edinburgh, 1963.
Wilde, W. R., 'Memoir of the Dublin Philosophical Society', *Proceedings of the Royal Irish Academy*, III (1845).
Wormell, D. E. W., 'Latin Verses by William Thompson spoken at the Opening in 1711 of the first scientific Laboratory in Trinity College Dublin', *Hermathena*, XCVI (1962).

Notes to Chapters

CHAPTER ONE

[1] T. Sprat, *The History of the Royal Society of London for the improving of Natural Knowledge* (London, 1667), p. 438. See the annotated edition by J. I. Cope and H. W. Jones (St Louis, Missouri, 1958).

[2] T. K. Rabb, 'Puritanism and the Rise of Experimental Science in England', *Journal of World History*, VII (1962), 63.

[3] R. F. Jones, *Ancients and Moderns: A Study of the Rise of the Scientific Movement in Seventeenth Century England* (2d edn., St Louis, Missouri, 1961), p. 89.

[4] W. Petty, *The Advice of W.P. to Mr Samuel Hartlib for the Advancement of some particular Parts of Learning* (London, 1648), pp. 7–9.

[5] W. Petty, *The Discourse made before the Royal Society the 26 of November 1674 Concerning the Use of Duplicate Proportion in sundry Important Particulars: Together with a New Hypothesis of Springing or Elastique Motions* (London, 1674), pp. 2 and 5.

[6] M. Astell, *An Essay in Defence of the Female Sex* (London, 1696), quoted in W. E. Houghton, 'The English Virtuoso in the Seventeenth Century', *Journal of the History of Ideas*, III (1942), 53.

[7] H. Stubbe, *The Lord Bacons Relation of the Sweating-sickness Examined* (London, 1671), quoted in R. F. Jones, *Ancients and Moderns*, p. 237.

[8] R. Boyle, *Some Considerations touching the Usefulnesse of Experimental Naturall Philosophy* (Oxford, 1663), Second Part, First Section, p. 3.

[9] R. Hooke, *Micrographia: Or some Physiological Descriptions of Minute Bodies made by Magnifying Glasses* (London, 1665), Preface.

[10] T. Sprat, *History of the Royal Society*, p. 434. The Royal Society's motto was *Nullius in Verba*.

[11] S. Parker, *A Free and Impartial Censure of the Platonick Philosophie, Being a Letter written to his much Honoured Friend Mr N.B.* (Oxford, 1666), p. 57.

[12] T. Sprat, *History of the Royal Society*, p. 427.

[13] H. Stubbe, *Campanella Revived: Or an Enquiry into the History of the Royal Society* (London, 1670), p. 2.

[14] H. Stubbe, *A Relation of the Strange Symptomes Happening by the Bite of an Adder* (London, 1671), quoted in R. F. Jones, *Ancients and Moderns*, p. 260. Stubbe was a medical doctor.

[15] John Beale to Robert Boyle, 27 November 1671, *The Works of the Honourable Robert Boyle*, ed. T. Birch, 6 vols. (London, 1772), VI, 434.

[16] See, F. R. Johnson, 'Gresham College: Precursor of the Royal Society', *Journal of the History of Ideas*, I (1940), 413–38.

[17] W. Molyneux to Flamsteed, 3 December 1681, Southampton Civic Centre Archives MS D/M 1/1. This is a collection of some seventy loose holographs exchanged between Molyneux and Flamsteed, and inserted in a blank volume. There is no foliation or pagination. But the letters are arranged by date.

[18] C. Hill, *Intellectual Origins of the English Revolution* (Oxford, 1965), pp. 93–4.

[19] See, R. F. Jones, *Ancients and Moderns*, pp. 171–80.

[20] J. Wallis, *A Defence of the Royal Society and the Philosophical Transactions, particularly those of July 1670, in answer to the Cavils of Dr William Holder* (London, 1678), p. 7.

[21] The most recent account of the society's origins can be found in M. Purver, *The Royal Society: Concept and Creation* (London, 1967), which stresses the importance of the Oxford meetings. Some criticisms of this view are put forward in C. Hill, 'The Intellectual Origins of the Royal Society – London or Oxford?', *Notes and Records of the Royal Society*, XXIII (1968), 144–56 and A. R. and M. B. Hall, 'The Intellectual Origins of the Royal Society – London *and* Oxford', *ibid.*, pp. 157–68.

[22] T. Sprat, *History of the Royal Society*, pp. 53–7.

[23] D. McKie, 'The Origins and Foundation of the Royal Society' in *The Royal Society its Origins and Founders*, ed. H. Hartley (London, 1960), p. 8.

[24] R. H. Syfret, 'The Origins of the Royal Society', *Notes and Records*, V (1948), 85.

[25] C. C. Gillispie, 'Physick and Philosophy: A Study of the Influence of the College of Physicians of London upon the Foundation of the Royal Society', *Journal of Modern History*, XIX (1947), 213–17.

[26] The title 'Royal' was not granted until 1662.

[27] A. Wolf, *A History of Science, Technology, and Philosophy in the Sixteenth and Seventeenth Centuries* (2d edn., London, 1950), p. 63.

[28] Quoted in D. McKie, 'Origins and Foundation of the Royal Society', *op. cit.*, p. 31.

[29] Written in 1663 and quoted in H. Lyons, *The Royal Society 1660–1940: A History of its Administration under its Charters* (Cambridge, 1944), p. 41.

[30] These figures include foreign members, but not royal patrons. They are taken from the annual printed lists of fellows, of which the Royal Society Library has originals or photostats. They are not always entirely reliable.

[31] Until the middle of the eighteenth century the production of the *Philosophical Transactions* was the private concern of the secretary.

[32] Quoted in A. Bryant, *Samuel Pepys: The Years of Peril* (Cambridge, 1935), p. 337.

[33] R. K. Bluhm, Remarks on the Royal Society's Finances', *Notes and Records*, XIII (1958), 83 and 95–6.

[34] R.S. MS DM.5.12.

[35] *The Record of the Royal Society* (4th edn., London, 1940), p. 386.

[36] Boyle to Oldenburg, 30 September 1665, R. T. Gunther, *Early Science in Oxford*, 14 vols. (Oxford, 1923–45), IV, 5.

[37] T. Birch, *The History of the Royal Society of London for Improving of Natural Knowledge, from its First Rise*, 4 vols. (London, 1756–7), IV, 180. Birch prints, more or less in their entirety, the Royal Society's minutes from 1660 to 1687.

[38] These minutes are contained mainly in Bodl. MSS Ashmole 1810–12. They are printed in full in R. T. Gunther, *Early Science in Oxford*, IV, 17–220.

[39] The established church in Ireland, especially after the appearance of the 104 Articles of 1615, was always on average more Calvinistic than the Church of England.

[40] G. H. Turnbull, *Hartlib, Dury, and Comenius* (Liverpool, 1947), p. 204. Ussher also supported Comenius's proposed College of Science.

[41] Adams to Hartlib, 5 August 1640, *ibid.*, p. 207 note 3.

[42] *D.N.B.* In 1627 Carpenter published at Dublin *Achitophel or the Picture of a Wicked Politician* (reprinted London, 1629). This originally contained passages attacking Arminianism, which was described as part of a Jesuit plot to undermine true religion. These were however removed by Laud's agents. See, E. R. McC. Dix, *Catalogue of Early Dublin Printed Books 1601–1700*, 5 Parts (Dublin, 1897–1912), p. 44. On Carpenter in general, See, R. F. Jones, *Ancients and Moderns*, pp. 65–71.

[43] See, *The Whole Works of the Most Reverend James Ussher D.D.*, ed. C. R. Elrington, 17 vols. (Dublin, 1864), XV, 63, 89–90, 98, 213, 351–3, 394, 447–8.

[44] Briggs to Ussher, August 1610, *ibid.*, p. 63.

[45] Ussher to Camden, 28 April 1614, *ibid.*, p. 78.

[46] W. O'Sullivan, 'Ussher as a Collector of Manuscripts', *Hermathena*, LXXXVIII (1956), 42. On Ussher; see also H. F. Kearney, 'Puritanism, Capitalism, and the Scientific Revolution', *Past and Present*, No. 28 (1964), 88.

[47] F. V. Emery, 'Irish Geography in the Seventeenth Century', *Irish Geography*, III (1958), 264. Other works with similar aims had already appeared, such as John Woodhouse's *A Guide for Strangers in the Kingdome of Ireland* (London, 1647). Y. M. Goblet refers to Boate's work as 'le premier ouvrage moderne'. See his *La Transformation de la Géographie politique de l'Irlande au XVIIe Siècle*, 2 vols. (Paris, 1930), I, 147.

[48] *D.N.B.*

[49] Hartlib to Boyle, 28 February 1654, *Works of Boyle*, ed. T. Birch (London, 1772), VI, 81.

[50] Hartlib to Boyle, 8 May 1654, *ibid.*, p. 88.

[51] See K. T. Hoppen, 'Sir William Petty 1623–87', *History Today*, XV (1965), 126–34.

[52] E. Lynam, *The Mapmaker's Art: Essays on the History of Maps* (London, 1953), p. 76. See also E. G. R. Taylor, *The Mathematical Practitioners of Tudor and Stuart England* (Cambridge, 1954), pp. 177, 185, and 187, and J. H. Andrews, 'The Irish Surveys of Robert Lythe', *Imago Mundi*, XIX (1965), 22–31.

[53] W. Molyneux, *Dioptrica Nova* (London, 1692), p. 188. Here Molyneux also recalls the many 'disquisitions' he and Osborne had had on astronomical subjects.

[54] E. G. R. Taylor, *Mathematical Practitioners of Tudor and Stuart England*, p. 240.

[55] H. Osborne, *A More Exact Way to Delineate the Plot of any Spacious Parcel of Land as Baronies, Parishes, and Townlands, as also of Rivers, Harbours, and Loughs etc.* (Dublin, 1654). The only copy of this piece that I have discovered is in Marsh's Library Dublin, Pressmark LA.3.18(1).

[56] See two articles by W. P. Pakenham-Walsh, 'Captain Josias Bodley: Director-General of Fortifications in Ireland 1612–1617', *The Royal Engineers Journal*, VIII (1908), 253–64, and 'Captain Thomas Rotheram Knt. and Nicholas Pinnar, Directors-General of Fortifications in Ireland 1617–1644', *ibid.*, X (1909), 125–34. All three were Englishmen.

[57] Information on this matter has been drawn from: (a) E. R. McC. Dix, *Catalogue of Early Dublin Printed Books 1601–1700*, 5 Parts (Dublin, 1897–1912), (b) *Short-Title Catalogue*, (c) D. Wing's *Short-Title Catalogue*, (d) J. Alden, *Bibliographica Hibernica: Additions and Corrections to Wing* (Charlottesville, Virginia, 1955), (e) The author's own research. Further items will no doubt come to light. It should be noted that all proclamations, printed acts of parliament, and broadsheets have been omitted from the above table.

[58] See P. Logan, 'Dermot and Edmund O'Meara: Father and Son', *Journal of the Irish Medical Association*, XLIII (1958), 312–16.

[59] See W. R. Le Fanu, 'Two Irish Doctors in England in the Seventeenth Century', *Irish Journal of Medical Science*, No 463 (1964), 303–9.

[60] Two of these, that for 1681 and one of those for 1695, are reprints of English almanacs. See E. R. McC. Dix, 'Early Dublin-Printed Almanacs', *The Bibliographical Society of Ireland, Publications*, I (1918–20), No 2. For a somewhat disjointed account of early Irish almanacs, see also, E. Evans, *Historical and Bibliographical Account of Almanacks, Directories, etc. etc. published in Ireland from the Sixteenth Century* (Dublin, 1897).

[61] J. Booker, *A Bloody Irish Almanack: Or Rebellious and Bloody Ireland* (London, 1646). Booker was answered from a royalist position by George Wharton in *Bellum Hybernicale: Or Ireland's War Astrologically Demonstrated* (London, 1647).

[62] *A New Almanack for the yeare of Our Lord 1646 . . . by a Manapian* (Waterford, 1646).

[63] See E. R. McC. Dix, 'A Dublin Almanack of 1612', *Proceedings of the Royal Irish Academy*, Section C, XXX (1913), 327–30.

[64] J. Whalley, *Mercurius Hibernicus: Or an Almanack for the year of Christ 1693* (Dublin, 1692).

[65] *D.N.B.*

[66] J. Whalley, *Vox Urani* (Dublin, 1685).

[67] J. Whalley, *Syderus Nuncius* (Dublin, 1686).

[68] This is stated in J. Whalley, *Mercurius Hibernicus* (Dublin, 1692).

[69] J. Whalley, *Ptolemy's Quadripartite: Or Four Books concerning the Influence of the Stars* (Dublin, 1701).

[70] *Calendar of Ancient Records of Dublin*, ed. J. T. Gilbert and Lady Gilbert, 19 vols. (Dublin, 1889–1944), V, 461–2. On 8 March 1688 Bourke was paid twenty pounds by the corporation for a survey he had undertaken of the River Liffey from the Bar at Essex Bridge, 'with the soundings both at high

and low watermarks, with all sholes, bankes, and creekes, with as much exactness and as little charge as possible'. *Ibid.*, pp. 470–71. This Bourke may have been related to the John Bourke who published almanacs at Dublin in 1684 and 1685.

71 Hartlib to Boyle, 16 November 1647, *Works of Boyle*, ed. T. Birch (London, 1772), VI, 76.

72 *The Double-Bottom or Twin-Hulled Ship of Sir William Petty*, ed. Marquis of Lansdowne (Oxford, 1931), pp. xiii–xiv and 34–5.

73 B. M. Sloane MS 360, f. 73. This poem is quoted at greater length in M. H. Nicolson, *Pepys' Diary and the New Science* (Charlottesville, Virginia, 1965), pp. 181–9. Petty was knighted shortly after the Restoration.

74 *The Double-Bottom*, ed. Marquis of Lansdowne, p. 91.

75 J. Fleetwood, *History of Medicine in Ireland* (Dublin, 1951), p. 29.

76 G. Clark, *A History of the Royal College of Physicians of London*, 2 vols. (Oxford, 1964–6), I, 249–50.

77 J. D. H. Widdess, *A History of the Royal College of Physicians of Ireland 1654–1963* (Edinburgh, 1963), p. 10.

78 J. Fleetwood, *History of Medicine in Ireland*, p. 43.

79 J. D. H. Widdess, *History of the Royal College of Physicians of Ireland*, p. 21.

80 W. Doolin, 'Dublin's Surgeon-Anatomists' *Annals of the Royal College of Surgeons of England*, VIII (1951), 7 note. After 1680 it was stipulated that the president of the College of Physicians should be a member of the established church. The new charter of 1692 declared that henceforth all fellows were to be Anglicans. John Crosby, elected fellow in 1674 and treasurer in 1676, acted as president in the years 1687–90, although a Roman Catholic.

81 In August 1687 James II sent letters patent to Ireland for the establishment of a College of Physicians at Kilkenny, in which were listed fourteen fellows, some of whom have names which might indicate their having been Catholics. A charter was actually granted in 1687, but the war presumably prevented its implementation. See, J. D. H. Widdess, *History of the Royal College of Physicians of Ireland*, p. 29. In the previous year Bishop Otway of Ossory reported an attempt by 'six of the natives who have studied at Paris' to establish a university at Kilkenny. Again nothing seems to have come of the plan. See, T. Corcoran, *Education Systems in Ireland from the Close of the Middle Ages* (Dublin, 1928), p. 19.

82 This information is given in two letters written by Sir Patrick Dun and dated 1697 and 1698 in Bodl. MS Rawlinson C. 406, and noted in Ir. MSS Comm., *Analecta Hibernica*, II (1931), 10.

83 Robert Molesworth to Hon. Mrs Molesworth, 29 October 1696, H.M.C., *Reports on Various Collections*, VIII (1913), 218 (Clements MSS).

84 Tollet to Mr Collins, 19 August 1675, R.S. MS Early Letters T.45. The addressee was almost certainly John Collins, elected F.R.S. in 1667.

85 E. G. R. Taylor, *Mathematical Practitioners of Tudor and Stuart England*, p. 226.

86 *The Double-Bottom*, ed. Marquis of Lansdowne, p. 129.

87 Petty to Aubrey, 12 July 1681, Lord Edmond Fitzmaurice, *The Life of Sir William Petty 1623–87* . . . *chiefly derived from Private Documents, hitherto unpublished* (London, 1895), p. 262.

[88] A. Mullen, *An Anatomical Account of the Elephant accidentally burnt in Dublin on Fryday June 17 in the year 1681: . . . Together with a Relation of new Anatomical Observations in the Eyes of Animals* (London, 1682). Thirty years later Patrick Blair, a Scottish surgeon, dissected an elephant at Dundee. See his 'Osteographia Elephantina', *Philosophical Transactions*, XXVII (1710–12), 51–168.

[89] A. Mullen, *Anatomical Account of the Elephant*, pp. 1–2.

[90] E. G. R. Taylor, 'The English Atlas of Moses Pitt', *Geographical Journal*, VC (1940), 295.

[91] Two copies survive; the first is Bodl. MS Ashmole 1820a, f. 221, the second Bodl. MS Aubrey 4, f. 245. The former is photographically reproduced in K. T. Hoppen, 'Queries for a Seventeenth Century Natural History of Ireland', *The Irish Book*, II (1963), 60–1. It is given in full in Appendix A.

[92] Quoted in R. H. Syfret, 'The Origins of the Royal Society', *Notes and Records*, V (1948), 97.

[93] Marsh to Michael Boyle, 18 May 1682, Bodl. MS Rawlinson Letters 45, f. 14.

[94] Capel Molyneux, *An Account of the Family and Descendants of Sir Thomas Molyneux Kt., Chancellor of the Exchequer in Ireland to Queen Elizabeth* (Evesham, 1820), p. 61. This book contains (pp. 51–78) a 'Memorial of the Life of Wm. Molyneux by Himself, July 1694'. The original of this seems to have been lost.

[95] S. E. Morison, *The Intellectual Life of Colonial New England* (2d edn., New York, 1956), p. 255 and K. B. Murdock, *Increase Mather: The Foremost American Puritan* (New York, 1966: First published, 1925), pp. 147–8.

[96] B.M. Add. MS 4223, f. 34. This manuscript contains (ff. 34–8) an anonymous 'Memorial Molyneux', almost certainly written about 1730. Palliser, a future Bishop of Cloyne and Archbishop of Cashel, joined the Dublin Society in 1684. For an account of Molyneux, see K. T. Hoppen, 'The Royal Society and Ireland: William Molyneux F.R.S.', *Notes and Records*, XVIII (1963), 125–35.

[97] B.M. Add. MS 4223, f. 34.

[98] *Ibid.*

[99] C. Molyneux, *An Account of the Family*, p. 60.

[100] *Ibid.*

[101] Over twenty replies were received as a result of the geographical queries. All but two are among the Molyneux Papers at Trinity College Dublin. The others are in Royal Irish Academy MS 12/W/22.

[102] See, R. A. Butlin, 'The Population of Dublin in the later Seventeenth Century', *Irish Geography*, V (1965), 57, and J. G. Simms, 'Dublin in 1685', *Irish Historical Studies*, XIV (1965), 212. Dublin in 1685 was more than twice as large as the biggest English provincial centres like Bristol and Norwich.

[103] R. Munter, *The History of the Irish Newspaper 1685–1760* (Cambridge, 1967), p. 11.

[104] C. Molyneux, *An Account of the Family*, pp. 63–4.

[105] Molyneux to Flamsteed, 17 September 1681, Southampton MS D/M 1/1.

106 Molyneux to Flamsteed, 3 April 1683, *ibid.*

107 William to Thomas Molyneux, 30 October 1683, *Dublin University Magazine*, XVIII (1841), 472. This volume of the magazine contains four anonymous articles on Sir Thomas Molyneux, which include long extracts from the correspondence between the two brothers, the originals of which seem to be lost.

CHAPTER TWO

1 For a discussion of Trinity College and its attitude towards science in the seventeenth century, see Chapter 3.

2 B.M. Add. MS 4811, f. 160. This is the minute and register book of the society. Besides minutes it contains copies of papers read at meetings and of correspondence received. Hereafter it is referred to as 'Minutes', followed by date and folio number. The names of the original members are:

Charles Willoughby	Samuel Foley
William Molyneux	Robert Huntington
St George Ashe	John Keogh
Mark Baggot	Narcissus Marsh
John Baynard	Allen Mullen
Richard Bulkeley	William Petty
Francis Cuffe	George Tollet

3 Two of these have survived. They are: *The Ancient and Moderne Doctrine of Holy Fathers and Judicious Divines Concerning the Rash Citation of the Testimony of Sacred Scripture in Conclusions meerly Natural, and that may be Proved by Sensible Experiments and Necessary Demonstrations* (Marsh's Library Dublin, MS Z3.1.10) and *Tractatus Galilei de Motu Locali, cum Appendice de Centro Gravitatis. Transscriptus ex Originali . . . Anno Domini 1686–7* (Marsh's Library Dublin, MS Z4.2.8(8)).

4 J. G. Simms, *The Williamite Confiscation in Ireland* (London, 1956), pp. 141–4.

5 Baggot to King, 19 December 1700, T. C. D. Lyon MS No. 745. This is part of a large collection of King's Papers.

6 Narcissus Marsh to Archbishop Sancroft, 13 November 1688, Ir. MSS Comm., *Calendar of the Tanner Letters*, ed. C. McNeill (Dublin, 1943), p. 496.

7 E. G. R. Taylor, *The Mathematical Practitioners of Tudor and Stuart England* (Cambridge, 1954), p. 270.

8 Clarendon to Pepys, 1 July 1700, *Private Correspondence and Miscellaneous Papers of Samuel Pepys*, ed. J. R. Tanner, 2 vols. (London, 1926), II, 2.

9 Unless otherwise indicated, general biographical information on the members of the society is taken from, *D.N.B.*, H. Cotton, *Fasti Ecclesiae Hibernicae*, 6 vols. (Dublin, 1845–78), and G. D. Burtchaell and T. V. Sadlier, *Alumni Dublinensis* (2d edn., Dublin, 1935).

10 Southampton MS D/M 2/1, f. 4. This is a survey and rent roll of the Castle Dillon estate.

11 *The Diary of John Evelyn*, ed. E. S. de Beer, 6 vols. (Oxford, 1955), IV,

56. Entry for 24 March 1675. See, K. T. Hoppen, 'Sir William Petty 1623–87', *History Today*, XV (1965), 126–34.

12 *The Diary of John Evelyn*, ed. E. S. de Beer, IV, 58.

13 Petty's 'Directions to my deare Wife, 15 Aprill 1679', B. M. Lansdowne MS 1228, f. 28v.

14 For an account of the eighteen members of the Dublin Society who were also fellows of the Royal Society, see K. T. Hoppen, 'The Royal Society and Ireland II', *Notes and Records*, XX (1965), 78–99.

15 For a list of those new members who joined the Dublin Society between January and December 1684, see Note 85 below.

16 John Wilkins of Chester and Thomas Sprat of Rochester. In England there was of course a large non-clerical group of intellectuals which could provide fellows of the Royal Society. This was far less so the case in Ireland.

17 See, *The Record of the Royal Society* (4th edn., London, 1940), pp. 384–91. Philip Bisse, Bishop of Hereford, was the only bishop never to hold an Irish see to join the Royal Society between 1672 and 1719.

18 See King to Jenkins, 23 April 1698, T.C.D. King Correspondence MS N.3.1, p. 216, and J. C. Beckett, *Protestant Dissent in Ireland 1687–1780* (London, 1948), pp. 41 and 76–9.

19 See Ashe to King, 24 January and 30 August 1700, T.C.D. Lyon MSS Nos. 656 and 717.

20 J. C. Beckett, *Protestant Dissent in Ireland*, p. 35.

21 *Ibid.*, p. 53.

22 H.M.C., *Calendar of Ormonde MSS*, New Series, VII (1912), 314–15. See also J. G. Simms, 'Dublin in 1685', *Irish Historical Studies*, XIV (1965), 225.

23 J. C. Beckett, *Protestant Dissent in Ireland*, p. 121.

24 *D.N.B.*

25 See Membership List for December 1693, T.C.D. MS F.4.24, ff. 48v–9. This is given above as Appendix C.

26 Quoted in J. C. Beckett, *Protestant Dissent in Ireland*, p. 56.

27 *Ibid.*, p. 37.

28 See above, p.40.

29 W. Hamilton, *The Life and Character of James Bonnell Esq.* (Dublin, 1703), pp. 84 and 239.

30 *The Autobiography of the Rt Hon Sir Richard Cox*, ed. R. Caulfield (London and Cork, 1860), p. 15.

31 *The Petty Papers: Some Unpublished Writings of Sir William Petty*, ed. Marquis of Lansdowne, 2 vols. (London, 1927), II, 251.

32 *The Economic Writings of Sir William Petty*, ed. C. H. Hull, 2 vols. (Cambridge, 1899), I, 262; taken from the *Political Arithmetick* (London, 1690), which was probably written in the early 1670s.

33 T. Smith, *Admodum Reverendi et Doctissimi Viri D. Roberti Huntingtoni* (London, 1704), p. xxxi.

34 W. Molyneux, *The Case of Ireland's being bound by Acts of Parliament in England Stated* (Dublin, 1698), p. 3.

35 See B. J. Shapiro, 'Latitudinarianism and Science', *Past and Present*, No. 40 (1968), 16–41. This point has also been developed, using a more strictly

theological definition of 'Latitudinarianism', by H. R. McAdoo in *The Spirit of Anglicanism: A Survey of Anglican Theological Method in the Seventeenth Century* (London, 1965), pp. 156–239.

³⁶ O. T. Beall, 'Cotton Mather's Early "Curiosa Americana" and the Boston Philosophical Society of 1683', *William and Mary Quarterly*, 3rd Series, XVIII (1961), 361.

³⁷ Quoted from Nicholas Bernard's *The Life and Death of . . . Dr James Usher D.D.* (1656) by C. Hill in *Puritanism and Revolution: Studies in Interpretation of the English Revolution of the 17th Century* (London, 1958), p. 244.

³⁸ Many have written on the matter, among them R. Merton, who has tried to establish a connection between the growth of Puritanism and the rise of experimental science in England in 'Science, Technology, and Society in Seventeenth Century England' *Osiris*, IV (1938), 360–632. A more recent expression of a similar attitude is to be found in C. Hill, *Intellectual Origins of the English Revolution* (Oxford, 1965). The contrary opinion is put forward by T. K. Rabb in 'Puritanism and the Rise of Experimental Science in England', *Journal of World History*, VII (1962), and in two articles by H. F. Kearney, 'Puritanism, Capitalism and the Scientific Revolution', *Past and Present*, No. 28 (1964) and 'Puritanism and Science: Problems of Definition', *Past and Present*, No. 31 (1965). L. S. Feuer, in *The Scientific Intellectual* (New York, 1963), pp. 420–3, argues that the early membership of the Royal Society was predominantly Royalist and sympathetic to what he rather vaguely calls a 'Hedonist–Libertarian ethic'. While M. Purver, in *The Royal Society: Concept and Creation* (London, 1967), p. 152, maintains that 'the supposition that the Royal Society was a manifestation of "the Puritan ethic" is refuted by the society's own testimony, as well as by its conduct in action.'

³⁹ I. Masson and A. J. Youngson, 'Sir William Petty' in *The Royal Society its Origins and Founders*, ed. H. Hartley (London, 1960), p. 81.

⁴⁰ T. P. C. Kirkpatrick, 'Charles Willoughby M.D.', *Proceedings of the Royal Irish Academy*, Section C, XXXVI (1923), 240.

⁴¹ Willoughby to Ormonde, 16 September 1682, H.M.C., *Calendar of Ormonde MSS*, Old Series, I (1895), 104.

⁴² For this, see above, pp. 91–2.

⁴³ See J. Lodge, *The Peerage of Ireland*, Revised by M. Archdall, 7 vols. (Dublin, 1789), III, 376 and 380, Arran to Ormonde, 26 January 1684, H.M.C., *Calendar of Ormonde MSS*, New Series, VII (1912), 184, and *Liber Munerum Publicorum Hiberniae ab An. 1152 usque ad 1827*, ed. R. Lascelles, 5 Parts (London, 1824–30), II, 103.

⁴⁴ Keogh to Molyneux, 14 March 1684, R.I.A. MS 12/W/22, pp. 9–14. This MS also contains (pp. 1–7) a description of Leitrim by Teague O'Roddy.

⁴⁵ Keogh to Molyneux, 4 June 1684, T.C.D. MS I.4.18, ff. 96–7.

⁴⁶ Molyneux to Keogh, 22 March 1684, R.I.A. MS 12/W/22, p. 15.

⁴⁷ *D.N.B.*

⁴⁸ W. Molyneux, *Dioptrica Nova* (London, 1692), 'To the Reader' (unpaginated). This introduction is dated April 1690.

⁴⁹ *The Life and Times of Anthony à Wood*, ed. A. Clark, 5 vols. (Oxford, 1891–1900), I, 274.

⁵⁰ See E. Bernard, *Catalogi Librorum Manuscriptorum Angliae et Hiberniae* (Oxford, 1697), Tom. II, Part II, pp. 52–6 and 61–5. Most of Marsh's oriental manuscripts are now in the Bodleian Library Oxford.

⁵¹ Marsh to Boyle, 30 September 1682, *Works of Boyle*, ed. T. Birch, 6 vols. (London, 1772), VI, 606.

⁵² Copies of three letters from Wallis to Marsh, dated 16 June, 17 August, and 21 August 1681, are preserved in R.I.A. MS 12/D/34, pp. 1–19. This is the manuscript referred to in the following sentence. Copies of these letters can also be found in the Bodleian Library, see C. J. Scriba, 'A Tentative Index of the Correspondence of John Wallis F.R.S.', *Notes and Records*, XXII (1967), 74.

⁵³ G. T. Stokes, *Some Worthies of the Irish Church* (London, 1900), pp. 110–11.

⁵⁴ I. Ehrenpreis, *Swift: The Man, His Works, and the Age*, 2 vols. to date (London, 1962–), I, 49, from which Swift's description of Marsh is also taken.

⁵⁵ H. N. Clokie, *An Account of the Herbaria of the Department of Botany in the University of Oxford* (Oxford, 1964), p. 187.

⁵⁶ Dudley Loftus to Archbishop Sancroft, 18 August 1682, Ir. MSS Comm., *Calendar of the Tanner Letters*, ed. C. McNeill, p. 448.

⁵⁷ Marsh's Library Dublin MS Z2.2.3B, p. 3. This is a typescript of MS Z2.2.3, which is a contemporary copy of a diary kept by Marsh.

⁵⁸ Arran to Ormonde, 1 and 7 April 1683, H.M.C., *Calendar of Ormonde MSS*, New Series, VII (1912), 5 and 8.

⁵⁹ *The Whole Works of Sir James Ware*, ed. W. Harris, 2 vols. (Dublin, 1739–46), I, 278.

⁶⁰ T. Smith, *Admodum Reverendi et Doctissimi Viri D. Roberti Huntingtoni*, pp. xxviii–xxix. An English translation of the biographical (as opposed to epistolary) section of this work can be found in the *Gentleman's Magazine* for 1825, from p. 218 of which the above version has been taken.

⁶¹ Minutes, 7 and 14 April 1684, f. 162. The paper on the porphyry pillars is printed in *Philosophical Transactions*, XIV (1684), 624–9. For the bottles of mineral water, see Minutes, 2 June 1684, f. 163v.

⁶² Minutes, 2 November 1685, f. 174.

⁶³ See I. Ehrenpreis, *Swift: The Man, His Works, and the Age*, I, 51–6.

⁶⁴ J. W. Stubbs, *The History of the University of Dublin* (Dublin and London, 1889), pp. 115 and 332.

⁶⁵ In December 1684 in addition to the provost (Huntington), six fellows of Trinity College were members of the society, namely, Richard Acton, St George Ashe, Samuel Foley, William King, William Palliser, and Edward Smyth. At this period it was laid down that the college should contain no more than sixteen fellows.

⁶⁶ See above, p. 64.

⁶⁷ Addison to Swift, 20 March 1718, *The Correspondence of Jonathan Swift*, ed. H. Williams, 5 vols. (Oxford, 1963–5), II, 286.

[68] William to Thomas Molyneux, Spring 1684, *Dublin University Magazine*, XVIII (1841), 478.

[69] Marsh to Boyle, 23 June 1682, *Works of Boyle*, ed. T. Birch (London, 1772), VI, 604.

[70] See A. Mullen, 'An Account of an Experiment of the Injection of Mercury into the Blood', R.S. Classified Papers XIV(1), 34. Printed, *P.T.*, XVII (1691), 486–8.

[71] Mullen to Boyle, 26 February 1686, R.S. MS Boyle Letters 4, ff. 83–4.

[72] 'The Diary of Robert Hooke from 1 November 1688 to 8 August 1693' printed in R. T. Gunther, *Early Science in Oxford*, 14 vols. (Oxford, 1923–45), X, 92, 94, 103, 123, 132, and 135.

[73] See J. Clayton, 'A Letter . . . giving a farther Account of the Soil of Virginia, . . . as likewise a Description of the several Species of Birds observed there', *P.T.*, XVII (1693), 990. This and other papers by Clayton are printed in *The Reverend John Clayton: A Parson with a Scientific Mind, His Scientific Writings and other Related Papers*, ed. E. and D. S. Berkeley (Charlottesville, Virginia, 1965), which also includes a biographical sketch of Clayton.

[74] *D.N.B.* The *Dictionary's* date of 1690 for Mullen's departure is presumably in the New Style. He actually left on 27 December 1689 Old Style. See R. T. Gunther, *Early Science in Oxford*, X, 174.

[75] Quoted in I. Ehrenpreis, *Swift: The Man, His Works, and the Age*, I, 41.

[76] See Foley's will, T.C.D. Lyon MS No. 432. He appointed his fellow member William King to be executor. Dominick was a fellow of the Irish College of Physicians, and acted as censor until his death in 1692. See MS Minute Book of the Royal College of Physicians of Ireland Vol. I, f. lv. This is kept in the library of the college.

[77] Foley to Sancroft, 5 July 1684, Ir. MSS Comm., *Calendar of Tanner Letters*, ed. C. McNeill, p. 469.

[78] *The Whole Works of Sir James Ware*, ed. W. Harris, I, 214.

[79] S. Foley, 'An Account of the Giant's Causeway in the North of Ireland', *P.T.*, XVIII (1694), 170–3.

[80] *D.N.B.* wrongly gives the date as 1644. But see *Alumni Dublinensis* and J. Lodge, *The Peerage of Ireland*, V, 23–4. In my 'The Royal Society and Ireland', *Notes and Records*, XX (1965), 82, the date is misprinted as 1651.

[81] J. Lodge, *The Peerage of Ireland*, V, 23.

[82] Boyle to Ormonde, 2 May 1683 and Ormonde to Boyle, 7 July 1683, H.M.C., *Calendar of Ormonde MSS*, New Series, VII (1912), 19 and 66.

[83] See *Warnings of the Eternal Spirit spoken by Abraham Withro, with a Preface by Sir R. Bulkeley* (London, 1709). In the preface Bulkeley claims that Whitterow had miraculously cured him of headaches, stone, and rupture.

[84] Berkeley to Sir John Perceval, 1 March 1710, *The Works of George Berkeley, Bishop of Cloyne*, ed. A. A. Luce and T. E. Jessop, 9 vols. (London, 1948–57), VIII, 31.

[85] W. Molyneux to Francis Aston (Secretary to the Royal Society), 27 December 1684, R.S. MS Early Letters, M.1.88. The relevant part of this letter is printed in T. Birch, *The History of the Royal Society of London*, 4 vols. (London, 1756–7), IV, 352–3. The new members were:

Richard Acton	*Dr John Madden
*John Bulkeley	Viscount Mountjoy
*Dr Paul Chamberlain	*Dr William Palliser
*R. Clements	William Pleydall
*Dr Christopher Dominick	Sir Robert Redding
Henry Ferneley	Edward Smyth
*J. Finglass	John Stanley
Dr Daniel Houlaghan	Dr Jacobus Sylvius
William King	*Dr John Worth

*Sir Cyril Wyche

Those with asterisks against their names are not again mentioned in the minutes of the society. Some of these, like Finglass and Palliser, seem to have taken part mainly in the theological meetings, for which, see above, pp. 88–9.

[86] Ashe to Dodwell, 18 December 1684, Bodl. MS English Letters c. 29, f. 2.

[87] See *Liber Munerum Publicorum Hiberniae*, V, 115, and *The Diary of William King*, ed. H. Lawlor (Dublin, 1903), p. 9. (Reprinted from the *Journal of the Royal Society of Antiquaries of Ireland*, XXXIII (1903).)

[88] E. MacLysaght, *Irish Life in the Seventeenth Century* (2d edn., Cork, 1950), pp. 447–8.

[89] B.M. Add. MS 4811, ff. 4lv-3.

[90] Minutes, 1 November 1684, f. 166. At the next election of officers in November 1685 he was succeeded by George Tollet, an original member.

[91] R. Acton, 'Of the Scoter Duck', see Minutes, 27 July 1685, f. 172. No copy of this paper has survived.

[92] Minutes, 1 February 1686, f. 176.

[93] Minutes, 19 January 1685, f. 168.

[94] C. Molyneux, *Account of the Family* (Evesham, 1820), pp. 63–4. As Chief Engineer, Molyneux designed a small part of Dublin Castle.

[95] A description of the dispute can be found in G. T. Stokes, *Some Worthies of the Irish Church*, pp. 178–80.

[96] J. C. Beckett, 'William King's Administration of the Diocese of Derry 1691–1703', *Irish Historical Studies*, IV (1944), 180.

[97] *The Diary of John Evelyn*, ed. E. S. de Beer, V, 597. Entry for 4 June 1705. King was elected F.R.S. in November 1705, and was obviously thought an important member. See Isaac Newton to Hans Sloane, 17 September 1705, *The Correspondence of Isaac Newton*, ed. H. W. Turnbull and J. F. Scott, 4 vols. to date (Cambridge, 1959–), IV, 448.

[98] T. Birch, *History of the Royal Society*, IV, 248. The early minutes of the Dublin Society, from October to December 1683, are not in the minute book (B.M. Add. MS 4811), but were sent to London in Huntington to Plot, 18 December 1683, R.S. MS Early Letters, H.3.72.

[99] *Liber Munerum Publicorum Hiberniae*, V, 18.

[100] T. P. C. Kirkpatrick, 'The *Novissima Idea de Febribus* of Jacobus Sylvius', *Irish Journal of Medical Science*, No. 96 (1933), 667.

[101] T.C.D. MS I.1.2, p. 82.

[102] T. P. C. Kirkpatrick *op. cit.*, p. 668.

[103] H. F. Berry, 'The Ancient Corporation of Barber-Surgeons or Guild of St Mary Magdalene, Dublin', *Journal of the Royal Society of Antiquaries of Ireland*, XXXIII (1903), 231.

[104] *The Petty Papers*, ed. Marquis of Lansdowne, I, 200.

[105] The testimonial and description of the operation performed by Proby can be found in B. M. Sloane MS 1786, ff. 152–3.

[106] Petition of John Meagher, Dr of Phisick, Bodl. MS Rawlinson A.482, noted in Ir. MSS Comm., *Analecta Hibernica*, I (1930), 112–13.

[107] Minutes, 7 April 1684, f. 162. This paper has not survived, but another, 'Observations on the Body of One Dying of the Stone' can be found in B.M. Add. MS 4811, ff. 11v–12.

[108] Minutes, 1 February 1686, f. 176.

[109] See especially his *The Present State of the Ottoman Empire* (London, 1668).

[110] Minutes, 25 January 1686, f. 176.

[111] Minutes, 15 November 1686, R. T. Gunther, *Early Science in Oxford*, XII, 196. The minutes for the period 15 November 1686 to 11 April 1687 are not in the minute book, but, having been sent to Oxford, are printed in *Early Science in Oxford*, XII, 196–201. Another version of them can be found in R.S. MS Early Letters, S.1.135.

[112] Minutes, 16 June 1684, f. 164.

[113] Minutes, 21 July 1684, f. 165.

[114] T. P. C. Kirkpatrick, 'Charles Willoughby M.D.', *Proceedings of the Royal Irish Academy*, Section C, XXXVI (1923), 248.

[115] C. Hill, *The Century of Revolution 1603–1714* (London, 1961), p. 248.

[116] This argument owes much to Q. Skinner's interesting article 'Thomas Hobbes and the Nature of the Early Royal Society', *Historical Journal*, XII (1969), 217–39.

[117] This problem is discussed in M. 'Espinasse, 'The Decline and Fall of Restoration Science', *Past and Present*, No. 14 (1958), 71–89.

[118] D. McKie, 'Origins and Foundation of the Royal Society', in *The Royal Society its Origins and Founders*, ed. H. Hartley, pp. 32–3.

[119] In 1683 Huntington was aged 46. The average age of the fourteen original members was then about 35.

[120] *D.N.B.*

[121] Perceval to Sir Robert Southwell, 2 February 1686, H.M.C., *Calendar of Egmont MSS*, II (1909), 177. Perceval had some interest in scientific matters. In October 1683 he thanked Southwell for obtaining for him a copy of Nehemiah Grew's *Anatomy of Plants* (London, 1682), *ibid.*, p. 135.

[122] Quoted in R. H. Murray, *Revolutionary Ireland and its Settlement* (London, 1911), p. 316.

[123] The address is printed in full in G. T. Stokes, *Some Worthies of the Irish Church*, pp. 171–2.

[124] William Sheridan, Bishop of Kilmore, was deprived of his see after the Williamite Revolution, as the only Irish episcopal non-juror. See King's 'Letter to the Reader' in his *St Paul's Confession of Faith, or a Brief Account of*

his Religion (Dublin, 1685). King however was one of several Irish bishops who gave funds to Sheridan in his distress.

[125] King to Ashe, 24 March 1702, R. Mant, *History of the Church of Ireland*, 2 vols. (London, 1840), II, 125.

[126] C. Molyneux, *Account of the Family*, p. 69.

[127] William to Thomas Molyneux, March 1685, *Dublin University Magazine*, XVIII (1841), 605.

[128] The others were Ashe, Bulkeley, Huntington, Marsh, Thomas Molyneux, Smyth, and Tollet.

[129] F. C. Turner, *James II* (2d Impression, London, 1950), p. 393.

[130] B.M. Lansdowne MS 1228, f. 4v.

[131] J. G. Simms, *The Treaty of Limerick* (Dundalk, 1961), p. 12.

[132] Minutes, 31 October 1683, T. Birch, *History of the Royal Society*, IV, 248.

[133] Thomas to William Molyneux, 26 May 1683, *Dublin University Magazine*, XVIII (1841), 319. This portrait was presented by Aubrey in 1670. It seems probable that Molyneux's shock was brought about by his dislike of Hobbes's specifically political and perhaps religious views, and not necessarily by the English thinker's general philosophical outlook, which, as Q. Skinner in 'Thomas Hobbes and the Nature of the Early Society', *Historical Journal*, XII (1969), 217–39, points out, was by no means antagonistic to the Royal Society's intellectual position.

[134] These were Ashe, Bulkeley, W. Molyneux, Mullen, Petty, Tollet, and Willoughby.

[135] These were King, Redding, Rycaut, Smyth, Sylvius, Wetenhall, and Wyche. See K. T. Hoppen, 'The Royal Society and Ireland II', *Notes and Records*, XX (1965), 78–99.

[136] W. Molyneux to Flamsteed, 27 January 1690, *A General Dictionary, Historical, and Critical in which a New and Accurate Translation of that of the Celebrated Mr Bayle, with the Corrections and Observations printed in the late Edition at Paris is included*, ed. J. P. Bernard, T. Birch, and J. Lockman, 10 vols. (London, 1734–41), VIII, 612. The life of W. Molyneux in this work includes several letters from his correspondence with Flamsteed which are no longer extant in Southampton MS D/M 1/1.

[137] R. T. Gunther, *Early Science in Oxford*, X, 103, 107, and 135.

[138] *Record of the Royal Society*, p. 10.

[139] W. Molyneux to Francis Aston, 14 November 1685, R.S. MS Early Letters, M.1.93. Molyneux had already become friendly with the Duke of Ormonde, who in the Spring of 1684, had attended some gunnery experiments carried out by the society, and had given Molyneux 'his discourse on various subjects for a great while'. William to Thomas Molyneux, 12 April 1684, *Dublin University Magazine*, XVIII (1841), 480.

[140] Three peers joined in 1693. They were the Earl of Longford, Viscount Blessington, and Lord Shelburne. The last was of course the eldest surviving son of Sir William Petty.

CHAPTER THREE

[1] F. Watson, *The Beginnings of the Teaching of Modern Subjects in England* (London, 1909), p. 242. M. Curtis's *Oxford and Cambridge in Transition 1558–1642* (Oxford, 1959) has somewhat modified the view that the English universities in the early seventeenth century were invariably inimical to modern forms of learning. For a brief criticism of Curtis, See C. Hill, *Intellectual Origins of the English Revolution* (Oxford, 1965), pp. 301–14. P. Allen, in 'Scientific Studies in the English Universities of the Seventeenth Century', *Journal of the History of Ideas*, X (1949), 219–53, also tends to be critical of Oxford and Cambridge in this period.

[2] N. Biggs, *Mataeotechnia Medicinae Praxews. . . . With an humble Motion for the Reformation of the Universities* (London, 1651), Section 305.

[3] J. Hall, *An Humble Motion to the Parliament of England Concerning the Advancement of Learning and Reformation of the Universities* (London, 1649), pp. 15 and 26–7.

[4] C. Hill, *The Century of Revolution 1603–1714* (London, 1961), p. 248.

[5] F. S. Taylor, 'An Early Satirical Poem on the Royal Society', *Notes and Records*, V (1947), 38.

[6] I. Parker, *Dissenting Academies in England* (Cambridge, 1914), pp. 59 and 70.

[7] *A Great Archbishop of Dublin William King, D.D. 1650–1729*, ed. C. S. King (London, 1908), p. 5 (Part of an autobiographical fragment by King) and J. C. Beckett, *Protestant Dissent in Ireland 1687–1780* (London, 1948), p. 41. An attempt was made to establish another such school at Antrim in 1685. But it failed because of a shortage of pupils. *Ibid.*, p. 22.

[8] The above is based on the best account of the matter, A. Gwynn, 'The Medieval University of St Patrick's, Dublin', *Studies*, XXVII (1938), 199–212 and 437–54. I am grateful to Dr J. A. Watt for bringing this article to my attention.

[9] E. Curtis, *A History of Medieval Ireland from 1086 to 1513* (2d edn., London, 1938), p. 329 and T. Corcoran, *Education Systems in Ireland from the Close of the Middle Ages* (Dublin, 1928), p. 7.

[10] A. Gwynn, *op. cit.*, p. 454.

[11] T. Corcoran, *Education Systems*, p. 4.

[12] J. P. Mahaffy, *An Epoch in Irish History: Trinity College, Dublin, its Foundation and early Fortunes, 1591–1660* (London, 1903), pp. 99–103.

[13] T. Corcoran, *State Policy in Irish Education A.D. 1536 to 1816* (Dublin, 1916), pp. 49–51 and 12. In 1600 Hugh O'Neill demanded the setting-up of a university 'wherein all sciences shall be taught according to the manner of the Catholic Church'. *Ibid.*, p. 58.

[14] T. P. C. Kirkpatrick, 'A Short History of the Medical School, Trinity College Dublin', *Hermathena*, LVIII (1941), 40.

[15] J. W. Stubbs, *The History of the University of Dublin* (Dublin and London, 1889), p. 44.

[16] *Ibid.*, p. 30.

[17] J. E. L. Oulton, 'The Study of Divinity in Trinity College Dublin since the Foundation', *Hermathena*, LVIII (1941), 3.

R

[18] J. P. Mahaffy, *An Epoch in Irish History*, p. 194. In his sermons Bedell 'used still rather to contract the differences between protestants and papists than to widen them.' *Two Biographies of William Bedell*, ed. E. S. Shuckburgh (Cambridge, 1902), p. 26.

[19] See S. J. Knox, *Walter Travers: Paragon of Elizabethan Puritanism* (London, 1962), p. 147, E. H. Pearce, *Sion College and Library* (Cambridge, 1913), p. 244, and C. Hill, *Intellectual Origins of the English Revolution*, p. 277 note 4. This does not of course mean that the whole college was suffused with a scientific glow. Travers's interests seem to have been purely private, and did not impinge upon the teaching, or, as far as one can judge, the atmosphere of the college. See H. F. Kearney, 'Puritanism and Science: Problems of Definition', *Past and Present*, No. 31 (1965), 104.

[20] This speech was delivered in 1595 and is printed in J. W. Stubbs, *Archbishop Adam Loftus and the Foundation of Trinity College Dublin* (Dublin and London, 1892), pp. 14–21.

[21] They are printed in J. P. Mahaffy, *An Epoch in Irish History*, pp. 327–75.

[22] Quoted in C. Maxwell, *A History of Trinity College Dublin 1591–1892* (Dublin, 1946), p. 42. Borlase however (see J. W. Stubbs, *The History of the University of Dublin*, p. 75) claims that Chappel was a Ramist.

[23] The 1637 statutes can be found in R. Bolton, *A Translation of the Charter and Statutes of Trinity-College, Dublin* (Dublin, 1760), pp. 24–118.

[24] J. W. Stubbs, *The History of the University of Dublin*, p. 81.

[25] J. P. Mahaffy, *An Epoch in Irish History*, p. 143, and J. G. Smyly, 'The Old Library: Extracts from the Particular Book', *Hermathena*, XLIX (1935), 173–5.

[26] Printed in J. P. Mahaffy, 'The Library of Trinity College, Dublin: The Growth of a Legend', *Hermathena*, XII (1903), 76–7.

[27] T.C.D. MS D.1.2. The date written on the volume, namely 1604, may be the year in which it was begun.

[28] J. P. Mahaffy, *An Epoch in Irish History*, p. 255.

[29] A catalogue is in the college archives, T.C.D. MS D.1.3. See also H. J. Lawlor, 'Primate Ussher's Library before 1641', *Proceedings of the Royal Irish Academy*, XXII (1900–1902), 216–64.

[30] See the two Trinity Library Loan Books, T.C.D. MSS R.2.20 and R.2.21. Crossings-out make these difficult to use.

[31] St J. D. Seymour, *The Puritans in Ireland 1647–1661* (Oxford, 1921), pp. 104 and 29.

[32] T. Corcoran, *State Policy*, p. 75.

[33] *Ibid.*, p. 79.

[34] W. Urwick, *The Early History of Trinity College Dublin 1591–1660* (London, 1892), pp. 63–4.

[35] Symner to Boyle, 13 March [No year given], R.S. MS Boyle Letters 7, f. 49. I am grateful to Mr T. C. Barnard for bringing this and the next reference to my attention.

[36] Symner to Hartlib, 24 October 1648, B.M. Sloane MS 427, f. 85.

[37] The information on salaries can be found in W. Urwick, *The Early History of Trinity College Dublin*, p. 78. Symner's references to geography and to Greaves were remembered in 1686 by a member of the Dublin Society,

Richard Acton. See Minutes, 15 March 1686, f. 177v. Copies of the reports to the Commissioners for the Affairs of Ireland on lands in Ireland by Petty and Symner for July 1656 to May 1659 are in the Oireachtas Library, Dublin, MS 3.G.12.

[38] Donegal's foundation was welcomed by Anthony Dopping, fellow of Trinity and later Bishop of Kildare and then Meath, in a public oration. This speech, which contains little more than conventional praise of learning in general, can be found in Dopping's Commonplace Book, Cambridge University Library Add. MS 711, pp. 169–75. It is however noteworthy that Dopping thought the new lectureship might advance the study of astrology.

[39] T. Salusbury, *Mathematical Collections and Translations* (London, 1661), Part I, 'To the Reader'. Some confusion as to Symner's identity is caused by the fact that *Alumni Dublinensis* lists two men of this name. 1. Scholar 1626; Fellow 1652; D.D. 1664. 2. Scholar 1640; Chief Engineer of the Army. On the other hand H. Cotton's *Fasti Ecclesiae Hibernicae* mentions only one man, who corresponds with *Alumni*'s No. 1, and who became Archdeacon of Kildare in 1668, and is not noted as having been Professor of Mathematics at Dublin University. Now if only one Miles Symner existed, the fact that he became an archdeacon, after having been a parliamentary major, is interesting. However it seems most probable that the mathematician was Scholar 1640; Fellow and Professor 1652; and again Professor in the late 1670s, and that the archdeacon was a different person.

[40] C. Maxwell, *A History of Trinity College Dublin*, pp. 51–2.

[41] J. Taylor, *Via Intelligentiae: A Sermon preached to the University of Dublin, shewing by what Means the Scholars shall Become most Learned and most Useful* (London, 1662), p. 58.

[42] H. L. Murphy, *A History of Trinity College Dublin from its Foundation to 1702* (Dublin, 1951), p. 201.

[43] W. Molyneux to Flamsteed, 22 December 1685, Southampton MS D/M 1/1. Although Molyneux mentions the sum of twenty pounds, the College's 'General Registry from 1640' (kept in its Muniment Room), notes for 21 November 1685, 'Thirty pounds appointed to be lay'd out in mathematical instruments'.

[44] Ashe to William Musgrave, 15 July 1687, R.S. MS Early Letters, A.39.

[45] E. St J. Brooks, 'Henry Nicholson: First Lecturer in Botany and the earliest Physic Garden', *Hermathena*, LXXXIV (1954), 3.

[46] 'St George Ashe's Speech to Lord Clarendon', T.C.D. MS I.4.17, ff. 32–3v. It is printed in I. Ehrenpreis, *Swift: The Man, His Works, and the Age*, 2 vols. to date (London, 1962–), I, 275–8. A fuller dicussion of this important speech can be found above, pp. 78–9.

[47] H. L. Murphy, *A History of Trinity College Dublin*, pp. 181–2, and J. W. Stubbs, *The History of the University of Dublin*, p. 137. But for Ashe's important sermon delivered on this occasion, see above, p. 170.

[48] Shadwell to Howell, 26 September 1703, Howell Papers, Bodl. MS Rawlinson D.842, f. 35. Printed in Ir. MSS Comm., *Analecta Hibernica*, II (1931), 74–5. Peter Browne (Provost 1699–1710), Benjamin Pratt (Provost 1710–17), and Owen Lloyd, were all, at one time or another, members of

the Dublin Society. Locke had been introduced to the college by St George Ashe (Provost 1692–5), see above, p. 174. Browne was a metaphysician of ability, and author of *The Procedure, Extent, and Limits of Human Understanding* (London, 1728), in which he asserted that Locke's philosophy tended towards scepticism. He was appointed Bishop of Cork and Ross in 1710.

⁴⁹ *Remarks and Collections of Thomas Hearne*, ed. C. E. Doble, D. W. Rannie, and H. E. Salter, 11 vols. (Oxford, 1885–1921). I, 62. The note is dated 2 November 1705. In November 1709 George Berkeley, who had been appointed librarian in that month, referred to the 'damps and mustly [*sic*] solitudes' of the library. Berkeley to S. Molyneux, 26 November 1709, *The Works of George Berkeley Bishop of Cloyne*, ed. A. A. Luce and T. E. Jessop, 9 vols. (London, 1948–57), VIII, 24.

⁵⁰ *Some Proposals humbly offered to the Consideration of the Parliament, for the Advancement of Learning* (Dublin, 1707), p. 3. The only copy of this work that I have been able to locate is in the Cashel Diocesan Library.

⁵¹ *Ibid.*, p. 11. Referring to contemporary lampoons, the author writes on p. 6 of 'that natural philosophy that has raised our knowledge so much above the ancients, that we can see now plainly what they never dream't of; however ridicul'd by some lavish wits not worth our notice.'

⁵² B.M. Add. MS 4223, f. 34.

⁵³ See J. W. Stubbs, *The History of the University of Dublin*, pp. 42 and 114.

⁵⁴ Petty's table can be found among the Lansdowne Papers at Bowood, Wiltshire, in a box labelled 'Royal Society etc.' I am grateful to the Most Hon. the Marquis of Lansdowne for permission to examine and use this document.

⁵⁵ The Cambridge figure is based on the table in J. B. Mullinger, *The University of Cambridge*, 3 vols. (Cambridge, 1873–1911), III, 679. The number of medical degrees awarded at both institutions in the period 1660–99 follow roughly the same proportion, Trinity awarding 28 and Cambridge 330 (excluding those by royal mandate). The Cambridge figures can be found in A. Rook, 'Medicine at Cambridge 1660–1760', *Medical History*, XIII (1969), 112.

⁵⁶ The figures for 1682–1704 have been taken from the 'Entrance Book 1637–1725' preserved in the Trinity College Muniment Room. Those for 1661–81 from Petty's table, which has been checked against the Entrance Book and found accurate. The years referred to are calendar years old style up to 1668, and thereafter academic years beginning in July. The nine 'noblemen' admitted between 1661 and 1704 have been included among the fellow and scholar commoners.

⁵⁷ For the earlier period detailed figures are available in the Entrance Book only for the three years 1657–9, when 88 students matriculated. The classification of 12 is not given. Of those for whom it is provided no less than 50% were fellow or scholar commoners – a strange commentary on conditions in the Commonwealth college.

⁵⁸ Occupations are given as in the Entrance Book. The years 1662, 1683, and 1700 have been chosen because for them comparatively full details are available. The large number under the heading 'generosus' for 1683 indi-

cates that entries for that year were probably done with less discrimination than for the other two.

⁵⁹ D. McKie, 'The Origins and Foundation of the Royal Society' in *The Royal Society its Origins and Founders*, ed. H. Hartley (London, 1960), p. 35.

⁶⁰ This has been done in R. T. Gunther, *Early Science in Oxford*, 14 vols. (Oxford, 1923–45), I, 49.

⁶¹ Oxford Minutes, 15 June 1686, p. 183.

⁶² There was at this time no longer the heavy concentration on Wadham College which had been a feature of Oxford science in the 1650s. In the society of the 1680s fellows of the following colleges were represented: New College, University College, All Souls, Balliol, Brasenose, Magdalen, Merton, St John's, Trinity, Wadham, and Worcester.

⁶³ C. Molyneux, *Account of the Family* (Evesham, 1820), p. 64.

⁶⁴ William to Thomas Molyneux, 10 May 1684, *Dublin University Magazine*, XVIII (1841), 481.

⁶⁵ C. H. Josten, 'Elias Ashmole' in *The Royal Society its Origins and Founders*, ed. H. Hartley, p. 228.

CHAPTER FOUR

¹ For an analysis of the philosophy lying behind the activities of the Dublin Society, see K. T. Hoppen, 'The Dublin Philosophical Society and the New Learning in Ireland', *Irish Historical Studies*, XIV (1964), 99–118.

² W. Petty, *The Advice of W.P. to Mr Samuel Hartlib for the Advancement of some particular Parts of Learning* (London, 1648), p. 2.

³ W. Molyneux, *Sciothericum Telescopicum: Or a new Contrivance of adapting a Telescope to an Horizontal Dial for observing the Moment of Time by Day or Night* (Dublin, 1686). All quotations, unless otherwise noted, are taken from the Epistle Dedicatory.

⁴ W. Molyneux, *Dioptrica Nova: A Treatise of Dioptricks in Two Parts* (London, 1692). All quotations, unless otherwise noted, are taken from the Dedication.

⁵ W. Petty, *Political Arithmetick* (London, 1690), from the Preface. This work was actually written in the early 1670s.

⁶ W. Molyneux, *Sciothericum Telescopicum*, Epistle Dedicatory.

⁷ W. Molyneux to Francis Aston, 9 October 1684, R.S. MS Early Letters, M.1.86. Copy, Bodl. MS Ashmole 1813, f. 275. Printed, *P.T.*, XV (1685), 876–9.

⁸ Marsh to Ashe, 19 June 1685, B.M. Add. MS 4811, ff. 95v-6. See also Minutes, 6 July 1685, f. 171v.

⁹ W. Molyneux, 'Why Bodies Dissolved in Menstrua specifically Lighter than themselves, Swim therein', B.M. Add. MS 4811, f. 114. Printed, *P.T.*, XVI (1686), 88–93.

¹⁰ W. Molyneux, 'Concerning the Apparent Magnitude of the Sun and Moon', R.S. MS Copy Record Book, 7, 78. Printed, *P.T.*, XVI (1687), 314–23.

¹¹ W. Molyneux, 'Remarks on Mons Hautefeuille's Method for Shortening Telescopes', R.S. MS Early Letters, M.1.100.

[12] S. Foley, 'Of Formed Stones', B.M. Add. MS 4811, f. 37.

[13] St G. Ashe, 'A Discourse of the Air', B.M. Add. MS 4811, f. 136.

[14] St G. Ashe, 'Concerning the Squaring of the Circle', B.M. Add. MS 4811, f. 54. Copy, R.S. MS Early Letters, A.34 and R.S. MS Copy Letter Book, 10, 94–114.

[15] W. Molyneux, *Dioptrica Nova*, Dedication

[16] Thomas to William Molyneux, 11 October 1690, *Dublin University Magazine*, XVIII (1841), 611.

[17] Thomas to William Molyneux, 2 June 1684, *ibid.*, p. 483.

[18] 'St George Ashe's Speech to Lord Clarendon', T.C.D. MS I.4.17, ff. 32–3v. Printed, I. Ehrenpreis, *Swift: The Man, His Works, and the Age*, 2 vols. to date (London, 1962–), I, 275–8.

[19] A. R. Hall, *From Galileo to Newton 1630–1720* (London, 1963), pp. 151–2.

[20] W. Petty, *The Discourse made before the Royal Society the 26 of November 1674 Concerning the Use of Duplicate Proportion* (London, 1674), p. 1.

[21] See W. Petty, *A Declaration Concerning the Newly Invented Art of Double Writing* (London, 1648), and also above, pp. 17–18, 143–4, and 147–8.

[22] W. Molyneux to Halley, 8 April 1686, R.S. MS Early Letters, M.1.94. Printed, T. Birch, *The History of the Royal Society of London*, 4 vols. (London, 1756–7), IV, 475–9.

[23] C. Molyneux, *Account of the Family* (Evesham, 1820), p. 67.

[24] See for example St G. Ashe, 'A Discourse of the Air', B.M. Add. MS 4811, ff. 136–7v.

[25] P. M. Rattansi, 'The Intellectual Origins of the Royal Society', *Notes and Records*, XXIII (1968), 129.

[26] Marsh's Library Dublin, MS Z2.3.2B, pp. 12, 13, and 15.

[27] H. Power, *Experimental Philosophy* (London, 1664), quoted in R. F. Jones, *Ancients and Moderns* (2d edn., St Louis, 1961), p. 195.

[28] W. Petty, *A Declaration Concerning the Newly Invented Art of Double Writing*, p. 4.

[29] Petty to Sir Robert Southwell, 14 November 1676, *The Petty–Southwell Correspondence*, ed. Marquis of Lansdowne (London, 1928), p. 9.

[30] R. S. Westfall, *Science and Religion in Seventeenth Century England* (New Haven, 1958), p. 133.

[31] *D.N.B.*

[32] *Six Metaphysical Meditations Wherein it is Proved that there is a God*, translated and introduced by W. Molyneux (London, 1680), Preface to the Reader.

[33] T. Sprat, *The History of the Royal Society* (London, 1667), p. 349.

[34] W. Molyneux to Flamsteed, 19 May 1688, *A General Dictionary . . . of the Celebrated Mr Bayle*, ed. J. P. Bernard, T. Birch, and J. Lockman, 10 vols. (London, 1734–41), VIII, 611.

[35] W. Molyneux, *Dioptrica Nova*, p. 195.

[36] C. Molyneux, *Account of the Family*, p. 67.

[37] W. Molyneux, *Dioptrica Nova*, Dedication.

[38] A. A. Luce, *The Life of George Berkeley, Bishop of Cloyne* (London, 1949), p. 44.

[39] T. Molyneux, 'Concerning Swarms of Insects', R.S. MS Copy Record Book, 7, 229. Printed, *P.T.*, XIX (1697), 741–56.

[40] T. Molyneux, 'Some Additional Observations on the Giant's Causeway' in a letter to Martin Lister, 25 March 1698, R.S. MS Early Letters, M.1.105. Another version, T.C.D. MS I.4.19, ff. 296–308v. Printed, *P.T.*, XX (1698), 209–23.

[41] Francis Nevil to Ashe, 19 November 1694, T.C.D. MS I.4.19, f. 5. Partial copy, T.C.D. MS I.1.2, pp. 13–15.

[42] T. Molyneux, 'A Discourse concerning Large Horns', R.S. MS Classified Papers XV(1), 51. Printed, *P.T.*, XIX (1697), 489–512.

[43] See Q. Skinner, 'Thomas Hobbes and the Nature of the early Royal Society', *Historical Journal*, XII (1969), 230–6.

[44] Quoted in S. Toulmin and J. Goodfield, *The Fabric of the Heavens* (London, 1961), p. 251.

[45] *The Works of the Honourable Robert Boyle*, ed. T. Birch, 6 vols. (London, 1772), V, 515.

[46] S. Foley, 'Of Formed Stones', B.M. Add. MS 4811, f. 38.

[47] C. Molyneux, *Account of the Family*, p. 64.

[48] William to Thomas Molyneux, 8 January 1684, *Dublin University Magazine*, XVIII (1841), 477.

[49] These rules are printed in *The Petty Papers*, ed. Marquis of Lansdowne, 2 vols. (London, 1927), II, 88–90.

[50] William to Thomas Molyneux, November 1684, *Dublin University Magazine*, XVIII (1841), 489.

[51] These are written on a stray sheet inserted in the first minute book of the later (1683) Oxford Society, Bodl. MS Ashmole 1810, which is photographically reproduced in M. Purver, *The Royal Society: Concept and Creation* (London, 1967), Plate VI.

[52] *The Record of the Royal Society* (4th edn., London, 1940), pp. 9–10.

[53] Oxford Minutes, 11 March 1684, p. 46.

[54] Minutes, 3 November 1684, f. 166. The rules are to be found in B.M. Add. MS 4811, f. 48v, and are given above as Appendix B.

[55] Aston to W. Molyneux, 11 December 1684, T.C.D. MS I.4.18, f. 117. Copy, B.M. Add. MS 4811, f. 63v.

[56] *The Life and Times of Anthony à Wood*, ed. A. Clark, 5 vols. (Oxford, 1891–1900), III, 107.

[57] H. Lyons, *The Royal Society 1660–1940* (Cambridge, 1944), p. 41.

[58] T. Sprat, *History of the Royal Society*, p. 53.

[59] *The Spectator*, No. 262 (31 December 1711). See *The Spectator*, ed. D. F. Bond, 5 vols. (Oxford, 1965), II, 519.

[60] Minutes, 3 December 1683, T. Birch, *History of the Royal Society*, IV, 248.

[61] Huntington to Plot, 18 December 1683, R.S. MS Early Letters, H.3.72.

[62] Ashe to Dodwell, 18 December 1684, Bodl. MS English Letters c. 29, f. 2.

[63] Ashe to Dodwell, 23 June 1685, Bodl. MS English Letters c. 29, f. 6.

[64] Ashe to Dodwell, 31 July 1685, Bodl. MS English Letters c. 29, f. 7.

[65] B.M. Add. MS 4811, f. 48v.

[66] B.M. Sloane MS 1008, ff. 233, 251, 301, and 333.

[67] Huntington to Plot, 18 December 1683, R.S. MS Early Letters, H.3.72.

[68] T. Birch, *History of the Royal Society*, IV, 249.

[69] Aston to W. Molyneux, 26 February 1684, T.C.D. MS I.4.18, f. 115. Copy, B.M. Add. MS 4811, f. 7.

[70] Musgrave to W. Molyneux, 23 February 1684, T.C.D. MS I.4.18, f. 135. Copy, B.M. Add. MS 4811, f. 8.

[71] Flamsteed to W. Molyneux, 2 May 1684, Southampton MS D/M 1/1.

[72] Petty to Southwell, 17 March 1685, *The Petty–Southwell Correspondence*, ed. Marquis of Lansdowne, p. 136.

[73] C. Molyneux, *Account of the Family*, p. 60.

[74] W. Molyneux to Flamsteed, 3 April 1683, Southampton MS D/M 1/1.

[75] W. Molyneux to Flamsteed, 13 May 1684, Southampton MS D/M 1/1.

[76] W. Molyneux to [Halley], 7 July 1687, R.S. MS Copy Letter Book, 11(1), 101.

[77] W. Molyneux to Flamsteed, 13 May 1684, Southampton MS D/M 1/1. See also, T.C.D. Lyon MS, No. 27a. This is a bill from Pitt to King and Dun, dated 9 October 1684, for three copies each of the 'Lipsick Transact'.

[78] Thomas to William Molyneux, 15 August 1684 (New Style), *Dublin University Magazine*, XVIII (1841), 486. Thomas also sent a copy of Huygens's *Astroscopia Compendiaria* (The Hague, 1684) to Dublin at this time.

[79] Thomas to William Molyneux, April 1684, *Dublin University Magazine*, XVIII (1841), 479.

[80] William to Thomas Molyneux, June 1684, *ibid.*, p. 485.

[81] Bibliothèque Nationale Paris, Fonds Français MS 13050, f. 248. This is an unsigned letter to Boulliau, dated 27 March 1684 (?New Style), which mentions the Dublin 'Society of Arts' and 'Mr Petti'.

[82] Huntington to Trumbull, 11 September 1685, H.M.C., *Calendar of Downshire MSS*, I, Part 1 (1924), 42. Huntington and Trumbull had been together at Oxford in the 1650s and 1660s. In the *Dioptrica Nova*, p. 224, Molyneux refers to a visit he paid to Giovanni Cassini at the latter's obervatory in Paris.

[83] T. Molyneux to Bayle, 6 January 1685 (New Style), Royal Library Copenhagen, MS Thott. 1208 b–c 4°. (In Latin). This letter is No. 339 in E. Labrousse, *Inventaire Critique de la Correspondance de Pierre Bayle* (Paris, 1961).

[84] Sylvius to Bayle, 1 September 1686, Royal Library Copenhagen, MS Thott. 1208 b–c 4°. Labrousse No. 579.

[85] *Nouvelles de la République des Lettres*, VI (1686), 790–96. In *Ibid.*, p. 708 Sylvius is described as 'Docteur en médecine, et membre de l'Académie qui s'est formée à Dublin depuis quelque temps pour perfectionner les sciences.'

[86] Smyth to Bayle, Prid. Id. Decemb. [12 December] 1686, B.M. Add. MS 4811, f. 141. Another copy, B.M. Add. MS 4226, ff. 256v–7. Labrousse No. 630. Printed, *Lettres de Mr Bayle, publiées sur les Originaux*, ed. P. Desmaizeaux, 3 vols. (Amsterdam, 1729), I, 272–3.

[87] Bayle to Smyth, 8 Kalend. Feb. [25 January] 1687 (New Style), B.M. Add. MS 4811, f. 141v. This letter is not listed in Labrousse.

88 Articles by members of the Dublin Society which were printed in continental journals include: T. Molyneux's 'Essay on Bodies dissolved in a menstruum', *Nouvelles de la République des Lettres*, II (1684), 581–5; 'Further Reflections on the Same', *ibid.*, III (1685), 50–3; Jacobus Sylvius's 'Account of the Horny Girl', *ibid.*, VII (1686), 790–96; St George Ashe's 'Account of the Horny Girl', *Acta Eruditorum*, (1686), 487–8; W. Molyneux's 'Solution of a Dioptric Problem', *Bibliothèque Universelle et Historique*, III (1686), 329–34; 'Account of the Connaught Worm', *Acta Eruditorum*, (1686), 300–2; 'Account of the Hygroscope', *Ibid.*, 388–91; 'Circulation of the Blood in the Water-Newt', *Journal des Sçavans* (15 April 1683). An abridgement of W. Molyneux's book, *Sciothericum Telescopicum*, appeared in *Acta Eruditorum*, (1687), 623–6.

89 *The Diary of John Evelyn*, ed. E. S. de Beer, 6 vols. (Oxford, 1955), III, 110. Entry for 13 July 1654.

90 Huntington to Plot, 18 December 1683, R.S. MS Early Letters, H.3.72.

91 W. Molyneux to Flamsteed, 17 September 1681, Southampton MS D/M 1/1.

92 W. Molyneux to Flamsteed, 8 April 1684, Southampton MS D/M 1/1.

93 'St George Ashe's Speech to Lord Clarendon', T.C.D. MS I.4.17, ff. 32–3v.

94 H. F. Berry, 'The Ancient Corporation of Barber-Surgeons, or Guild of St Mary Magdalene, Dublin', *Journal of the Royal Society of Antiquaries of Ireland*, XXXIII (1903), 237.

95 William to Thomas Molyneux, 10 May 1684, *Dublin University Magazine*, XVIII (1841), 481.

96 William to Thomas Molyneux, 14 June 1684, *ibid.*, p. 483.

97 C. Molyneux, *Account of the Family*, p. 75.

98 *A Catalogue of the Library of the Honble. Samuel Molyneux Deceas'd, . . . Consisting of many Valuable and Rare Books in Several Languages, . . . With Several Curious Manuscripts, and all his Mathematical, Optical, and Mechanical Instruments* (London, 1730), pp. 56–7 and 60–2.

99 C. Molyneux, *Account of the Family*, p. 64.

100 See above, pp. 166–7.

101 W. Molyneux to Flamsteed, 5 January 1684, Southampton MS D/M 1/1. Part One had been published at Danzig in 1676 and Part Two in 1679. Halley had visited Hevelius to examine his instruments (see above, p. 115). In the Autumn of 1685 the Royal Society presented the Dublin Society with a copy of Hevelius's *Annus Climactericus* (Danzig, 1685). See W. Molyneux to Aston, 12 November 1685, R.S. MS Early Letters, M.1.92.

102 W. Molyneux to Flamsteed, 16 December 1684, Southampton MS D/M 1/1.

103 *A Catalogue of the Library of the Honble. Samuel Molyneux.* This lists about 3500 titles, of which it is estimated that about 2000 probably belonged to William Molyneux.

104 *Ibid.*, pp. 22, 48, 9, and 21. The library also contained works by Hobbes, Evelyn, and Locke, and a number of legal, historical, and genealogical pieces.

105 Part of William Molyneux's library is still kept together at the Public Library Southampton, where it is interspersed with some of Samuel Molyneux's books and those which belonged to Nathaniel St André, who married Samuel's widow, and who made his home at Southampton. St André bequeathed the books to George Frederick Pitt, who sold some of them, most importantly the medical works to the Royal College of Surgeons in 1818, and presented the remainder to the Southampton authorities in 1831. See City of Southampton Public Libraries Committee, *A Catalogue of the Pitt Collection* (Southampton, 1964).

106 The catalogue of Willoughby's library is T.C.D. MS E.4.9. This MS is not foliated, but the books are listed alphabetically under author. About 800 works are noted.

107 T.C.D. MS E.4.9. The first two leaves contain rough notes of books lent, e.g. Hobbes's *Leviathan* to Dr Chamberlain, Descartes's *Geometry* to Narcissus Marsh, and Hooke's *Micrographia* to Mark Baggot.

108 From the title page of the auction catalogue given in Publications of the Bibliographical Society of Ireland, VI, No. 3, F. O'Kelley, *Irish Book-Sale Catalogues before 1801* (Dublin, 1953), p. 45. 'Philosophical' books were also being read in rural parts. Swift's friend Richard Dobbs of County Antrim, for example, owned a copy of Joseph Glanvill's *Scepsis Scientifica*, which Swift thought 'a fustian piece of abominable curious virtuoso stuff'. See, Swift to John Winder, 13 January 1699, *The Correspondence of Jonathan Swift*, ed. H. Williams, 5 vols. (Oxford, 1963–5), I, 30.

109 Minutes, 3 March 1684, f. 160v.

110 T.C.D. MS I.4.18, f. 38v. The minute book itself (B.M. Add. MS 4811) contains at least three different hands.

111 The only known copy is in Bodl. MS Ashmole 1813, ff. 356–7.

112 William to Thomas Molyneux, Spring 1684, *Dublin University Magazine*, XVIII (1841), 485.

113 William to Thomas Molyneux, 12 April 1684, *ibid.*, p. 480.

114 See the report on the Wyche Papers (now in the Public Record Office of Ireland) in, *Fifty-Seventh Report of the Deputy Keeper of the Public Records and Keeper of the State Papers in Ireland* (Dublin, 1936), p. 479.

115 William to Thomas Molyneux, October 1684, *Dublin University Magazine*, XVIII (1841), 489, and Minutes, 3 November 1684, f. 166.

116 Minutes, 25 January 1686, f. 176.

117 T.C.D. MS I.4.17, ff. 32–3v.

118 Minutes, 1 February 1686, f. 176.

119 Minutes, 19 April 1686, f. 178v.

120 See Bulkeley to Lister, 8 May and 24 June 1686, Bodl. MS Lister 35, ff. 118 and 121.

121 Minutes, 17 January 1687, R. S. MS Early Letters, s.i. 135.

122 C. Molyneux, *Account of the Family*, p. 64.

CHAPTER FIVE

[1] M. Boas, *Robert Boyle and Seventeenth Century Chemistry* (Cambridge, 1958), p. 52.

[2] Minutes, 5 May 1684, f. 162v, and 22 October 1683, R.S. MS Early Letters, H.3.72.

[3] Minutes, 5 May 1684, f. 162v.

[4] Oxford Minutes, 19 August 1684, p. 87.

[5] T.C.D. MS E.4.9.

[6] Willoughby to King, December 1691, T. P. C. Kirkpatrick, 'Charles Willoughby', *Proceedings of the Royal Irish Academy*, Section C, XXXVI (1923), 244–5. Willoughby had sensible views on prescriptions and the use of drugs. See his comments on Thomas Sydenham's use of opium, Bodl. MS Rawlinson C. 406, f. 68, partly printed in K. Dewhurst, *Dr Thomas Sydenham 1624–1689* (London, 1966), p. 58. On his return from Holland in the late 1680s Thomas Molyneux brought with him a fine herbarium, which is now in the National Museum of Ireland.

[7] William to Thomas Molyneux, Spring 1684, *Dublin University Magazine*, XVIII (1841), 479.

[8] Oxford Minutes, 23 November 1686, p. 189.

[9] W. H. G. Armytage, 'The Royal Society and the Apothecaries 1660–1722', *Notes and Records*, XI (1954), 23.

[10] Minutes, 20 July 1685, f. 172.

[11] Oxford Minutes, 12 May 1685, pp. 145–8.

[12] They were sent in a letter dated 21 May 1685, B.M. Add. MS 4811, f. 90.

[13] Oxford Minutes, 12 May 1685, p. 145.

[14] *Johann Kunckels . . . Chymischer Probier-Stein, De Acido et Urinoso, Sale Calid. et Frigid. Contra Herrn Doct. Voigts Spirit. Vini Vindicatum, An Die Weltberühmte Königl. Societät in Engeland* (Berlin, 1684). See the summary in *P.T.*, XV (1685), 896–914.

[15] T. Birch, *History of the Royal Society*, 4 vols. (London, 1756–7), IV, 325, Note Q.

[16] Aston to W. Molyneux, 8 November 1684, B.M. Add. MS 4811, f. 51v. See also Minutes, 24 November 1684, f. 167.

[17] Minutes, 23 March 1685, f. 169.

[18] Minutes, 15 June 1685, f. 171.

[19] M. Boas, *Robert Boyle and Seventeenth Century Chemistry*, p. 154.

[20] Minutes, 4 February 1684, f. 160. The paper itself is T.C.D. MS I.4.18, ff. 123–4, with a copy in B.M. Add. MS 4811, f. 1. Ashe actually refers simply to 'Mr Boyl's book'. It is however obvious that he was using the second edition of *New Experiments*.

[21] St G. Ashe, 'Experiments of Freezing', T.C.D. MS I.4.18, ff. 123–4.

[22] R. Boyle, *New Experiments*, p. 124.

[23] Oxford Minutes, 1 February 1684, p. 33.

[24] St G. Ashe, 'Experiments of Freezing', T.C.D. MS I.4.18, f. 124.

[25] Minutes, 18 January 1686, f. 175v.

[26] B.M. Add. MS 4811, f. 27. Printed, *P.T.*, XIV (1684), 802–3.

27 W. Petty, 'Diary of a Journey in August 1683', B.M. Lansdowne MS 1228, f. 23.

28 Minutes, 2 June 1684, f. 163v, and 23 June 1684, f. 164v.

29 Oxford Minutes, 17 March 1685, pp. 130–2.

30 Minutes, 11 May 1685, f. 170.

31 H. C. Cameron, 'The Last Alchemist', *Notes and Records*, IX (1951), 109.

32 R. K. Merton, 'Science, Technology, and Society in Seventeenth Century England', *Osiris*, IV (1938), Table 6, p. 406. This table, which henceforth will be referred to as '*Osiris*, IV, Table 6', gives a thematic breakdown of the articles published in the *Philosophical Transactions* from 1665 to 1702. In Appendix D of the present work a detailed numerative breakdown is given of the nature of the work performed at the Royal, Oxford, and Dublin Societies for the period 1684 to 1687. This is based on the minutes of the three societies.

33 C. Willoughby, 'Observations on the Bills of Mortality and Increase of People in Dublin 1690', *Proceedings of the Royal Irish Academy*, VI (1856), 414.

34 T. Molyneux, 'Concerning Swarms of Insects', R.S. MS Early Letters, M.1.106. Printed, *P.T.*, XIX (1697), 741.

35 Minutes, 19 January 1685, f. 168.

36 Minutes, 26 January 1685, f. 168.

37 W. Molyneux to Musgrave, 21 February 1685, T.C.D. MS I.4.18, f. 281. Printed (from a copy in Bodl. MS Ashmole 1813), R. T. Gunther, *Early Science in Oxford*, 14 vols. (Oxford, 1923–45), XII, 164–5.

38 Minutes, 23 February 1685, f. 168v.

39 *Ibid.*

40 A. Mullen, 'Discourse on the Dissection of a Monstrous Double Cat', B.M. Add. MS 4811, ff. 83–4. Printed, *P.T.*, XV (1685), 1135–9.

41 Minutes, 18 May 1685, f. 170v, and 22 March 1686, f. 177v. Members of the Academia naturae curiosorum also reported on humans with 'horns'. See L. Thorndike, *History of Magic and Experimental Science*, 8 vols. (New York, 1929–58), VIII, 236. The Oxford Society twice mentioned similar phenomena. See Oxford Minutes, 21 December 1686, p. 195, and 1 February 1687, p. 198.

42 Oldenburg to Boyle, 24 December 1667, *The Correspondence of Henry Oldenburg*, ed. A. R. and M. B. Hall, 6 vols. to date (Madison, 1965–), IV, 78.

43 Minutes, 18 May 1685, f. 170v.

44 L. Thorndike, *History of Magic and Experimental Science*, VIII, 253.

45 Minutes, 18 May 1685, f. 170v.

46 'St George Ashe's Speech to Lord Clarendon', T.C.D. MS I.4.17, ff. 32–3v.

47 L. Thorndike, *History of Magic and Experimental Science*, VIII, 236.

48 Oxford Minutes, 1 February 1687, p. 198.

49 F. Watson, *The Beginnings of the Teaching of Modern Subjects in England* (London, 1909), p. 242.

50 Minutes, 26 May 1684, f. 163.

51 T. Birch, *History of the Royal Society*, IV, 306.

52 W. Molyneux to Grew, 7 June 1684, *Ibid.*

53 Oxford Minutes, 6 October 1685, p. 161.

54 A description of this experiment is to be found in T. Sprat, *The History of the Royal Society* (London, 1667), p. 232. See also Hooke to Boyle, 10 November 1664, *The Works of the Honourable Robert Boyle*, ed. T. Birch, 6 vols. (London, 1772), VI, 498.

55 *Works of Boyle*, ed. T. Birch (London, 1772), VI, 498.

56 Minutes, 26 May 1684, f. 163v. See also his undated paper 'On Injecting Mercury into the Blood and its Effects on the Lungs', R.S. Classified Papers XIV (1), 34. Printed (posthumously), *P.T.*, XVII (1691), 486–8. On this question in general, see W. Shugg, 'Humanitarian Attitudes in the Early Animal Experiments of the Royal Society', *Annals of Science*, XXIV (1968), 227–38.

57 Minutes, 10 November 1684, f. 166v.

58 A. Mullen, 'A Conjecture of the Quantity of Blood in Men, together with an Estimate of the Celerity of its Circulation', *P.T.*, XVI (1687), 433–4.

59 Minutes, 17 March 1684, f. 161v.

60 Oxford Minutes, 13 May 1684, pp. 68–9.

61 A brief examination of the diary of the prominent Limerick physician Thomas Arthur (*Kilkenny Archaeological Journal*, New Series, VI (1867)), shows that venereal diseases, especially gonorrhoea, were not uncommon among seventeenth century Ireland's social élite.

62 Minutes, 29 November 1686, R.S. MS Early Letters, S.1.135.

63 J. Fleetwood, *History of Medicine in Ireland* (Dublin, 1951), p. 80.

64 Ashe to John Benbrigge, 26 March 1687, R. T. Gunther, *Early Science in Oxford*, XII, 202.

65 See Y. M. Goblet, *La Transformation de la Géographie politique de l'Irlande au XVIIe Siècle*, 2 vols. (Paris, 1930), I, 153, note 1. I have been unable to locate a copy of the 1652 pamphlet.

66 Minutes, 17 January 1687, R.S. MS Early Letters, S.1.135.

67 T. Sprat, *History of the Royal Society*, p. 223.

68 T. Birch, *History of the Royal Society*, IV, 278.

69 Minutes, 8 March 1686, f. 177.

70 C. Allen, *The Operator for the Teeth shewing how to Preserve the Teeth and Gums from all Accidents they are Subject to* (Dublin, 1686), p. 28.

71 *Ibid.*, p. 58.

72 His observations were later confirmed by Christopher Pitt at Oxford. See Oxford Minutes, 3 May 1687, p. 204. Mullen's paper was published after his death in *P.T.*, XVII (1693), 711–16.

73 *Osiris*, IV, Table 6.

74 R. K. Merton, 'Science, Technology, and Society in Seventeenth Century England', *Osiris*, IV (1938), 391.

75 W. Molyneux to Flamsteed, 17 September 1681, Southampton MS D/M 1/1.

76 These figures, which, as records are incomplete, are minimum ones, have been obtained from an analysis of G. Fennell, *A List of Irish Watch and Clock Makers* (Dublin, 1963).

77 W. Molyneux to Flamsteed, 3 December 1681, Southampton MS D/M 1/1.

78 W. Molyneux to Flamsteed, 3 April 1683, *Ibid.*

79 W. Molyneux to Flamsteed, 2 May 1683, *Ibid.*

80 W. Molyneux to Flamsteed, 22 December 1685, *Ibid.*

81 E. G. R. Taylor, *The Mathematical Practitioners of Tudor and Stuart England* (Cambridge, 1954), p. 240.

82 W. Molyneux to Flamsteed, 22 December 1685, Southampton MS D/M 1/1.

83 *P.T.*, XIV (1684), 749. Edmond Halley recorded Osborne's observations of a solar eclipse in his edition of Thomas Streete's *Astronomia Carolina* (London, 1716).

84 W. Molyneux to Flamsteed, 8 April 1684, Southampton MS D/M 1/1. Wood was thanked in 1661 by Thomas Salusbury, the translator of Galileo, for 'more than ordinary encouragement'. See T. Salusbury, *Mathematical Collections and Translations* (London, 1661), Part I, 'To the Reader'.

85 *The Double-Bottom or Twin-Hulled Ship of Sir William Petty*, ed. Marquis of Lansdowne (Oxford, 1931), p. 129.

86 C. Molyneux, *Account of the Family* (Evesham, 1820), p. 64.

87 *P.T.*, XVI (1686), 213–16, and Wallis to W. Molyneux, 1691, *P.T.*, XVII (1691–2), 844.

88 D. J. Price, 'The Early Observatory Instruments of Trinity College Cambridge', *Annals of Science*, VIII (1952), 3.

89 Minutes, 7 July 1684, f. 164v.

90 Oxford Minutes, 29 July 1684, p. 81.

91 *P.T.*, XV (1685), 1162–83.

92 E. F. MacPike, *Hevelius, Flamsteed, and Halley: Three Contemporary Astronomers and their Mutual Relations* (London, 1937), p. 95.

93 W. Molyneux to Aston, 12 November 1685, R.S. MS Early Letters, M.1.92.

94 E. F. MacPike, *Hevelius, Flamsteed, and Halley*, p. 97.

95 W. Molyneux, 'Concerning Telescopic Sights as adapted to Astronomicall and other Instruments', B.M. Add. MS 4811, f. 6.

96 W. Molyneux to Halley, 8 April 1686, R.S. MS Early Letters, M.1.94. Hooke's reply to Molyneux can be found in *The Posthumous Works of Robert Hooke*, ed. R. Waller (London, 1705), pp. xvi–xix.

97 Minutes, 15 October 1683, R.S. MS Early Letters, H.3.72.

98 Halley to Wallis, 9 April 1687, *The Correspondence and Papers of Edmond Halley*, ed. E. F. MacPike (Oxford, 1932), p. 82.

99 W. Molyneux, 'A Way of Viewing Pictures in Miniature', B.M. Add. MS 4811, ff. 13v–14.

100 Flamsteed to W. Molyneux, 2 January 1690, Southampton MS D/M 1/1.

101 Oxford Minutes, 29 July 1684, p. 81.

102 W. Molyneux, 'Concerning Telescopic Sights', B.M. Add. MS 4811, f. 5v.

103 *Osiris*, IV, Table 6.

[104] A. R. Hall, *The Scientific Revolution 1500–1800* (2d edn., London, 1962), p. 171.

[105] Minutes, 31 October 1683, R.S. MS Early Letters, H.3.72.

[106] Minutes, 14 April 1684, f. 162.

[107] R. T. Gunther, *Early Science in Oxford*, VII, 610.

[108] St G. Ashe, 'Concerning the Squaring of the Circle', B.M. Add. MS 4811, ff. 53–7. Copies, R.S. MS Early Letters, A.34, and R.S. MS Copy Letter Book, 10, 94–114. See also Minutes, 3 and 17 November 1684, f. 166.

[109] In 1596 van Ceulen had given the result to 20 places by finding the perimeters of the inscribed and circumscribed regular polygons of 60×2^{33} sides. Snell, who calculated to 34 places, used a more elegant method, obtaining his result by the use of a polygon from which van Ceulen had obtained only 14 (or possibly 16) places. Grienberger, who calculated to 39 places in his *Elementa Trigonometrica* (Rome, 1630), was the last to use the classical method of finding the perimeters of inscribed and circumscribed polygons. Most subsequent practitioners relied on converging infinite series, a method hardly practicable before the invention of the calculus. It was not however until 1761 that J. H. Lambert provided analytical proof of the incommensurability of π.

[110] Oxford Minutes, 16 December 1684 and 10 March 1685, pp. 109 and 129.

[111] St G. Ashe, 'Of Mathematicks and a new Method of Demonstration', T.C.D. MS I.4.18, ff. 8–9. Copy, B.M. Add. MS 4811, ff. 21v–3. Printed, *P.T.*, XIV (1684), 672–6. See also Minutes, 14 April 1684, f. 162.

[112] W. Petty, *The Discourse made before the Royal Society . . . concerning the Use of Duplicate Proportion* (London, 1674), p. 5. On this see R. Kargon, 'William Petty's Mechanical Philosophy', *Isis*, LVI (1965), 63–6.

[113] Minutes, 19 November 1683, R.S. MS Early Letters, H.3.72.

[114] W. Molyneux, *Dioptrica Nova* (London, 1692), Epistle.

[115] Minutes, 28 January 1684, f. 160.

[116] R.S. Classified Papers I, 20 (Copy, R.S. MS Copy Letter Book, 10, 221–4), and R.S. Classified Papers VI, 38.

[117] *Private Correspondence and Miscellaneous Papers of Samuel Pepys*, ed. J. R. Tanner, 2 vols. (London, 1926), I, 82–4 and 92–3.

[118] *Ibid.*, I, 75–6, 78–81, and 91–3. For Newton's solutions, See also *The Correspondence of Isaac Newton*, ed. H. W. Turnbull and J. F. Scott, 4 vols. to date (Cambridge, 1959–), III, 294–6, 298–300, and 302–3, as also the editor's note No. 4 on p. 301.

[119] R.S. Classified Papers I, 5. Printed, *P.T.*, XVII (1693), 677–81.

[120] W. Molyneux to Flamsteed, 19 May 1688, *A General Dictionary . . . of the Celebrated Mr Bayle*, ed. J. P. Bernard, T. Birch, and J. Lockman, 10 vols. (London, 1734–41), VIII, 611.

[121] *Osiris*, IV, Table 6.

[122] M. 'Espinasse, 'The Decline and Fall of Restoration Science', *Past and Present*, No. 14 (1958), 72.

[123] W. Molyneux to Flamsteed, 20 February 1686, Southampton MS D/M 1/1.

[124] E. Smyth, 'Concerning the Method of Demonstrating Independently' B.M. Add. MS 4811, f. 138v.

[125] This society did not receive the title 'royal' until some years after its foundation. I refer to it as such to distinguish it from the earlier Philosophical Society.

[126] B.M. Add. MS 4811, ff. 31v–5. Copy, R.S. MS Early Letters, F.2.1a.

[127] T. Hobbes, *De Cive*, ed. S. P. Lamprecht (New York, 1949), p. 3. It is also probable that Foley had read the then influential *Idea Matheseos Universae* (1669) by the German Erhard Weigel, in which a general all-embracing science, based on mathematics, was presented as a tool by which all things could be measured. See L. I. Bredvold, 'The Invention of the Ethical Calculus' in R. F. Jones and Others, *The Seventeenth Century: Studies in the History of English Thought and Literature from Bacon to Pope* (Stanford, California, 1951), pp. 165–80.

[128] Oxford Minutes, 13 October 1685, p. 162.

[129] W. Molyneux, *Dioptrica Nova*, Admonition to the Reader.

[130] W. Molyneux to Flamsteed, 17 May 1687, Southampton MS D/M 1/1.

[131] W. Molyneux to Flamsteed, 19 May 1688, *A General Dictionary . . . of the Celebrated Mr Bayle*, ed. J. P. Bernard, T. Birch, and J. Lockman (London, 1734–41), VIII, 611.

[132] *Ibid.*

[133] Petty to Southwell, 9 July 1687, Lord Edmond Fitzmaurice, *The Life of Sir William Petty* (London, 1895), p. 306.

[134] W. Molyneux to Hans Sloane, 13 November 1697, B.M. Sloane MS 4036, f. 367.

[135] W. Molyneux to Flamsteed, 18 April 1682, Southampton MS D/M 1/1.

[136] A. Armitage, 'William Ball F.R.S.' in *The Royal Society its Origins and Founders*, ed. H. Hartley (London, 1960), p. 168.

[137] Oxford Minutes, 30 November 1683, p. 25.

[138] Oxford Minutes, 30 November 1683 and 8 April 1684, pp. 25 and 55–8.

[139] *P.T.*, XIV (1684), 472–88.

[140] Oxford Minutes, 15 February 1684, p. 38.

[141] Minutes, 7 July 1684, f. 165. Morland (1625–95) was a prodigious inventor and described his speaking trumpet in *Tuba-Stentoro-Phonica* (London, 1671).

[142] T. Shadwell, *The Virtuoso*, ed. M. H. Nicolson and D. S. Rodes (London, 1966), pp. 111–12 (Act V, Scene ii).

[143] F. Robartes, 'A Discourse concerning the Musical Notes of the Trumpet and Trumpet-Marine, and the Defects of the Same', *P.T.*, XVII (1692), 559–63.

[144] *P.T.*, XI (1677), 839–42.

[145] M. Nicolson and N. Mohler, 'The Scientific Background to Swift's Voyage to Laputa' in M. Nicolson, *Science and Imagination* (Ithaca, N.Y., 1956), p. 122.

[146] *Osiris*, IV, Table 6. But see Appendix D.

147 Minutes, 11 February 1684, f. 160v.
148 W. King, 'Of Hydraulic Engines', T.C.D. MS I.4.18, ff. 105–12.
149 Minutes, 2 June 1684, f. 163v.
150 Minutes, 3 May 1686, f. 175v. Papin's engine is described in *P.T.*, XV (1685), 1093–4 and 1274–8.
151 W. Molyneux, 'An Optic Problem', R.S. MS Copy Letter Book, 10, 43–51. See P. Gassendi, *De Apparante Magnitudine Solis Humilis et Sublimis* (Paris, 1642), p. 167ff.
152 'Extrait de trois Lettres écrites à l'Auteur du Journal contenant quelque chose de fort curieux', *Journal des Sçavants* (Amsterdam ed.), XIII (1685), 466.
153 W. Molyneux, 'A Dioptric Problem', R.S. Classified Papers II, 14. Printed, *P.T.*, XVI (1686), 169–72, and *Bibliothèque Universelle et Historique*, III (1686), 329–34.
154 B.M. Add. MS 4223, f. 36. See Chapter One, Note 96.
155 C. Molyneux, *Account of the Family*, p. 76.
156 Powys to Pepys, 19 January 1697, *Private Correspondence and Miscellaneous Papers of Samuel Pepys*, ed. J. R. Tanner, I, 136. Another reason for Flamsteed's anger may have been his dislike of Halley.
157 Two versions of the manuscript exist: Southampton MS D/M 4/15 (rough copy) and Southampton MS D/M 4/16 (fair copy). I quote from the preface to the latter.
158 T.C.D. MS I.4.19a.
159 A. R. Hall, *From Galileo to Newton 1630–1720* (London, 1963), p. 102.
160 M. 'Espinasse, *Robert Hooke* (London, 1956), p. 50.
161 Hooke's 'Method for Making a History of the Weather' is printed in T. Sprat, *History of the Royal Society*, pp. 173–9.
162 W. Molyneux to Musgrave, 17 April 1685, B.M. Add. MS 4811, ff. 84v–8v. Copies, Bodl. MS Ashmole 1813, ff. 284–5, and R.S. MS Copy Letter Book, 10, 156–62. Printed, *P.T.*, XV (1685), 1032–5.
163 Minutes, 23 March 1686, f. 174v.
164 Aston to W. Molyneux, 3 April 1684, T.C.D. MS I.4.18, f. 35. Copy, B.M. Add. MS 4811, f. 16.
165 Minutes, 10 November 1684, f. 166v.
166 Minutes, 2 June 1684, f. 163v.
167 Oxford Minutes, 6 May 1684, pp. 65–6.
168 Minutes, 10 March 1684, f. 161.
169 Bodl. MS Ashmole 1813, f. 347. The first half of this sheet is reproduced in R. T. Gunther, *Early Science in Oxford*, XII, 208.
170 Minutes, 8 March 1686, f. 177.
171 Minutes, 24 May 1686, f. 179.
172 Minutes, 3 August 1685, f. 172v. George Garden (1649–1733) was a Scottish divine and regent of King's College Aberdeen. His paper on the weather is printed in *P.T.*, XV (1685), 991–1001. See also Oxford Minutes, 7 April 1685, pp. 137–8, and Garden to George Midleton, 2 March 1685 (N.S.), R. T. Gunther, *Early Science in Oxford*, XII, 270–2.
173 Oxford Minutes, 6 May 1684, p. 66.

S

174 Minutes, 25 October 1686, f. 180v, and St G. Ashe, 'A Discourse of the Air', B.M. Add. MS 4811, ff. 135v-8.

175 D. C. Douglas, *English Scholars 1660-1730* (2d edn., London, 1951), p. 25.

176 Halley to Ashe, 27 March 1686, R.S. MS Early Letters, H.3.42 (draft). Copy, B.M. Add. MS 4811, f. 117. Printed, *The Correspondence and Papers of Edmond Halley*, ed. E. F. MacPike, pp. 61-2 (from the draft).

177 W. Petty, 'The Scale of Animals' (undated), *The Petty Papers*, ed. Marquis of Lansdowne, 2 vols. (London, 1927), II, 25-34.

178 R. Hooke, *Micrographia* (London, 1665), p. 112.

179 M. 'Espinasse, *Robert Hooke*, p. 76.

180 T. Molyneux, 'A Discourse Concerning Large Horns', R.S. Classified Papers XV(1), 51. Printed, *P.T.*, XIX (1697), 489-512.

181 S. Foley, 'Of Formed Stones', B.M. Add. MS 4811, ff. 37-8v. See also Minutes, 30 June 1684, f. 164v.

182 *P.T.*, VI (1671), 2281-4.

183 Redding to Lister, 28 September 1684, R.S. MS Copy Letter Book, 10, 164-7.

184 Minutes, 4 May 1685 and 10 March 1684, ff. 170 and 161.

185 Ray to Lhuyd, 8 October 1695, *Further Correspondence of John Ray*, ed. R. T. Gunther (London, 1928), p. 260.

186 T. Molyneux to Lhuyd, 26 June 1698, Bodl. MS Ashmole 1816, f. 361.

187 Oxford Minutes, 18 January 1684, p. 31.

188 Lhuyd to Lister, 3 July 1694, R. T. Gunther, *Early Science in Oxford*, XIV, 239.

189 T. Molyneux to Lhuyd, 26 June 1698, Bodl. MS Ashmole 1816, f. 361.

190 *P.T.*, XVIII (1694), 170-82.

191 R.S. MS Copy Journal Book, 8, 247. Entry for 27 June 1694.

192 W. Molyneux to Sloane, 13 November 1697, B.M. Sloane MS 4036, f. 367.

193 R.S. MS Copy Journal Book, 8, 280. Entry for 20 February 1695.

194 *P.T.*, XX (1698), 209-23.

195 *Osiris*, IV, Table 6.

196 Marsh to Ashe, 19 June 1685, B.M. Add. MS 4811, ff. 95v-6. See also Minutes, 6 July 1685, f. 171v. The full title of Lister's translation is *Johannes Godartius Of Insects, Done into English and Methodized with the Addition of Notes by M.L.* (York, 1682).

197 Minutes, 27 July 1685, f. 172.

198 T. Molyneux, 'Observata quaedaem Anatomica in Vespertilione dissecto 22do die Septembris 1682' B.M. Add. MS 4811, f. 15. See also Minutes, 24 March 1684, f. 162.

199 *Osiris*, IV, Table 6.

200 S. Foley, 'The Anatomy of a large Garden Bean', T.C.D. MS I.4.18, ff. 161-2v. Copy, B.M. Add. MS 4811, ff. 10v-11. See also Minutes, 10 March 1684, f. 161.

201 N. Grew, *The Anatomy of Plants* (London, 1682), Book I, pp. 1-10.

202 Minutes, 17 May 1686, f. 179. The paper itself is no longer extant.

203 Minutes, 13 October 1684, f. 166.

204 *The Double-Bottom or Twin-Hulled Ship of Sir William Petty*, ed. Marquis of Lansdowne, p. 129.

205 They were Baggot, J. Bulkeley, R. Bulkeley, Huntington, Marsh, W. Molyneux, Petty, and Tollet.

206 W. Molyneux to Flamsteed, 13 May 1684, Southampton MS D/M 1/1.

207 W. Molyneux to Aston, 22 April 1684, R.S. MS Early Letters, M.1.84.

208 Quoted in I. Ehrenpreis, *Swift: The Man, His Works, and The Age*, 2 vols. to date (London, 1962–), I, 84.

209 W. Molyneux to Aston, 23 December 1684, R.S. MS Early Letters, M.1.87.

210 Petty to Southwell, 23 December 1684, *The Double-Bottom or Twin-Hulled Ship of Sir William Petty*, ed. Marquis of Lansdowne, pp. 140–1. The matter of the double-bottom is also discussed in M. H. Nicolson, *Pepys' Diary and the New Science* (Charlottesville, 1965), pp. 179–89.

211 Minutes, 4 February 1684, f. 160. The paper is to be found in B.M. Add. MS 4811, f. 2.

212 W. Molyneux to Flamsteed, 11 August 1683, Southampton MS D/M 1/1.

213 *P.T.*, XVI (1686), 192–3.

214 See T. Birch, *History of the Royal Society*, IV, 469, 502, and 550.

215 W. Molyneux to Flamsteed, 17 May 1687, *A General Dictionary . . . of the Celebrated Mr Bayle*, ed. J. P. Bernard, T. Birch, and J. Lockman (London, 1734–41), VIII, 611.

216 See MS notes in W. Molyneux's hand on the flyleaf of the first edition of the *Dioptrica Nova*, B.M. Pressmark 537.k.17.

217 See B.M. Add. MS 4811, ff. 124–5.

218 See E. G. R. Taylor, *The Haven-Finding Art* (London, 1956), pp. 245–53.

219 Minutes, 25 May and 1 June 1685, f. 170v. For a copy of the paper, see, B.M. Add. MS 4811, ff. 88–9. At various times throughout the 1680s Aland served as sheriff, common councilman, and alderman at Waterford. See, Ir. MSS Comm, *Council Books of the Corporation of Waterford 1662–1700*, ed. S. Pender (Dublin, 1964), p. 378.

220 W. Molyneux to Flamsteed, 20 February 1686, Southampton MS D/M 1/1.

221 J. Whalley, *Syderus Nuncius: Or an Ephemeris for the Year of the Humane Redemption 1686* (Dublin, 1686), from the Preface, dated 7 July 1685. The only copy of this almanac known to me is in the Public Library, Pearse Street, Dublin.

222 Minutes, 25 May 1685, f. 170v.

223 J. Herne [*sic*], *Longitude Unvailed* (London, 1678), Broadsheet, B.M. Pressmark 533.l.16(1). On Hearne, see E. G. R. Taylor, *The Mathematical Practitioners of Tudor and Stuart England*, p. 236.

224 For Tollet's reply to Hearne, see R.S. MS Early Letters, T.46. In this Tollet shows evidence of acquaintance with the works of Blaeu, Clavius, Dechales, Galtruchius, Mercator, Oughtred, Riccioli, Schottus, Tacquet, and Varenius.

[225] W. Hearne, *An Answer to Two Arguments produced by the Learned the Society of the City of Dublin, as their Judgements upon a Thesis relating to the Line of Latitude and the Line of Longitude upon the Terrestrial Globe* (Dublin, 1685). This eight-page pamphlet, which is not noted in Wing's *Short-Title Catalogue*, seems to have survived in only one copy in the Pitt Collection (Bound with Item No. 330) in the Southampton Public Library. It was printed by Joseph Ray who also acted as printer to the Dublin Society. Ashe called it an 'impertinent pamphlet'. Ashe to Aston, 4 July 1685, R.S. MS Early Letters, A.29. For Molyneux's view of the affair, see C. Molyneux, *Account of the Family*, pp. 64–3 [*sic*].

[226] Oxford Minutes, 28 July 1685, p. 159. T. Birch, *History of the Royal Society*, IV, 422.

[227] W. Petty, *The Advice of W.P. to Mr Samuel Hartlib for the Advancement of some particular Parts of Learning* (London, 1648), p. 7.

[228] W. Petty, 'Experiments to be made relating to Land Carriage', B.M. Add. MS 4811, ff. 11v–12. Printed, *P.T.*, XIV (1684), 666–7.

[229] Minutes, 10 December 1683, R.S. MS Early Letters, H.3.72. Printed, T. Birch, *History of the Royal Society*, IV, 249.

[230] W. Molyneux to Aston, 22 April 1684, R.S. MS Early Letters, M.1.84.

[231] Bulkeley to Lister, 5 May 1685, R.S. MS Copy Letter Book, 10, 162–3. Printed, *P.T.*, XV (1685), 1028–9.

[232] W. Petty, 'Experiments to be made relating to Land Carriage', B.M. Add. MS 4811, ff. 11v–12, and Minutes, 24 March 1684, f. 161v.

[233] Minutes, 7 July 1684, f. 165.

[234] Oxford Minutes, 12 August 1684, pp. 84–5. A copy of Walker's paper is in T.C.D. MS I.4.18, f. 128.

[235] Aston to W. Molyneux, 31 May 1684, T.C.D. MS I.4.18, f. 113.

[236] R. T. Gunther, *Early Science in Oxford*, VII, 666.

[237] *Ibid.*, pp. 666–79.

[238] M. 'Espinasse, *Robert Hooke*, p. 21.

[239] *P.T.*, XV (1685), 1028–9.

[240] Bulkeley to Ashe, 11 July 1685, R.S. MS Copy Letter Book, 10, 242–9.

[241] *The Diary of John Evelyn*, ed. E. S. de Beer, 6 vols. (Oxford, 1955), IV, 483–4. Entry for 28 October 1685.

[242] Oxford Minutes, 20 October 1685, p. 163.

[243] Bulkeley to Lister, 3 August 1686, Bodl. MS Lister 35, f. 123.

[244] Robert to Mrs Molesworth, 1 June 1706, H.M.C., *Reports on Various Collections*, VIII (1913), 234.

[245] *The Petty Papers*, ed. Marquis of Lansdowne, II, 10.

[246] I have been unable to discover the place or date of publication of this book. The only copy known to me is at Trinity College Dublin (Pressmark L.nn.15) and has the title-page wanting. It is not listed in Wing's *Short-Title Catalogue*.

[247] The translation is now Southampton MS D/M 4/18.

[248] W. Molyneux to Flamsteed, 11 August 1683, Southampton MS D/M 1/1.

[249] Minutes, 23 November 1685, f. 174v.

[250] W. Molyneux to Flamsteed, 1 August 1682. Southampton MS D/M 1/1.

[251] Minutes, 7 July 1684, f. 165.

[252] Minutes, 2 March 1685, f. 169.

[253] Minutes, 23 November 1685, f. 174v.

[254] G. Tollet, 'On Gunnery', R.S. Classified Papers I, 20.

[255] Minutes, 2 February 1685, f. 168v. See also a paper on the subject B.M. Add. MS 4811, f. 71v.

[256] Minutes 26 January and 9 February 1685, f. 168.

[257] T. Birch, *History of the Royal Society*, IV, 539.

[258] *Ibid.*, I, 461.

[259] Minutes, 21 July 1684, f. 165.

[260] Minutes, 15 December 1684, f. 167v.

[261] Minutes, 5 July 1686, f. 180.

[262] W. King, 'Of the Bogs and Loughs of Ireland', B.M. Add. M.S 4811, ff. 57v–61. Printed, *P.T.*, XV (1685), 948–60. See F. V. Emery, 'Irish Geography in the Seventeenth Century', *Irish Geography*, III (1958), 268. It seems likely that King had read the fourteenth chapter of Gerard Boate's *Irelands Naturall History* (London, 1652) which is entitled 'Original of the Bogs of Ireland'.

[263] That on maize was originally written in the form of a letter to Martin Lister, dated 23 October 1693, Bodl. MS Lister 36, ff. 70–1. Printed, *P.T.*, XVII (1693), 938–40. That on elms is printed, *P.T.*, XVII (1693), 971.

[264] *P.T.*, XVII (1693), 940.

[265] Seth Ward to Sir Justinian Isham, 27 February 1652, *Notes and Records*, VII (1949), 69.

[266] W. Petty, *The Advice of W.P. to Mr Samuel Hartlib*, pp. 2–3, and *Petty Papers*, ed. Marquis of Lansdowne, I, 205–7. Petty was involved in the Royal Society's scheme.

[267] Minutes, 7 April 1684, f. 162.

[268] *P.T.*, XVII (1693), 581.

[269] J. Wilkins, *Essay towards a Real Character and a Philosophical Language* (London, 1668). See E. N. da Costa Andrade, 'The Real Character of Bishop Wilkins', *Annals of Science*, I (1936), 4–12. A similar language was put forward in George Dalgarno's *Ars Signorum* (London, 1661).

[270] H. Hartley, 'Epilogue' in *The Royal Society its Origins and Founders*, ed. H. Hartley, p. 263.

[271] Minutes, 1 December 1684, f. 167.

[272] Ashe to Aston, 16 September 1685, R.S. MS Early Letters, A.31.

[273] Minutes, 3 December 1683, T. Birch, *History of the Royal Society*, IV, 248.

[274] Minutes, 18 February 1684, f. 160v.

[275] Minutes, 14 April 1684, 30 June 1684, and 15 June 1685, ff. 162, 164v, and 171.

[276] Minutes, 3 November 1684, f. 166v.

[277] Minutes, 19 October 1685 and 3 August 1685, ff. 174 and 172v.

[278] Anthony Irby to Mullen, 16 June 1685, B.M. Add. MS 4811, f. 93.

[279] Minutes, 23 March 1685, f. 169.

[280] Minutes, 30 March 1685, f. 169v.

[281] Minutes, 28 June 1686, f. 180.

[282] See R. H. Kargon, *Atomism in England from Hariot to Newton* (Oxford, 1966), p. 104.

[283] O. W. Ferguson, *Jonathan Swift and Ireland* (Urbana, Ill., 1962), p. 74.

[284] *Ibid.*, p. 73.

[285] *P.T.*, XV (1685), 1269–71.

[286] Minutes, 18 May 1685, f. 170.

[287] Minutes, 8 February 1686, f. 176.

[288] Minutes, 19 April 1686, f. 178v.

[289] Countess of Clarendon to Evelyn, 29 January 1687, *The Correspondence of Henry Hyde, Earl of Clarendon*, ed. S. W. Singer, 2 vols. (London, 1828), II, 149.

CHAPTER SIX

[1] R. F. Jones, *Ancients and Moderns: A Study of the Rise of the Scientific Movement in Seventeenth Century England* (2d edn., St Louis, 1961), p. 261.

[2] The best account of Loftus can be found in G. T. Stokes, *Some Worthies of the Irish Church* (London, 1900), pp. 35–62, originally published in *Journal of the Royal Society of Antiquaries of Ireland*, 5th Series, I (1890), 17–30.

[3] C. McNeill, 'Reports on the Rawlinson Manuscript Collection in the Bodleian Library Oxford', Ir. MSS Comm., *Analecta Hibernica*, I (1930), 157.

[4] *The Whole Works of Sir James Ware*, ed. W. Harris, 2 vols. (Dublin, 1739–46), II, 254.

[5] Loftus to Archbishop Sancroft, 19 October 1680, Ir. MSS Comm., *Calendar of Tanner Letters*, ed. C. McNeill (Dublin, 1943), p. 437.

[6] *The Whole Works of Sir James Ware*, ed. W. Harris, II, 254.

[7] Minutes, 22 October 1683, R.S. MS Early Letters, H.3.72. Richard Simon's *Histoire Critique* was published in 1678 with the intention of converting Protestants to Catholicism by undermining their faith in the authoritativeness of the bible as they knew it. The book was condemned by Bossuet and was translated into English in 1682. Unfortunately Loftus's discourse has been lost.

[8] Huntington to Plot, 18 December 1683, R.S. MS Early Letters, H.3.72. See above, pp. 87–8.

[9] H. Fisch, 'The Scientist as Priest: A Note on Robert Boyle's Natural Theology', *Isis*, XLIV (1953), 257.

[10] Loftus's criticisms of the Dublin Society are contained in King's Inns Library Dublin MS No. 33. There is no printed catalogue of King's Inns MSS, nor is this MS listed in the library's inadequate handlist. The MS, which dates from the year 1684, contains several items by Loftus. It is paginated, but a separate series of page numbers runs from the back of the volume. I indicate these thus, 1a, 2a, etc.

[11] King's Inns MS No. 33, pp. 217–19.

[12] *Ibid.*, p. 218.

[13] *Ibid.*, p. 220.

[14] 'A Character of 3 persons of the society occasioned by a difference amongst the society', *ibid.*, pp. 11a–14a.

[15] John Prideaux (1578–1650) was appointed Bishop of Worcester in 1641. He was a strong apponent of Arminianism and was a friend of Meric Casaubon.

[16] This paragraph is based on a passage in King's Inns MS No. 33, pp. 220–5.

[17] 'A letter to a person concerning the Society', *ibid.*, pp. 226–30. A copy of this item is to be found in B.M. Add. MS 38856, ff. 158–61. Internal evidence makes it clear that it was written on 29 January 1684.

[18] King's Inns MS No. 33, p. 221.

[19] Loftus to Archbishop Sancroft, 2 August 1680, Ir. MSS Comm., *Calendar of Tanner Letters*, ed. C. McNeill, p. 426.

[20] A certainly incomplete list of Loftus's books can be found in Marsh's Library Dublin MS Z4.5.14, ff. 273–4. A discussion of contemporary reactions to the Royal Society is included in R. H. Syfret, 'Some early Critics of the Royal Society', *Notes and Records*, VIII (1950), 20–64.

[21] 'A Reflection on the Society's new Invention', King's Inns MS No. 33, pp. 61a–2a. Loftus's claim in this matter is a little wide of the mark. Athenaeos the Mechanician actually speaks of two ships lashed together, rather than of a single double-bottomed vessel. See the edition of his *On Siege Engines*, ed. R. Schneider in the series of 'Griechische Poliorketiker', No. III in *Abhandlungen der Königlichen Gesellschaft der Wissenschaften zu Göttingen* (Philologisch-Historische Klasse), Neue Folge, XII, No. 5 (Berlin, 1912), 30–33.

[22] Quoted in R. H. Syfret, 'Some early Critics of the Royal Society', *Notes and Records*, VIII (1950), 55.

[23] King's Inns MS No. 33, p. 223.

[24] *Ibid.*, p. 224.

[25] T.C.D. MS I.4.17, ff. 32–3v.

[26] 'A Tripos or Speech delivered in the University of Dublin att a Comencemt. held there the 11th of July 1688 by Mr John Jones then Batchelr. of Arts, afterwards D.D.' Printed, J. Barrett, *An Essay on the Earlier Part of the Life of Swift . . . to which are subjoined Several Pieces ascribed to Swift* (London, 1808). Harold Williams, in *The Poems of Jonathan Swift*, 3 vols. (2d edn., Oxford, 1958), III, 1056, says, 'All that can be said of the Tripos . . . is that a share in the composition by Swift is not impossible.'

[27] J. Barrett, *An Essay on the Earlier Part of the Life of Swift*, pp. 66–7.

[28] *Ibid.*, pp. 73–4.

[29] *Ibid.*, pp. 60–61. Gwithers was a fellow of the Dublin College of Physicians and acted as its anatomist from 1693 until his death in 1700.

[30] *The Poems of Jonathan Swift*, ed. H. Williams, III, 780.

[31] Printed, *The Prose Works of Jonathan Swift*, ed. H. Davis, 14 vols. (Oxford, 1939–68), IV, 257–9.

[32] D. E. W. Wormell, 'Latin Verses by William Thompson spoken at the Opening in 1711 of the first scientific Laboratory in Trinity College Dublin', *Hermathena*, XCVI (1962), 24.

CHAPTER SEVEN

[1] Ashe to Musgrave, 15 July 1687, R.S. MS Early Letters, A.39.

[2] C. H. Josten, 'Elias Ashmole' in *The Royal Society its Origins and Founders*, ed. H. Hartley (London, 1960), pp. 228–9.

[3] R. T. Gunther, *Early Science in Oxford*, 14 vols. (Oxford, 1923–45), X, 107 and 135. In Harvard University Library is a copy of John Evelyn's *Kalendarium Hortense* (8th edn., London, 1691) with an inscription to Ashe. (See G. Keynes, *John Evelyn: A Study in Bibliophily with a Bibliography of his Writings* (2d edn., Oxford, 1968), p. 162.) The two may well have met at this time.

[4] Clarendon to Trumbull, 11 May 1686, H.M.C., *Calendar of Downshire MSS*, I (Part 1), (1924), 166.

[5] Ashe to the Royal Society, 17 July 1690 (N.S.), R.S. MS Early Letters A.40.

[6] W. Molyneux to Flamsteed, 27 January 1690, *A General Dictionary . . . of the celebrated Mr Bayle*, ed. J. P. Bernard, T. Birch, and J. Lockman, 10 vols. (London, 1734–41), VIII, 612.

[7] Ashe to Halley, [early 1690], R.S. MS Copy Letter Book, 11(1), 186–90. In July 1690 Ashe sent two papers on the lunar eclipse of March 1690 by Wurzelbau and Eimmart to the Royal Society. These can be found in R.S. Classified Papers VIII(1), 41 and 45.

[8] Seven of Ashe's letters to Magliabcchi covering the period November 1690 to September 1691 are preserved in the Biblioteca Nazionale Centrale-Firenze, Cl. VIII, Ser. I, Tom. I, ff. 78–89v. Ashe reported on the correspondence to the Royal Society in Ashe to Halley, 18 June 1691 (N.S.), R.S. MS Copy Letter Book, 11(1), 191–5, while the relevant letters of Magliabechi to Lcibniz can be found in Deutsche Akademie der Wissenschaften zu Berlin, *Gottfried Wilhelm Leibniz saemtliche Schriften und Briefe*, Erste Reihe (Allgemeiner politischer und historischer Briefwechsel), VI (Berlin, 1957), 326, and VII (Berlin, 1964), 639–40.

[9] St G. Ashe, *A Sermon preached in Trinity-College Chappell before the University of Dublin January the 9th, 1693–4, Being the first Secular Day since its Foundation by Queen Elizabeth* (Dublin, 1694), pp. 3–14.

[10] See the MS list (in Molyneux's hand) of people to whom copies were presented on the flyleaf of the copy of the first edition in the British Museum (Pressmark 537.k.17). Others who received copies include Boyle, Wallis, Plot, King, Willoughby, Wyche, and Tollet.

[11] Willoughby to King, 10 March 1693, T.C.D. Lyon MS No. 224.

[12] W. Molyneux, *Dioptrica Nova* (London, 1692), p. 273.

[13] Huygens to Faccio of Duillier, 5 April 1692 (N.S.), Société Hollandaise des Sciences, *Œuvres Complètes de Christiaan Huygens*, 22 vols. (The Hague, 1888–1950), X, 279. The extracts from the *Dioptrica* together with Huygens's remarks can be found in *ibid.*, XIII, 826–44. Note the generous comment, 'Egregia est dedicatio ubi scolastica ac barbara philosophia exagitatur, nova experimentalis laudatur.'

[14] See the MS extracts (in Molyneux's hand) from a letter from Sturm to Ashe, 7 April 1693 (N.S.), on a sheet at the back of the copy of the first

edition of the *Dioptrica* in the British Museum (Pressmark 537.k.17). The review is in *Acta Eruditorum*, (January 1693), 1–5.

[15] Locke to W. Molyneux, 16 July 1692, *The Works of John Locke*, 10 vols. (11th edn., London, 1812), IX, 290. The Molyneux-Locke correspondence was first published in *Some Familiar Letters between Mr Locke and Several of his Friends* (London, 1708). It covers the period 16 July 1692 to 25 January 1699, and consists of thirty-four letters from Molyneux to Locke, twenty-nine from Locke to Molyneux, five from Thomas Molyneux to Locke, and four from Locke to Thomas Molyneux, as well as a number of enclosures. Locke, who had been at Leyden in October and November 1684, had there met Thomas Molyneux, then studying medicine in Holland.

[16] W. Molyneux to Locke, 2 March 1693, *Works of John Locke*, IX, 311. On the problem, see C. M. Turbayne, 'Berkeley and Molyneux on Retinal Images', *Journal of the History of Ideas*, XVI (1955), 339–55, and J. W. Davis, 'The Molyneux Problem', *ibid.*, XXI (1960), 392–408.

[17] Bodl. MS Locke c. 16, f. 92. This version has now also been noted by D. Park in 'Locke and Berkeley on the Molyneux Problem', *Journal of the History of Ideas*, XXX (1969), 253–60. Park argues that Locke's analysis of the problem is inadequate partly because of his neglect of the section on changing distances.

[18] See E. C. Graham, *Optics and Vision: The Background of the Metaphysics of Berkeley* [Columbia Ph.D.], printed 1929, p. 41.

[19] W. Molyneux, *Dioptrica Nova*, pp. 104–5.

[20] J. Locke, *An Essay Concerning Human Understanding* (2d edn., London, 1694), pp. 67–8.

[21] C. M. Turbayne, 'Berkeley and Molyneux on Retinal Images', *Journal of the History of Ideas*, XVI (1955), 344.

[22] Synge to Dr Quayl, 6 September 1695, *Works of John Locke*, IX, 372. Molyneux refused to accept this. See his letter to Locke, 24 December 1695, *ibid.*, p. 370.

[23] Quoted in J. W. Davis, 'The Molyneux Problem', *Journal of the History of Ideas*, XXI (1960), 397.

[24] M. von Senden, *Space and Sight: The Perception of Space and Shape in the Congenitally Blind before and after Operation* (London, 1960), p. 326.

[25] R. L. Gregory, *Eye and Brain: The Psychology of Seeing* (London, 1966), p. 198.

[26] See K. MacLean, *John Locke and English Literature of the Eighteenth Century* (New Haven, 1936), p. 107, and M. H. Nicolson, *Newton Demands the Muse* (Princeton, 1946), pp. 83–5. The latter is however not correct when she says that the problem is discussed in the *Dioptrica Nova*.

[27] Locke to W. Molyneux, 20 September 1692, *Works of John Locke*, IX, 293.

[28] W. Molyneux to Locke, 22 December 1692, *ibid.*, p. 298. Thus Locke was introduced to Trinity some time before his writings were accepted at Cambridge. At Oxford they were of course greeted with little sympathy in the eighteenth century. See C. Wordsworth, *Scholae Academicae: Some Account of the Studies at the English Universities in the Eighteenth Century* (Cambridge, 1910), pp. 126–7.

[29] W. Molyneux to Locke, 2 March 1693, *Works of John Locke*, IX, 308.

[30] W. Molyneux to Locke, 2 June 1694, *ibid.*, p. 337. Two other members of the Dublin Society were in contact with Locke during the 1690s. In 1691 Willoughby produced an account of the Dublin bills of mortality in response to a query from Locke, while two letters dating from about 1698 from Patrick Dun to Locke on medical matters have survived. All three items are printed in K. Dewhurst, 'The Genesis of State Medicine in Ireland', *Irish Journal of Medical Science*, No. 368 (1956), 370–83.

[31] See Appendix C for a list of members in late 1693.

[32] Plot to Charlett, 26 March 1694, Bodl. MS Ballard 14, f. 58, quoted in M. Purver, *The Royal Society: Concept and Creation* (London, 1967), p. 127, note 114.

[33] Minutes, 26 April 1693, f. 182.

[34] Huntington to Wyche, 22 June 1693, Public Record Office of Ireland, Wyche Papers, Lot 158, No. 80.

[35] Taken from a second version of the minutes for 26 April 1693 in Marsh's Diary, Marsh's Library Dublin, MS Z2.2.3B, p. 30.

[36] Cox to W. Molyneux, 3 November 1685, printed in S. P. Johnston and T. A. Lunham, 'On a Manuscript Description of the City and County of Cork . . . written by Sir Richard Cox', *Journal of the Royal Society of Antiquaries of Ireland*, XXXII (1902), 353–76.

[37] *The Autobiography of the Rt Hon Sir Richard Cox*, ed. R. Caulfield (London and Cork, 1860), p. 9.

[38] J. C. Beckett, *Protestant Dissent in Ireland 1687–1780* (London, 1948), p. 33. In 'To the Reader' in *Hibernia Anglicana* Cox refers to Geoffrey Keating's *History* (which dates from about 1629) as 'an ill-digested heap of very silly fictions'.

[39] Marsh's Diary, Marsh's Library Dublin, MS Z2.2.3B, p. 30.

[40] Lloyd to Waller, 3 June 1693, R.S. MS Early Letters, L.5.124.

[41] Minutes, 10 May 1693, f. 183. Cox contributed the section on Ireland to Edmund Gibson's edition of Camden's *Britannia* (London, 1695), towards which his papers to the society were presumably preliminary.

[42] Minutes, 3 May 1693, f. 182v.

[43] Bulkeley to Lister, 13 April 1697, Bodl. MS Lister 36, f. 182. Edward Lhuyd in a letter to Lister, 6 July 1698 (R. T. Gunther, *Early Science in Oxford*, XIV, 378) mentions the Dublin Society as if it were still in existence. But Lhuyd, then in Cardigan, may have been misinformed.

[44] B. M. Sloane MS 1786, ff. 152–3. The operation was performed in 1695, and a slightly condensed description appeared in *P.T.*, XXII (1700), 455–9.

[45] The paper is R.S. Classified Papers XIV(1), 37. It was sent by Lloyd to Royal Society, 31 March 1694, R.S. MS Early Letters, L.5.127, and is printed in *P.T.*, XVIII (1694), 105–11.

[46] R.S. Classified Papers XV(1), 52. Printed, *P.T.*, XIX (1697), 405–12.

[47] R.S. MS Early Letters, M.1.106 (incomplete), and R.S. MS Copy Record Book, 7, 216–29. Printed, *P.T.*, XIX (1697), 741–56. See W. Molyneux to Locke, 5 January 1697, *Works of John Locke*, IX, 392; Sloane

to Locke, 18 April 1696, Bodl. MS Locke c. 18, ff. 120–21; and Locke to Sloane, 22 March 1697, B.M. Sloane MS 4036, ff. 294–5.

48 R.S. Classified Papers XV(1), 51. Printed, *P.T.*, XIX (1697), 489–512.

49 Lloyd to Royal Society, 13 June 1694, R.S. MS Early Letters, L.5.128.

50 T. Molyneux to Sloane, 22 May 1697, B.M. Sloane MS 4036, f. 314.

51 See a letter written by Dunton in 1698 printed in E. MacLysaght, *Irish Life in the Seventeenth Century* (2d edn., Cork, 1950), p. 378.

52 Lloyd to Royal Society, 13 June 1694, R.S. MS Early Letters, L.5.128.

53 R.S. Classified Papers XVII, 26. Printed, *P.T.*, XVIII (1694), 118–20.

54 Lloyd to Royal Society, 13 June 1694, R.S. MS Early Letters, L.5.128. A 'Digression concerning Physiognomy' can be found attached to Evelyn's *Numismata: A Discourse of Medals* (London, 1697).

55 R.S. Classified Papers II, 4. Printed, *P.T.*, XIX (1697), 625–31.

56 R.S. Classified Papers I, 5. Printed, *P.T.*, XVII (1693), 677–81.

57 R.S. Classified Papers VIII(1), 49. Printed, *P.T.*, XVIII (1694), 101–3.

58 The first can be found in R.S. Classified Papers IX(1), 48, printed, *P.T.*, XIX (1696), 228–30, the second in R.S. Classified Papers XI(1), 40, printed, *P.T.*, XIX (1696), 288–90.

59 Ashe to Southwell, 12 February 1694, R.S. MS Early Letters, A. 42.

60 Bulkeley to Lister, 15 February 1694, Bodl. MS Lister 36, f. 44. See also Bulkeley to Lister, 2 November 1694, Bodl. MS Lister 36, f. 105v: 'This society at present are upon a philosophic ferment, and to make comparisons these 5 months past, have produced many curious discoveries in earths, formed stones, and minerals, and other fossils.'

61 Lloyd to Sloane, 7 May 1695, B.M. Sloane MS 4036, f. 209.

62 Bulkeley to Lister, ?[1694], Bodl. MS Lister 3, f. 43.

63 R.S. Classified Papers IX(1), 46a, also R.S. MS Copy Record Book, 7, 342–4. Printed, *P.T.*, XVIII (1694), 170–2.

64 R.S. Classified Papers IX(1), 46b, also R.S. MS Copy Record Book, 7, 344–6. Printed, *P.T.*, XVIII (1694), 173–5. Bulkeley had already sent a very short account of the causeway to Lister. See Bodl. MS Lister 36, ff. 46v–7v. Printed, *P.T.*, XVII (1693), 708–10.

65 R.S. Classified Papers IX(1), 46c, also R.S. MS Copy Record Book, 7, 347–53. Printed, *P.T.*, XVIII (1694), 175–82.

66 See J. Kenntmann, 'Nomenclaturae Rerum Fossilium' in Conrad Gesner, *De Omni Rerum Fossilium* (Zurich, 1565).

67 W. Molyneux to Sloane, 4 November 1697, R.S. MS Early Letters, M.1.99. The 'prospect' was included as a frontispiece to *P.T.*, XIX (1697), No. 235, and was the work of Edwin Sandys. Bulkeley told Lister (13 April 1697, Bodl. MS Lister 36, f. 182) that this had cost the society thirteen pounds.

68 R.S. MS Early Letters, M.1.105. Printed, *P.T.*, XX (1698), 209–23.

69 W. Molyneux to Mr Grey, 10 June 1693, T.C.D. MS I.4.18, f. 196. The other commissioners were Sir Michael Mitchell, Charles Dering, John Weaver, and John Nelmes.

70 H.M.C., *Calendar of Treasury Books 1693–6*, X, Part 1 (1935), 157, and Part 3 (1935), 1227.

[71] W. Molyneux to Sloane, 4 November 1697, R.S. MS Early Letters, M.1.99.

[72] This paper is enclosed in W. Molyneux to Sloane, 22 January 1698, R.S. MS Early Letters, M.1.100.

[73] W. Molyneux to Sloane, 4 November 1697, R.S. MS Early Letters, M.1.99. See also W. Molyneux to Sloane, 13 November 1697, B.M. Sloane MS 4036, ff. 367–8, 'We have in some measure already an instance of the relish many would have of such a work in what Mr Whiston has published in his *New Theory*' (London, 1696).

[74] W. Molyneux, *The Case of Ireland* (Reissue, Dublin, 1725), p. 101.

[75] W. Molyneux to Locke, 19 April 1698, *Works of John Locke*, IX, 455.

[76] R. H. Murray, *Revolutionary Ireland and its Settlement* (London, 1911), p. 328.

[77] King to Bishop T. Lindsay of Killaloe, 7 June 1698, T.C.D. King Correspondence MS N.3.1, p. 241.

[78] Cox to ——, 28 October 1699, H.M.C., *Fourteenth Report*, Appendix II, p. 609 (Portland MSS).

[79] Ashe to King, 10 February 1700, T.C.D. Lyon MS No. 658.

[80] Locke to T. Molyneux, 10 February 1699, *Works of John Locke*, IX, 468.

[81] A. M. Fraser, 'The Molyneux Family', *Dublin Historical Record*, XVI (1960), 11.

[82] T. Molyneux to Sloane, 29 November 1698, B.M. Sloane MS 4037, f. 157, paraphrasing Sloane's no longer extant letter of condolence.

[83] Baggot to King, 19 December 1700, T.C.D. Lyon MS No. 745.

[84] Quoted in R. H. Murray, *Revolutionary Ireland and its Settlement*, p. 316.

[85] H.M.C., *Calendar of Ormonde MSS*, Old Series, II (1899), 475, 'Licenses to Roman Catholics to carry arms'.

[86] Bulkeley to King, 9 December 1699, T.C.D. Lyon MS No. 649.

[87] See Sloane to Bulkeley, 1 April 1699, R.S. MS Copy Letter Book, 12, 103, and Bulkeley to Lister, 31 May 1701, Bodl. MS Lister 37, f. 36, 'To make amends for the neglect of my promise of sending you Sir Wm. Petty's advice to the Dublin Society, when he was president thereof, I have sent you also his *Supellex Philosophica*.'

[88] Bulkeley wrote on their behalf. See, *Warnings of the Eternal Spirit spoken by Abraham Withro, with a Preface by Sir R. Bulkeley* (London, 1709). In this preface Bulkeley claimed that Whitterow had miraculously cured him of headaches, stone, and rupture.

[89] Berkeley to John Perceval, 1 March 1710, *The Works of George Berkeley, Bishop of Cloyne*, ed. A. A. Luce and T. E. Jessop, 9 vols. (London, 1948–57), VIII, 31.

[90] Ashe to King, 18 January 1701, T.C.D. Lyon MS No. 749. In December 1698 Ashe, then Bishop of Clogher, attended the Dublin book auctions held by John Dunton, who claims that Ashe had encouraged him to visit Ireland. See J. Dunton, *The Dublin Scuffle* (London, 1699), pp. 50–1 and 130–1.

[91] Tollet to Pepys, 24 January 1702, *Private Correspondence and Miscellaneous Papers of Samuel Pepys*, ed. J. R. Tanner, 2 vols. (London, 1926), II, 251.

⁹² R.I.A. MS 12/D/34, ff. 20v–26v.

⁹³ Sloane to T. Molyneux, 1 April 1699, R.S. MS Copy Letter Book, 12, 104, and T. Molyneux to Sloane, 29 August 1702, B.M. Sloane MS 4039, f. 18.

⁹⁴ The first is in *P.T.*, XXII (1700), 487–508, the second in *P.T.*, XXIII (1702), 1267–78.

⁹⁵ R. T. Gunther, *Early Science in Oxford*, XIV, 256.

⁹⁶ T. Molyneux to Lhuyd, 27 July 1689, Bodl. MS Ashmole 1816, f. 359.

⁹⁷ P. W. Carter, 'Edward Lhuyd the Scientist', *Transactions of the Honourable Society of Cymmrodorion* (1962), 53.

⁹⁸ Lloyd to Lhuyd, 6 October [?1694], Bodl. MS Ashmole 1816, f. 254.

⁹⁹ Lhuyd to Lister, 1 January 1695, R. T. Gunther, *Early Science in Oxford*, XIV, 256.

¹⁰⁰ W. Molyneux to Lhuyd, 7 February 1695, Bodl. MS Ashmole 1816, f. 37.

¹⁰¹ P. W. Carter, 'Edward Lhuyd the Scientist', *op. cit.*, p. 54.

¹⁰² These were sheets left over from the Welsh survey. Many are preserved in Bodl. MS Ashmole 1820a.

¹⁰³ T. Molyneux to Lhuyd, 21 June 1698, Bodl. MS Ashmole 1816, f. 361.

¹⁰⁴ See J. L. Campbell, 'The Tour of Edward Lhuyd in Ireland 1699 and 1700', *Celtica*, V (1960), 218–28.

¹⁰⁵ Lhuyd to T. Molyneux, 7 May 1700, T.C.D. MS I.4.19, ff. 312–13. The books were *Auctarium Musei Balfouriani* (Edinburgh, 1697) and *Memoria Balfouriana* (Edinburgh, 1699). On Lhuyd's tour of Scotland, see J. L. Campbell and D. Thomson, *Edward Lhuyd in the Scottish Highlands 1699–1700* (Oxford, 1963).

¹⁰⁶ Lhuyd to T. Molyneux, 29 January 1700, T.C.D. MS I.1.3, pp. 284–92. For Lhuyd's views on New Grange, including quotations from his accounts of the passage and chamber, see M. Herity, 'From Lhuyd to Coffey: New Information from unpublished Descriptions of the Boyne Valley Tombs', *Studia Hibernica*, No. 7 (1967), 128–33.

¹⁰⁷ Lhuyd to T. Molyneux, 15 May 1700, R.I.A. MS 12/W/22 (loosely inserted).

¹⁰⁸ *Ibid.*, pp. 1–7.

¹⁰⁹ J. H. Todd, 'Autograph Letter of Thady O'Roddy', *Miscellany of the Irish Archaeological Society*, I (1846), 122.

¹¹⁰ T. Molyneux to Lhuyd, 4 May 1699, Bodl. MS Ashmole 1816, f. 363v.

¹¹¹ O'Flaherty's letters are in Bodl. MS Ashmole 1817a, ff. 11–61.

¹¹² T. Molyneux to Lhuyd, 10 August 1702, Bodl. MS Ashmole 1816, f. 365. The dictionary is listed in Edward Bernard's *Catalogi Librorum Manuscriptorum Angliae et Hiberniae* (Oxford, 1697), Tom. II, Part 2, 50 as belonging to Marsh, and is described as 'Focloir Hibernicum, id est, vocabularium Hibernicum et Latinum, in folio, magnum et copiosissimum'. It is now Marsh's Library Dublin, MS Z4.2.5, and dates from 1662.

¹¹³ *The Works of George Berkeley*, ed. A. A. Luce and T. E. Jessop, IV, 203.

¹¹⁴ S. Molyneux to Hawksbee, 25 January 1707, Southampton MS D/M 1/2, p. 2. This MS is Samuel Molyneux's letter book for the years 1707–9.

An air-pump of this period after Hawksbee's design is illustrated in R. T. Gunther, *Early Science in Oxford*, I, plate between pp. 250 and 251.

[115] Hawksbee to S. Molyneux, 27 February 1707, Southampton MS D/M 1/2, p. 3.

[116] Churchill to S. Molyneux, 8 March 1707, *ibid.*, p. 8. See also, S. Molyneux to Churchill, 10 June 1707, *ibid.*, p. 9.

[117] S. Molyneux to Churchill, 6 December 1707, *ibid.*, pp. 24–5.

[118] S. Molyneux to Churchill, 24 June 1707, *ibid.*, p. 10.

[119] S. Molyneux to Derham, 24 June 1707, *ibid.*, pp. 11–12. Derham's paper can be found in *P.T.*, XXV (1707), 2411–12.

[120] Derham to S. Molyneux, 13 August 1707, Southampton MS D/M 1/2, pp. 13–16.

[121] S. Molyneux to Derham, 27 September 1707, *ibid.*, pp. 17–19. A list of the large number of instruments belonging to Molyneux can be found in *A Catalogue of the Library of the Honble. Samuel Molyneux Deceas'd* (London, 1730).

[122] S. Molyneux to Derham, 27 September 1707, Southampton MS D/M 1/2, p. 18.

[123] Ashe to S. Molyneux, 30 November 1707, *ibid.*, p. 22.

[124] S. Molyneux to Ashe, 27 November 1707, *ibid.*, p. 20.

[125] S. Molyneux to Ashe, 6 December 1707, *ibid.*, pp. 22–3.

[126] S. Molyneux to Keogh, 29 November 1707, *ibid.*, p. 21.

[127] *The Works of George Berkeley*, ed. A. A. Luce and T. E. Jessop, IX, 4.

[128] S. Molyneux to Atkin, 6 December 1707, Southampton MS D/M 1/2, pp. 25–6.

[129] Atkin to S. Molyneux, 10 April 1708, *ibid.*, pp. 47–8.

[130] Keogh to S. Molyneux, 22 December 1707, *ibid.*, pp. 26–7, and Norman to S. Molyneux, 29 January 1708, *ibid.*, pp. 31–2.

[131] O'Flaherty to S. Molyneux, 9 April 1708, *ibid.*, pp. 45–6. See E. Stillingfleet, *Origines Britannicae* (London, 1685), pp. 266–76.

[132] O'Flaherty to S. Molyneux, 17 December 1708, Southampton MS D/M 1/2, pp. 103–5.

[133] O'Flaherty to S. Molyneux, 9 April 1708, *ibid.*, pp. 45–6. Molyneux's diary of his journey is printed in A. Smith, 'Journey to Connaught . . . 1709', *Miscellany of the Irish Archaeological Society*, I (1846) from T.C.D. MS I.4.12, and ascribed to Thomas Molyneux. However, the handwriting of the MS and other evidence make it clear that the journey was made, and the diary kept, by Samuel Molyneux.

[134] T. Molyneux to Sloane, 7 August 1707, B.M. Sloane MS 4041, f. 10.

[135] R.S. MS Copy Journal Book, 10, 170 (31 December 1707), and Sloane to S. Molyneux, 3 January 1708, B.M. Add. MS 4812, f. 32. The latter MS also contains a number of papers read to the society in 1707 and 1708.

[136] B.M. Add. MS 4812, ff. 4, 24–5v, and 26–7.

[137] *Ibid.*, ff. 9–11. Printed, *P.T.*, XXVI (1708), 59–64.

[138] B.M. Add. MS 4812, ff. 13–14. Copies, B.M. Sloane MS 3329, f. 141, and T.C.D. MS I.4.17, f. 102. Printed, *Calendar of Ancient Records of Dublin*, ed. J. T. Gilbert and Lady Gilbert, 19 vols. (Dublin, 1889–1944), VI, 613–16.

139 B.M. Add. MS 4812, ff. 15–17v.

140 T.C.D. MS I.4.18, ff. 46–8. Printed, *The Works of George Berkeley*, ed. A. A. Luce and T. E. Jessop, IV, 235–8.

141 George Cheyne (1671–1743), a London physician, published *Fluxionum Methodus Inversa* (London, 1703) and *Philosophical Principles of Natural Religion* (London, 1705). Joseph Raphson (d. about 1715): His 'De Spatio Reali' appended to the second edition of *Analysis Æquationum Universalis* (London, 1702) made a profound impression on Berkeley because of its virtual deification of space. See *The Works of George Berkeley*, ed. A. A. Luce and T. E. Jessop, IV, 237, notes 1 and 2, as also A. Koyré, *From the Closed World to the Infinite Universe* (Baltimore, 1957), pp. 190–205.

142 *The Works of George Berkeley*, ed. A. A. Luce and T. E. Jessop, IV, 233.

143 There are two copies of this paper, (*a*) T.C.D. MS I.4.19, ff. 245–8v, (*b*) T.C.D. MS I.4.19, ff. 249–53v. Printed, *The Works of George Berkeley*, ed. A. A. Luce and T. E. Jessop, IV, 257–64.

144 T. Molyneux to Sloane, 10 May 1706, B.M. Sloane MS 4040, f. 164.

145 B.M. Add. MS 4812, f. 27.

146 *Ibid.*, f. 28. Molyneux, like Lhuyd (see Lhuyd to T. Molyneux, 29 January 1700, T.C.D. MS I.1.3, pp. 284–92), thought that Muiredach's Cross at Monasterboice dated from the mid-sixth century. This is an error, and it is now thought that the cross was erected in the early tenth century.

147 Thomas to William Molyneux, 2 June 1684, *Dublin University Magazine*, XVIII (1841), 483.

148 B.M. Add. MS 4812, f. 28v.

149 J. H. Todd, 'Autograph Letter of Thady O'Roddy', *Miscellany of the Irish Archaeological Society*, I (1846), 124.

150 S. Molyneux to O'Flaherty, 5 August 1708, Southampton MS D/M 1/2, p. 76.

151 C. H. Josten, 'Elias Ashmole' in *The Royal Society its Origins and Founders*, ed. H. Hartley, pp. 228–9.

152 S. Molyneux to Domvile, 5 March 1709, Southampton MS D/M 1/2, p. 119.

153 *Ibid.*, pp. 141–8. The letters are printed in *The Works of George Berkeley*, ed. A. A. Luce and T. E. Jessop, VIII, 19 and 24–7.

154 Southampton MS D/M 1/3, pp. 77–8. This MS is a fragment of Molyneux's letter book for 1712 and 1713. The letters are not addressed.

155 *Ibid.*, p. 101.

156 *Ibid.*, p. 125.

157 See Bodl. MSS Bradley 38, 39, and 44, which contain descriptions of these observations. A collated version is printed in *The Miscellaneous Works and Correspondence of the Reverend James Bradley*, ed. S. P. Rigaud (Oxford, 1832), pp. 93–115.

158 See A. W. Badcock, 'Physical Optics at the Royal Society 1660–1800', *British Journal for the History of Science*, I (1962), 106.

159 Printed in Robert Smith, *A Compleat System of Opticks*, 2 vols. (Cambridge, 1738), II, 281–312.

160 *Ibid.*, II, 301 and 363–6. See also Fig. 617.

APPENDIX A

[1] A copy of the queries can be found in Bodl. MS Ashmole 1820a, f. 221. It has been photographically reproduced in K. T. Hoppen, 'Queries for a Seventeenth Century Natural History of Ireland', *The Irish Book*, II (1963), 60–1.

APPENDIX B

[1] B.M. Add. MS 4811, f. 48v.

APPENDIX C

[1] T.C.D. MS F.4.24, ff. 48v-9.

APPENDIX D

[1] R. K. Merton, 'Science, Technology, and Society in Seventeenth Century England', *Osiris*, IV (1938), 563.

APPENDIX E

[1] Newton to Aston, 23 February 1685, *The Correspondence of Isaac Newton*, ed. H. W. Turnbull and J. F. Scott, 4 vols. to date (Cambridge, 1959–), II, 415.

[2] *Ibid.*

[3] See C. R. Weld, *A History of the Royal Society With Memoirs of the Presidents*, 2 vols. (London, 1848), I, 232.

[4] Musgrave to W. Molyneux, 3 July 1684, B.M. Add. MS 4811, f. 39v.

[5] Middleton to John Wallis, 27 December 1684, R. T. Gunther, *Early Science in Oxford*, 14 vols. (Oxford, 1923–45), XII, 249.

[6] Garden to Middleton, 2 March 1685, *ibid.*, XII, 271.

[7] A. Skene to John Wallis, 12 January 1685, *ibid.*, XII, 251.

[8] L. Cunninghame to Dr Bernard, 16 January 1685, *ibid.*, XII, 253. By the beginning of the eighteenth century St Andrews had, of course, already begun to sink into a condition of extreme intellectual torpidity.

[9] C. R. Weld, *A History of the Royal Society*, I, 383.

Index

T